John L. Williams is a biographer, novelist and crime writer from Cardiff. His non-fiction includes his account of the Cardiff Three miscarriage of justice case, *Bloody Valentine* ('A bloody good book' Benjamin Zephaniah). His biography of his fellow Cardiffian Shirley Bassey was proclaimed the music book of the year by *The Times*. He is the co-founder and literary director of the Laugharne Weekend Festival in west Wales. He is a left arm swing bowler and a confirmed tail-ender.

Praise for *CLR James*

'A fascinating biography' Clive Davis

'John L. Williams's exciting and briskly written biography, *CLR James: A Life Beyond the Boundaries*, offers the perfect introduction to this titan of 20th-century politics and culture' *The Times*

'This is an unrivalled storehouse of information about one of the twentieth century's most important revolutionaries. John Williams' sparkling biography counterpoints understanding of James' ideas with a richly-detailed account of his itinerant life and times.' Paul Gilroy

'As John Williams states at the beginning of his absorbing biography, CLR James may have been born in the Victorian age but he belongs very much to ours . . . [The book] may be a single biography, but it describes multiple lives.' *New Statesman*

'A genius, a seducer . . . the firebrand author, historian and critic was a complex, fragile human being, as John L. Williams's biography reveals' *Observer*

'This is a passionate, timely and challenging portrait. CLR James was decades ahead of his time in challenging our thoughts about empire, colonialism, black history and, not least, in writing brilliantly about cricket. He finally has the biography his extraordinary influence deserves.' Barney Ronay

'It's a testament to this generous biography that the idiosyncratic personality of the great silver-tongued enthusiast comes shining through' *Prospect*

'CLR's life has been chronicled many times in film, memoirs and biographies. This one . . . should rank as definitive.' *Tablet*

Also by John L. Williams

Non-fiction

Into the Badlands: Travels Through Urban America
Bloody Valentine: A Killing in Cardiff
Michael X: A Life in Black and White
Miss Shirley Bassey
America's Mistress: The Life and Times of Eartha Kitt

Fiction

Faithless
Five Pubs, Two Bars and a Nightclub
Cardiff Dead
The Prince of Wales
Temperance Town
Fade to Grey (as John Lincoln)

CLR JAMES

A LIFE BEYOND THE BOUNDARIES

JOHN L. WILLIAMS

CONSTABLE

CONSTABLE

First published in Great Britain in 2022 by Constable
This paperback edition published in 2023 by Constable

1 3 5 7 9 10 8 6 4 2

A CIP catalogue record for this book
is available from the British Library.

ISBN: 978-1-47213-012-9

Typeset in Bembo by Hewer Text UK Ltd, Edinburgh
Printed and bound in Great Britain by Clays Ltd, Elcograf S.p.A.

Papers used by Constable are from well-managed
forests and other responsible sources.

FSC www.fsc.org
MIX
Paper from responsible sources
FSC® C104740

Constable
An imprint of
Little, Brown Book Group
Carmelite House
50 Victoria Embankment
London EC4Y 0DZ

An Hachette UK Company
www.hachette.co.uk

www.littlebrown.co.uk

For Pete Ayrton

Introduction

CLR James, at eighty years old, was wearing his good suit and sitting outside the Oil Workers' building in San Fernando, Trinidad, waiting for a cab he greatly feared wasn't coming.

They had been kind to him, the Oil Workers Union, given him a place to live when he needed one. But he couldn't let himself die here, alone and forgotten, re-reading Proust in a room on the Circular Road. He had left the island as a young man, to make his way in the world, and he would leave it again as an old man.

Darcus Howe had a place waiting for CLR in London. And once he was there he would sing for his supper, write more essays, give more talks. Just as he always had done. And, with luck, people would listen. They had listened in the thirties and in the sixties. Maybe the time was right again in the eighties. There was a new edition of *The Black Jacobins* coming. That was a lesson that still needed teaching. So he would retrace the journey of fifty years ago. And this time there would be no coming back. In London there would be newspapers and journals and cricket on the television and opera in the theatres and people to talk to about Shakespeare. It would do.

CLR was right to be worried about the cab. It didn't come. He was sure he would miss the plane and be stuck in San Fernando. He couldn't let that happen. And then his luck changed. His good friend David Abdulah came by. When he heard what was happening, he bundled CLR into his Mazda and told him to hold on tight. And so CLR James set off for the last leg of his long life in a headlong rush, at a hundred miles an hour down the Sir Solomon Hochov Highway.

When CLR James arrived back in London at the beginning of the eighties he was yesterday's man. The books he'd written over the past half-century were almost all out of print. He had barely appeared in the mainstream press in decades. There were a few circles in which his name rang a bell: serious students of Black history; obsessive cricket fans. But that was it. In the last few years he had rarely left his bed and was in danger of losing the ability to walk. He was dependent on sleeping pills and barely eating a thing.

Nine years later, when he died in Brixton, he was internationally famous – lauded as the greatest of Black British intellectuals: the 'Black Plato', according to *The Times*.

And now, thirty years after his death, CLR James is the thinker we need – but he's too important a figure to be left to scholarly study alone.

So many of the ideas we take for granted now – of the importance of identity and culture – start with his work. These days he is practically an academic subject in himself – no discussion of Black history or postcolonial studies can take place without his work being front and centre. Outside academia, though, his name remains unjustly obscure.

For CLR James was one of the truly revolutionary voices of the last century. He debated with Trotsky, was published by Leonard and Virginia Woolf, inspired Kwame Nkrumah, and was a profound influence on the British Black Power movement.

And his two great books, *The Black Jacobins* and *Beyond a Boundary*, have the power to change readers' understanding of the world.

The Black Jacobins tells the story of the only successful slave rebellion in history, the Haitian Revolution of the 1790s. It showed how history could not only dig into the past but inspire the future. It became a key text for Black radicals, from Apartheid South Africa to Black Power America. Its enduring appeal to new generations was neatly symbolised by its repeated invocation in Steve McQueen's *Small Axe* series of films.

Beyond a Boundary appears less radical: it's ostensibly a book about cricket, but as its famous epigram has it, 'What do they of cricket know, who only cricket know?' *Beyond a Boundary* brilliantly unpicks the way colonialism changes its subjects but is in turn changed by them, as exemplified by the way West Indian cricketers revolutionised the game. It was a book that profoundly influenced this writer – its echoes were plain to see in eighties London, where the children of the Windrush generation were confidently transforming the streets and the sounds of the city.

So why was it only at the end of his life that CLR James's true importance began to be recognised? It is difficult to look beyond the matter of race. CLR James was a Black polymath, a historian and political philosopher and cultural theorist at a time when Black people were not expected to be any of those things.

Everything he strove for, in his writing and his political activism, was to move beyond the racial strictures – both legal and social – that tried to limit who he could be. But of course the question of race was always there. CLR James may not have wanted to see the world simply through the prism of colour, but when the world looked at him, it saw a Black man. His friend, the great West Indian poet Derek Walcott, pointed out how hard it was for James 'to have been so brilliant and yet to have been thought of as a brilliant black man'.[1]

But if 'race' did affect how others saw him, James still refused to let it prevent him from living his life beyond its arbitrary boundaries. He always followed his own path, all the way from Trinidad at the end of the Victorian era to London at the end of the Thatcher era. He was born in a remote outpost of the British Empire but died in a Britain struggling to come to terms with the post-colonial era. He lived through two world wars and the Russian Revolution. As a child he had an elderly aunt who had been born a slave. And yet by the end of his life, Trinidad had become an independent republic with a Black prime minister.

In his life's work, CLR James was a true all-rounder. Much of that work attracted some attention: as an historian, an architect of Pan-Africanism, a novelist, the *éminence grise* of Trinidad's independence, a cricket reporter for the *Guardian*, a playwright, a pioneering Trotskyist. And yet despite all these highlights, it's surprising how much of his long career was lived far from the spotlight.

For while the work has been much examined, the long and remarkable life story has never before been told in detail. No previous book has shown just how varied his actual life was: the places he lived and the work he did. It's often said of CLR James that everyone has their own version of the man. Perhaps it's because there were so many different versions in real life.

There's the young literary gent who lived in Port of Spain in the twenties, writing short stories and aspiring to be the Trinidadian O. Henry. There's the Trotskyist firebrand who discovered Marxism in a Lancashire mill town and toured the halls and meeting rooms of thirties Britain, in the years between the Depression and the war. There's the New York intellectual of the forties, debating the 'Negro question' with Trotsky himself and refashioning Hegel's dialectic for the modern world. There's the Trinidadian politician of the fifties and sixties, playing his part as his island moved towards independence. There's the Washington DC teacher of the seventies, educating Black Power devotees about Lenin and Herman Melville, while schooling himself in feminism. And there's the grand old man of the eighties, listening to Mozart operas in his Brixton bedsit and appearing on TV to talk about Shakespeare.

Too many lives for one man, surely, but somehow he contrived to live them all. And there's a common thread that runs throughout: an undimmed belief in a better world. In his youth he believed in the power of literature to change the world. Later he put his faith in Marxist politics. He saw many of his hopes come to fruition in the anti-colonial struggle of the post-war years – and at the end of his life he drew succour from the rise of the Polish Solidarity movement. He never lost his faith in the power of the common people of the world, Black and white, to make their own history.

In fact, the older he got, the more fully he believed in the power of the spontaneous uprising of the oppressed. He'd seen it among the millworkers of Nelson in Lancashire. He saw it among the sharecroppers of south-eastern Missouri. He saw it in the Hungarian uprising of 1956 and the Parisian student riots of May 1968. He would most certainly have recognised it in the Black Lives Matter protests of 2020.

And there are few Black lives that offer more for us to learn from than that of CLR James. As far back as 1938, he recognised the power of identity politics, but also its limitations when it came to effecting true social change. In *The Black Jacobins* he made his position clear:

> The race question is subsidiary to the class question in politics, and to think of imperialism in terms of race is disastrous. But to neglect the racial factor as merely incidental is an error only less grave than to make it fundamental.

He saw Black people across the diaspora as allied groups because of their experience of colonial oppression and, for the same reason, he saw them as potential revolutionaries. His focus, though, was always on the way forward, rather than on the wounds of the past. When he did write on history, it was with the aim of inspiring people to change their own situation. To that end he found his perfect subject in the Haitian Revolution. Years later he explained the reasons why:

> I was tired of reading and hearing about Africans being persecuted and oppressed in Africa, in the Middle Passage, in the USA and all over the Caribbean. I made up my mind that I would write a book in which Africans or people of African descent instead of constantly being the object of other peoples' exploitation and ferocity would themselves be taking action on a grand scale and shaping other people to their own needs.[2]

And just as the story of the Haitian Revolution and its leaders, particularly Toussaint Louverture, still has much to teach us, so too does the life of CLR James. Like Toussaint Louverture he is not a man without flaws, or political misjudgements. His personal life did not always match up to his ideals, but he never ceased trying to make a way forward, to envision a society in which Black and white, men and women, would have an equal say in the circumstances of their lives.

At great personal cost he sought to live by these ideals. His was a life of great sacrifices and great rewards. He was a man who cared nothing for money and possessions, other than books and records, but nonetheless loved fine wine and good food. A man every bit as happy talking to the janitor as the judge, a man who genuinely believed that – in the favourite phrase he took from ancient Athens – 'every cook can govern'. Having grown up in the surprisingly multicultural world of early twentieth-century Trinidad, he went on to live in Black worlds and white worlds, Harlem and Hampstead, but preferred, if possible, to live in the in-between places. In his own life he treated overt racism less as a barrier blocking his way than as something foul you stepped in occasionally and had to scrape off your shoes. He was a man who knew where he came from, but refused to be defined by it. He was a man who lived his life beyond the boundaries.

PART ONE

Trinidad

Chapter One

It was not impossible for a Black boy, born in Trinidad in 1901, to make it to the top of his society, but there was only one route that anyone knew of, and that road was a long and a hard one, and its entrance gates were exceedingly narrow.

First they would need to go to elementary school and work hard on their reading and writing and mathematics so that, at the age of eleven, they might win one of four exhibitions – scholarships – to one of the island's two private secondary schools, either Queen's Royal College or the Catholic St Mary's College. Once there they would have to study relentlessly at a curriculum modelled on an English public school so that, aged eighteen, they might win one of the three annual Island Scholarships. These would pay for a boy to travel to England and go to university there. And if they pulled that off, they could return to Trinidad and take up a job as a lawyer or doctor or senior civil servant.

It was possible, then, but the odds against were overwhelming and most of Trinidad's Black people were resigned to setting their sights rather lower. However, the James family, from the village of Tunapuna, were not inclined to aim low for their firstborn son, Cyril Lionel Robert. They had already travelled a long way in the past sixty years, since the abolition of slavery in the British Empire.

Robert Alexander James was in his mid-twenties when his son was born, the headmaster of the elementary school in Tunapuna. His grandfather had been a slave in Barbados. His father had come to Trinidad in search of betterment. He had found a good job as a pan-boiler on a sugar estate. It was a skilled but dangerous job, and one that had ended in serious injury, leaving Robert to carry the family's fortunes. He had taken on the responsibility, winning a scholarship to the teacher-training college in Tranquility, and rising fast to become head of one of the government-run schools.

In Tunapuna he met and married Bessie Rudder. His brother had spotted her at the railway station, rushed home and told Robert he'd found the perfect girl for him. According to family tradition he announced that 'I was coming from the station and see her just getting off. She is a tall girl, she is friendly, she is slim and she is elegant, she is ladylike.'[1]

Bessie had come to Trinidad from Barbados as a baby. Her father Josh had made a pioneering career for himself on the Trinidad railways, the first Black engine driver on the island and an expert mechanic. Bessie's mother had died young, so she was sent to a convent to be educated in the ways of Victorian ladyhood.

The two of them were part of a generation of young Black people who were starting to move up in society, to take jobs in teaching and government. And, of course, they wanted better still for their son. So when he turned out to be a precociously bright little boy, the course was set.

Before going any further there needs to be some scene setting, some sense of Trinidad in the last years of the reign of Queen Victoria.

Basics first: Trinidad is the southernmost Caribbean island, less than ten miles off the coast of Venezuela. It's approximately fifty miles long and thirty miles wide. The main town is Port of Spain in the northwest. When CLR was born, Trinidad was a booming island, with a population of around a quarter of a million, three times what it had been forty years before. It was largely dependent on agriculture. Traditionally sugar had been the major product, but in recent years cocoa had become a fashionable crop, driving the population increase as workers arrived from other Caribbean islands and, particularly, from India.

Trinidad's population was always unusually mixed for a Caribbean island. It had been inhabited by Arawaks and Caribs when Columbus first landed there in 1492. A hundred years later the Spanish finally took control and established permanent but small-scale settlements. It never had a population of more than a few thousand, many of whom were French Creoles, until 1777, when the Spanish encouraged immigration from elsewhere in the Caribbean, allowing slave owners (some of whom were 'free people of colour') to settle on the island.

By the time the British captured the island in 1797, the population was around 17,000, including 10,000 African slaves, and increased slowly over the next few decades. The slave trade was outlawed by the British in 1807 and slave ownership made illegal in 1833. By this time the total slave population had reached 17,000 (compared to 360,000 in Jamaica).

Following the final liberation of the slaves in 1838, the island plantation owners had a problem. The freed slaves had no enthusiasm for returning to the land, so the owners came up with the idea of importing 'indentured labourers' from elsewhere in the Empire. This was essentially slavery v2.0. Poverty-stricken labourers were shipped to the Caribbean in conditions barely preferable to the slave boats. In return for this they would be credited with a substantial debt, which they would have to work off by labouring on the plantations for years. The first indentured labourers to be imported were Chinese, but their mortality rate was so extraordinarily high that plantation owners decided to turn to India next, and across the next seventy years more than 140,000 Indian indentured labourers came to Trinidad, doubling its population.

By 1901, then, the island had a population north of two hundred thousand. The two largest ethnic groups by far were those of African and Indian origin. There was also a significant mixed-race or 'coloured' population, plus a motley assortment of white Europeans, ranging from the ruling English to the lowly Portuguese, topped off by a few thousand Chinese and a small but significant Syrian community. Unusually, the people of Black African origin were not at the bottom of the social pile. The Indian 'coolies' had that role, labouring on the plantations, while the Black people tended to live in the towns, where some of them were starting to move into professional jobs, as well as labouring, dock work and so forth.

It was a society in a permanent state of flux and pregnant with opportunities: the 'promised land' of the Caribbean, according to the press, particularly if you had a starting position some way up the ladder.

If you were part of the 'coloured' elite, or Portuguese perhaps, the way forward was simple, but there were real chances of advancement for the Black population too, if you were determined and ambitious enough.

CLR James was born in Chaguanas, a settlement in the west of the island between the two major towns of Port of Spain and San Fernando. It had a small hospital, which is very likely where he was born. CLR himself suggests the family may actually have lived there for a while: 'All I remember of it was that my godfather was a Chinese shopkeeper whose sons were taught by my father. There was some understanding between them which at the time was rather unusual and I vaguely remember being taken to the Chinese gentleman's living quarters behind the Grocery Store and their coming to our house.'[2]

By this time, though, the James family were living in or near the village of Arouca, just outside the town of Arima. We know this because when CLR was little more than a year old, Robert James was mentioned in the *Trinidad Mirror* as being one of the founding members of a debating association in Arouca. A few months later Robert was recorded as leading the choir in the Arouca Presbyterian Church.

The details of his life become clearer from the time CLR was around four years old. He was now known to one and all as 'Nello' – from his middle name Lionel – and had acquired two younger siblings, Olive and Eric. At that point his father was transferred to a new job, as headmaster of the government school in the remote rural village of North Trace, in the south of the island, amid the sugar and cocoa plantations. CLR described his earliest memories of life there in a letter to his second wife, Constance Webb:

> My first memory is at the age of about four. My mother brought myself and my sister, two years younger, in a cab to North Trace. The train brought us to Princes Town, and then a cab carried us the six miles to North Trace. My father had gone there to be a village schoolmaster. I sat in the cab looking out. Then I remember in the

> first days going to the wooden latrine . . . I remember too that one day my brother and I were allowed by my mother to run out in the street and bathe naked in the rain.[3]

This was a difficult posting for Robert James on a number of levels. Firstly, he was stuck in the back of beyond, trying to provide a basic education to the rural poor. CLR describes what he was up against in another letter:

> Everything was very primitive. There were about 120 children, boys and girls, most of them bare-footed for they were very poor. The schoolhouse was about eighty feet by forty, with a few maps on the wall and benches.

There was also a headmistress, whose task was to teach the infants while Robert concentrated on the older children, teaching them reading, writing, arithmetic, geography, singing and drill (PE, more or less). He also had some assistants ('of varying degrees of ignorance', according to CLR).[4]

The second problem the James family now had to deal with was the climate. Trinidad, in the tropics, has only two seasons, known as the rainy and the dry. The rainy season lasts approximately from June to December, and down in the rural south it was believed to be unhealthy, especially for children ('We got fever', wrote CLR). It had been responsible for an alarming level of mortality when the indentured workers first arrived from India to work these fields. The solution the James family found was to send the children north to Tunapuna to stay with their aunts, Robert's sisters, during the rainy seasons.

Tunapuna may have been a bigger, busier town with shops and churches and a train station, but CLR's new living quarters were basic in the extreme. The house was only twelve feet by eighteen in its entirety. There were two rooms, one divided by a paper blind. This was now home to the three children, plus CLR's grandmother and his two aunts. The house had a thatched roof that let the rain in, and holes in the floor.

CLR couldn't sleep for fleas. The adults in the house were washerwomen and seamstresses. Times were hard, but Robert sent money and there was always food on the table.

The house's singular benefit was its location, directly opposite the recreation ground. If you stood at the front window you could watch the games of cricket there, from right behind the bowler's arm. This window is where the legend of CLR James starts. It's where he begins his masterpiece, *Beyond a Boundary*:

> By standing on a chair a small boy of six could watch practice every afternoon and matches on Saturdays – with matting one pitch could and often did stand for both practice and matches. From the chair also he could mount on to the window-sill and so stretch a groping hand for the books on top of the wardrobe. Thus early the pattern of my life was set.

There's no use trying to better James's own description of watching the cricketers, as related in *Beyond a Boundary*. But it's worth recapping the key elements. The great excitement for James was watching Matthew Bondman* bat. Bondman was a young man who lived a few doors down. He was everything CLR's hard-working, God-fearing aunts disapproved of – uncouth, unemployed, unshod. This was the final straw: to care so little for the values of society that you didn't even bother with shoes. But on the cricket pitch, for a year or two until he lost interest, he was transformed into a natural batsman with a flair for the sweep and the cut shot, which he would play with one knee low to the ground – elegant shots that seemed so at odds with the man playing them. In Bondman, CLR saw early the contradictions inherent in every aspect of life for a Black boy in Trinidad – the chasm between lofty aspiration and grimy reality.

Bondman exemplified the rough life of the street. CLR's home life sought to protect him from the street and ultimately to deliver him from it. And for his aunts and grandmother escape was via the books

* Matthew Bondman was a pseudonym used by CLR so as not to upset his family.

that sat on top of the wardrobe and would occupy the young CLR before and after cricket.

These books were all religious in character. Unsurprisingly so. The older of the sisters, his aunt Judith, something of a second mother to him, was later described by CLR as 'the English Puritan incarnate'.[5] The family attended church every Sunday morning, and the children stayed on for Sunday school in the afternoons. This was an utterly unremarkable given. It was no more something to rebel against than the weather. And he would later credit this relentless exposure to the English of the King James Bible as the foundation of his own use of the English language.

> There was a series of brightly coloured religious pamphlets telling the story of Jacob and the Ladder, Ruth and Naomi and similar stories. There was a large book called The Throne Of The House Of David. One day somebody told me that these stories could be found in the many bibles that lay around the house. Detective-like, I tracked down the originals and must have warmed the souls of my aunts and grandmother as they saw me poring over the bible. It fascinated me. When the Parson read the Lessons I strove to remember the names and numbers. Rev Allen had a fine voice and was a beautiful reader. I would go home and search and read half aloud to myself. Somewhere along the way I must have caught the basic rhythms of English prose. My reading was chiefly in the Old Testament and I may have caught too some of the stern attitude to life that was all around me, tempered by family kindness.

When he returned to his parents with the dry season in December each year, CLR was exposed to a wider variety of reading matter. Surprisingly, this didn't come from his father the schoolteacher, as much as from his mother. Over the years he would talk again and again about the extent of her passion for reading. His letters to Constance Webb offer a vivid description of his beloved Bessie:

> My chief memory is of my mother sitting reading and I lying on the floor near her reading until it was time for me to go to bed – 9

> o'clock. She was a very tall woman, my colour, with a superb carriage and so handsome that everybody always asked who she was. She dressed in the latest fashion – she had a passion for dress and was herself a finished seamstress. But she was a reader. She read everything that came her way. I can see her now, sitting very straight with her book held high, her pince-nez on her Caucasian nose.* As she read a book and put it down I picked it up. My father read nothing – a book a year perhaps.[6]

She was a voracious but indiscriminate reader, doubtless limited by the fact that the only source of books was an itinerant bookseller who would come by every couple of weeks, carrying a sack of books on his shoulders. Bessie would buy books by the popular writers of the day, whether literary folk like the Brontës or Thackeray, classic romancers like Sir Walter Scott or Fenimore Cooper, or forgotten popular hits like Mrs E. D. E. N. Southworth or Nat Gould.

On occasion his father would buy a book specifically for CLR, a copy of *The Pickwick Papers*, for instance, because he knew of its reputation, rather than through having read it himself. The bookseller carried magazines too, so Robert would buy copies of *Pearson's* and *Tit-Bits*, which would feature short stories but also profiles of the leading cricketers of the day.

This interest, at least, he shared with his father, who was a hard-hitting batsman and an admirer of W. G. Grace, the great cricketing hero of the Victorian era, perhaps the first true sporting hero of the modern age. CLR started to keep cuttings about cricketers and cricket matches, a habit that would persist through his life, and an early indicator of his supremely organised, if highly individual, approach to learning.

He didn't just follow cricket. He played too: his father had given him a bat and ball for his fourth birthday and when in Tunapuna he'd ask friends and neighbours to bowl at him, among them the local blacksmith and cricketing star, Cudjoe, and local boys called Kelvin,

* The legacy of a white French ancestor, so CLR told his friend Alfred Mendes

Buller, George and Aldrick. At other times he had to make do with playing with his little brother Eric, three years younger. This was less satisfactory:

> He was a sickly boy and lazy and not too much inclined to play. When I had no books to read, I would beg him to play with me ... My brother would never play unless I allowed him to bat first. If he got out at once he would say he wasn't playing any more. I used to cry bitter tears (I remember them now). It wasn't fair. He had cheated me, and the idea revolted me. I complained to my mother. She sometimes compelled him to play – a stupid thing ... I gave him two innings to my one. No use. He always cheated me. He cheated naturally and I was naturally honest and fair-minded.[7]

It is possible, of course, that Eric might have had a different perspective.

CLR also records that he used to love to roam around with an air gun, shooting at birds or tin cups. He may have felt himself to be a fair-minded boy, but the birds and little brothers might have kept their own counsel with regards to that judgement.

CLR was undeniably a very bright child, taking easily to the three Rs. His father knew what needed to happen next. That would be the annual scholarship examination, in which the cleverest boys from around the island under the age of twelve all competed for the exhibitions to Queen's Royal College and St Mary's.

This was in addition to the regular island-wide examinations. Once a year, inspectors would come to each of Trinidad's elementary schools. The pupils would take the exam and the school's performance would be assessed on the basis of these results. More pupils marked 'very good' meant more money for the school – 'the bonus' went directly to the headteacher, who, if they were a decent man like Robert James, would distribute some of it among their assistants.

This system of payment by results led, according to CLR, to institutionalised corruption:

> The chief part of the examination was the written part; all the standards had for example Arithmetic Cards with sums on them. The cards were imported by the examiner from England. Groups of teachers got together and imported cards from every maker of cards in England. They had all the possible cards. When the [inspector's] tour began, the first teacher passed the word along that this year, Mr, Robinson was using Craul's cards or Johnson's as the case might be. At once the teachers all along the route had their pupils furiously working out those cards over and over again so that when the day came and they were handed out each pupil knew his sums already . . . There was this cheating going on in every school . . . The curious thing is that no one considered it immoral.

The scholarship examination, though, was a very different matter. Robert James was determined that CLR should pass, and when his son was eight he decided to take him in hand. It was a decision so momentous that the date remained in CLR's mind decades later: 26 April 1909. From then on he would stay in North Trace all year round and study with his father.

Before and after school Robert would give his son extra tuition. At the same time CLR was now really starting to leap forward in his reading:

> I was way beyond the average boy. Because I had been reading. We used to use a kerosene lamp. At nine o'clock my parents would go to bed. I would have brought a candle. And in my room where I slept, my father always put me alone by myself, I would light my candle and read till about two or three in the morning.[8]

His choice of reading matter was becoming more sophisticated. Just as he was being made aware of the ambitions his parents had for him and the tasks he had ahead, he became fascinated by one of the great nineteenth-century novels, one that centred around a bright outsider called Becky Sharp trying to make her way in society: Thackeray's *Vanity Fair.*

> My mother had an old copy with a red cover. I had read it when I was about eight, and of all the books that passed through the house this one became my Homer and my bible. I read it through from the first page to the last, then started again. For years I had no notion that it was a classical novel. I read it because I wanted to.[9]

In December 1909 CLR sat the examination, just before his ninth birthday. He was two or three years younger than the boys he was up against, and his father claimed that he was just doing the exam for practice, this little kid from North Trace up against all the smart town boys.

> On the day of the examination a hundred boys were brought from all parts of the island by their teachers, like so many fighting cocks. That day I looked at the favourites and their trainers with wide-open eyes, for I was a country bumpkin.

He didn't win an exhibition but, remarkably, he was placed seventh. And unlike his competitors, CLR would have three more chances before reaching the cut-off age of twelve.

As it happened, the following year he would no longer be a country bumpkin. The month after he first took the exam, in January 1910, Robert got a new job. It was a serious promotion. From the backwoods of North Trace, he was picked to be the new headmaster of St Ann's School in Port of Spain, close by the Governor's house and the great Savannah Park.

CLR went with his father to live in Port of Spain. It's unclear whether the rest of the family came too, or whether they stayed behind in either North Trace or Tunapuna. CLR's memoirs never mention either his mother or his siblings being there, but then he does focus very heavily on his own fortunes. His brother and sister, in particular, very rarely get a look in. Either way, he certainly enjoyed his new quarters:

> St Ann's was a remarkably situated school. It was around the Queen's Park Savannah and just next to a famous sporting club, the Shamrock Sporting Club. So there was a house where the head teacher lived within the same yard and there was a little room in the front, and there I was well installed and having a fine time.[10]

The Savannah, the city's central park, was essentially a big open space and it was full of cricket and football pitches, even a horse-racing track. From his new home the young CLR could walk straight out on to the Savannah and see all the leading players of the day in club matches.

> So just a few weeks from North Trace and I am catapulted into the heart of what is taking place, I was extremely well educated on cricket, football and horse-racing. In addition to that an English team came to play international cricket at the Queen's Park Oval, just across the Savannah. My father took me. I began to be very much interested in football because I am not only learning to play, but I could watch the games take place in the Savannah and read about them the next morning.

Reading newspaper sports reports became one of CLR's great interests – and a lifelong habit. He would read about his special interests, cricket, football, great boxing matches and even horse racing, then cut out any articles that particularly interested him for his scrapbooks.

Robert James hadn't brought CLR to Port of Spain just to read the sports pages and watch cricket, though. His focus was firmly on the next year's scholarship examination. He gave CLR an hour's tuition before and after the school day. He was soon sure that his son was going to have little trouble with the exam. Aged nine, CLR was holding his own in the same class as teenagers.

> I remember him looking at me in a very peculiar way when I did some of these things. And one week before the exams he told me

– 'Boy I have nothing more to teach you, I am not going to do any work with you this week, you are ready, do what you like, come to class, I am not giving you any extra lessons just take it easy.' So my mother was a little bit concerned – 'You are not teaching him anything more, Robert?' she said. 'No,' said my father, 'I cannot teach him anything more than what he knows at the present time. He is going to go there, he is coming first, nobody is going to beat him.'

And I went into the examination and everybody understood that I was going to come out first. I got one hundred marks for arithmetic. I did everything.

CLR was never a man afflicted by false modesty. Having the benefit of a quite extraordinary memory, studying always came easy. Winning a scholarship to Queen's Royal College, when still just nine years old, was no more than he expected. He was officially the brightest boy on the island. The way forward, once so narrow and remote, was starting to open up in front of him.

Chapter Two

Queen's Royal College, looking out over the western edge of the Savannah, was a remarkable institution; a school that would produce prime ministers and presidents, Olympic medallists and a Nobel prize-winner, radicals and reactionaries, cricketers and carnival designers. It was the apogee of the school system that the British had set up once they took control of Trinidad.

In 1851 the Governor General, Lord Harris, established a system of primary schools across the island. Education was to be made available to all, 'however humble their birth'. In 1857 the new Governor, Arthur Hamilton-Gordon, decided to add a secondary, or collegiate, school. This would be set up so that, in the words of the Governor, 'Its advantages should be open to those of every race and every religion, and that the education given should be of a decidedly superior character.'[1]

The school opened in 1859, as the Queen's Collegiate School, and by 1863 it was the first school in a British colony to enter students for the Cambridge Entrance exam, with considerable success. The original school site was in Lord Harris Square, in the centre of town, but its remarkable results attracted further funding from England. In 1904, by now renamed Queen's Royal College, it moved into spectacular new premises by the Savannah, one of a string of ornate Edwardian buildings known as the Seven Sisters.

It was still a very new building when CLR James arrived in January 1911, immediately after his tenth birthday. It can't fail to have made an impression on him, this grand building, after the primitive establishments he'd attended in Tunapuna and North Trace. And one can only imagine his father's pride, taking his boy across the Savannah for his first day.

But while Queen's Royal College may have had something of the look of a British public school – and certainly its curriculum was broadly the same as that of Rugby or Winchester – its mix of pupils was very different. In later years CLR remembered his fellow pupils as a harmonious bunch, whose numbers included the white children of British officials and businesspeople; the children of the Black middle class; lawyers, doctors, pharmacists and so on; as well as Indian and Chinese children whose parents were more likely to be shopkeepers. 'There was, as far as I can remember, no racial conflict.'[2]

And then there were the scholarship boys like CLR. He was in no way overawed by his new surroundings. He was the brightest boy on the island, after all. He started learning Latin and French. Greek would follow a year or so later. And he started making friends. He recalled that the Black boys generally tended to mix with the East Indians, while the white boys and the Chinese boys generally stuck in their own groups. CLR, however, quickly made friends with some white boys, sons of doctors and senior civil servants – 'obviously their families were of notable status in the community. But I never felt it and they didn't seem to be aware of it and year after year we fought to sit next to each other in class.'

It's worth pausing to consider this cheery account. Can CLR's first interactions with the island's white ruling class really have been so simple? It's hard to imagine that there was no racism in a school on an island where skin colour and racial origin were key factors in determining your chances in life. So how to explain this? It seems likely that much of it comes from CLR's own person and personality. He was good-looking, confident and well spoken. All of this doubtless mitigated against him being a target for bullying, racist or otherwise. Credit must also be due to the teachers at QRC. Generally white Englishmen, they nevertheless seem to have treated their multi-racial pupils with fairness.

Certainly, CLR enjoyed his time there. The teaching he remembered as first rate – the masters were all bar one Oxbridge men. He soon achieved distinction by winning a prize in an essay competition. Students from all over the island were invited to send in contributions on 'The British Empire'. CLR, still only ten, came second and won two volumes of Kipling's stories.

His appetite for reading remained prodigious and after the first year he was able to access what he saw as the school's greatest asset: its extensive library. There he found the complete works of his beloved Thackeray – thirty-eight volumes, mostly illustrated by the novelist himself – plus Dickens and George Eliot and the other Victorian novelists, as well as collections of poetry selected by Matthew Arnold. He dived into all of these but found time too for less elevated material. He devoured the adventure stories of G. A. Henty and the school stories of P. G. Wodehouse, plus copies of the *Boy's Own Paper*. He was always on the lookout for anything written about the game of cricket. There wasn't much – just things like the *Jubilee Book of Cricket* by Ranjitsinhji – but CLR scoured them for information.

Cricket was becoming more and more of a passion. He had grown into a tall, athletic boy and could both bat and bowl to a decent standard. QRC had its own grounds. Up to five teams could play at once, and the school's first team was good enough to play in the all-island competitions. A sporting ethos was much encouraged by the headmaster, William Burslem – described by CLR as part Pickwick, part Dr Johnson, part Samuel Smiles. Burslem had been an assistant master at Harrison College in Barbados, the elite school of the British Caribbean and the crucible for the popularity of cricket in the area. Alumni included Pelham 'Plum' Warner, the English cricket captain and pioneering cricket writer. All shared a belief that sport had a civilising power, cricket most of all. The game's explicit moral code was elevated to the level of a religious faith – a faith CLR would cleave to with perhaps excessive fervour.

At the start of CLR's second year at QRC, his father was transferred once again, from St Ann's to Arima, a sizeable town twenty miles east of Port of Spain. This presented a problem, as it was too far for CLR to travel to and from school each day, given the limitations of public transport. The first solution was for CLR to board in town, at the house of a friend of his father's, a teacher called Mr Brown.

This stay lasted for a few months. And while there is precious little evidence as to what happened there, many years later CLR would refer – in an anguished letter to his second wife – to the trauma he experienced when he was sent away to board. In a fragment of memoir, he describes Mr Brown as 'a very peculiar man'.[3] It was from this period on that CLR started to become a more wilful, wayward boy, rather than the exemplary son he'd been up to this point. But he was also entering adolescence, so it's hard to definitively give responsibility for these changes to the 'peculiar' Mr Brown.

Whatever happened there, after a few months CLR left Mr Brown's place and returned to Tunapuna to live once again with his aunts. Tunapuna was about halfway between Port of Spain and Arima, and the commute was easier for a schoolboy.

Over the next few years CLR entered into what he would later describe as a war. Ironically perhaps, as these were also the years of the Great War in Europe, which some of his older schoolmates would sign up for.

CLR's war was a hard-fought one, memorably described in *Beyond A Boundary*:

> In reality my life up to ten had laid the powder for a war that lasted without respite for eight years, and intermittently for some time afterwards – a war between English Puritanism, English literature and cricket, and the realism of West Indian life.

It was an asymmetrical war too. On one side were CLR's parents and family, family friends, masters and the headmaster, even the Board of Education. And, on the other side, the young CLR James.

The front line was between CLR and his father. CLR's increasing independence of mind led him to read what he wanted when he wanted, rather than to follow the approved curriculum. It led him to play cricket when he should be studying, and to explore the streets. According to a later girlfriend, Louise Cripps, he told her: 'I played hooky – I ran around with a group of boys intent as I was on wild doings, mischief.'[4]

There was only one way such behaviour was dealt with in Trinidad back then – corporal punishment, brutally applied:

I remember when I was going to the Tunapuna school as a small boy I saw Mr Jordan, the headmaster, a very polite and well-mannered man, beating a boy not on his behind but putting him to sit down and beating him across the thighs. He must have given him at least a dozen strokes. But beating was the practice at all schools, Queen's Royal College as well. Mr Burslem, the principal, was always not only ready but alert to beat a boy who was reported to him or whom he caught doing something that he ought not to do, such as wearing a felt hat and not a straw hat.

But if at Queen's Royal College there was regular beating, it was nothing compared to the beatings which were administered by the headmasters of the elementary schools. The boys were beaten without mercy. Boys were badly beaten for not knowing the lessons which should have been prepared the evening before. Any rudeness or impertinence or lack of manners to a teacher was immediately met with blows. The headmaster had two or three rods available and often as well a thick leather strap.[5]

So Robert was no stranger to beating a boy, and when his son defied him he was merciless. He rarely talked about it, but Louise Cripps remembers seeing the marks on CLR's back, scars from the beatings he'd endured. And later, writing to Constance Webb and trying to explain his emotional repression, he stated baldly that 'I was badly beaten as a little boy. Father fierce Puritan.'[6] Even his mother was unable to come to his rescue.

When my father beat me badly she did not interfere and said nothing, except that I was made to understand that she was ready to do any rubbing down that was necessary. She did not want to take my side against his.[7]

Years later James tried to rationalise the brutality he and so many others received at the hands of men like his father:

> They were not cruel men . . . I have talked over this merciless beating of which they were guilty with some of my old schoolfellows. Some of us today believe that, as with so much in the Caribbean today, it was a heritage of slavery, and secondly there was so much vice and ignorance around us that a teacher who was responsible for the moral standards of his community thought it his duty to exercise the severest discipline, and the only discipline he could exercise was the extensive use of the rod.
>
> But the same men not only taught with extreme concentration and responsibility, they told us how to behave in school and out of school. If your clothes were not fixed as they ought to be they not only told us what to do but gave a little lecture on the importance of being tidily dressed . . . some serious study ought to be made of these men who were born and received their education in the second generation after slavery . . . modelling themselves on the conduct and style of the English men and women who ruled over them, established a standard of behaviour which laid the foundation of what became in the next generation the black middle class.

Robert James, then, strove to beat his son into respectability. It didn't work. The beatings served only to alienate him. CLR continued to follow his own intellectual path. The more he saw of life outside the home, exploring Port of Spain, the more he was convinced that the rigid beliefs of his father's generation were simply inadequate. In particular he could see that that the ordinary people of Trinidad lived their life with a vigour and individuality that seemed so much more rewarding than the puritanical lifestyle the teachers were attempting to impose:

> In Shakespeare I had the clash of passion and lust and love and revenge and friendship and all that, that I could see around me with the ordinary people.

CLR was determined to find his own way forward. At school, aged fourteen, he started his own little magazine, taking a few sheets of paper and folding them over to make twenty-four small pages that he would singlehandedly fill up every week:

> I wrote all sorts of things in it. Gossip about the boys and masters, I would include cricket and football, news about the school play, short stories, very short, jokes, anything that will fill the 24 pages. I spent hours writing the thing to hand it to my class. And they read it with interest and there was competition as to who should get it and how long a boy would take to read it. I hadn't the faintest idea why I was doing it. It took an awful amount of time which meant I was neglecting my schoolwork.

Even when he was paying attention to his studies, he was determined to follow his own interests. It's easy to see the precocious schoolboy in his later recollections:

> My schoolwork followed an individual course of its own. I did some studies in integral calculus and differential calculus but soon got tired of them, or rather was too busy with other things to pay proper attention to them. Not that I was weak in mathematics. Not at all. Whenever I paid attention to it I could do as well as anybody else. But I was very busy now with Greek literature . . . having to study Euripides and Thucydides in class I, as usual, read not only the introductions but went off to the library to find all that other people had said about these writings.

Even the college library was not enough to satisfy his intellectual curiosity. He didn't eat lunch with the other boys, but brought his own food – beef sandwiches made by his aunt. Left alone in the school he discovered the inner sanctum: the masters' room, with its own, more rarefied library.

At fifteen he discontinued the magazine but wrote a novel, sixty thousand words or so, based around his school life. To his later regret he tore it up not long afterwards: 'That I regret very much . . . Often I wanted to see what it was I thought when I was fifteen years old . . .

Nobody told me to do any of these things. I had no models on which to mould myself. I simply felt like doing them and did what I wanted to do.'

Also at fifteen, CLR made it into the school's first eleven (he made the football first team as well, playing in goal, but that impacted rather less on his life and work). The cricket team was almost entirely self-administered. They elected their own captains, secretaries and committees ('a master presided, but that's all he did').[8] CLR took to the administration side enthusiastically. He became secretary of the first eleven and at the beginning of every term went off to the shops in town to buy the sports equipment for some 200 boys.

Meanwhile, his approach to the game was very similar to his approach to ancient Greek. Ironically, the cricket that others saw as distracting him from his studies, was, for CLR himself, simply one more academic discipline. He read books on cricket fanatically and the newspaper reports of cricket matches religiously. While still at school he turned himself into an expert in the history and analysis of the game.

More than that, it was cricket that actually inculcated the kind of Victorian values his father had attempted to imbue via rod and leather strap. In *Beyond a Boundary*, CLR describes how the omnipresent public-school code was ignored or subverted in the classroom, but obeyed without question or demur on the sports field:

> As soon as we stepped on to the cricket or football field, all was changed. We were a motley crew. The children of some white officials and white businessmen, middle-class blacks and mulattos, Chinese boys, some of whose parents still spoke broken English, Indian boys, some of whose parents spoke no English at all, and some poor black boys who had won exhibitions or whose parents had starved and toiled on plots of agricultural land and were spending their hard-earned money on giving their eldest boy an education. Yet rapidly we learned to obey the umpire's decision without question, however irrational it was. We learned to play with the team, which meant subordinating your personal inclinations, and

> even interests, for the good of the whole. We did not denounce failures, but 'Well tried' or 'Hard luck' came easily to our lips. We were generous to opponents and congratulated them on victories, even when we knew they did not deserve it.

There's the contradiction that would both trouble and inspire CLR for the rest of his life. He would always and at once be both fierce critic and committed devotee of Western culture, as refracted through the public-school code. It's a mix that is not exclusively, but is definitely very strongly, Trinidadian.

How singular was CLR within his own time is harder to be sure of. So much of what we know of his life comes from his own accounts. There are one or two external sources on which to draw, however. In particular, his schoolmate William Besson narrated a memoir in his eighties,* which includes a vivid portrait of the young CLR.

Besson was from a mixed Black and Chinese background (CLR refers to him as 'a Chinese boy' in various memoirs, showing the keen awareness of racial gradations endemic among Trinidadians at the time). Like CLR, Bill Besson had been educated in Tunapuna and won a scholarship to QRC. He was the same age as CLR but a school year or two behind because of his friend's precociously early start. Unsurprisingly, he was somewhat in awe:

'I think everybody in the island must have known about him,' he recalled. 'Nello took me to his house and I remember seeing a room in his house where the floor was covered with books and I think those books belonged to Nello!'[9]

They didn't see much of each other at first. Besson was not a sportsman like CLR. What brought them together was a tragedy. On 6 March 1915, the two boys were both, separately, on the train from Tunapuna to Port of Spain. It was a single-track line, dangerously overused, and as they approached McKenzie Bridge, just east of San Juan station, the train crashed into an oncoming goods train coming

* Featuring a warmly affectionate foreword by CLR, one of the last pieces he ever wrote.

in the opposite direction. It was a horrific accident. Eleven people died in the carnage. Bill Besson and his two brothers were in one of the worst-affected carriages:

> When this collision took place I lost consciousness for some time and when I regained consciousness I found myself under a lot of wreckage through which I could see twilight and then I heard a voice calling my name. It was Nello calling for me and I replied, and he removed all the wreckage and pulled me out and took me to the embankment. Well, it happened that the friends of my two brothers with whom they were travelling were killed, and this schoolboy friend of mine with whom I was travelling was killed. Nothing happened to Nello . . .

To Besson, then, CLR seemed to have a charmed existence, one that ran on different rails to that of his contemporaries. But if CLR's progress seemed effortless, the reality was very different. The school did not approve of CLR's free and easy approach to the curriculum. For years his exam results were regularly disappointing, definitely below what was expected of a scholarship boy. It was accepted that a pupil funded by public money was not just letting himself down, but the whole community. Now that he was living back home again, his father would beat him and CLR would do as he was told for a while, then head off on his own path once again.

> [My father decided to] give me a beating, which had not happened for a year or two. Disciplined and respectful as I always was to him and other members of my family, I made him understand from early that I was not going to be beaten. I was too big for that. The threat and my calm but determined defiance went on for a day or two, and one night he entered my little bedroom with a strap and said he was going to show me who was master. We held on and though he was a big strong man, I was also very fit and we struggled together. My mother, in tears, came in and somehow she put herself between us, put an end to the conflict.[10]

Robert kept on threatening retribution, so Bessie packed CLR some clothes and told him to go and stay with their neighbours, the Rankeesons. He spent the night there and they gave him money to take the train down south, where he stayed with his uncle, a station master in the village of California.

CLR stayed there for some days, borrowing books and playing cricket and debating with his uncle, an autodidact starved of intellectual conversation. Finally a letter arrived from his father. It was an effective surrender. CLR returned home, went back to school and his father never laid a hand on him again.

Years later CLR would comment, 'He decided to accept me as I was and I became a respectable and self-respecting member of society and have remained so to this day.'[11]

For a while CLR's interests started to coincide more closely with the academic expectations of the school as he prepared for the Oxford & Cambridge Higher Certificate, particularly demanding examinations that Mr Burslem was very keen on. CLR latched on to two elements that particularly appealed to him. The English examination focused on the British romantic movement: Keats, Shelley, Wordsworth, De Quincey ... More exciting yet was the French paper, which introduced him to the great writers of the French romantic movement, Victor Hugo, Gauthier, Lamartine, Balzac and more.

However, CLR being CLR, the fact that there were areas of the new curriculum that excited him meant that he focused on those to the exclusion of all else. As a result, he achieved a prodigious mark for his French literature paper, but a poor one for French prose, and an appalling one for applied mathematics.

From CLR's point of view this was a reasonable enough outcome. He had acquired a lifelong interest in and knowledge of French literature. From the point of view of his family and the hopes they had pinned on him, it was more frustration.

The story of CLR's intransigence was passed down through the James family. His niece Erica, daughter of Eric and herself a long-time preschool educator, remembers the legend of Nello James, the boy who preferred to sit outside the classroom reading his own book rather than sitting inside and listening to the teacher:

> He never wanted to stay in any schoolroom, to sit down, because he knew everything! His father was a headmaster and could not understand it. He knew CLR was very bright, but he couldn't understand why he didn't want to sit in a class like a regular person, but his mother knew that he had really special gifts. It was very difficult for his father.[12]

Robert's frustration with his brilliant, self-willed son is easy to understand. However, it is clear that, in many ways, CLR was absolutely his father's son. Robert too was a proud man, unwilling to compromise. In later years CLR liked to tell the story of how one day, when his father was still headmaster of St Ann's, the Governor stopped by for an impromptu visit.

His father had the children stand up and sing 'God Save the King', then he made a little speech about the work they were doing there. After that the Governor inspected a collection of rocks and stones the children had collected from the nearby Dry River. He liked what he saw and invited Mr James to come up to Government House to see the geological collection they had there.

This was a considerable honour for a Black elementary school teacher and Bessie and the rest of the family were duly impressed. But come the day of the visit, she was amazed to see Robert putting on his regular teaching outfit:

> My mother was startled, she said: 'Robert, I have been dusting down your three-piece suit.' My father told her 'This is my day to day clothes. I am not going to be there as a friend of his. I am there as the teacher and he is the Governor. I am not going to wear all my three-piece suit as if I am an honoured guest.'[13]

Like his son, Robert James was an ambitious man, but constitutionally incapable of being false to himself. And the family were steadily starting to prosper. They were the very epitome of Black middle-class respectability. In his memoirs, CLR testified to the public and private rectitude of his parents and how much their values stayed with him in later life:

> No one has ever seen me drunk, because I have never been drunk. In a society largely undisciplined, my father was never the worse for liquor. As for my mother, the idea was unthinkable. They were not teetotallers, not even critical of drinkers. At Christmas time there would be in the house a bottle or two of Vermouth, some rum, some whiskey, some Madeira wine, gin and one or two other bottles . . . One day, one Christmas day, I saw my father and his friends a little more talkative than usual, but that was all. No one has ever heard me use one of the four letter words in public. I don't do it. It is not a moral question. I simply don't do it because my mother and father never at any time used such words, either in the world outside, or in private in the house.

CLR's sister Olive gets little mention in his memoirs. His one extended reminiscence involves her piano-playing, and offers a vivid illustration of the stern improving regime that Robert presided over:

> In Arima my father bought a piano. He was as fanatically dedicated to music as ever and he was concerned that my sister should play. He taught her for a while, then sent her to the most well-known professor of music in the island, Professor Northalgo, who taught her year after year. Morning after morning, my father made her play scales and day after day, year after year, she sat at the piano at about 7 a.m., playing scales which ran up and down the piano and my father in bed interrupting – 'C sharp not C, F major not minor'. And my sister made a face and played it over.

Olive, of course, never had the chance to go to Queen's Royal College. The only secondary school for girls at the time was a Catholic convent, St Joseph's. She was another great reader, like her mother and older brother, but there was no scholarship path for women at that time. The totems of respectability – playing the piano, dress-making, gardening – were all she was allowed.

CLR's final year at QRC was 1918. The Great War in Europe was still going on and CLR decided that he would like to join the QRC contingent who had signed up to fight. Clearly news of the realities of life in the trenches had failed to make its way back to Port of Spain:

> I was underage but I got it into my head that I would like to see the world, and the best way would be to go to the war. We had been deluged with propaganda, but I don't think that had much to do with it.[14]

The QRC boys had joined up via the Merchant's Contingent, officer-class boys financed by local merchants. On the face of it CLR was an ideal candidate – fit, strong and bright. However, the recruiting agent took one look and shook his head. His dark skin instantly disbarred him. It was a sharp reminder that outside the tolerant precincts of his school, Trinidad's racial hierarchy was still very much in place. The QRC masters were outraged but CLR himself, with a characteristic unwillingness to dwell on his experiences of racism, later said it had only been the most passing of disappointments.

So, instead of heading off to Flanders, CLR returned to his studies, ready to take the O&C Certificate exam on the results of which the Island Scholarship would be awarded. His teachers still had faith in him, not least the redoubtable Mr Burslem:

> He was immensely kind to me and often after telling me at the end of a term that he hoped he would never see my face again (implying that he would report me to the Board of Education – which meant the guillotine) he would write mitigating words in my report, call me to do some personal task for him (a way of showing favour) and in the course of it try to show me the error of my ways.

However, while CLR's attitude may have been changed – less running around town, more studying – so too had his enthusiasm for the project itself. He was no longer convinced that it was worth the candle. If he won the Island Scholarship he would be launched on a set path, to become a lawyer or a doctor or civil servant. Friends and family, his whole community, could see no higher ambition. But CLR could. He had divined a calling. His love of literature had claimed him for its own.

This was plain to see for Bill Besson, who was also studying for the scholarship, though a year behind CLR.

> It was then that CLR James and I became very friendly, because he had no interest in winning the scholarship as he wanted to become a writer. I don't think that anybody could have prevented Nello from winning the scholarship, if he had wanted to ... So he was reading extensively to embark on the career of a writer ... I realised how much Nello knew because when he ought to have been doing his homework he was reading history and literature, that is in the classroom; I mean instead of doing the class work he would actually be reading! ... he would read the masters' text books and he used to read Shakespeare and books which were entirely out of the curriculum. I used to lend him my text books and he would make marginal notes ... I likened him to Samuel Taylor Coleridge. Because it was said ... that if Coleridge borrowed your book, never mind, when you got it back it was worth more than when he had borrowed it. ... So it was in those days, then, that Nello used to come up to our house and we used to study by candlelight or lamplight, because in those days there was no electricity ... And I remember late at night after we had finished our studies we used to go a few yards along the road to the Chinese bakery to get hot loaves ...[15]

And so it came to pass that the brightest boy on the island fell at the final hurdle.

> It was the newness and the excitement of the French literature that I concentrated on for a whole year. The result was that I failed in the

> Higher Certificate Exam. Everyone, including the Principal, was so shocked that they believed a mistake had been made, and a cable was sent to the Oxford & Cambridge examiners asking for papers to be reviewed in case a mistake had been made. The reply came as I at least had expected it would be, that no mistake had been made. I had failed. There was a general crisis among my friends and family, among all except me. I didn't care or thought I didn't.[16]

Besson won the scholarship the following year and went to medical school in Edinburgh, before going on to a distinguished career as a doctor in the colonial medical service in British Guiana and, later, a psychiatrist in Edinburgh. CLR stayed in Trinidad, determined to launch himself on the literary life.

Curiously, his most enduring impression on the school records at QRC was with an achievement that he scarcely mentioned in later life. That was the school high jump record, which he held for twenty years with a mark of 5' 5".

Chapter Three

CLR James's adult life began in the new year of 1919. And for the time being it was to take place in Trinidad. He would not be going to Europe, either to study or to fight, now that the Great War was over. In fact, the scholarship-winners he knew from QRC, Bill Besson and an older boy, George Busby, would not yet be travelling to Britain either, as their awards were deferred until the world had settled down.

CLR had two immediate priorities. First, he needed to find a job. Second, he needed to find a cricket team.

A job came along easily enough, courtesy of a man he'd met while staying with his uncle following the big bust-up with his father. The man in question worked on the Brechin Castle sugar estate, north of San Fernando. Much of the work in the sugar factory was brutally hard and hot labour, but for a QRC boy like CLR it was another story. He found himself with a wonderfully cushy job in the estate offices. All he had to do was venture into the main body of the factory every half hour and take a sample of the cane juice; to the rest of his time he could devote to reading.

So CLR sat in an office otherwise populated by English and Scottish engineers, reading Hume or Kant or a history of the French revolution. When one of them asked what he was reading, CLR gave the lofty answer that it was a work of philosophy, just something a person of some education should read. The engineer, with some self-restraint, would respond that they were a person of some education too!

While he was at Brechin Castle the ill-paid field labourers threatened to strike but CLR took little interest, happy enough in the office with his books. Neither does he seem to have paid much mind to the series of strikes that rolled out across Trinidad later that year, led by the Trinidad Workingmen's Association. At this stage his interest in politics was very much more on the theoretical level than the practical.

After a while he was allowed to actually carry out tests on the samples he'd been collecting. It turned out, not entirely surprisingly, that he was measuring the sugar content. Another pleasant month or two of measuring and testing and reading passed, and then he was offered a more challenging job, one that would bring him back to Port of Spain.

A Mrs Regis ran the mellifluously named Pamphyllian High School. This was a private school that offered secondary education to mostly Black children whose parents either couldn't afford the fees at QRC or saw it as socially beyond them. It offered Latin and other subjects that weren't available in the elementary schools. The school was looking for a new principal. It might seem unlikely that anyone would pick an eighteen-year-old for the job, but CLR himself saw it as entirely natural, given his QRC education and his sporting reputation.

Sure enough, he was offered the post at a salary of $30 a month. So he left Brechin Castle and his uncle's place in Carapachaima, and moved to lodgings in Port of Spain.

The school was clearly a very small operation, most likely with CLR as the sole teacher, as in Bill Besson's memory: 'He started his own school, which he called the Pamphyllian High School and I remember on my way walking down from the college to the railway station I used to drop in and have a chat with him.'[1]

So, with no little irony, the boy who was notorious for sitting outside the classroom following his own curriculum was now a teacher himself, just like his father before him. The most notable feature of his time running the school was his decision to stage a production of *The Merchant of Venice*. This is how CLR remembered it fifty years later:

> Boys played the girls' parts. Among the performers were black, white, Chinese, East Indians. It did not matter in the slightest, the play lasted until about two o'clock in the morning to a full house at the Empire Theatre and was talked about for years after.[2]

Which contrasts markedly with Bill Besson's memory of the show:

> Nello told me he was going to stage *The Merchant of Venice* in a cinema in Port of Spain; and he actually got his pupils to learn Shakespeare and put on the show. But unfortunately Port of Spain had not reached the stage to appreciate that. I remember I took a young lady to see the play and there was just a sprinkling of people in this huge cinema. But Nello pressed on. The play was staged in front of the curtain and his pupils performed the whole of *The Merchant of Venice*.[3]

All of which suggests that much of CLR's character was already in place. In particular, his lifelong willingness to press on in the face of public indifference, and also a valuable ability to ignore said indifference and see enthusiasm instead. Besson remembers taking his date to a half-empty theatre; CLR remembers the twelve-year-old who played Bassanio and from scratch 'picked up the Shakespearean rhythm to perfection'.[4]

If anything, the experience of putting on the play only increased CLR's passion for Shakespeare. The following year he took a summer holiday to Trinidad's sister island of Tobago and spent his time there in intensive study:

> I would get up in the morning early, go down to the sea which was only a few yards away, have an early dip, come back and have some breakfast and settle down to reading a Shakespeare play. At about mid-day down to the sea again back to lunch and then Shakespeare again. I had no other books with me and had purposely left everything else behind. At about 5 o'clock I would go down for another dip and meet some boys playing cricket on the beach. I would have a game with them then back to dinner and after that Shakespeare again. I read the 37 plays, also Venus & Adonis and the Rape of Lucrece.[5]

This is evidently pretty much CLR's ideal holiday, but his hosts were baffled by it. He tried to address their confusion by explaining the plots of several plays to them. This did not help. Finally they decided that he must have 'a gift'.

* * *

William Besson may have bemoaned the lack of cultural awareness in Port of Spain, but a nascent intelligentsia was starting to make its presence felt. For Black people like CLR it focused around the Maverick Club. This was a brand-new cultural and debating society for the rising generation of Trinidadians ready to take a more prominent place in society than their forebears had been allowed.

There is one surviving photo of the Maverick Club. It's a formal outdoor group shot, taken in 1919. It's also the earliest known photo of CLR James, eighteen years old at the time. He's second from the left in the middle row. A tall young man with a natty bow tie and his arms folded. He must be one of the youngest members, but looks entirely at home.

There are twenty-six Mavericks in the picture, arranged in rows. Half men, half women: the men in smart dark suits, women in white dresses, ages looking to range from late teens to late fifties. It's a photo that positively radiates pride. Pride forged in adversity. As CLR commented, 'People said that Negroes could not organise anything. The Maverick club consisted of Negroes. We met every Saturday night in a hall attached to All Saints Church. Later we progressed to a new house in Woodbrook.'[6]

Many of the Mavericks went on to distinguished careers in Trinidad or abroad. Audrey Jeffers would launch a women-only offshoot, the Coterie of Social Workers, which began pioneering charity work among the poor. A highway is named after her now, while her house has recently been restored. George Busby would become a doctor in Britain and Ghana. His future wife, Beryl Davis, would be the first Trinidadian woman to qualify as a doctor, before giving it up for showbusiness.

Meta and her sister Kathleen,* whose father was one of the wealthiest Black men in Trinidad, were both prominent members. Years later Kathleen would tell a Trinidad newspaper that CLR had given her her first kiss. It may have been Kathleen who proposed that he should become secretary of the club when it became riven by factionalism.

* Later Kathleen Warner, an actress and radio broadcaster. As Auntie Kay she presented a talent show on Trinidad radio for over forty years, from the forties to the eighties.

CLR, never a shrinking violet, accepted the challenge, and in combination with the new chairman, Mr Berridge, one of the older members, took charge.

Much of the business of the Mavericks consisted of putting on concerts. The Grosvenor sisters were fine musicians, while Elise Braithwaite was a remarkably talented vocalist, whose praises CLR would sing for decades to come. They even staged a musical comedy (which one, CLR couldn't remember, sadly). There were also debates and talks. CLR naturally gave several of them – on Wordsworth, on Longfellow, on the American Revolution. Some of the other lectures served to broaden his own education, especially when it came to racial politics. The older members, like Mr Berridge and a Mr Worrell, had a long-term interest in Black nationalism. They read books by the Black American writer W. E. B. Du Bois and the newspaper *The Crisis*.

Meanwhile, CLR's career was advancing rapidly. He hadn't been at the Pamphyllian long when he received a summons from his old headmaster, the revered Mr Burslem. He offered CLR a job at QRC teaching the preparatory class, the mostly white children waiting their turn to start the school proper. The pay would be $80 a month – a vast increase on the $30 Mrs Regis paid him.

CLR was delighted to accept the offer and he would teach at QRC on and off until 1930. He rapidly moved on from teaching the preparatory class. The new principal, Mr A. M. Lowe, was in charge of teaching the scholarship pupils, but when he had to go abroad for six months he took the remarkable step of offering this prestigious role to the very junior (and very Black) CLR James.

One of the first things CLR had to do in this new role was to escort the Prince of Wales (the future Edward VIII) on an inspection of the school. CLR himself professed to be unimpressed by this honour. He may not have been a political man yet, but his devoted reading of Thackeray had given him a profound cynicism towards the British aristocracy. However, his friend Audrey Jeffers assured him that it would send a powerful message both to the established power structures and the watching boys to be seen with the Prince.

★ ★ ★

Most of his prestige with his pupils, however, came from his sporting prowess. The year 1919, after he had left QRC, was the high point of his cricketing career. In *Beyond a Boundary* he refers to it as 'my year of cricketing glory'. He played for the QRC old boys' team, Old Collegians, also in the second division, and headed the divisional batting figures with an average of over 70. At the end of the season, though, the club broke up and CLR looked around for a new team in the first division.

He had no shortage of suitors, but the choice was far less simple than it might appear. The range of cricket clubs precisely reflected the complex social and racial divisions in Trinidadian society. CLR laid these out elegantly in *Beyond a Boundary*, running through the options in descending order of prestige, though not playing strength.

Top of the pile was the Queen's Park Club. This was the wealthy club of the island's elite. They had a private ground, the Queen's Park Oval, that was and is the best in Trinidad and the venue for international or inter-island matches. Most of the members were both white and well off. There were also some members drawn from what CLR describes as 'old well-established mulatto families'. Any Black members needed to be remarkably distinguished – or very rich. And, as CLR observes, 'by the time he had acquired status or made enough money to be accepted he was much too old to play'.

Next in line was Shamrock, which drew from the established white Catholic families and barely had any non-white members. Neither Shamrock or Queen's Park would have been remotely willing to admit a young Black man like CLR as a member, so they could be ruled out. He wasn't eligible for the next in line either, but that's because it was Constabulary, reserved for policemen.

Beneath them came Maple, the club for 'the brown-skinned middle class', and then Shannon, 'the club of the black lower-middle class'. Finally there was Stingo, the club of the Black masses, 'the butcher, the tailor, the candlestick-maker'.

A QRC man like CLR was never going to play for Stingo. The real choice was between Maple and Shannon. And this was the hard one. In some ways Maple was the obvious choice, as many of his friends were members.

However Maple, as CLR saw it, was the pure product of an unequal society in which gradations of skin colour were absurdly fetishised. Its *raison d'être* was to separate the 'brown' from the 'black'. As he went on to explain, 'A lawyer or a doctor with a distinctly dark skin would have been blackballed, though light-skinned department store clerks of uncertain income and still more uncertain lineage were admitted as a matter of course.' What he's alluding to here is a world in which a darker-skinned woman having an illegitimate child as a result of a liaison with a light-skinned – or white – man would be a cause for celebration.

Edgar Mittelholzer, a Guyanese writer who lived and worked in Trinidad in the thirties, offered a brilliantly detailed account of the intricacies of the island's social hierarchy in his first novel, *A Morning at the Office*. He satirises the Maple Club as the Poui Club:

> It was exclusively for members within a certain range of shades, beginning from sallow and ending at very light brown and taking into consideration at the same time, quality of hair (anything from passably good – small waves but not outright kinky – to straight hair would satisfy the committee). A pure-blooded negro stood no chance of admittance in the Poui Club.

Shannon was Maple's great rival, and had the players CLR most admired. Lebrun Constantine, the first great Black West Indian cricketer, was captain. His son Learie Jr, their star player, was already on his way to being one of the greatest all-rounders and most inspirational figures in the history of the game. But in Trinidad terms he was simply a dark-skinned law clerk, so Shannon was the club for him. Similarly, Wilton St Hill, CLR's batting idol, who was a dark-skinned department store clerk.

CLR's heart was with Shannon. His reading of Dickens and Thackeray had imbued in him a deep dislike of snobbery and artificial class distinctions. Plus Shannon were a simply thrilling cricket team.

On the other hand, Maple were making him an offer. And that was remarkable in itself. CLR already had such a reputation as an intellectual and sportsman that the Maple colour snobs were prepared to relax their standards. Viewed one way, it was a chance to break apart the colour caste system. Viewed another way, it could be seen as a betrayal of his roots, allowing himself to be the exception that proved the rule of Maple's discrimination.

CLR was caught between his principles and his ambition, which was considerable. He took advice from peers and elders. In particular he talked to the father of his contemporary Clifford Roach. Clifford was a fine batsman who would go on to play for the West Indies. He had darkish skin but 'good'-enough hair to have been let into Maple.

His father was a political man, with no time for colour snobbery, so CLR felt he'd be able to see both sides. He explained his dilemma and Mr Roach said he'd think it over.

> A couple of days later he came back with his verdict. 'I understand exactly how you feel about all this God-damned nonsense. But many of the Maple boys are your friends and mine. These are the people whom you are going to meet in life. Join them: it will be better in the end.'[7]

It was pragmatic, well-meant advice and CLR took it. He joined Maple and became their opening batsman alongside Clifford Roach. He would come to regret it, though. Looking back in *Beyond a Boundary* he saw it as a decision that had retarded his political development. He had chosen self-interest over the greater good and in the process had distanced himself from men and cricketers he deeply admired like St Hill and Constantine.

CLR spent his early twenties teaching at QRC, taking part in debates and amateur dramatics with the Mavericks, romancing young women, reading – of course – and starting to write. And playing cricket for Maple.

How good a cricketer CLR was is hard to assess. In a contributor's note to E. W. Swanton's sixties compendium, *The World of Cricket*, he describes himself as 'a sound right-hand batsman and right-arm fast-medium bowler'. He also records that he was eventually made vice-captain of Maple and, on one occasion, represented North Trinidad against South, a definite achievement. As far as his bowling went, he admits that he lacked the ability to sustain a level of pace and accuracy. However, he also described himself as a born bowler, going so far as to say that on his day he would have backed himself against any batsmen in the world, Bradman included. Which is no small boast.

There is no way to assess this extravagant claim. His batting, however, does have an independent reference. When, in 1976, Mike Dibb made a film companion to *Beyond a Boundary* for the BBC, Clifford Roach was interviewed, and he gave this wry appraisal of his one-time opening partner's batting style:

> So far as cricket is concerned he himself was artificially cultivated in that he practised cricket before a looking-glass. How he didn't break it the Lord knows! But he stand before it, take his cricket books, read out how the stroke was made, practice it without a ball, and go on to the field, make the stroke, but his timing was, very often, faulty: stroke perfect, timing faulty, wicket lost! But that didn't stop him from enjoying his game and we continued playing the game together for many years.

CLR did his best to defend himself – 'Many famous cricketers have practised in front of the mirror!' he replied to Roach in the film – but the point was made: CLR James's famously detailed observation of cricketers' techniques began with his study of himself.

Chapter Four

While his interest in cricket has come to be perhaps the best-known aspect of CLR's life and character, it did not define how he thought about himself at the time. He illustrates the sport's significant but minor place in his pantheon by listing all the English magazines he subscribed to at the time – a list that also gives a marvellous picture of the young Caribbean intellectual:

> Not only the *Cricketer*, but the *Times Literary Supplement*, the *Times Educational Supplement*, the *Observer*, the *Sunday Times*, the *Criterion*, the *London Mercury*, the *Musical Review*, the *Gramophone* . . . the editions of the *Evening Standard* when Arnold Bennett wrote in it, and the *Daily Telegraph* with Rebecca West.[1]

Not content with this list, he also added, from France, the *Nouvelle Revue Française* and the *Mercure de France*, and, from the USA, the *Nation* and the *New Republic*. He presumably didn't pay for all of these but read them at the public library, where his lifelong friend Carlton Comma would order in whatever publications his peers wanted to read.

Gradually CLR began to make friends with other young men of similarly intellectual bent. First and most important of these was a Portuguese Creole called Alfred Mendes. Years later CLR said that 'if I have to single out a single individual in the Caribbean with whom my life was inextricably bound then Alfred Mendes is the person'.[2] Much later he summed up the mutually beneficent nature of their relationship neatly: 'I can't say how much I owe to Mendes; all I can say is he probably owes as much to me.'

Alfie Mendes was only four years older than CLR, but by the time they met in the early twenties he had already had an extremely eventful life. His father was a wealthy man, having made good in the provisions business. Following his mother's death, Alfie was sent to an English boarding school for a couple of years, before the outbreak of war led to his recall to Trinidad. In 1915, though, he joined the Merchants' Contingent and went off to Europe to fight. He spent two years in Flanders as a rifleman, a bona fide war hero who won the Military Cross after one particular operation of foolhardy bravery. He was finally invalided out after inhaling poison gas. His wartime experience provided the inspiration for his grandson Sam Mendes's film *1917* a century later.

Back in Trinidad, Alfie met his first wife, Jessie. They married, had a son and Jessie died of pneumonia, all within two years. In 1922 he married his second wife, Juanita. Meanwhile he was working for his father and starting to write. Like CLR he was active in a literary society – the Richmond Street Literary and Debating Association, named for Mendes's Port of Spain home. The Association published its own *Quarterly Review*, featuring much writing by Mendes. In a society as compact as Port of Spain, it was inevitable the two young men of letters would meet.

CLR made an immediate impression: 'He stood about six feet three inches, as lean as a pole, and possessed the kind of rough charm that women of all complexions succumb to so easily. His intelligence was of the highest order, his memory for music and literature phenomenal; all of this was seasoned with a sharp wit and a sardonic sense of humour.'[3]

Mendes notes that while CLR was very clearly 'a Negro', 'he always assured me that one of his forebears was a European, French as far as my memory serves me'. He also observes that as a teacher at QRC, CLR was immensely popular, teaching English and history; 'with a style so austere and at the same time so colourful that his pupils listened to him in thrall'. It's an observation that suggests that the key elements of CLR's speaking style were in place well before he ever left Trinidad.

For his part, CLR was simply delighted to meet someone as fanatical in their love of literature as himself. He was particularly impressed that Alfie Mendes had his own library. His father had bought him the house at 45 Richmond Street when he married, and he had since added on an extra room to house his library, which already ran to more than two thousand volumes, mostly novels and poetry. The two men started to meet regularly. After he finished teaching CLR would cycle down to the Mendes business premises and together the two friends would head back to Alfie's house and settle down in his study. 'Countless are the hours I spent there,' he later recalled.[4]

Together they would read the literary periodicals, order the books they read about and then discuss them. 'Mendes being the son of a wealthy father, he bought more books than I did, but I don't think there was any great gap between us.'[5] Indeed not. CLR's healthy salary enabled him to start on a prodigious book-buying habit, one that would carry on throughout his life, even at times when he was living in the most straitened of circumstances. When it came to assessing life's essentials, books always came first for him.

Mendes and James's friendship saw them exchanging letters on a daily basis, despite the fact they saw each other most days and lived in the same town. Few of their letters survive, but a sprinkling of those written by CLR give the flavour of their friendship. They address each other by their surnames, as per the public-school code. The earliest surviving letter dates from December 1925 and begins, 'Dear Mendes, I return the two books I borrowed last evening' before going on to discuss Thomas Hardy's *The Dynasts* (it's worth considering that Thomas Hardy was still alive at this point and *The Dynasts* published less than twenty years earlier). CLR comments that 'Unfortunately I have neither the time nor the energy just yet to give a book like that the attention it deserves. Reading such a book is a landmark in one's literary life, and I would like to see a few days clear before me.'[6]

CLR's letter asks for feedback on something he's written: 'How do you like my sketch? It is rather annoying of me I admit, but I like to hear your opinion on what I have written. You know how isolated you can feel in this God-forsaken hole.'

Further letters see him sending Mendes volumes of Chekhov stories, and a work by the Austrian Schnitzler. Gramophone records – an exciting new phenomenon – are exchanged too. CLR had a gramophone in his room.* Mostly they swap classical music – Beethoven, Brahms, Debussy etc. – though on one occasion CLR has to apologise for not sending back a recording of Gershwin's *Rhapsody in Blue* because 'a lady borrowed it'.

This is about as forthcoming as CLR ever was in referring to his many relationships with women. His published writings, when they touch on the matter of sex at all, tend to see him presenting himself as an upright puritan, a prisoner of the strict moral code of his upbringing. The truth was generally a long way from that. As Alfie Mendes suggests in his pen portrait, CLR spent a lot of energy in the pursuit of women and continued to do so throughout his life.

When he came to attempt an autobiography in the seventies, he was encouraged to write a chapter on his relations with women. Sadly it's one of the least persuasive pieces he ever produced. He offers a remarkably detached account of losing his virginity at sixteen, with a girl the same age. After he succeeded in overcoming her initial resistance he says only that 'she obviously wanted me to come back again but I was through with it by that time'.[7]

He says that in his twenties he acted like a typical middle-class boy in Port of Spain, going to parties, meeting girls and trying to sleep with them – 'she would or she would not, and you could persuade her or you could not'. Carnival time, he noted, was the best time to make your advances.

As to what type of women he liked, or what characterised any of the women he went out with, he says nothing. The only known girlfriend is the one who would later become his first wife. He barely wrote a word about her, but he did at least talk about her a little to later partners. Her name was Juanita Young. She was a stenographer in a legal office. She was mixed Black and Chinese, perhaps part Spanish or Venezuelan. Her sister was reputed to be the most beautiful girl in

* Mendes was impressed by CLR's record collection. CLR apparently found a shop that was selling off old records on the Red Seal label cheaply. He was earning $6 a week writing a sports column on top of his regular wages and would spend the money on records. Particular favourites were operatic arias from singers like Enrico Caruso, Amelita Galli-Curci, Marcel Journet and Emmy Destinn.

Trinidad. Apparently, he wrote to her every Friday evening for three years before they got married in 1929.

Alfred Mendes was rather more forthcoming about his romantic life. He reports that his second marriage was disastrous and soon became sexless, a situation to which Mendes reacted as men generally did in a firmly macho society like Trinidad: 'It wasn't long before I found a mistress, a young uneducated Indian girl who was as knowledgeable in the technique of making love as any sophisticated woman.'[8]

Apart from the sexual side, Mendes also found that his relationship with this unnamed girl, and the other working-class folk he met through his father's business, offered valuable grist to his fictional mill. He had been working for some time on a novel whose guiding principle was the destructiveness of racial prejudice, but it lacked characters or plot. Now he was taking inspiration from the life around him: 'I met numbers of Indian and Chinese shopkeepers and commission agents of all ethnic groups . . . I was writing short stories all of which flowed from these people whose lives, I discovered, were being more honestly lived than those I consorted with socially.'[9]

CLR was of like mind. His early experiences of watching the ne'er-do-well Matthew Bondman playing cricket with aristocratic ease had given him the sure sense that culture was not the sole property of the formally educated and, like Mendes, he could see the richness of the lives of Port of Spain's poor.

Port of Spain's working classes tended to live in 'barrack yards' – barrack-like lodgings organised around a central courtyard – so CLR and Mendes started to characterise the stories they were writing of working-class life as 'barrack yard stories'.

They sent each other their stories to critique and published them wherever they could. Both men dreamt of being published abroad, in London or New York, those places where there was real literary culture, not the 'godforsaken hole' they lived in. They sent stories to the major magazines of the time and did their best to make contact with the London literary world. And they succeeded in this aim when they had the good fortune to meet a man called Robert Cunninghame Graham, who was visiting Trinidad.

Robert Cunninghame Graham was one of the extraordinary figures of the late Victorian and Edwardian age. Born in 1852 to a family of notorious Scottish lairds and slave owners, after he left school he went to Argentina, living the gaucho life as a cattle rancher known as Don Roberto. Subsequently his world travels saw him visiting the forbidden cities of Morocco in disguise, meeting Buffalo Bill in Texas, and teaching fencing in Mexico City. Back in Scotland in the 1880s, he met the likes of William Morris and George Bernard Shaw and became a committed socialist. He founded the Scottish Labour Party with Keir Hardie and became the first-ever socialist MP to be elected to the House of Commons, before moving into a literary career. He wrote history, biography, travel and many volumes of short stories. His literary associates included Shaw and G. K. Chesterton, and, particularly, Joseph Conrad, a fellow adventurer who he helped with the research for *Nostromo*.*

Graham was a devout anti-imperialist and, when his travels brought him to Trinidad, it's unsurprising that he took an interest in the work of the two young bohemians. CLR was the first to strike gold. Thanks to Graham, who had a long association with the journal, the prestigious *Saturday Review* took a story of CLR's called 'La Divina Pastora' and published it in October 1927, the first story to be published in London by a Caribbean writer. 'That created a sensation in Trinidad amongst those of us who were really interested in the arts . . . it meant that we had the talent for making the metropolitan markets,' remembered Mendes later.[10]

'La Divina Pastora' had fallen into CLR's lap:

> It was a story that my grandmother told me and she took about five minutes to tell it. It was just a casual story . . . but there was something particularly interesting about this one. I set out to make a literary short story out of it.[11]

It's a short but complex tale of a maturity which betokens the hard, unpublished labour CLR had put in beforehand. It's set in North

* There is a portrait of Graham on the cover of one of the Penguin editions of *Nostromo*.

Trace, the southern village in which he'd spent much of his early childhood, and features a woman called Anita Perez, one of the remaining Trinidadians of Spanish descent. She's a labourer on a cocoa plantation, smitten with Sebastiano, the owner. He's her one chance of escape from the drudgery of her daily life. To try to secure his love, she seeks the magical help of the statue of La Divina Pastora at the Catholic shrine in the remote village of Siparia.

The story has a pioneering mix of magic and realism, plus the kind of surprise ending much beloved of popular short story writers of the time, writers like O. Henry, whose work, according to Mendes, CLR knew so well he could recite whole stories from memory.

It was an auspicious beginning, and all the more so when the story was selected for inclusion in a hardback anthology of the 'Best Stories of 1928'. But it wasn't easy to follow up, working so far away from the publishing industry.

Then there was the question of what else he had to write about. Mendes had his job, bringing him into daily contact with Port of Spain's colourful street life. There is a suggestion that by 1926 he'd already written a novel about the lives of the 'barrack yarders'. CLR, by contrast, was living the life of a middle-class young bachelor with his debating societies and his Debussy recordings and his job teaching the children of the elite at QRC. On one level he was about as removed as he could be from the lives of the people in the slums and tenements. And yet as a Black man living in a city as small as Port of Spain, he was inevitably well aware of their existence:

> Every street in Port of Spain proper could show you numerous examples of the type: a narrow gateway leading into a fairly big yard, on either side of which run long, low buildings, consisting of anything from four to eighteen rooms, each about twelve feet square. In these live the porters, the prostitutes, carter-men, washer-women and domestic servants of the city.
>
> In one corner of the yard is the hopelessly inadequate water-closet, unmistakable to the nose if not to the eye; sometimes there is a structure with the title of bathroom, a courtesy title, for he or she

> who would wash in it with decent privacy must cover the person as if bathing on the banks of the Thames; the kitchen happily presents no difficulty; never is there one and each barrack-yarder cooks before her door.[12]

He became very much more intimately familiar with them when in early 1928, aged twenty-seven and already engaged to Juanita, he moved into a barrack house. The reasons are opaque. Talking about it later, he makes it sound as if it was a deliberate move in order to help his understanding of the 'common people', perhaps wanting to keep up with his friend and rival Mendes. At some point during this period Mendes rented a place in a barrack yard on Park Street ('I did not live completely there, but I ingratiated myself. They knew of what I was doing: they knew what I felt about their way of life – that I was sympathetic to it').[13] Whether Mendes copied James or vice versa is moot. Their twin literary trajectories were extraordinarily close at that time. All that said, it seems more than likely that CLR's motives for moving into the barrack yard were, in the first instance at least, financial.

While he earned a good wage at QRC, he was not a permanent staff member and there were definitely gaps in his employment. He may have made up any shortfall from freelance teaching and journalism, but shortfall there very likely was. Throughout his life he struggled to balance income and outgoings. One of his early short stories, 'Turner's Prosperity', concerns a young man trying to dodge his many creditors, and has a definite ring of lived experience as his protagonist attempts to escape tailors and grocers alike. Moving from respectable lodgings into a barrack yard had a profound effect on him:

> I was about 27 or 28 . . . I was already engaged to be married. I went to live there, the people fascinated me, and I wrote about them from the point of view of an educated youthful member of the black middle class.[14]

James appears to have realised right away that his surroundings offered perfect material for his fiction. While living in the barrack yard he wrote a short story called 'Triumph', directly inspired by the domestic dramas going on all around him, dramas that came out of lives that had rejected the colonial values he'd grown up with:

> They lived their life independently of the kind of pretence or desire to imitate the British style which so preoccupied the middle classes. It was the vitality and collectivity of that life which fascinated me.[15]

'Triumph' is the story of a young woman called Mamitz. CLR describes her carefully, with the precise attention to ethnic mix that Trinidadians were accustomed to make, as 'a black woman, too black to be pure Negro, probably with some Madrasi East Indian blood in her, a suspicion which was made a certainty by the long thick plaits of her plentiful hair'.

He's clear, too, as to her particular attractions: 'She was shortish and fat, voluptuously developed, tremendously developed, and as a Creole loves development in a woman more than any other extraneous allure, Mamitz (like the rest of her sex in all stations of life) saw to it when she moved that you missed none of her charms.'

This might suggest that CLR really did see women as no more than sex objects. Thankfully, though, the rest of the story demonstrates precisely the opposite. Mamitz and her friend Celestine are drawn with great care and sensitivity. Their situation is objectively desperate. They can make a pittance from taking in washing or working as cooks, but really they are dependent on men to keep their heads above water. Not men as husbands, but men as other people's husbands who would come to the barrack yard for sex and throw their chosen woman a few dollars each week for the privilege. Mamitz had a tram conductor, but then he had accused her of infidelity, beaten her even more badly than usual, and left. Celestine had a policeman, and her enemy Irene a cab driver.

CLR, like a Caribbean Zola or Balzac, sets out the lives of these women without moralising. He shows their suffering but makes time too for their raucous joys on the days when they have money in their pockets and a chicken in the cooking pot. There is no twist as in 'La

Divina Pastora', just a fully drawn picture of barrack-yard life and one that puts the female experience at its heart.

'Triumph' was a great step forward in CLR's writing, but he still faced the problem of isolation, Robert Cunninghame Graham having gone back to Britain. So he, and Mendes too, were delighted when a man called Hulbert Footner arrived in Trinidad around May 1928. Footner was another classic example of that now long-vanished species, the writer/adventurer. He made his name by writing about his several epic journeys across Canada by river, travelling thousands of miles in a canoe. He went on to write novels of adventure and, by the twenties, detective fiction. The great humourist H. L. Mencken called him 'one of the most charming men who was ever on earth'. Why he was in Trinidad is not recorded, though a decade later he published a novel called *The Obeah Murders*, set on a fictional Caribbean island whose capital was called Port of Grace.

Whatever the reason for his visit, Footner evidently met James and Mendes and offered to show their work to New York editors on his return to the US. He was as good as his word and dropped off some of their stories with an editor at *Harper's*. Then he wrote to CLR, summing up his feelings about his work. He tells him that he admires the craft of one story and the immorality of another, before coming to 'Triumph'. That's the one for him. There, he tells CLR, he has found his subject and his voice: 'In the barrack yard you are unique and unrivalled. Consider what an advantage that gives you. The barrack yard is all your own artistically.'[16]

He also suggested that the short story, contrary to the advice CLR had previously received (perhaps from the short-story specialist Graham), was not the easiest form to sell, particularly a longer story like 'Triumph'. Instead, he said, 'I adjure you to write a novel.'

CLR clearly took Hulbert Footner's advice to heart. He decided to write a full-scale novel set in the barrack yard. He had the subject matter and he had the opportunity.

> About 1928 I had nothing to do for a summer vacation. I decided to write a novel about certain events and people with whom I happened

> at the time to be closely associated. I was living in Port of Spain in an alley, which I called Minty. But when vacation time came I left Minty Alley and went to St Joseph to spend time with my parents. Many of the incidents of the novel actually happened . . . I showed it to Mendes, chapter by chapter, when I was writing it, and he said at the time that he found it very interesting. I remember that what struck him most was the speed at which I did a chapter every day. I finished the novel in about six weeks and then put it away.[17]

The role of Alfred Mendes in all this should not be underestimated. The two young men, always competitive, were both writing novels set in the barrack yard, and they were constantly reading and commenting on each other's work. This spirit of competition must surely have helped CLR keep up the momentum of writing a chapter a day.

In the end there were thirty-five chapters to the novel, which would eventually be published some eight years later as *Minty Alley*. Mendes's novel, called *Pitch Lake*, appeared two years earlier.

The setting of *Minty Alley* is a barrack yard broadly similar to that of 'Triumph', but this time it has a presiding landlady, Mrs Rouse, and where CLR himself was only present in the earlier story as an omniscient narrator, in *Minty Alley* there is a central character, Haynes, who is very clearly a proxy for the author. Haynes is a twenty-year-old from a middle-class family. Despite a regular job in a bookshop he can no longer afford to live in his family home following the death of his mother, and he decides to take the cheapest place he can find. Which turns out to be in Minty Alley.

The plot is feather-light. There is a love triangle involving Mrs Rouse, her handsome lover Benoit and the enviably light-skinned Nurse Jackson. At first Haynes tries to remain aloof, with his books and his meals prepared by his family's former cook Ella, but he is steadily drawn into the life of the barrack yard, not least by Mrs Rouse's teenage servant Maisie, a girl who has all the lust for life that Haynes lacks.

As with 'Triumph', it's notable for its consistently humane and empathetic treatment of female characters. In CLR James's fictional world women are at the centre, striving to get through their difficult lives, hoping to find some joy along the way. The trouble, all too often, is that that joy is found in the arms of shiftless, untrustworthy men like Benoit.

It's a remarkably feminist perspective from a young man in a distinctly unfeminist world and who, by his own account, had grown into adulthood seeing women as prospective sex partners and little else. It's tempting to hypothesise that his relationship with Juanita may have had something to do with that. It more than likely explains why CLR later pointed out that the significant way in which *Minty Alley* differed from real life was that 'I never slept with Maisie, but I imagine at 20 [like Haynes] I would have found it very exciting to sleep with Maisie'.[18]

The baffling thing about *Minty Alley* is the fact that CLR claimed he made no effort to get it published. Just filed it away. He said he saw it as an exercise, a prentice piece rather than a serious piece of work. This despite Mendes's rivalrous encouragement. Furthermore, it was the last piece of fiction that CLR would set in the barrack yard. He had found his own, personal fictional territory but then abandoned it, and all within a year.

So what explains this? The most plausible scenario is that he was derailed by the ordinary matter of life. In late 1928, when he finished the manuscript and went back to teaching, he was a young man engaged to be married, with good, but insecure, employment prospects, and a tendency to the spendthrift.

His financial circumstances were clearly an ever more pressing worry. In December, he took the drastic and clearly embarrassing step of asking Mendes for some assistance in borrowing money:

> I am awfully sorry to trouble you but I want your assistance in an important matter – strictly between us. I am in straits for money – rather desperate straits, because a man who promised to lend me some put me off today at the last minute. What I want you to do for me is to put me on to someone who will be able to lend me $100 at a reasonable rate of interest ... If you can introduce me to

someone and say 'I know Mr James. He is a master at the College', etc, etc, I shall be very grateful. It is Xmas time and although I don't care a straw about that, yet I have certain obligations around me to fulfil . . . and the idea that I wouldn't be able is enough to make me feel to commit suicide.[19]

It's an uncharacteristically emotional appeal. And it certainly seems likely that the level of stress relates to his upcoming marriage, rather than simply his Christmas present buying. Mendes responded to the appeal, not with cash but with a plan:

One day James came to me and confided that he was in a money jam: could I help him in any way other than cash? I immediately suggested a magazine under our joint editorship: the advertisements could bring in tidy returns which, after meeting the cost of the magazine, could leave a substantial net profit for him, as I did not want to share any of it.

CLR enthusiastically agreed with this scheme and together the two men started work on a journal that they would simply call *Trinidad*. However, it would not actually appear until Christmas 1929. By that time CLR had clearly overcome his financial problems sufficiently to get married. He and Juanita were living in a small house in Jerningham Avenue, one of the main roads heading east from the Savannah into the lower-middle-class, mostly Black suburb of Belmont.

There is frustratingly little known about Juanita. CLR's niece and nephew, Erica and Heno, remember seeing her around Port of Spain later in her life, an elegant, intelligent woman who kept herself to herself. His cousin Cyril Austin recalled that Juanita would come home from her job typing in the law office and then set to typing CLR's work by night. CLR, like many a male writer of the time, never learned to type and relied on women to type up his handwritten articles and manuscripts.

CLR's second wife, Constance, offers a little more, not necessarily entirely reliable, detail:

> Juanita was of Spanish and Chinese descent, from Venezuela . . . Eric, Nello's brother, told me she was beautiful, but Nello had not been passionately in love; theirs was a traditional West Indian marriage. She was to keep the house in order, cook, and be his bedmate when desired. She was not interested in politics. On weekends he would gather up the gramophone, records, books and they would take themselves to Tunapuna to stay with his mother and father.[20]

All CLR said to Constance was that the marriage was 'pleasant'. And yet he also told her a far from pleasant story:

> Juanita became pregnant, but nearing term the baby died as a result of the umbilical cord twisted around his neck. Nello did not seem particularly saddened, only described the infant as a fine-looking baby boy.

However sanguine he may have been about the matter twenty years later, talking to his new wife, it's hard to imagine that this awful event did not traumatise both parents. What is surely the case is that, from late 1929 onwards, there was a new seriousness in CLR's work and life. He didn't turn his back on literature, but he began to look at the world from a political perspective as well as a literary one.

Chapter Five

CLR and Mendes started in earnest on their new magazine in October 1929. *Trinidad* came out at Christmas 1929. They drew on their small circle of fellow artists and intellectuals for contributions, including the violinist Henry 'Sonny' Carpenter, who would write about music, while fiction contributions came both from the white upper class, with the likes of Frank Evans, the future QC Algernon 'Pope' Wharton and Kathleen Archibald, and from Black Trinidadians such as Ernst Carr and the future Trinidad MP C. A. Thomasos, who contributed a barrack-yard story, as well as CLR himself. It was a decently mixed group for the times: Black, white and Creole; men and women. According to Alfred Mendes, there were Indian and Chinese writers in their circle too, though none of them appear in the magazine.

The writer CLR and Mendes were most excited about, however, was a young Creole called Ralph de Boissière, no more than twenty-one years old. Mendes was impressed by a story de Boissière had written, 'Miss Winter', and decided to include it in *Trinidad*. Looking back later, Ralph provided vivid pictures of the magazine's editors. First Alfred Mendes, who immediately intimidated him with his worldliness and his upper-class accent: '[He] came of a rich, long-established Portuguese family. He had been educated in England, been through the First World War, had been gassed and had earned a medal ... He was small, swarthy, with a quick mind that appeared to miss nothing.'[1]

Mendes, according to de Boissière, had come back from the war thoroughly disillusioned. Any belief in the virtues of Empire was gone. Instead he set his face against the bourgeois values of his upbringing, 'angered his father with outrageous views and in every way made himself the *enfant terrible* of his family'.

CLR he knew already. As 'Mr James', he had been Ralph's history teacher in his last year at QRC. He was hugely impressed by CLR's depth of knowledge and keenly aware that his background was far less secure than most of his associates: 'Being black he was careful in his dealings with Alfie. He did not call him Alfie but Mendes, and Alfie called him not Nello, as we did, but James. He had none of Alfie's spontaneous enthusiasms, he frowned on his flaunting of eccentricities. He had to make his way as a teacher, he had no father to fall back on.'

In de Boissière's memory, Mendes was the older, worldly wise charismatic leader, bringing in new recruits to his vision of radical bohemianism in the Caribbean. He liked to provoke, strip naked and walk around the veranda of his house.

When it came to the actual production of the magazine, CLR, who was the one who stood to benefit financially, was in charge. He went for a simple format, 8" x 12", printed and stitched by the cheapest printer he could find.

When it came out at Christmastime it was an immediate *succès de scandale*. In Mendes's memory it was the frank sexual content – led by CLR's 'Triumph' – that was particularly controversial:

> This was anathema to the island's bourgeois public. The Church of Rome was extremely strong in Trinidad at that time and naturally created quite a disturbance. Letters began to appear in the press condemning the magazine out and out, stating that it was an immoral publication and as such harmful to the youth of the island.[2]

Ralph de Boissière has a more nuanced recollection of *Trinidad*'s publication. He remembers 'Triumph', in particular, being attacked, but he also remembers long, largely positive reviews in both the establishment *Trinidad Guardian* and the more liberal *Port of Spain Gazette*. In a revealing glimpse of bourgeois Trinidadian mores of the time, he recalls his father being pleased to read a warm review of Ralph's story, but not actually bothering to read the work itself, being firmly subscribed to the view that 'good literature could not come out of our Trinidad world'.[3]

The magazine announced that the island now had a literary scene, whether it liked it or not. And if critics at home were divided, the response from abroad was encouraging. Mendes again:

> We received quite a lot of letters, including one from Aldous Huxley, who commended the magazine very highly, and several from Edward J. O'Brien, who was *the* anthologist of the day in short fiction. He listed five of the stories as being amongst the best of the year without actually reprinting any one.*[4]

Trinidad did also succeed in its initial aim, which was to help CLR pay off his debts. That having been achieved, thanks to sales of over a thousand copies plus advertising revenue, the editorial group decided to make the next issue a more lavish affair – with considerably higher production values. Mendes and Wharton took care of this and CLR, perhaps feeling a financial snub or perhaps worried for his job following the controversy, asked not to be listed as a co-editor this time, though he still contributed work and helped with the editorial process.

The second issue came out in March 1930. It featured an editorial by Mendes inveighing against those who criticised the first issue – 'all nonsense, all canting hypocrisy'.

But despite its improved appearance, its content was weaker and it failed to match the financial success of the first issue. In particular, the opposition of the Catholic Church had made it impossible to find advertisers. Disappointed by this, their collective energy fizzled out for the moment.

A contributory factor may have been CLR's decision to do something that he had up till now always refused to do. He took a full-time government job, working as an instructor at the teacher training college in Port of Spain.

> My mother told me, 'Boy you are busy with your writing and your teaching, why don't you go and get in the government service?

* O'Brien had already reprinted 'La Divina Pastora' in his 1928 anthology and he included a story co-written by Mendes and Pope Wharton in his 1929 anthology.

> They would be glad to have a young fella like you and you would start at $80 a month. I told her, 'But mother, I don't want to go into the government service, I am very busy as it is.' She told me 'you could go to the government service and still do your writing in your spare time. Remember when you are sixty, the pension.' That time I am about twenty-five.[5]

Five years later and newly married, he finally took his mother's advice and signed on for a secure job with a pension at the end of it – all his parents had wanted for him. What they might not have predicted was the effect the new job would have, which was to propel him into the world of politics:

> I got a job finally teaching history and literature at the government training college and then I began in addition to reading history and literature and the books and papers which I used to get, I began to listen seriously to Captain Cipriani, who was leading the labor movement.

Captain A. A. (Arthur Andrew) Cipriani had come to prominence over the past decade as the leader of the movement towards self-government. He was the leader of the powerful Trinidad Workingmen's Association (TWA), a Port of Spain councillor and sometime mayor, and a member of the legislature.

He came out of the white elite – from a French Creole family with Corsican roots (they were allegedly related to Napoleon) – but he had had a strong Black following since 1917, when, having volunteered at the age of forty, he had been a captain in the British West Indies Regiment fighting in Europe.

West Indian soldiers were treated with appalling racism by the British Army. They were put onto the most demeaning duties that could be found – cleaning latrines and so forth – and no Black soldier was permitted to rise beyond the rank of sergeant. Cipriani took the side of his men. He helped to make sure that they did at last see battle. However, the worst troubles occurred when the regiment were waiting to be demobbed in the Italian port of Taranto. Riots broke out as the Black soldiers had finally had enough of being treated as second-class. Again Cipriani stood by his men when other white officers didn't.

On his return to Trinidad his reputation preceded him as a champion of the Black man. Meanwhile, he had been radicalised by his experience of war. He had left the cocoon of Trinidad and discovered that the British Empire was scarcely the benevolent mothership it claimed to be. And, like all the returning troops, he heard the drums of the Russian Revolution. One great empire was no more. Winds of change were coming.

He joined the TWA and quickly transformed it into a powerful island-wide force. He had a similarly transformative effect on the island's legislature. This was a toothless talking shop that existed only to do what its British masters thought best, but Captain Cipriani used his position to expose the injustices all around, even if he did not yet have the power to change them.

Particularly telling is the transcript of a hearing he conducted with leading plantation owners on their employment practices. He quizzed a Mr Robinson, who had a huge labour force made up almost entirely of Indian indentured workers. He established that among them were hundreds of children, some as young as seven, and that during the four months of harvesting the crops, the workers were lucky to get more than three hours' sleep a night. Finally, he asked Robinson if he felt his child labourers might be better served by receiving an education. Robinson's response is breathtaking in its pragmatic brutality, making it clear that indentured labour was only slavery cynically reframed:

> No. Give them some education in the way of reading and writing, but no more. Even then I would say educate only the bright ones; not the whole mass. If you do educate the whole mass of the agricultural population, you will be deliberately ruining the country.[6]

Cipriani, then, was the man who ignited CLR's serious interest in politics. The interesting question is why it had only happened now, as he approached his thirties.

The answer would appear to lie deep within the culture of the island. Trinidad was a place curiously lacking in either history or context. It was essentially an immigrant society less than a century old. It was independent, remote and unique but still completely dependent, a half-forgotten possession of the British Empire. So even for someone like CLR, growing up in an educated family, the matter of politics, particularly racial politics, was simply not something people talked about. Not even the brute fact of slavery. Indeed, up to the point at which he left school, CLR recalled that

> I have to state that the continent of Africa and the ancestral slavery never entered into any serious relation either actual, intellectual or psychological with my life. Slavery was not a historical fact. It was a term of warning against people who attempted to impose an unofficial authority. 'You watch your step with me. These are not slavery days.' That was a fairly often-heard statement.[7]

Ten years later he was no longer so politically ignorant. The Mavericks had debated the issues of the day. At QRC, he had taught history as well as literature and had started to dig into the history of the West Indies. He had learned about early Trinidad reformers and radicals. He was aware, of course, that the society he lived in was an unjust one, in which gradations of skin tone counted for more than education, but for the most part he'd been content to deal with it by ignoring it. He had trusted in his intellect to lift him above the everyday prejudices, and to some extent he had succeeded. He had a convivial bubble, moving between the cocoons of the QRC masters' room and Mendes's book-lined study. He read the literary magazines not the political ones. He knew his times were radical, but it was the radicalism of the artist that attracted him, not that of the street-corner politico.

That is, until he heard Captain Cipriani speak. He was an unlikely candidate for a popular hero, this middle-aged white fellow, but CLR gives a good impression of that man and his popular appeal:

He is below middle height, very solidly built and giving at first glance an impression of squareness and power. He has a big fleshy clean-shaven face, and his eyes, of a peculiar greenish colour, though small, sometimes in conversation, and always in public speech blaze with a fire which increases the impression of force so characteristic of his general appearance. He wears always a khaki suit of military cut, brown boots, and a white helmet. There is no democratic affectation in this. That simplicity has always been his way. (But he does not wear the same in London. When the boat leaves Barbados he dons the regulation tweeds.)[8]

It's very typical of CLR, this fondness for the insider detail. He goes on to detail Cipriani's curious, though very Trinidadian, mix of business interests:

For his living he still trains horses and is also an auctioneer. During the day he can always be found in a dusty auctioneer's office in St Vincent Street. But he does very little auctioneering and his chief business is his politics. He has a cocoa estate, but although himself a planter, his political work caused him to neglect it so much that had not two of his supporters taken it over he would have lost it long ago. He represents the people so well, chiefly because he is so much one of them. All through the day persons pass in and out, coming to see him usually for help of some kind, some with grievances, some with information, some asking for advice, many begging. They stop him in the street. They pursue him to his house, for his purse is always open.

The picture he paints is of a classic populist small-town politician. But then he gets on to Cipriani's actual beliefs and his appeal becomes clearer. In particular, he quotes at length a speech the captain gave to the Labour Commonwealth Conference in London in July 1930:

It is all very well and good to talk of us as 'subject races'. I laugh that to scorn. We are free people of the British Empire. We are entitled

> to the same privileges and the same form of government and administration as our bigger sisters, the Dominions, and we have got to use everything in our power, strain every nerve, make every effort – I go further and say to make every sacrifice to bring self-government and Dominion status to these beautiful Colonies.
>
> The first question is the important one of self-government for the West Indies, and our claim to this right is the reasonable and practical one that we have the education, ability, culture, and civilisation, necessary to undertake and successfully administer the affairs of our country.

These demands – accompanied by a request that Trinidad be given the rights to its own mineral wealth – may not seem terribly radical now, but back then they were revolutionary, a sign that the ripples from Russia had made their way across the Atlantic and reinvigorated the island's home rule movement.

CLR was sold. Over the next two years he immersed himself in studying the political system and compiling material for a proposed book on Cipriani and his mission to free Trinidad from its shackles.

He didn't completely desert the literary world, however. While at the government training college he put on two plays with his students, first Molière's *Le Bourgeois gentilhomme* and then Sheridan's *The Rivals*. And later in 1930 when plans came together for a new magazine, he immediately became involved. The catalyst for this was the return to Trinidad of an extraordinary young man called Albert 'Bertie' Gomes. Ralph de Boissière remembered their first meeting – at Alfie Mendes's place – very well. This Bertie Gomes was a supremely self-confident nineteen-year-old, his ego only matched in size by his physical bulk:

> He reclined, looking like a Japanese wrestler in the broadest and most comfortable rattan cane armchair. All taken up with what he was saying in his loud and youthful voice, which he loved, he paused a moment to acknowledge our introduction with careless affability, 'Hello, boy, how?' and went on with a triumphant laugh to demolish some idea that had come up in the conversation.[9]

Bertie Gomes, like Alfie Mendes, was of Portuguese stock. But where the Mendes family had already succeeded in moving up in society by the time Alfie was born, the Gomes family lagged behind. Bertie was born to unmarried parents, living in poverty in Belmont. By the time he was a teenager, however, his father had managed to build up a small network of shops and, while they still lived in Belmont, they were newly prosperous. As a result, Bertie, aged seventeen, had been able to head off to New York, notionally for his education, but actually to spend his time immersing himself in Greenwich Village's literary world.

By the time he returned to Trinidad he was an unusually worldly nineteen-year-old. He had been sent a copy of *Trinidad* while in the US and was much excited by it – 'Did this mean a cultural break-through was imminent in Trinidad?' he wondered[10] – so on his return home he had promptly sought out Mendes and was invited into this charmed circle of young intellectuals who 'met regularly and informally at Mendes' house, where they listened to recorded music, argued way into the night, and read excerpts from each other's writings. This was the tiny oasis of artistic appreciation I found in the vast philistine desert of Trinidad,' as he recalled in his memoirs.

Gomes quickly decided that this group, though interesting enough, were ultimately mostly hopeless romantics, prone to 'a self-flattering aestheticism'. The only exceptions, he felt, were CLR and Ralph de Boissière, who had real hunger for actual political change, rather than just enjoying the roles of *enfants terribles*.

He decided what was needed to shake the group out of its torpor was this new magazine. It would be called *The Beacon* and he would be the editor and publisher. His adoring mother persuaded his father to finance the venture and he was in business. *The Beacon* came out more or less monthly for two years, achieving a decent circulation but always struggling to find enough advertising to be financially viable. The Catholic Guild, as disapproving as ever, sought to dissuade businesses from supporting such a venture.

The Beacon, like *Trinidad*, ran short stories and poems, but there was a much greater emphasis on current affairs and politics. CLR was a regular writer from the beginning. His first contributions included a piece called 'The Problem of Knowledge', and another called 'Revolution', presented as a short story but really closer to reportage, as it relates a conversation with a long-time veteran of Venezuela's revolutionary movement. Another short story, 'The Star That Would Not Shine', was also laid out as a conversation, this time with a man who'd had a brief brush with Hollywood. It's a squib somewhat in the O. Henry, or even Damon Runyon, mode.

It's clear that as a writer CLR was in a period of flux, trying out this direction and that. On the one hand his political interests were coming to the fore; on the other he was writing a column about Arnold Bennett, one of the major British literary figures of the early twentieth century, and the most unlikely of CLR's long-time heroes, who had recently died.

Now largely forgotten, Arnold Bennett was the great chronicler of the new classes – a middle-class boy from the unfashionable Midlands who'd made his way first as a journalist and then as an enormously successful novelist. Interestingly, just as politics were becoming central to his own view of the world, CLR says he admired Bennett for not seeing the world through political blinkers: 'Rather more than less, he took the world as he found it . . . he had as much as any English novelist of his time, the rare virtue of a scrupulous intellectual honesty. Bennett never tried to deceive the reader nor, what was worse, allowed himself to be deceived.'[11]

Bertie Gomes surely helped to push CLR towards politics, racial politics in particular. He was determined to make *The Beacon* a provocative read, one that would breed controversy. So he commissioned a piece by a resident English scientist, Dr Sidney Harland, which attempted to prove 'that Negroes were as a race inferior in intelligence to whites', as CLR would later write.[12]

Harland's piece is a bizarre mishmash of prejudices, dressed up with sporadic attempts at 'scientific' justification. It was an obviously provocative thing to publish in a place like Trinidad, and one can only presume that Gomes ran it in order to set the stage for the following issue, in which CLR delivered a magisterial rebuttal of Harland's genteel bigotry.

In a piece baldly titled 'The Intelligence of the Negro', CLR begins by stating the simple fact that science, even then, had definitively disproved the notions of 'races' having innate levels of intelligence. Then he picks up on Harland's citation of Toussaint Louverture, the eighteenth-century Haitian revolutionary, as an example of an exceptionally intelligent 'negro' – perhaps 'about equal to the foreman of an English jury'. As CLR so rightly observes, 'What respect can anyone have for a man who in the midst of what he would have us believe is a scientific dissertation produces such arrant nonsense!'[13]

But the mention of Toussaint clearly inspired him, as he then composes a brief tribute to the Haitian's extraordinary achievements and says that he would much sooner have written more about the great Toussaint than respond to Harland's nonsense. And there we can see the genesis of one of James's great works.

James finished his piece with an intriguing statement of his own personal, rather than collective, feelings about the race question. It's a charitable view, for sure, perhaps excessively so. He stresses the virtues of his particular white friends and mentors and downplays the direct effects of racism on his life. It was a principle that he followed throughout his life:

> I am not 'touchy' on the race question. If at times I feel some bitterness at the disabilities and disadvantages to which my being a negro has subjected me it is soon washed away by remembering that the few things in my life of which I am proud, I owe, apart from my family, chiefly to white men, almost all Englishmen and Americans . . . Looking back at my life I see that on the whole white people have befriended me far more than negroes have done.

CLR had reached a turning point. He would write no more fiction, for *The Beacon* or anyone else. He wrote one more article for the magazine, in effect a further rebuttal of Harland's thesis, but a more subtle one. This was a profile of Michael Maxwell Philip, the first great product of Trinidad's emerging mixed-race (or 'coloured') community, a brilliant lawyer and advocate. And meanwhile he redoubled his historical studies, reading everything he could on Toussaint Louverture. His political convictions were starting to come together – not just rooted in a specifically racial sense of injustice, but seeing that as part of the wider cause of anti-colonialism.

In the summer of 1931, armed with this new perspective, CLR started serious work on two book projects, both ostensibly biographies of notable Trinidadians, but both concerned with much more than that.

The first of these was the biography of Captain Cipriani he had been planning, which would simultaneously serve as a manifesto for Trinidadian self-government. To this end he started systematically interviewing the Captain, while also immersing himself in the island's political history, a process that had a profound effect upon him:

> My hitherto vague ideas of freedom crystallized around a political conviction: we should be free to govern ourselves. I said nothing to anyone. After all, I was working for the government. When I told my brother some of my ideas his only comment was: 'You will end up in gaol.'[14]

At the same time, he became involved in a project that most people would have seen as being as far from politics as you could get.

His old acquaintance and cricketing hero Learie Constantine Jr had become one of the game's great stars. A sensationally gifted all-rounder, an attacking batsman, skilful bowler and phenomenal fielder, he had toured England with the West Indies team in 1925 and made an extraordinary impression. So much so that, in 1929, the Lancashire league team Nelson offered him a contract as a professional.

That was a considerably more exciting opportunity than it might sound at this remove. In a mostly amateur game there were few well-paid opportunities. The Lancashire leagues were enormously popular and each team had one professional player. The wages were the best in the business and, before Constantine, no West Indian had ever been offered the job. He took it and his fame spread far and wide.

At the end of the 1931 summer season, Constantine came back to Trinidad and met up with CLR, as he often did, to talk cricket and racial politics. This time, however, Constantine had an idea: 'I want to write a book. All the things I am telling you, they should be in print.'[15]

This was a radical notion. Cricketers generally only wrote books after they retired, and no West Indian had ever written one. But Constantine was confident he could find a publisher. He just needed someone to help him write it, and CLR was the obvious choice.

> I agreed that it was quite an idea. I agreed to do the actual writing. He began to talk more systematically and I to listen with a writing pad on my knee . . . The plans were as rapid in the making as in the telling. At the time he had, I think, dined at my house once. I doubt if his wife and mine had yet met.

There was much in CLR's life that Juanita was not privy to. Before consulting her, CLR and Constantine had agreed not only to collaborate on the book but that CLR would come to England to continue the work when Constantine returned for the new cricket season in the spring of 1932.

In *Beyond a Boundary* CLR presents this as a simple decision easily carried through. The reality must have been more complicated. He was a married man, thirty years old, with a good job working for the government. Men of his background didn't easily give up such security. The trip to the mother country was one you made when you were a bright young student, before taking up a comfortable life back home in Trinidad. To head off into the unknown, with no financial security, must have given him pause for thought.

Meanwhile, CLR was working to finish his Captain Cipriani book. This was starting to run into problems. Cipriani's formerly unassailable status as a popular leader was coming under severe threat as he became embroiled in the Divorce Bill controversy and found himself in opposition to the island's young radicals.

The Legislative Council had brought in a bill in 1926 to legalise divorce. The TWA, led by Cipriani, had supported the bill as a progressive measure, but it had been withdrawn after fierce opposition from the Catholic Church. Now, in 1931, the bill was reintroduced and this time Cipriani bowed to pressure from the Church and his fellow French Creoles, and decided to oppose the bill.

Bertie Gomes used *The Beacon* to rail against this reactionary change of heart. CLR was caught between his contemporaries and his political hero and did his best to stay neutral in an increasingly bitter and personal battle.

The Beacon was becoming a focus of Trinidadian radicalism. Not only did it deal with racial politics – including a notably fierce broadside from Gomes encouraging the Black man to rise up against oppression – but its young contributors were starting to take an interest in communism. Visiting sailors would bring contraband literature to Gomes's house on De Castro Street.

But despite setting itself against both the Catholic Church and the legislature – the two great powers in the land – it was from a very different source that *The Beacon* met its greatest challenge.

Alfred Mendes had written a story called 'Sweetman' for the magazine. This was a barrack-yard story with a remarkable amount in common with 'Triumph'. Both had a heroine with the unusual name of Mamitz, for instance. But where CLR's story revolved around women looking for men, Mendes flipped it around and wrote about men looking for women to support them – good-looking Lothario types known as sweetmen. The problem was that Mendes's protagonist Seppy was not only clearly modelled on a real individual, but carried his actual name. As a result, Septimus 'Seppy' Louhard sued for libel, something that had never happened before in Trinidad in relation to a work of literature.

Mendes fought the case but lost. Louhard did just as a sweetman might have been expected to: he blew his winnings on a huge party. Meanwhile, Mendes was threatened with another court action. This time it was a charge of blasphemous libel, relating to the passionate anti-Catholic broadsides he'd written for the *Trinidad Guardian* at the height of the Divorce Bill controversy. He was advised that he might go to jail and instead made plans to leave Trinidad.

That his closest friend for the past decade was considering leaving the island must surely have influenced CLR's thinking. Particularly as, shortly beforehand, Alfie had received a letter from Aldous Huxley, who he had met on a brief visit to Trinidad. Huxley told Mendes that he had passed his novel, *Pitch Lake*, to the publisher Duckworth with his recommendation and the offer of writing an introduction. It was as good as guaranteed that Alfie would have a novel published in London, the very thing both young men had dreamed of.

So when CLR received a letter from Learie Constantine reiterating his suggestion that he should come to England, and offering to help out if he needed financial assistance, he made his decision.

He told almost nobody what he was planning. He waited till the day the boat actually left before handing in his resignation and informing his dismayed students of his decision. There was a loose arrangement made that his wife Juanita might join him in due course, but nothing was fixed. Thirty-one years old, CLR James was ready to leave his native land for the first time, abandoning a secure career to leap into the unknown. It would be more than a quarter of a century before he returned. After a long seasick journey he arrived in London in March 1932.

PART TWO

England

Chapter Six

'It is a pleasant thing to be no longer that model of all propriety, a teacher, and that model of subservience, a government servant.'[1]

CLR James left Trinidad on the MS *Magdalena* on 27 February 1932 and arrived in Plymouth on the MS *Colombia* on 18 March. The change of ship was made in Barbados, where he stopped off for a week, delivered a lecture and wrote a piece for the *Port of Spain Gazette*, for whom he had also arranged to send back a series of despatches from London once he'd settled in.[2]

On arriving in London he hit the ground running. While he'd surprised his students with his sudden departure, he had actually done some forward planning. He had a few connections, mostly boys he'd taught at QRC who were now over there studying, plus he had various letters of introduction provided by Captain Cipriani and Alfie Mendes.

Some of his former students found him a room in a house on Southampton Row, on the edge of Bloomsbury, just around the corner from the British Museum. And within twenty-four hours he was not just starting to adjust but eagerly immersing himself in the culture. He was thrilled to be able to read the newspapers and magazines as they came out. He went to museums and bookshops, talks and meetings: he met students and intellectuals and talked till late at night in rented rooms and late-night cafés, of which his favourite was the one next to Russell Square tube ('I do not want to start to talk about that café at all, because I would never stop,' he wrote).

He seems to have met a lot of girls, starting on his first day when he visited a firm in the City, armed with a letter of introduction (from Mendes, perhaps?) to a young woman who worked there. With admirable *savoir faire* she told him that 'it's rather awkward here' and, having ascertained his address, arranged to visit him that evening. 'It was a good introduction to women in London,' he would tell the readers of the *Port of Spain Gazette*, with a casual chauvinism that thankfully vanished from his writing thereafter. 'She was pretty, she was tidy, she was not intellectual, far from it, but she spoke well. Best of all she was very much at home: that is what I admired in her chiefly, her independence, her ease, her total lack of constraint.'

He was also on the lookout for opportunities to earn money. He had saved up a little, but London was expensive and his funds were going fast. He started well. Within two weeks of arriving, he'd managed to get a piece in *The Times* – a brief tribute to Lord Harris, who had died a few days earlier. Lord Harris was the son of the former Trinidad governor general and had followed his father into colonial administration, but had also managed to become captain of the England cricket team. CLR's piece is written in perfect *Times*-speak, slightly pompous and Victorian. It's hard to imagine that the author was any sort of radical.

Once he had been in London for a few weeks, CLR wrote the promised dispatches for the *Port of Spain Gazette*. They offer a fascinating picture, not just of CLR, but of multiracial bohemian life in thirties London. The two most interesting pieces essentially detail his activities over a long weekend in Bloomsbury. Here are the edited highlights.

It begins on Wednesday 18 May, in the afternoon. CLR was not in the best of shape. He'd slept badly, couldn't face eating and was suffering with an affliction that would loom large over the rest of his life: what he calls writer's cramp. Overall, he says, he was suffering from nervous strain – hardly surprising after the exertions of his first ten weeks in London. He tried to relax, couldn't and decided to go out instead. A girl – not the one he'd been given the introduction to, but another one, this time definitely an intellectual type – had invited him to hear Edith Sitwell speak at an event at the Student Movement House (essentially a hostel for foreign students on Russell Square).

He headed off to the girl's room, met her and one of her friends there and they went to the meeting. Sitwell was a major literary celebrity of the time and CLR was immediately impressed: 'a striking figure, decidedly good-looking and even more decidedly a personality'. She read from her work and gave her thoughts on modern writing. At one point she talked about a talented young American novelist, but declined to name him. CLR saw his opening and replied from the floor that he was sure she must be referring to William Faulkner. Naturally he was right, and further literary peacocking followed. Impressed, Sitwell asked to speak to CLR afterwards and took his address and phone number. He had been seeking to make an impression and, gratifyingly, succeeded.

After the reading, at around half past eleven, CLR and his two new friends went back to the first girl's lodgings. There they sat and talked for an hour before the second girl cycled back to Chelsea, 'the artists' quarter'. CLR and the first girl carried on talking, of Tagore's poetry and much else, till he looked outside and saw it was dawn, at which point he had a cup of Oxo and went home to bed.

He hadn't actually gone to sleep though, when at half past eight a male friend arrived, a poet much given to reading aloud, who proceeded to entertain a drowsy CLR with a selection of Edith Sitwell's poems and then a Handel aria. When the extrovert poet left, CLR got up and went for a walk, ending up at Bumpus's bookshop on Oxford Street, where he looked at an exhibition of John Locke ephemera. A quick nap on the sofa and then he was out for dinner with the girl from the night before, plus a West African student. Together they read Chekhov's *Three Sisters* before CLR finally made it home around midnight.

He had a lie-in in the morning, reading the newspapers and weekly magazines, a highlight being 'the delightful Miss Rebecca West in the *Daily Telegraph*'. At lunchtime he set off for Middle Temple, to meet two friends and spend time walking and arguing and stopping in cafés till six, when he headed over to the Society for International Studies. There he delivered a lecture (on what, he does not say). That done, he says, 'you might think that was enough for one day. You simply do not know Bloomsbury.'

No indeed. After the lecture, CLR and a party of friends went to the Russell Square tube café just before midnight to talk and drink coffee. He might have eaten too, except the president of the Friends of India society invited him to come for dinner at a friend's house half a mile away (of this dinner he notes, somewhat surprisingly, how little the average middle-class English person seems to drink). They talked about art for hours. CLR got to see 'a reproduction of some Pompeian wall paintings which I had heard about and wanted to see', before leaving at around four in the morning. His Indian friends then went to the all-night post office to send an airmail, but CLR actually called it a night.

On Saturday morning CLR got up to visit the *Times* book club,* before a couple came round to visit him. She was pretty and 'most charmingly dressed'; her boyfriend was 'not at all good-looking, dresses even more carelessly than I do, but is in many respects one of the most stimulating and amusing men I have ever met'. They went for a high tea at which they talked about Mussolini, before going to the pub. They left the pub with three large bottles of beer, a half bottle of whisky and about fifty cigarettes.

They went back to CLR's room and argued about music and literature till ten, when the provisions ran out. At which point they took a taxi over to the couple's own lodgings, where they read extracts from *Cyrano de Bergerac* before the boyfriend read out a reportedly hilarious short story. Then they ate sardines and olives, and CLR finally made it home around two, before getting up in the morning and doing it all again.

Finally, CLR tried to make up his mind as to what he thought about the world he'd landed in, so far from Port of Spain. He had mixed feelings. On the one hand he felt that 'in one important sense it is not a life at all. It is a highly artificial form of living and I would not be surprised if a great deal of what modern works suffer from is not to be traced to that very cause ... Wordsworth did not learn to write like that running around in Bloomsbury or any other literary quarter talking about books and art and music. These things come from deeper down.'

* A reading room, lending library and bookshop in Wigmore Street.

It's a complaint that could reasonably have been made about all bohemias through the ages, right up to the Williamsburgs or Peckhams of today. And yet CLR is well aware that while it may not be deep, it's the kind of life he loves:

> Even though I see the Bloomsbury life for the secondary thing that it is, nevertheless both by instinct and by training I belong to it and have fit into it as naturally as a pencil fits into a sharpener. Birds of a feather will flock together.

All that said, it is not an unmixed picture of life in Britain that CLR offers his readers back in Trinidad. There is, he explains, no shortage of racial prejudice. Interestingly, he locates it as essentially a male problem: 'The average man in London is eaten up with colour prejudice,' he writes. They are superficially polite, he says, but if they see you with a white girl, then it's a very different matter. And the London girls, he observes, are generally very well disposed to 'coloured' men, West Indians in particular:

> The English native is so dull and glum and generally boorish in his manners, that the girls turn with relief from these dreadful Englishmen to the smiling and good-natured West Indians. At which the Englishman sits in a corner and scowls and makes himself as unpleasant as possible.

The matter of racial prejudice 'is a big question', he writes, 'and I am going to tackle it someday in the way it deserves'. This, however, he did not do. There is very little discussion of the racism he must have personally experienced in any of his writing over the next few years. Presumably, on one level, he simply decided to ignore it as beneath him. And, on another level, his whole political outlook was about to change profoundly. It was a small town in the north of England that would be the catalyst.

Just a week or so after his long weekend in Bloomsbury, CLR left London. He had run out of money and it was time to take Learie

Constantine up on his offer of help. He headed off to a place about as far from Bloomsbury as you could get, both literally and figuratively: the Lancashire mill town of Nelson.

Learie Constantine had arrived in Nelson three years earlier when the Nelson Cricket Club had made him an offer of a three-year contract at £500 a year to play for them in the Lancashire League, from the 1929 season onwards. That was roughly three times the average wage in Britain at the time.

It wasn't an easy decision for Constantine to make. On the one hand the money was far better than anything available to him in Trinidad. On the other, he would have to take his wife and baby daughter across the Atlantic to live in a town where they would be the only Black people for miles around.

In the end the financial incentive won out. The Constantine family came to Nelson, a town of around forty thousand people that had prospered in the Victorian heyday of the cotton mills but was now struggling. The first year had been tough socially. They suffered a certain amount of straightforward racism and a much greater amount of simple gawping. Kids would peer through the windows of their house to get a glimpse of these exotic newcomers. Cricketing-wise, however, it was a triumph. Constantine's all-action game was ideally suited to the one-day format of the Lancashire League.

At the end of the first season the Constantines took stock. Learie was prepared to take the family back home, but his wife Norma persuaded him to honour the contract. They decided to spend their winters in Trinidad and return to Nelson for the cricket season. They lost out to Bacup in 1930, but won the league again in 1931. And over the two summers the family started to make real friends in the area.

By the time CLR arrived, near the beginning of the 1932 season, Constantine had negotiated a new contract, this time for £650 a season, an amount that made him one of the highest-paid sportsmen in Britain. It was nearly twice as much as the highest-paid footballer received, for instance. Despite that, the family lived simply in a two-bedroom house on Meredith Street, with a view over a bowling green to the town centre and, beyond that, Pendle Hill.

It wasn't the smallest of houses. Nevertheless, there was already a couple, plus their four-year-old daughter, living there, so CLR's arrival for an indefinite stay had the potential to be quite a stressful addition. And so it proved.

CLR was not the easiest of lodgers. He hit Nelson, as he had hit London, with a fierce determination to discover everything he could about his new home. Within the first couple of weeks he had joined the Labour Club and the Cricket Club, and he'd embarked on teaching law to Learie and, at the same time, himself. The two men also enjoyed extensive political discussions.

All of this was, as CLR acknowledges in *Beyond a Boundary*, a terrific strain on the great man:

> All these discoveries and excitements had one disastrous consequence. They ruined Learie's batting for nearly a whole season. Despite the objective circumstances, I believe the responsibility was largely mine. I was adjusting myself to British life. I was reading hard. Night after night I would be up till three or four. I must have seriously discommoded that orderly household, Often I was abstracted and withdrawn. Literature was vanishing from my consciousness and politics was substituting itself. There hung over me for part of the time the great question mark: How was I to earn my living?

Lancashire was not exactly the place that CLR discovered organised politics, but it was the place that changed his political outlook for ever. He arrived in Nelson with the manuscript for the life of Captain Cipriani, with its plea for Britain to allow Trinidad self-government. This was in one sense a revolutionary work – in that Britain was still determined to keep control of its empire – but its demands were simply for Trinidad to be allowed the same sort of parliamentary democracy that Britain had. It was not advocating communism or anything like it. Indeed, Cipriani had charged CLR with the task of talking to the British Labour Party and reminding them of their commitment to West Indian self-government, the commitment they had signally failed to honour in their recent time in government.

CLR had been too busy running around Bloomsbury to deliver on this promise, but once in Nelson he at least arranged for the publication of his manuscript. Learie Constantine agreed to pay for it to be published by a printer in Nelson, and they would ship copies back to Trinidad.

The printer was a man named Fred Cartmell, and it was a choice that would have unexpected results.

> Mr Cartmell ... was not only a reader but a great buyer of books. On learning that I also was a wide reader, Mr Cartmell became very friendly with and towards me, told me that in Nelson he was quite isolated in his concern with books, invited me to his house and pressed his library upon me.[3]

The first book that Fred Cartmell lent to CLR was the opening volume of Trotsky's newly published *History of the Russian Revolution*. It made an immediate and profound impression. Not only did it detail this still recent history, but it put it in the context of Marxist theory while also being written in elegant, even on occasion humorous, prose with plentiful references to literature – Tolstoy in particular – as well as politics.

Thus, even as *The Life of Captain Cipriani* was being printed, CLR's own politics were taking a decisive turn to the radical left. And it wasn't just his reading that was causing that shift, it was also the real-world politics that were taking place all around him. As he arrived in Nelson, the mill workers were voting to strike, and across the summer a bitter industrial battle gradually gained intensity.

Within days, CLR had learnt of another recent piece of collective action. The local cinema had attempted to cut the wages of its staff, and the town had responded with a mass boycott. CLR relayed news of this back to Trinidad in the last of his dispatches for the *Port of Spain Gazette*:

> The whole town of Nelson, so to speak, went on strike. They would not go to the cinema. The pickets were put out in order to turn back those who tried to go. For days the cinemas played to empty benches. In a town of forty thousand people you could find sometimes no more than half a dozen in the theatres. The company went bankrupt, and had to leave. Whereupon local people took over and the theatres again began to be filled. It was magnificent and it was war . . . I could forgive England all the vulgarity, and all the depressing disappointment of London for the magnificent spirit of these north country working people.[4]

CLR was helped, of course, in his efforts to get to know these working people by the fact that he was the guest of the local celebrity. Constantine had made inroads and CLR was able to travel in his wake. Quite literally so, when it came to cricket itself. Within days of arriving in town, CLR was practising in the nets at Nelson Cricket Club and a week or so later he was given a game in the second team. He made a duck coming out to bat at the elevated position of number three, but took two wickets with his bowling. A week later he played in a friendly alongside Constantine, and again failed with the bat but partially redeemed himself with the ball.

But his new-found enthusiasm for radical politics quickly consumed him, to the extent that he didn't even make space for playing cricket. Instead he read and read. After Trotsky's *History*, Fred Cartmell lent him another key text, Oswald Spengler's *Decline of the West*. This was a fashionable tome that argued that Western society had run out of road and legitimacy, and was therefore vulnerable to the rise of fascist leaders. It was timely reading matter. Mussolini was well established as the increasingly dictatorial ruler of Italy. Hitler was on the rise in Germany and Oswald Mosley had just formed the British Union of Fascists. CLR was utterly taken up by the sense that the world was on the cusp of violent change. He needed urgently to understand the forces at work and started reading even more voraciously. Which made him an ever less ideal lodger. The Constantines' daughter Gloria remembers one particular incident:

> My mother and I were in the living room and his bedroom was directly above the living room and my mother said to me, 'Do you smell something burning?' and so I said 'I think so'. She said 'Oh my goodness' and went up the stairs. There is Nello very busy writing or reading, sitting in a cardigan near an electric fire and his cardigan is on fire. And when my mother pointed out to him 'Nello, you are on fire' he said 'Oh my goodness, oh my goodness', but the thing is he hadn't a clue ...[5]

As CLR read Trotsky in Lancashire, *The Life of Captain Cipriani* was printed and shipped out to Trinidad in remarkably short order. By September reviews were already starting to appear, both in Trinidad and in the wider West Indies.

It's a curious book, and would certainly have benefited from a firm editorial hand. On one level it's a polemic aimed at the complacent, racist Trinidadian political system and its supine acceptance of British authority. At the same time, it makes some gestures towards being a biography of the leading player in this struggle, Captain Cipriani. Finally – and least successfully for contemporary readers – it tries to marry the two elements by detailing particular legislative struggles in which Cipriani was engaged and gets bogged down in transcripts of political debates. There is also a chapter in which CLR attempts to defend his hero's disastrous about-turn on the Divorce Bill. Overall, it's the work of a journalist who had not yet quite worked out how to transfer his talents to a book-length project.

In later years, CLR would remember the book as having been 'a grand success. When the letters and notices came Constantine and I rejoiced.'[6]

The reality was rather more complex. The book did receive some very positive reviews, but these were mostly from elsewhere in the West Indies. In Trinidad it had a decidedly mixed reception. Not least in *The Beacon*, CLR's old literary stamping ground. A long review by the future labour activist Ralph Mentor gave a balanced account of its strengths and weaknesses. In particular, Mentor identifies the Divorce Bill chapter as an unworthy piece of special pleading. Albert Gomes, still in his early twenties but precociously confident in his opinions, gave a flippant but not entirely unfair summary when he suggested that the book might have been better titled 'Some incidents in the Legislative Council of Trinidad and Tobago with their Colour Implication'.

For Gomes, Cipriani's politics and his desire for self-government for Trinidad, while remaining part of the British Empire, wasn't nearly enough. He was now agitating for a classless, communist society. Cipriani was rapidly becoming yesterday's hero.

Still, there was no doubt that the book had helped stir up debate in the West Indies. Whether it sold enough copies to repay Constantine's investment is not recorded, but CLR also did what he could to launch the book in the UK.

Cipriani himself had given CLR an important contact, a Scot called William Gillies who was the international secretary of the Labour Party. Cipriani had written to Gillies, telling him to expect a visit from CLR, a few months earlier. On 10 August, once copies of the book were ready, CLR finally wrote to Gillies, offering to send him a copy and telling him that he was looking for an English publisher to take it on, to reach 'the few who are interested in West Indian affairs'.[7] He explained his failure to visit Gillies while he was in London was due to an attack of 'writer's cramp'.* Gillies wrote back, chiding CLR for his tardiness, but asking for a copy of the book.

A week or so later, on 27 August, CLR went to watch Nelson play an away game at Rawtenstall. This was no ordinary match. Rawtenstall were close rivals and both teams had great professional champions. Nelson had Learie Constantine, of course, but Rawtenstall had S. F. (Sydney) Barnes. Barnes was fifty-nine years old now, but in his prime he was reckoned to have been one of the greatest bowlers ever. He was essentially a leg-spinner who bowled at fast medium speed, with remarkable accuracy and disquieting bounce. He still has the best bowling figures for a Test series of any bowler in history. A proud, unbending man, with a keen sense of his own worth as a professional in an amateur era, he had quit Test cricket after the war and devoted himself to the

* This trivial-sounding but debilitating complaint would actually loom large throughout the rest of CLR's life.

Lancashire League, where he had taken thousands of wickets at a paltry average of around seven or so. The great *Guardian* cricket writer Neville Cardus offered this memorable one-line description: 'He was relentless, a chill wind of antagonism blew from him on the sunniest day.'

The year before, the two titans had met for the first time and Constantine had been the clear winner. A huge crowd had watched as he scored 96 not out in Nelson's 175 and then took four for 34 as Rawtenstall were bowled out for 103. Anticipation, then, for the rematch was sky-high, not least on the part of CLR.

Sydney Barnes was a living link to the golden-age players, W. G. Grace, Victor Trumper, Ranjitsinhji and all the other pre-war legends whose exploits CLR knew by heart, though he had never seen any of them in the flesh. His new studies had meant he'd missed many of Constantine's appearances for Nelson, but there was no way he was missing this one. He wrote about it immediately afterwards, beginning with this portrait of Barnes:

> To begin with, Barnes not only is fifty-nine, he looks it. Some cricketers at fifty-nine look and move like men in their thirties. Not so Barnes. You can almost hear the old bones creaking. He is tall and thin, well over six feet, with strong features. It is rather a remarkable face in its way and could belong to a great lawyer or a statesman without incongruity. He holds his head well back, with the rather long chin lifted. He looks like a man who has seen as much of the world as he wants to see.[8]

He goes on to describe the match, beginning with Rawtenstall, led by Barnes, bowling at Nelson. Barnes took seven wickets for 30 runs or so – 'it is impossible to imagine better bowling of its kind,' reckoned CLR. Sadly the battle with Constantine failed to live up to its potential as the West Indian hero was bowled by the journeyman operating from the other end.

Then came Nelson's turn to bowl, with precious few runs to defend. Constantine bowled at maximum speed, knocking over the first few wickets. Barnes came out to bat and defended stoutly for forty minutes before Constantine managed to bowl him leg stump. And that was that. Constantine and Nelson had prevailed again, and CLR had seen one of the game's greats in action and been in no way disappointed.

Back at Meredith Street, CLR wrote up his impression of Barnes and showed it to Constantine, who told him he should get it into print. He suggested sending it to Neville Cardus at the *Guardian*, with whom he was friendly. CLR did so and was utterly delighted when Cardus said he would run it in the paper. Not only that, but he asked CLR to come and see him in Manchester next time he was passing through, to discuss the possibility of further work.

This was terrific news. Firstly because it offered the prospect of paid work, but also because CLR had a tremendous personal admiration for Cardus. He was a working-class Lancashire boy who'd made himself into one of the country's foremost critics. The elegance of his style utterly belied the poverty of his upbringing as the illegitimate son of a prostitute. He had started as a classical music and theatre critic before falling ill with a chest infection and being asked to cover the cricket to keep his hand in during his convalescence. He took to it immediately, treating cricket with the same seriousness and careful observation as he would dedicate to a play or a symphony. He was, in short, a man absolutely after CLR's own heart when it came to his passions in life. And once he received the invitation to Manchester, CLR didn't hesitate. Forty years later, he told the BBC what happened:

> So I go in, in a day or two, and Cardus tells me, 'Now I am looking for someone to help me to do some work at matches that I am not able to do. Will you do it?' I told him, 'Most certainly I will do it.' And after a minute or two of casual conversation I went away. 'Come and see him when the next season began.' And I went and saw him and we worked it out together.[9]

It was an auspicious September week in the Meredith Street household. CLR had a job lined up for the following summer, and that Saturday Nelson won their final match, with Constantine making a half century, to secure the 1932 league title.

CLR James had been in Britain for six months and the success he had always envisaged was just starting to come within reach. There also appears to have been a romantic adventure. Anne Lamb,* who worked in the local café, remembered the impact he made on Nelson's female population:

> He was really very, very handsome – all the girls thought he was absolutely marvellous. He was very tall, very straight and there was nothing coarse about his features ... [there] was a girl, she was married and her husband was out in Persia. Her name was Kathleen Harrison ... a very attractive girl. Now they were very keen on each other and they used to sit in the café and have tea. There were two cafés – the top one was not used except for parties and they used to go up there. There was quite a bit of gossip ...[10]

While CLR's personal fortunes were starting to look up, the same did not go for the mill workers of Nelson. They were now engaged in a bitterly fought strike action. A week after their cricket team won the league, there was a major demonstration, led by the Labour Party, in support of the striking workers.

Support for the Labour Party itself, however, was starting to waver. People felt betrayed by Ramsay MacDonald's actions during the coalition government of the year before, cutting unemployment benefit. And those locals who had read CLR's *Captain Cipriani* were frankly cynical about its hope that the Labour Party would give self-government to the West Indies: 'They never gave us anything and we put them there; why do you think they would give you any?'[11]

Nevertheless, CLR pressed forward in his dealings with William Gillies. In November he went down to London and met Gillies. It evidently went well as Gillies provided him with an introduction to

* It seems likely CLR also had an affair with Anne Lamb. In the interview she says she visited him in London, probably in 1935, and he took her to the Proms for the first time. Decades later he sent her a copy of *Beyond a Boundary* with the inscription 'In memory of things past from Nello'.

Leonard Woolf, publisher of the Hogarth Press. Virginia's husband* was a Fabian and a former colonial administrator. He was also the man responsible for drawing up the Labour Party's 1928 statement in favour of West Indian self-government, the self-same statement that Cipriani had put much store by, and which had so far come to nothing.

CLR gave Woolf a copy of his book and a few weeks later Woolf wrote back to say that he liked it, but rather than print all of it he would like to extract a ten-thousand-word essay, as part of a series of 'day to day' pamphlets dealing with contemporary political issues.

Woolf wanted to cut out all the biographical material and discussion of internal issues, and focus on CLR's summing-up of Trinidad's racial pathology and his impassioned demand to treat its population as adults, not backward children. It was a smart move, both politically and in terms of highlighting what was best in the original book. CLR immediately agreed to the plan, writing to Gillies in January 1933 to let him know that the deal had been agreed.

There was one odd aspect to their correspondence. CLR appears to have mentioned the high price of shoes in Trinidad. Gillies responded by sending him several pairs of what sound like espadrilles, asking whether he thought they might sell well in Trinidad. Whether this was an abstract interest, or a prospective business opportunity, is never quite clear. In any event, CLR finally sent the shoes off to Juanita, with the promise that she would in turn show them to Captain Cipriani. There the matter ran out of steam, perhaps allowing a successful career in import/export to go begging (or, given CLR's general level of financial chaos, probably not).

This matter of finance was still a problem. There would be money next cricket season, but for the moment CLR was still dependent on the charity of Learie Constantine. His attempts to teach the cricketer law had fizzled out. The book they were writing together, now titled 'Cricket and I', was more or less done. He needed to find some other

* CLR did also meet Virginia Woolf, but sadly had very little to say about her when asked.

way to contribute to the household. Gradually he found one. He could, in effect, sing for his supper.

Constantine was deluged with requests to speak at different events, church gatherings, political meetings and so forth:

> It was something of a strain on him, but he was always ready to oblige. He began by taking me along to say a few words and soon substituted me wherever possible. By the winter we were in full cry all over the place. Sometimes I was paid and the money was useful . . . From my school debating-society days I had never had any difficulty on the public platform and here was an audience eager to listen to whatever I had to say.[12]

And so passed the winter. CLR read his books and talked to the Independent Labour Party about 'Coloured Peoples under British Rule', or to the Labour Party itself about 'The Present Policy of the Labour Movement'.

Meanwhile, he had made a new close friend, Harry Spencer, who with his wife Elizabeth ran a bakery and café in the centre of Nelson.* Harry was a reader and a music lover, and CLR got into the habit of dropping by the tearoom and spending hours talking to Harry about cultural and political matters. At weekends the Spencers would invite him to their house overlooking the moors, and CLR would listen to Harry's great collection of classical records. It was a friendship that would bear unexpected fruit later in the year.

* The site of his liaisons with Kathleen Harrison.

Chapter Seven

In late March 1933, CLR moved back to London determined to make his mark in journalism, and found a place to live at 29 Willow Road, Hampstead. His move coincided with the publication of his Hogarth Press pamphlet, now entitled *The Case for West Indian Self-Government*, on 21 March. He bought half the print run – five hundred copies – in the hope of being able to sell them himself. The pamphlet had already attracted a favourable mention in the *New Statesman*, which CLR had followed up by submitting a piece to them on the latest developments in Trinidad. Meanwhile, his regular *Guardian* cricket reporting would start in earnest in mid-April.

All around him, though, the world was changing. The Depression was grinding on and down. The Reichstag fire had taken place on 27 February and the Nazis had moved fast to use it to cement their grip on power in Germany. That same week, the *New Statesman* turned down his piece because it lacked 'topical interest'. In Britain in 1933, the issue of West Indian self-government was hardly anyone's most pressing concern. CLR was going to have to find some other drums to bang.

Over the next six months, he lived a curious kind of double life. Cricket reporter and revolutionary. Let's deal with the cricket side of things first.

Every week he covered a cricket match, generally three-day County Championship fixtures. So he would be at Edgbaston or Harrogate or Worcester, watching cricket with his forensic eye and getting to know England in the process.

By fortunate coincidence, the West Indies were the touring side in Britain that summer. They brought over a team featuring several people who were well known to him. There was Clifford Roach, CLR's one-time opening partner at Maple, and Cyril Merry, the son of his childhood pastor (and occasional Greek teacher) the Reverend Merry. Learie Constantine would only play in the second Test, at Old Trafford. Much of the excitement, in advance of the cricket, centred on the West Indies' new star, the twenty-four-year-old wunderkind George Headley. Headley was the first truly great West Indian batsman, second only to Bradman as the greatest of all time in many expert eyes, and in the years before the Second World War he carried their batting almost single-handedly. This was his first tour of Great Britain.

CLR profiled him for the *Guardian*, but sadly the demands of the job meant he was watching Lancashire play Surrey while Headley was making a brilliant 169 not out at Old Trafford, earning his team their only draw of the series. The other two matches were easily won by a very strong England team, featuring some of their own all-time greats: the batsman Wally Hammond, the spinner Hedley Verity et al. They were captained by the patrician Douglas Jardine, who had faced widespread criticism for launching bodyline against Australia the previous winter.

At Old Trafford, the West Indies decided to give Jardine a taste of his own medicine. Learie Constantine and Manny Martindale bowled fast and short leg theory* at the England batsmen. Constantine got Hammond, but the genuinely tough Jardine stood firm and scored his only Test century on what was ultimately a fairly placid track.

After the match there was considerable controversy about the West Indian use of bodyline. CLR and Constantine decided to address it in an extra chapter of their book. They justified it as a legitimate tactic, though not one that appealed greatly to Constantine himself, while pointing out the English hypocrisy in excusing this tactic when it was used by them against Australia. They concluded by pointing out the simple truth that 'Body-line bowling is the logical outcome of this "win at any cost" policy'.[1]

* Leg theory, aka 'bodyline', consisted of the bowler aiming a tight leg stump line at the batsman's body with an array of leg-side fielders. This meant the batsman either fended off the balls with his bat and risked being caught or had to take repeated blows to the body. It was a cynical but effective ploy, given suitably fast and accurate bowlers.

CLR's cricket writing for the *Guardian* shows little of its author's revolutionary side. He had grown up reading acres of cricket journalism and the style clearly came naturally to him. He comes over as cultured and erudite, fond of a classical allusion, and obviously particularly knowledgeable about West Indies cricket, but very much a pro journalist giving his readers what they expected. Along the way he picked up some further cricket reporting work, writing about the West Indies tour for *The Cricketer* and sending reports to the *Port of Spain Gazette* as well.

Perhaps the thing CLR enjoyed most of all about reporting cricket was the chance to sit in the press box and talk to his fellow experts, among them some of the legends of the game, starting with one of his boyhood heroes, the first of the cricketing intellectuals:

> C. B. Fry usually dominated the press box, reciting lines of poetry, warbling bits of opera, recalling great cricketing events, and all the time looking at the game and writing his column. Neville Cardus was lively and talkative, full of wit and humour. Jack Hobbs as he was then sat quiet, saying little, speaking usually only when spoken to. But how he watched the game! He never took his eyes off it.[2]

When he wasn't overnighting in the cricket towns of England, CLR seems to have split his time that summer between London and Lancashire. In Nelson he worked with Constantine on finishing the book and spent time with Harry Spencer discussing politics and books. One particular interest that came up again and again was the life of the Haitian revolutionary Toussaint Louverture. Ever since he'd mentioned Toussaint in his riposte to the racist Harland in *The Beacon*, and had read Percy Waxman's fascinating but unsatisfactory *Black Napoleon*, CLR had been taken with the idea that here was a subject he could write about.

In London he thoroughly immersed himself in the political and cultural life, and was once again more involved in anti-colonial politics. He returned regularly to the Student Movement House, where he would meet expats from all over the world, increasingly including young radicals fleeing Hitler's Germany.

He started to take a more active part in antiracist struggles, having joined the League of Coloured Peoples soon after coming to London. This was an organisation set up in 1931 by a Jamaican doctor called Harold Moody, who had lived in London since before the First World War. It was intended to be a British equivalent of the American National Association for the Advancement of Colored People, but unlike the NAACP, while being multiracial it would always have an all-Black leadership.

The LCP had held a three-day conference in Hertfordshire at the end of March 1933. CLR had attended and spoke on West Indian self-government alongside a number of speakers from elsewhere in the Empire, including several African activists.

The experience of meeting Africans in London would have a profound effect on CLR's thinking. Up to that point he had essentially accepted the imperialist propaganda that insisted Africa had no worthwhile culture, was simply the heart of darkness. Propaganda that insisted that Black West Indians like himself were, in effect, lucky to have been rescued by having had the good fortune to be educated into Western culture.

He started to read widely about African culture, and when an exhibition of African art opened at the Lefevre Gallery in mid-May he went along and was thrilled by what he saw there. Decades later he reflected on it:

> I went because it was African, and because it was art, something new. I was about thirty-two years old and for the first time I began to realise that the African, the black man, had a face of his own. Up to that time I had believed that the proper face was the Graeco-Roman face. If a black man had that type of face he had a good face, and if he didn't, well, poor fellow, that was his bad luck, that was too bad for him.[3]

The exhibition attracted a patronising review by Stanley Casson in the BBC magazine *The Listener*. CLR wrote in with an impassioned defence of the exhibition and by extension the African people:

> It is inconceivable to me how anyone looking at the Pahouin Venus in the present exhibition in the Lefevre Gallery, some of the masks in the British Museum ... can continue to base his criticism on the theory, daily more and more discarded by anthropologists, that the mind of the African, in his so-called 'primitive' condition was the mind of a child.[4]

The letters page for the next few weeks features a lively to and fro between CLR and Casson, in which CLR demonstrated how much he had recently read about anthropology and Africa.

At the same time, CLR, who was clearly making his presence known, was invited by the BBC to give a talk on the history of slavery, to coincide with the centenary of its abolition in Britain. As often happened with BBC talks, it was also printed in *The Listener*, coincidentally the same week as his letters appeared. It was a long, vigorous piece, obviously designed to be read aloud (like an enormous amount of CLR's work), and essentially summarising the arguments of *The Case for West-Indian Self-Government*. It ends, though, with a neat summary of his experience of life in Britain so far:

> As for myself, I have lived in the West Indies all my life. I came here just over a year ago and I have not had the slightest difficulty in entering into the phases of the life I see around me. I should do wrong not to say that, particularly from the intelligentsia (a horrible word, but I know no other), I have received a warm welcome and much kindness. But, were it not for a few institutions like the Student Movement House, and the League of Coloured Peoples, the average West Indian student would have a dreadful time. I say this and state our political aims because a centenary is a time when one should look not only backwards but forwards.
>
> A few weeks ago I wanted a typist and after some difficulty I found one. I started to dictate to her about the West Indies and after a few lines, she asked me what island I was from. I said Trinidad, and she told me that her people had lived there and held slaves before emancipation. When we had finished we walked down the steps together, she in front and I behind, for I had stayed to turn off the

> light. As we neared the end of the steps she said, 'Strange, isn't it, that your people used to work for mine and now I work for you?' At the bottom of the steps she waited for me and standing on the level we shook hands.[5]

He followed this up with a piece for *Tit-Bits* that August, and again tied to the centenary. In it CLR details the role of slavery in his family history, and goes on to say that slavery was far from dead in the world of the thirties. He talks about the continued existence of the slave trade in the Arab world and, particularly, in Abyssinia. It's time, he suggests, for the world to wake up and stamp out slavery once and for all.

As well as finding solidarity with the Black people of Africa, CLR would also have been keenly aware of the antiracist struggles going on in the USA. In particular, the case of the Scottsboro Boys had received enormous attention, and the LCP were very much involved in campaigning for justice. The Scottsboro Boys were nine Black teenagers who had been falsely accused of raping two white women on a train in Alabama in 1931. Eight were convicted and sentenced to death by all-white juries before a series of appeals took place. Public opinion outside the South was outraged and an international campaign, led by the Communist Party, lobbied to have the verdicts overturned.

The mother of two of the boys, Ada Wright, had toured Europe in 1932, rallying support. And now the latest of several retrials was due in the summer of 1933. To build support in London, the activist and socialite Nancy Cunard organised the Scottsboro Defence Gala at the Phoenix Theatre on 9 July, featuring British and American jazz musicians and singers including Sydney Bechet and Nina Mae McKinney, plus the African highlife group the Gold Coast Quartet. It's not recorded whether CLR was there but, given the cause and the fact that the LCP were heavily involved in the case, it's very likely. Certainly many people who would be significant figures in CLR's life over the next few years did attend, including the show's impresario.

Nancy Cunard was a remarkable figure. Born into the English upper classes as a member of the Cunard shipping family, she lived in

Paris in the twenties, at the heart of the world of avant-garde writing and art, publishing modernist poetry and acquiring a string of lovers. After a two-year liaison with the surrealist poet Louis Aragon she began a long relationship with Black American musician Henry Crowder, and this helped open her eyes to the cause of antiracism. The week after the Scottsboro Defence Gala, she won a libel case against three tabloids that had suggested her only interest in antiracism was a desire to have sex with Black men. She decided that she would use the money to fund an anthology of work by Black writers, from the USA, the Caribbean and Africa. She was a polarising figure, but one who got things done, and her range of contacts was remarkable.

One of them was a man named George Padmore. A thirty-year-old Trinidadian whose given name was Malcolm Nurse, he had been a childhood friend of CLR's. He had been to college in the US and embraced communism there. The Communist Party had identified him as a rising star, giving him the party name of George Padmore,* and he'd been taken to Moscow to further his political education. He spent a year there, becoming chief of the Negro Bureau at the Profintern, before moving to Germany to set up a CP front, the International Trade Union Committee of Negro Workers, bringing together for the first time Black radicals from all over the world. This was an extraordinary achievement from a man still only in his mid-twenties. He spent three years in Germany editing the organisation's journal, *The Negro Worker*, before Hitler's rise to power led to the sacking of their offices and his hasty retreat to London.

His was a well-known name in Black radical circles, so when he was announced as addressing a meeting on the edge of Bloomsbury that August, CLR was eager to attend.

> One night I heard that there was a man called George Padmore – he was a famous Moscow functionary – who was going to speak at Gray's Inn Road. I went to Gray's Inn Road to see the great George

* Members of revolutionary parties of the time customarily used adopted names to avoid identification by the authorities.

> Padmore because he was so widely known. And into the hall walked Malcolm Nurse, my old friend from Trinidad.[6]

The two men were delighted to meet again after many years apart. They talked long into that night and the next. However, Padmore was in the midst of a blazing internal row within the Communist Party and James was already, having read Trotsky, wary of getting too involved with the CP or its adherents. It would be a little while before they would meet again.

Trotsky was now a major obsession for James. He had read and re-read the *History of the Russian Revolution* 'as I had never read any books except *Vanity Fair* and Kipling's *Plain Tales from the Hills*'.[7]

He had bought copies of the second and third volumes, which were only available in French, in London, perhaps from the bookseller who was to become his unofficial political guru, a German anarchist called Charlie Lahr. Lahr was an archetypal bohemian, a tall free-thinker, a keen cyclist who favoured a beret and sandals in all weathers, and one whose kindness far exceeded his commercial sense.

Charlie Lahr's bookshop was between Bloomsbury and Holborn at 68 Red Lion Street, 'little bigger than a sentry box'.[8] The tiny shop was piled high with literary and political works. Lahr had done some publishing himself, most notably a D. H. Lawrence story called 'Sun'. For many of the shop's habitués – penniless poets who congregated in the shop hoping to cadge a couple of bob – Lahr was essentially a literary man.

For others, like James, he was a political man. Charlie was born in 1885 as Carl Lahr, left Germany in 1905 to avoid conscription, and devoted himself to anarchist politics apart from a brief dalliance with the CP around the time of the Russian Revolution, which ended when the Bolsheviks crushed the anarchist ship workers' uprising in Kronstadt. Unlike most politicos, however, Charlie didn't push a standard line. He was happy to find books by Trotsky for CLR, no matter that it was Trotsky himself who ordered the Kronstadt clampdown.

> Charlie did not so much argue a political issue. He disseminated information. 'Have you seen what these scoundrels have written about the United Front? Or the lies they are telling about Rosa

> Luxemburg and Carl Liebknecht? Here it is.' That was always the main part about Charlie, his anger at political lies and dishonesty, not only of Stalinism but of Social Democracy.[9]

For the people he liked, including CLR, he would order books and sell them at the publishers' wholesale price, not adding a commission. Through frequenting the shop, over the next few years CLR would be able to read a far wider range of source material than most of his contemporaries, who were already signed up to a fixed ideology with an approved reading list.

Charlie Lahr was not the only German to make an impact on CLR's life in 1933. One of the people he met at the Student Movement House was a young radical called Ernest Borneman. Borneman recalled their first meeting in his memoirs. He was washing his hands in the bathroom when heard someone in one of the stalls 'whistling the melody of Bella Figlia Dell'Amore so perfectly that I extended my hand-washing a little to see who it was. The answer was a two-metre-long black man with a beautifully shaped head and long pianist fingers.'[10] This, of course, was CLR James.

The two men became fast friends almost immediately. In some ways they could hardly have been more different: one a thirty-two-year-old Trinidadian schoolteacher turned cricket reporter and anti-colonial radical, the other an eighteen-year-old German Jewish communist who had escaped from Germany by posing as a member of the Hitler Youth on an exchange trip. And yet there was much they had in common. Both were fearsomely bright autodidacts, who never went to university but instead let their intellects roam around different areas as they reacted to life around them.*

Borneman knew Bertolt Brecht and had worked for the pioneering

* In *Beyond a Boundary* CLR mentions having met three truly brilliant people. These were Leon Trotsky, Amy Ashwood Garvey and 'a Hungarian refugee in London between the two wars – he was not twenty years old' – this could well refer to Borneman or, perhaps as Christian Hogsbjerg suggests, to a young Trotskyist called Hans Vajda.

psychologist Wilhelm Reich, who was about to publish *The Mass Psychology of Fascism*, the book that controversially rooted the phenomenon in sexual repression. Through his involvement in the Communist Party, he had already met George Padmore in Hamburg. He was also a pianist and anthropologist, a jazz critic, novelist, screenwriter, film editor and, later in life, a sexologist. Within days of arriving in London he had found himself at the Scottsboro Defence Gala. After the concert he went backstage where he was greeted by a 'slim very made-up woman with lots of bracelets', who asked him his name. 'And for the first time in my life I improvised this Anglicised version of my name. "Ernest Borneman. I'm a music critic from Berlin."'

This, of course, was Nancy Cunard. A decade earlier she had been pursued by Aldous Huxley, who had portrayed her in his novels as Lucy Tantamount and Myra Viveash. Borneman was less smitten: 'She didn't seem attractive to me at all, far too restless, too tense, too artificial, too intent on show.'

Nevertheless he accepted her invitation to an after-show party at her flat. There Borneman met a pianist called Garland Wilson who would introduce him to Soho's subterranean Black clubs, like the Nest ('dirty, cheap and dangerous') and the Shimsham, the latter fronted by a Black American with a minstrel show background called Ike Hatch, who had organised the Scottsboro Boys gala. The clubs attracted all the visiting Black American jazz stars. Borneman started playing the piano in both clubs, and before long found himself jamming the likes of Louis Armstrong, Cab Calloway and Duke Ellington.

Borneman lent CLR books by Marx, who CLR was still largely unfamiliar with, but he had no real interest in following his friend's enthusiasm for Trotsky. Where they did agree, though, was in their anticolonialism, which formed the bedrock of their intellectual friendship. More practically, both men needed somewhere to live and agreed to look for somewhere together, along with a friend of Borneman's, a German schoolteacher called Ernst Perl.

Borneman began by searching the area around the British Museum and the Student Movement House. Eventually he found an unfurnished three-room apartment on the upper floor with a kitchenette, but without a private toilet and bathroom, in a striking Georgian house on the fringe of Bloomsbury at 9 Heathcote Street. The rent was forty shillings a week. Borneman paid eight shillings as he had the smallest room, Ernst Perl paid twelve and CLR, who had the largest room, paid twenty. James and Perl had old-fashioned, beautifully proportioned arched windows. Borneman's room only had a small window, but he was able to use it to gain access to the flat roof of the neighbouring house, where he could sunbathe on summer days.

Number 9 Heathcote Street,* nicknamed the Hermitage by Borneman, would be CLR's home for the next four years – perhaps the most productive period of his life, at least in terms of books published.

* By a curious coincidence it was also the address at which Nancy Cunard had been living when she gave her party after the gala show. Her flat had a separate entrance, however, so it took Borneman some little time before he realised it.

Chapter Eight

Toussaint Louverture is a defining figure in Caribbean history. The great Haitian leader, the one who fought back and freed his people, is a hero to Black people, a bogeyman to white. His fame had spread around the world well before his death in 1803. Wordsworth wrote a sonnet in his honour, even as Louverture lay in a French dungeon. Later there would be books and plays, both celebrating and damning him.

For a people whose history had been deliberately erased – the Black people of the West Indies – his name was a rumour and the promise of hope. CLR would have grown up with Toussaint Louverture as a legend. He might have read Harriet Martineau's bestselling Victorian novel *The Hour and the Man*, or even Alphonse de Lamartine's verse play. What he did not have, what he could not access, was a true portrait of Toussaint, one that showed just how he had led what was generally believed to be the only successful slave rebellion in history.

The idea of writing about Toussaint Louverture had been steadily building in CLR since his last years in Trinidad, spurred on by reading Percy Waxman's *Black Napoleon*.* He was frustrated, however, by the lack of research materials. The books in English were unsatisfactory, partial accounts, always written by white writers full of colonial assumptions. What he wanted to do was to go back to primary sources wherever possible, to consult the historical record rather than just build up an imaginary portrait of the 'Black Napoleon' or 'Black Spartacus'. CLR wanted to write about Toussaint Louverture and the origins of the Haitian Revolution with the rigour of Trotsky on the Russian Revolution, not just peddle romantic quasi-history.

* Possibly also John W. Vandercook's novelistic *Black Majesty*. Vandercook was most likely in Trinidad at around the same time as CLR, given that he published a mystery, *Murder in Trinidad*, in 1933.

To do this, he needed to travel to Paris to look at the historical documents in the various archives there. The problem was money. Since he'd finished writing for the *Guardian* at the end of the cricket season, there was very little coming in. Help came from a rather unlikely source: his Nelson friend Harry Spencer.

> One day he said to me, 'Why are you always talking about this book – why don't you write it?' I told him that I had to go to France to the archives. I didn't have the money as yet, but I was saving. He asked me how much money I would need and I told him about a hundred pounds to start with. He left it there but a few days afterwards put ninety pounds in my hands and said, 'On to France, and if you need more let me know.'[1]

CLR reports that he was by then so well acquainted with the ways of northern folk that, rather than thanking Spencer fulsomely for this extraordinarily generous gift (very roughly £6000 in today's money), he just gave him a nod and a 'much obliged'.

Exactly when this exchange – one of the most repeated stories of CLR's life – took place is difficult to be sure about. CLR himself wrote that he went off and spent six months in France over the winter of 1933/34. However, Borneman's memoir makes it clear that CLR was in London for at least some of late 1933 and on 3 December, just after moving into Heathcote Street, he wrote to Leonard Woolf about the debt of £16 he owed the Hogarth Press for the five hundred copies of his pamphlet:

> I was sent to this country to study law, but with my own mind set on literature and politics. I asked for the money to publish the pamphlet and got it inasmuch as you had accepted the manuscript. But I received no encouragement to be allowed to live in London and try to write.
>
> In April I received one or two offers of articles about the W.I. cricket team and, realising that here was a chance to avoid the law, which I dislike intensely, I took the risk and come into London

> with the £16. I know I should have paid, but it was my only way out. I have not been unsuccessful. I have supported myself and have promises of work next summer for the *Manchester Guardian*. But the winter has been rather a blank. I am sure, however, that I shall raise the money before the end of the month ... I would not want you to think, the book being published, that I neglected the matter.[2]

This letter is fascinating and confusing in a couple of ways. Firstly, it suggests that CLR had glossed his trip to Britain as being a mission to study the law. And secondly because it's hard to understand how a man can be dodging his creditors in London while simultaneously digging in the archives in Paris.

There are two prime possibilities. Either CLR was keeping quiet about Harry Spencer's money and travelling back and forth between Paris and London all winter – easy enough to do, even in those pre-Eurostar days – or Spencer's gift didn't come till Christmastime and CLR actually headed to Paris in the new year, staying there for less than three months, rather than the six he later claimed. No matter, though: he certainly made good use of his time there.

On arrival in Paris he met up with two key contacts: Colonel Auguste Nemours and Léon-Gontran Damas. Nemours was a significant figure, a Haitian Creole in his fifties, a diplomat and historian and sometime delegate to the League of Nations. He was in Paris, at least in part, as a reaction to the American occupation of Haiti that had begun during the First World War and was now drawing to a close. In 1925 he had published a two-part military history of Haiti. His book gave CLR a basis for understanding the complex and confusing series of military confrontations that made up the decade-long war of independence. It was a great help to CLR to have the author himself at his disposal: 'He explained the whole thing to me in great detail, using books and coffee cups upon a large table to show how the different campaigns had been fought.'[3]

Nemours was a passionate advocate for the genius of Toussaint Louverture and convinced CLR that Toussaint and his fellow leader

Jean-Jacques Dessalines were military strategists on a par with Napoleon himself.

Léon-Gontran Damas was a very different figure. From French Guiana and only twenty-one years old, he was a student and nascent poet, with a passionate engagement in the anticolonial struggle. He had also thoroughly familiarised himself with the archives, libraries and bookshops of Paris. 'If you are working on the Haitian Revolution, this is the kind of material which you need,' he told CLR. 'I know Paris and sources of material very well and I put my knowledge at your disposal.'[4]

This was invaluable help for CLR, new in Paris and with limited time. Damas took him to the Bibliothèque nationale and the Archives nationales, as well as the bookshops that specialised in Caribbean history. He took full advantage, getting through an enormous amount of research, always delighted to surprise the librarians and archivists with his ability to speak and read French.

Paris being Paris, a city where even the archives closed for a two-hour lunch break, CLR was also able to eat and drink and meet a wide variety of Parisians. Colonel Nemours introduced him to the Haitian ambassador, who talked to him extensively. The ambassador was another member of the light-skinned elite and CLR observed that 'whether he knew it or not he gave me great insight into the mulatto side of the Haitian people'.[5]

He also had a more direct political experience while in Paris. The French fascists were on the rise and holding huge rallies. The Communist Party seemed unmoved, arguing that the fascists were no different to the bourgeois government. Only the Trotskyists saw the real menace at hand, and they were too few to have any great influence. However, the workers themselves – 'the proletariat, the stock of 1789' – came out and fought the fascists in the streets, halting them in their tracks.

Keen as his interest in politics was, CLR was never one to confine himself to a single social circle. He also met people at the heart of the city's artistic world, in particular the extremely well-connected – and newly married – pair of Théodore Fraenkel and Marguerite 'Ghita' Luchaire.

Théodore Fraenkel, five years older than CLR, had served in the Great War as a medic and then become one of the founders of surrealism, along with his close friend André Breton. After being at the heart of the movement through the early twenties, he decided to focus on his medical career. His first wife, the actress Lucie Morand,* died in mysterious circumstances, a possible suicide. He then married Ghita, daughter of the writer Julien Luchaire and younger sister of the literary dandy and newspaper editor (and later Nazi collaborator), Jean Luchaire.†

CLR talks little of Théodore, but rather more about his 'beautiful and charming wife', with whom he 'became very friendly'.[6] He would see Ghita again on future visits to Paris.

In March 1934, towards the end of his time in Paris, CLR got involved in one of the most unlikely writing projects of his career. Together with Learie Constantine, who came over from England to meet him, he was charged with undertaking an investigation into something called red butter.

Red butter was one of the staple foods of the Trinidad poor. It was low-quality butter adulterated with huge amounts of salt, which served as a preservative. It came in tins from France and was generally sold in spoonfuls. Many prominent Trinidadians, from Eric Williams to V. S. Naipaul, all ate it in their childhoods.

In 1934 a British butter company decided to launch a campaign against red butter and in favour of their own allegedly superior product, Green Pastures butter (named for the patronising musical of plantation life). They placed adverts in the Trinidad press decrying red butter as rancid, salty filth unfit for human consumption, and inviting readers to join the amusingly named Anti-Red League and promise to avoid red butter in favour of 'the all-purpose British butter'.

* A woman whose sister married both Georges Bataille and Jacques Lacan.

† He would face the firing squad wearing a coat that belonged to his former friend the writer Robert Desnos, who died in the Theresienstadt concentration camp. The coat was given to him in prison by Desnos's widow.

For one reason or another – and it's hard to look beyond money – Captain Cipriani became the public face of this campaign. And it was doubtless he who persuaded CLR and Constantine to become part of this unlikely crusade. Their task was to travel to Brittany, the home of red butter, and find out how it was made.

This implausible pair of investigative reporters travelled to Morlaix in Brittany, where they were invited into a peasant farm where butter was being made in decidedly unhygienic conditions; then to a bigger establishment, which was cleaner, but where the boss soon confided that 'of course we don't use that butter in France, we send it out to the colonies'.[7] Case closed. CLR duly returned to Paris and filed a series of stories in the *Trinidad Guardian*.

CLR must have followed Constantine back to Lancashire fairly promptly, no doubt eager to report to Harry Spencer on his progress, as by 14 March he was in Nelson, giving a talk on 'The Negro'. In it he contrasted the lots of Black people in England and France. He noted that the French record of colonial brutality was in many ways even worse than the British. But, as for how they treated Black people in the present, he came down on the French side. In Britain, he said, 'The average person . . . did not understand the negro. They saw him only dancing and kicking his heels like a half-crazy lunatic; the screen always presented him in an unfair position.' On the other hand, in France, 'They would find negroes in the French cabinet, in the ranks of retired naval and army men, in the professions, universities and colleges. France had already disregarded scientific theories, and judged the negro on results.'[8]

It's a contradiction that came up again and again as he researched the life of Toussaint Louverture. France was both saviour – the home of the revolution, of *liberté, égalité, fraternité* – and also the brutal, slave-owning, duplicitous devil.

Back in London, at the Hermitage, CLR's task was to decide what to do with the material he had gathered in Paris. The obvious course of action was to write another book, to try to take the model of Trotsky's *History of the Russian Revolution* and apply it to the Haitian Revolution of over a century earlier.

This would appear to have been his original plan, but instead he decided to take another tack entirely. He decided to write up the story of Toussaint as a play. After all, he'd always been a great lover of the theatre, and Shakespeare was the artist he revered above all. He had acted and produced plays in Trinidad. He is also said to have written one apprentice piece for the Maverick Club. But the actual catalyst for his change of plan was the arrival in his circle of one of the great figures of his age, the man who was Black Pride incarnate: Paul Robeson.

Paul Robeson was the son of a slave and yet, by the time he turned twenty-five in 1923, he had graduated from an Ivy League university, played professional American football and qualified as a lawyer. Since then he had established himself as one of the great acting and singing stars of the age. His recordings of spirituals had won him fans around the world, while on stage his extraordinary physical presence and magnificent speaking voice had made him an instant star, first in New York and then in London, where his 1928 performance in *Show Boat* had been an enormous hit, with its standout number, 'Ol' Man River', becoming his signature song.

Robeson loved London and had more or less settled there, buying a house in Hampstead. He was sick of the overt racism of his homeland and increasingly vocal politically. He made headlines again, starring in *Othello* opposite Peggy Ashcroft, accompanied by an affair ('How could one not fall in love in such a situation with such a man?' she later wrote).[9] Paul, never a faithful husband to his wife Essie, then had a more serious affair with a white English woman called Yolanda Wright. He was ready to divorce Essie and marry her when Yolanda's family put their foot down.

By the spring of 1934 Robeson, chastened by the recent break-up, was determined to immerse himself in positive, socially useful projects. In particular, he was determined to embrace his African-ness – a wholly alien concept for most Black Americans at the time. To this end, never a man for half measures, he enrolled at London's School of Oriental Studies* to work on African linguistics, with a view to

* Now the School for Oriental and African Studies (SOAS) University of London.

taking a PhD in philology. He began by starting to learn a selection of African languages. He was already a noted linguist, specialising in sourcing folk songs from different cultures.

During this period he was plunged into the world of African and colonial students and radicals in London. CLR recalled it as a small community in which it was easy to meet key players like Paul Robeson and Amy Ashwood Garvey. Getting to know Robeson was surely the catalyst in persuading CLR to take the Toussaint Louverture story and turn it into a play, with the great American as the star.

> Finally I ran him down at some party, told him about it and he agreed to read the script. He read it and, with great simplicity and directness said, yes, he would be ready to play the role: there were not too many parts in those days which gave a Black actor, however distinguished, a role that lifted him above the servants' quarters.[10]

Paul Robeson would have already been well aware of the story of Toussaint Louverture and the Haitian Revolution. This was partly because, in the US as in Trinidad, Toussaint's name had currency as an icon of successful Black struggle, but it was also because he had been approached four years earlier by the great Russian film director Sergei Eisenstein, who was interested in making a film based on the life of one of the other heroes of the Haitian Revolution, Henri Christophe. To this end he had bought the rights to John W. Vandercook's *Black Majesty*. The project had gone cold, however, so it is quite conceivable that Robeson encouraged CLR to work on his own play, changing the focus from Christophe to Toussaint in order to revive the film project. Robeson was always struggling to find a film role worthy of his talents.

So, over the summer of 1934, CLR worked on turning his researches into a play, all in between covering county cricket for the *Guardian*. Come September, he was able both to watch Bradman score a century at Scarborough and to see his first draft completed.

Meanwhile, CLR's political engagement was intensifying. Soon after returning from France, and perhaps directly inspired by the events of February in Paris, in which only the Trotskyists had seemed to intuit the true radicalism of the proletariat, he felt it was time to leave the Labour Party.

He decided to follow the example of Trotskyists he'd met in London and joined Labour's more radical rival, the Independent Labour Party (ILP).

Formed by Keir Hardie, along with CLR's early mentor Robert Cunninghame Graham,* in 1892, the ILP was the forerunner of the Labour Party and later a self-contained left-wing party within Labour, before its members decided to leave en masse in 1932, disgusted by Ramsay MacDonald's compromises. Aneurin Bevan called their decision one that rendered them 'pure, but impotent'. His view was borne out as the ILP haemorrhaged members over the next three years, from more than sixteen thousand in 1932 to fewer than five thousand in 1935. They were caught between the Labour Party to their right and the communists and, to a much lesser extent, the Trotskyists to their left.

So CLR joined a party in dire straits. He and his fellow Trotskyists started building their own group within the party. Throughout the summer they had regular meetings at the Hampstead home of a left-wing doctor. Among the comrades assembled there was a young woman called Louise Cripps:

> I first met C. L. R. James at the home of Dr Israel Heiger and his wife, Esther, in Hampstead Garden Suburb, London. There were eight of us to dinner. I noticed the West Indian sitting at the other end of the table.
>
> After dinner had finished, we went to sit in a horseshoe circle at the fireplace ... By this time I could concentrate on James. He was very tall, lean, handsome. He was telling us about Trotsky and the perfidies of Stalin; also, how the Communists in Great Britain were telling lots of lies and pursuing wrong policies. Normally, no one person monopolizes the conversation, and if they try, the others

* Though Graham later wrote off his comrades as 'piss-pot socialists'.

> around feel somewhat irritated. In this case, however, everybody was completely fascinated by James. They would ask questions; I do not know if I did or not, but everyone was quite prepared and pleased to have him, more or less, give us a lecture on his subject.[11]

Louise Cripps was far from the only person to notice CLR's remarkable gift for talking, whether in private with a handful of comrades or addressing a meeting, or even amid the free-for-all of public spaces like Speakers' Corner in Hyde Park. What was unusual about CLR was that his effectiveness as a public speaker was not based in the rhetorical tricks of the traditional street-corner agitator, or even the impassioned call and response of the Baptist minister.* Instead, he showed an extraordinary grip on a wide variety of material, thanks to a phenomenal memory that allowed him to quote at length and at will, without notes. People were less overwhelmed by emotion as struck quiet with wonder when they heard him speak.

Come November 1934, CLR and his fellow Trotskyists had formalised their association as the Marxist Group. Despite being only sixty or so in number, they developed a strategy to take over key constituency parties within the ILP. CLR and his Hampstead friends targeted the Finchley branch in north London. Before long, CLR was elected its chair. The Marxist Group were on their way to becoming a significant power in the ILP. Unfortunately, the ILP itself was fast sliding into irrelevance.

As for the Toussaint Louverture play, the first draft was written, but its intended star was a busy man. Robeson had spent the summer making a film called *Sanders of the River* at Elstree Studios. In December he headed off to Russia at the invitation of Sergei Eisenstein. They were to discuss, amongst other things, the long-mooted Haiti film.

The filming of *Sanders of the River* had been something of a sensation. The Korda brothers, Alexander and Zoltan, had determined to adapt Edgar Wallace's novel, and they wanted to make it as authentic

* Hardly surprising, given that CLR's childhood pastor was the very English Reverend Merry.

as possible, influenced by Robert Flaherty's *Nanook of the North*. This was to be the real Africa, shown on screen as never before. Zoltan Korda had travelled to Central Africa and shot stunning outdoor footage and recorded authentic African music. He came back to London and showed Robeson the footage, which persuaded him to come on board in the role of Bosambo. He could put his new-found knowledge of African language and custom to good use in what was promised to be a film that would uplift the race. Robeson told a reporter from the *Observer* about it with great enthusiasm, while playing African records in his London flat.

An 'African' village was built on the banks of the Thames in Surrey. The 'Africans' themselves were recruited from London's show-business circles and from the older established Black British communities of Liverpool and, particularly, Cardiff. The witch doctor, presented to the gullible *Observer* reporter as the real thing, was in fact a Mr Graham from Cardiff. There was at least one genuine African among these implausible villagers, however. That was a young Kenyan student called Jomo Kenyatta, later to become one of the great figures in the struggle for liberation from the colonial yoke.

CLR had doubtless met Kenyatta* during 1934, but their paths really came together in early 1935 with the political development that for the first time united London's different Black communities. This was Italy's aggression towards the country then called Abyssinia (now Ethiopia), the one African country to have held out against colonialism.

Italy's ruler, Benito Mussolini, had his eye on imperial expansion and Abyssinia was a prime target. Italy already owned the coastal lands to the immediate north and east – Italian Eritrea and Italian Somaliland. Now Il Duce wanted to take over the interior. He began by building

* Ernest Borneman had these, possibly exaggerated, things to say about the young Kenyatta: 'He lived in Victoria, the area around the train station. Although he was at least as poor as I was and sometimes had so little to eat after his separation from the CP in 1934, that he was too weak to stand up, he wrote his letters in green ink either wearing a Fes or an Astrakhan cap, a cape or a leather coat, a ring on each finger, and always wandered around with a walking stick that had a silver handle.' (*Die Ur-Szene.*)

a fort in Welwel, just over the border in Abyssinian territory. There was a violent confrontation in December 1934. Following this, an agreement with the other regional power, the French, gave the Italians a free run at Abyssinia, unless the British decided to intervene.

The British continued to sit on their hands, so Mussolini massed troops in the region throughout early 1935, obviously preparing for an invasion. Britain's small but vocal community of Black radicals were determined to launch a campaign, hoping to shame the government into action.

The key figures started to meet at a new hotspot for London's Black community, the International Afro Restaurant on New Oxford Street, close to the British Museum. It was run by Amy Ashwood Garvey, the first wife of Marcus Garvey, the pioneering populist Black nationalist. They had met in their native Jamaica and then moved to New York, where Garvey's fiery speeches had made him a hero. They divorced in 1922 (with Garvey confusingly going on to marry a second Jamaican woman called Amy).

Amy Ashwood Garvey was now keeping company with the Trinidadian entertainer Sam Manning, whose calypso recordings were popular across the Caribbean. They had recently arrived from New York and added some commercial knowhow to their political comrades' fervour, not to mention the chance to eat food that reminded them of home, rather than the blandness of the Lyons Corner House.

A remarkable crew came together at Amy's restaurant to form the International African Friends of Abyssinia (IAFA). Among them were a Guyanese doctor working in Manchester, Peter Milliard; Grenadian trade unionist T. Albert Marryshow; Guyanese activist Ras Makonnen (formerly known as George Griffiths); and the Barbadian sailor and trade unionist Chris Jones (aka Braithwaite). Jomo Kenyatta was appointed secretary, Amy Ashwood Garvey was treasurer, Sam Manning was in charge of 'propaganda'. The two leading figures, though, were CLR and, before long, George Padmore, who had now finally broken with the CP and returned to London to live.

While the International Afro Restaurant was the group's semi-official meeting place, informal conversations would take place at 9

Heathcote Street. Ernest Borneman went so far as to claim that 'A good part of the new Africa was created in this apartment'.[12] Among the regular visitors Borneman remembers were George Padmore and Ras Makonnen, as well as CLR's former pupil Eric Williams, then a student; Nnandi Azikiwe, later President of Nigeria;* Jomo Kenyatta, later President of Kenya; and Dr Hastings Banda, later head of state in Malawi.† The one notable woman in the mix was Amy Ashwood Garvey, 'who was running a restaurant on Oxford Street that fed some of us when we were starving'.

Occasional visitors included Prince Peter of Greece (Marie Bonaparte's son) who had studied with Malinowski at the LSE, alongside Borneman himself and Jomo Kenyatta, and, of course, Paul Robeson, whose wife Essie also studied with Malinowski and tried to hire Borneman to teach their son.

In summary Borneman felt that 'The atmosphere of those years had something in common with the years of the later student movement'. In the Hermitage the debates would carry on through the night at weekends, with people showing up at all hours to take part.

And so, in CLR James's flat, at the unfashionable end of Bloomsbury, the struggle to free Africa was joined. Strangely, this was not the only contribution to the cause that emanated from 9 Heathcote Street. Just a few months earlier, Nancy Cunard had finally published *Negro: An Anthology*, the first attempt to provide a survey of the arts and letters of Black people around the world. It included contributions from many of the great American names: Zora Neale Hurston featured prominently, alongside W. E. B. Du Bois, Langston Hughes, Countee Cullen and more. Some notable white writers featured too, William Carlos Williams and Ezra Pound among them, while Samuel Beckett provided translations from the French. Among the contributors to the section on African affairs were both Jomo Kenyatta and George Padmore. CLR James

* Borneman's memory may not be entirely reliable. Azikiwe doesn't appear to have been in London for any extended period of time, but could well have visited the flat.

† Also a man identified as 'Christie', probably Chris Jones.

had arrived on the scene too late to be a contributor, but was mentioned in passing.

The promise of change was in the air for Black people across the globe, as they woke up to the fact that they were going to have to take it for themselves, not wait meekly for it to be handed over.

Chapter Nine

The Pan-Africanists were not the only radicals to meet at the Hermitage: it also became a regular meeting place for the members of the Marxist Group. Ernest Borneman had no interest in this side of CLR's politics and kept well away. Louise Cripps, however, was thoroughly impressed by CLR. She offers a vivid description of the first time she attended a Marxist Group meeting at 9 Heathcote Street:

> We walked up a couple of flights of stairs, and when we went, we found a room with a fairly large window looking out onto the street. The room was moderately large, about twenty feet by sixteen feet. The walls had once been a cream colour. Now with age there were tinges of green and brown. Not exactly unpleasant, but not in any way a bright room. Short old curtains hung at the windows, curtains that had turned grey with age. The best aspect of the room was that it had large, half-length windows that overlooked the street. There was a tall street lamp immediately below. There was no fireplace, but a gas heater had been installed. It was operated by putting a shilling into a meter.
>
> The heater consisted of four asbestos-like bars with holes along them, and from these holes light and warmth emanated. There was also a single plate heater on a small stool. It also was coin-operated and allowed James to make tea. There was a kettle settled permanently on it. The only other fixture in the room was a small cupboard in which James kept a can of Carnation milk, Lipton's tea, and tins of biscuits. A milkman came by each day and left bottles of milk on the steps to the house for the tenants. James brought the milk up to this room. It was kept on the ledge outside the window or, if the weather was warm, hastily boiled on the hot plate to keep longer. It was not an attractive room, and James had done nothing to brighten

it. He seemed quite content with the way it looked. There were no pictures on the wall, framed reproductions, not any photographs at all . . . There was not much furniture in the room. The major piece was the large round table where everyone sat. There was also a divan in one comer and a small bookcase. But books were not confined to that small space. There were books everywhere: books up the walls, books on the floor, books and papers on the table.[1]

Despite the asceticism of his quarters, and despite being married, Louise Cripps was increasingly drawn to CLR. At some point during the spring of 1935, CLR made a further research trip to Paris, with some Trotskyist business to attend to as well. He suggested that Louise and her friend and comrade Esther Heiger come too.

The two women, both unhappy in their marriages, agreed to the trip. CLR found them a room in Montparnasse and they came over to join him:

It was springtime in Paris, the loveliest time of the year, and we sat outside the cafés, drinking wine and trying our first taste of absinthe. We went with some of the French comrades and also one or two of the *Partisan Review* people we met. James, as usual, tried to do most of the talking, with Esther and I being given little opportunity to join in the discussions of the men, though I stoutly intervened now and then. It was an exciting time: always with much more for the three of us to see and enjoy.

Louise suggests that CLR's spoken French was initially rather weaker than his ability to read it:

However, James could not bear to be silent. It really angered him that he could not fully express his views in French. He became almost fluent in French in three weeks because of his feeling of impotence when he could not talk and argue with people.

The three of them did a fair amount of sightseeing, looking at second-hand books along the Seine and so forth. One night CLR took Louise to the Black cabaret Le Bal Nègre, and they fox-trotted together (CLR refused to try the tango). CLR went off on his own to meet other comrades, including Trotsky's son Lev Sedov. His father – the Old Man, as Trotskyists liked to call him – was living in a village outside Paris at the time, under something close to house arrest.

One afternoon CLR took Louise on a cloak-and-dagger mission to meet a man called Adolf in a café.* This nervous young man offered her the job of working as Trotsky's secretary for three months. Louise thought it over, then turned it down:

> Obviously, James was disappointed in me. He had felt I would have suitably fit into the role, and that by offering my services, he was being of great help to 'the Old Man'. He had been sure of me: sure that I was free, was capable; would somehow find enough money to support myself and that my reason for refusing, to go home to look after my husband, was too trivial. But he made no effort to dissuade me.

As it happened, Trotsky was deported to Norway within weeks, but the excitement of being so close to one of the great revolutionaries of the time must have been palpable for the comrades of the Marxist Group. As Louise noted:

> Soon, Trotsky was in constant communication with us, sending us a letter, I imagine, about once a month, when any particular subject of importance came up, or when any new political event occurred . . . The thirties was a period of great political happenings throughout the world. There was the Italian war against Abyssinia, the Spanish Civil War, the Chinese Revolution, the rise to power of Hitler, the Moscow Trials. Trotsky wrote brilliantly on all these momentous events. He provided answers, suggested correct strategies. We were all, including James, his loyal followers. Our small

* This was actually Rudolf Klement, who was Trotsky's secretary for a while. He was murdered by Stalinist agents in Paris a few years later.

> group, though now in the ILP, still sat around James's bed-sitting room table, just a handful of us, enjoying one another's companionship ardently discussing political topics, with James, of course having the lion's share of the talk. We kept up our personal adherence to Trotsky through these regular meetings that were still held at James's rooming house. We had all become close comrades.

CLR and Louise were soon to become closer still. In May 1935 Paul Robeson opened in *Stevedore* at the Embassy, an important fringe theatre in Swiss Cottage. CLR invited Louise to come with him to see it.* *Stevedore* was an American play, a racial drama about a Black dock worker falsely accused of raping a white woman. Amy Ashwood Garvey and George Padmore had helped Robeson rustle up Black amateur actors to fill the minor parts. One of them, in the role of Ruby, was CLR's one-time girlfriend Kathleen Davis. Nancy Cunard reviewed the play very favourably for the NAACP magazine *The Crisis*, seeing it as Robeson's best, least patronising stage role yet.

After the show CLR took Louise back to his flat and they became lovers, and would remain so, on and off, for the next three years. 'We fell desperately in love,' he wrote. 'She was petite, yellow-haired and very, very beautiful.'[2]

The sexual side of their relationship is described in flowery detail in Louise Cripps's memoirs. Suffice to say, she was very happy with her new lover (and he would bring her tea and biscuits afterwards). Her husband was less pleased, but he had had his own affairs, notably with their former au pair.†

As would be the case throughout his life, the duties of being CLR's lover included a lot of typing. This became clear to Louise when CLR showed her a note he'd written to another woman, breaking off his relationship with her. This former girlfriend had been engaged in the

* Louise, in her memoir, misremembers the play as having been *Othello*, which would have been most appropriate, but took place three years earlier in 1932.

† A German girl who they sacked, not because of the relationship but because she turned out to be an enthusiastic member of the Hitler Youth.

task of typing up CLR's novel from the handwritten manuscript he'd brought over from Trinidad.

As well as being an able assistant, Louise Cripps was far from the only married woman with whom CLR would get involved. One might speculate that married women suited him, as they were unlikely to make too many demands on his time. Louise offers a pen portrait of the particular circumstances of their passionate but circumscribed relationship:

> Though he hated my having to return to my husband, he accepted it. I saw him go off on various political jaunts with no emotion except the knowledge we would soon be back together. I accepted perhaps better than he did that we could not live together. Later, I believed that it had kept our love woven within the limits of a tapestry, the edges defined.
>
> We were both happy during those years we had together. We did not have meals together except for a quick item on the menu of a Lyons Corner House, hurried suppers when we were going to meetings together, hardly tasting what we ate. They were never gourmet meals. Often I had to produce some cash to pay the bill, but it was of no importance between us. We shared the limited moments we had . . . Then we had to go back to our separate homes. But we knew we would meet again the next day. It was a matter-of-fact parting. At times I was vaguely aware that people looked at us a bit askance: a black man and a white woman. But we were not aware of them.[3]

CLR had not entirely given up on his literary aspirations, but there was little time for them as 1935 moved on. Much of the summer was once again spent covering cricket for the *Guardian*. There must have been a certain cultural dissonance in one August day reporting on the touring all-white South African cricket team, and the next addressing a public meeting in Trafalgar Square, right opposite South Africa House, protesting against imperialists in the Horn of Africa.

Two months later, the disaster that CLR and his friends in the IAFA had prophesied came to pass. Italy invaded Abyssinia on the morning of 3 October, attacking from the north. That night there was a huge meeting at the Memorial Hall on Farringdon Street in London. Twelve hundred people came to hear CLR, plus the ILP chairman James Maxton and senior comrade Fenner Brockway, denounce the imperialist aggression.

Members of the IAFA seriously discussed putting together some sort of foreign legion to go and fight in Abyssinia. CLR was right at the heart of this initiative, perhaps inspired by writing about the Haitian Revolution. Here was his chance to emulate Toussaint in real life. At one point he even suggested the Abyssinians imitate Toussaint: use scorched-earth tactics and burn Addis Ababa to the ground, so the Italians would gain nothing by conquering it.

It's hard to say how serious the IAFA plan was. It dissipated fairly quickly after the Abyssinian Minister in London told them their efforts would be better spent whipping up popular feeling in London, rather than getting killed in the Abyssinian highlands.

CLR accepted the point and spent the next months speaking out against the invasion wherever he could. He wrote articles for the ILP paper, *The New Leader*, and was sent on a lecture tour across England, Scotland, Wales and Ireland.

His message was simple at heart: this war was both terrible in itself and a harbinger of things to come. Europe was heading for another Great War unless capitalism could be stopped in its tracks. It was a message with plenty of resonance and CLR put it over with uncommon fluency and grasp of the wider picture. Moreover, here was a clear point of difference with the communists. Russia, far from supporting Abyssinia, had actually supplied oil to Mussolini, enabling his war effort. It was an action that had caused many Black people to finally quit the CP.

CLR was definitely starting to be noticed in the upper echelons of left-wing politics. A key ally was Fenner Brockway. Brockway came from a family of missionaries and had been a conscientious objector during the First World War, spending most of it in jail as a consequence. Afterwards he was a left-wing voice in the Labour Party and one of the prime movers in taking the ILP out of the Labour Party – 'a stupid and disastrous error', he said later.[4] Brockway was also a writer. He had written a book on the arms trade for the left-wing publisher of the moment, Victor Gollancz, and, in 1935, he'd just published a science fiction novel called *Purple Plague*, set in the wake of a pandemic.

Brockway, in turn, introduced CLR to a friend of his: Fredric Warburg, who was in the middle of setting up his own publishing house. This new venture, emerging from the remains of the distinguished Martin Secker imprint, was to be called Secker & Warburg and would publish a mix of literary fiction and politically oriented non-fiction.

However, the new house lacked the capacity to pay large advances, and Warburg was struggling to attract the calibre of writer he wanted when Fenner Brockway approached him with the suggestion that he might, in effect, become the in-house publisher for the leading lights of the ILP – people like Brockway himself, Jomo Kenyatta, Jennie Lee and CLR James. He even dangled the name of George Orwell as a possibility. Warburg took the bait and CLR was one of the first potential authors he met.

The two men liked each other immensely. Years later, in his memoirs, Warburg offered his impression of CLR at the time:

> James himself was one of the most delightful and easy-going personalities I have known, colourful in more senses than one. A dark-skinned West Indian Negro from Trinidad, he stood six feet three inches in his socks and was noticeably good-looking. His memory was extraordinary. He could quote, not only passages from the Marxist classics but long extracts from Shakespeare, in a soft lilting English which was a delight to hear. Immensely amiable, he loved the fleshpots of capitalism, fine cooking, fine clothes, fine furniture and beautiful women, without a trace of the guilty remorse to be expected from a seasoned warrior of the class war.[5]

It's as well to note here that, while CLR might have enjoyed the fleshpots, he was hardly a regular visitor. He was only in funds at all during the cricket season. Anyway, before long CLR had interested

Warburg in not one but two books. Warburg had been keen to get CLR to write something on African politics, but James declined, very likely because he was aware that George Padmore had a similar work due to be published by Victor Gollancz.

Instead, CLR suggested he write a political history of the upheavals worldwide since 1918. The CP's leading theorist, R. Palme Dutt, a devoted Stalinist, was preparing just such a book from an orthodox communist perspective; CLR proposed to write the Trotskyist alternative.

Warburg liked the idea and agreed to commission it as a book to be called *World Revolution*, but that was not all. During their discussions CLR had mentioned that he had already written a novel:

> He said to me 'You have written a novel?' I said, 'Yes, I scribbled a novel one vacation August I had nothing to do.' He says, 'Let me see it.' I said, 'It's of no use to you Fred. I'm getting ready to write *World Revolution* and *Black Jacobins*.' He said, 'Let me see it.' So one day I gave it to him. He read the manuscript and said, 'I'm going to print it. And I'm going to give you fifty pounds advance.'[6]

1936, then, may not have been a great year for the world in general – CLR's prediction that Italy's invasion of Abyssinia was just the harbinger of worse to come soon came to be terribly validated – but for CLR himself it was full of promise. He had achieved the dream of his Trinidad years, to have a novel published in London, and also the burning ambition of recent years – to have a book commissioned that would allow him to put forward his own revolutionary perspective on contemporary events.

And if all that wasn't enough, his Toussaint Louverture play was heading for the London stage. After he'd finished writing it, CLR had given a copy to the writer Marie Seton, who was close to the Robesons. She had taken it to the Stage Society, an august and gently radical outfit, who had started out by premiering work by the likes of Bernard Shaw and – CLR's particular favourite – Arnold Bennett, and had given English debuts to works by major playwrights from Chekhov to Ibsen.

The Stage Society told Seton they were interested, as long as Paul Robeson was prepared to star. This took a few months to arrange as Robeson's schedule was hectic. Finally, though, he agreed to appear in the play in the spring of 1936. He arranged to compress the filming of *Show Boat* into two months, so that he would be able to get back to London in time for rehearsals. This showed considerable commitment, as *Show Boat* was paying him a fortune and *Toussaint Louverture* a pittance.

That said, there was talk that the *Show Boat* team – director James Whale, plus the musical duo of Oscar Hammerstein and Jerome Kern – would turn *Toussaint Louverture* into a major movie (though still citing *Black Majesty* as the source material, rather than CLR's play). Robeson had been around long enough to be rightly cynical about the likelihood of this actually happening, but CLR may well have hoped that if his play went well, it would become the basis of a movie.

In February 1936 CLR broke off from a speaking tour agitating on the Abyssinian War in order to attend the rehearsals for the play. It was planned to run for two performances at the Westminster Theatre, with the hope of transferring to the West End in due course. Robeson's casting, while a commercial coup, was actually somewhat incongruous. The real Toussaint was a small man well into middle age at the start of the play, while Robeson was one of the most physically impressive men of his time. Several of the other parts were taken by actors who had performed alongside Robeson in *Stevedore*, Kathleen Davis among them.

Seeing Robeson at work and up close, however, CLR was enormously impressed:

> He was some six feet six inches in height and built in proportion, but he always had the silhouette and litheness of a great athlete. He was obviously immensely strong, strong enough to deal with two or three men at a time. Even in ordinary speech you were aware of his magnificent voice. He was obviously, not only from his reputation and his achievements, a man of unusual intelligence. But what was most important was that despite all these accomplishments and achievements he was as gentle a man as one could meet.[7]

Two performances took place, on the evening of Sunday 15 March and the afternoon of Monday 16 March. For the matinee, CLR himself stepped in to play the part of Macoya. So, by the age of thirty-five, he had both played cricket alongside Learie Constantine and acted alongside Paul Robeson!

The play itself received broadly positive but mixed notices. CLR does a good job of compressing over a decade of very complex historical action into a single script. At points it's clear that this is a play written by an historian rather than a natural-born playwright, and there's some clunky exposition at times. However, it builds well to a finale that moves confidently from tragedy to hope, as Toussaint is betrayed and killed but the revolution moves on.

Inevitably, it was Paul Robeson's performance that got the best reviews. Charles Darwin, the *Times* reviewer, was likely fair when he commented that 'the action is genuinely vitalised by Mr Robeson alone', and his observation that 'the sympathy evoked by Mr Robeson in his prison cell is not for a tricked Negro but for a statesman paying a price for his ideal' is one that would surely have pleased CLR. It was central to CLR's mission to make people understand that Toussaint was not simply a suffering slave who had risen up, but a brilliant revolutionary tactician.

Overall the play was neither a flop nor a hit. There was more talk of transfers to the West End and even to Broadway, but nothing came of it.

CLR likely didn't dwell on this as he had plenty more on his plate. There was the research to do for *World Revolution*, and also a lot going on with what was now very much his Marxist Group within the ILP. He continued to travel around Britain and Ireland, making the case for Trotskyism and against the Italian invasion of Abyssinia. He had become friendly with some key radical figures. In Dublin he'd got to know Nora Connolly O'Brien, the daughter of the Irish revolutionary James Connolly, and in Glasgow he'd become friendly with Nan Maclean. She was the daughter of John Maclean, the Scottish Marxist who was the nearest Britain had come to producing its own Lenin or

Trotsky. He had died young, and CLR and Nan had discussed working together on his biography (a project scuppered when CLR left the only copy of Nan's manuscript on a tube train).

Mostly he was engaged in hard, unglamorous slog, going into Labour Party and/or Communist Party heartlands and trying to put forward a Trotskyist analysis. As Warburg observed:

> He was brave. Night after night he would address meetings in London and the provinces, denouncing the crimes of the bloodthirsty Stalin, until he was hoarse and his beautiful voice a mere croaking on the throat. The Communists who heckled him would have torn him limb from limb, had it not been for the ubiquity of the police.[8]

This Marxist Group internal report, following an ILP speaking tour of South Wales, gives a flavour of political activism at the sharp end:

> Feb 10th (Mon) Neath
>
> We spoke at Neath Town Hall on Monday evening – the coldest day of the tour. Whilst quite a few tickets had been sold the bitter cold and gale kept a number away. About 150 present ... Despite the cold, the audience were absorbed in CLR's address and everyone stayed right through to the end. There were only a couple of CPers present and whatever remaining shreds of influence they may have had in Neath melted under CLR's withering fire.[9]

Within the ILP there was a fierce battle between the Parliamentary Group, who believed that both Italy and Abyssinia were essentially fascist dictatorships, and therefore there was no side to take, and the Marxist Group, who saw Italy as colonial aggressors and Abyssinia as a beacon of African resistance (albeit one that, as CLR and others acknowledged, still practised a form of slavery).

Meanwhile he and his comrades were working through enormous quantities of documents, piecing together the research materials for *World Revolution*. CLR James, as an activist and as a writer, was both determinedly individual and the most collective-minded of people. And, working with the real sense of urgency that the political situation demanded, he was happy to function more as the director of a group than a single author. Particularly useful to the project was Charlie Lahr, who, as ever, was able to steer CLR to the exact text he needed to demonstrate just what scoundrels the Stalinists were. In particular, he helped CLR with the chapter dealing with Hitler's rise to power:

> A great deal of what went into that chapter and made its foundations so clear came from my conversations, and often intricate discussions with Charlie. I could question him endlessly about what certain events meant, who were the leaders, who was the chief traitor and who was Mr Inbetween in the tangled political history of Germany.[10]

Also very helpful was Harry Wicks, a former communist turned leading British Trotskyist, who had a large library of his own. Wicks remembered how James 'laboured through an enormous literature, working from a small room in Gray's Inn Road, heated by the smallest of gas fires'.*[11]

By June, things were going well enough that James felt emboldened enough to write to Trotsky himself, who had been given asylum in Norway, to tell him that the project was well under way and asking if the Old Man might like to write a foreword to the book. He proposed that he could come to meet Trotsky in August.

Before that, in late July 1936, CLR was one of two British delegates to a planning conference for the Fourth International, held in France. This was meant to be the launching pad for a new worldwide Trotskyist movement. The name, the Fourth International, was an attempt to connect it with the previous Internationals that had marked key points

* Harry Wicks remembered CLR having secretarial and typing assistance from Dorothy Pizer, George Padmore's partner, rather than Louise Cripps. However, given the pace at which he was working, it makes sense that he would have needed more than one assistant.

in the development of communism. The Third International in 1919 took place soon after the Russian Revolution, when communism looked poised to sweep the Western democracies before it.

Trotskyism in 1936, by contrast, was a marginal faith, so styling their new organisation the Fourth International was somewhat optimistic. CLR, for instance, was a British delegate, but represented a group that had maybe forty members. The best they could all realistically expect was 'influence' based on the quality of their political analysis, which would soon be proved to be right, thus provoking the masses to turn as one to the Trotskyists in grateful recognition. Or so they hoped.

Attending the Fourth International planning conference made CLR painfully aware of the weakness of international Trotskyism, particularly in the UK. Delegates from other countries, France and Russia particularly, had an experience of real revolutionary situations. Whereas 'what was happening in Britain was nothing'.[12]

However, no sooner had the conference finished than European politics were shaken up by the first of the great convulsions that would lead inevitably to the Second World War. On 17 July the Spanish fascists, centred around the army, launched a coup against the democratic government. This was the start of the Spanish Civil War. The European left now had a cause to rally to. Over the next couple of months the various factions figured out how best to get involved and which side to join in a conflict that was never a simple clash of two opposing forces.

This was a very strange time for CLR to see his near-lifelong ambition of having a novel published realised. Nearly a decade had passed since he wrote *Minty Alley*, his fictionalised version of his time spent living in a Port of Spain barrack yard. It was a tangible relic of a life he'd left firmly behind him, along with the wife he no longer expected to join him (if he ever really had). And now it was to be published in London.

He wasn't the first of his generation of Trinidadians to get a novel published – Alfie Mendes had beaten him to it by two years – but it was no mean achievement. And yet it no longer had the meaning he might have expected. It was the culmination of an old dream. In the revolutionary, world-shaking year of 1936 he had new dreams. Nevertheless, here it was: his first novel.

Minty Alley came out in September and attracted generally positive reviews, particularly this very favourable one from the novelist A. G. Macdonell in the *Observer*:

> *Minty Alley* is a strange, passionate book . . . Mr James, a first novelist, describes the tragic life of . . . a small back lane with a most moving skill. As you read you feel that if ever a man knew what he was writing about it is Mr James. The big, swaggering unscrupulous Lothario, the timid bookseller's assistant, the vampire of a nurse, the discarded mistress, the sweated girl, they live out their small and vehement lives in *Minty Alley* . . . a remarkable book.

There was every indication that CLR might have made a success of the fiction-writing business. He enjoyed the literary world, spent a lot of time with the Warburgs at their country cottage in the village of West Hoathly ('In Sussex politics were forgotten,' said Warburg) where he would turn out occasionally for the village cricket team:* 'He was a demon bowler and a powerful if erratic batsman. The village loved him, referring to him affectionately as "the black bastard"'[13] – Warburg again. Warburg's artist wife Pamela, meanwhile, had real faith in him as a novelist as CLR would later note:

> [She] begged me almost with tears to settle down and write. I said 'No', a fine sight I would have been with two or three books or a play or two to my credit and hanging around the political world, as all these other writers do, treating as amateurs, what is the most serious business in the world today.[14]

* I visited West Hoathly in the course of writing this book, and the current captain of the village cricket team told me the story of how, almost 400 years ago, in 1624, a West Hoathly batsman, Edward Tye, accidentally killed a man. At that time the batsman was allowed to hit the ball twice before it bounced. In doing so Tye failed to notice an incoming fielder and struck him a fatal blow to the head.

It was as if different versions of CLR James were tumbling over each other, jostling for position: the novelist, the politically engaged playwright, the revolutionary polemicist. In another year, another decade, a very different CLR might have emerged.

But this was no ordinary year and, as it moved into autumn, it looked as if the radicals might be coming into their time. In Britain the menace of fascism, in the shape of Oswald Mosley's Blackshirts, received a definitive beating at the Battle of Cable Street; members of the Marxist Group were in among the action. And in Spain the democratically elected Popular Front was raising its banners, holding the great cities against the fascist insurrection. This was the people rising up in the cause of freedom. At least for a while.

The Marxist Group were doing their best to offer Trotskyist leadership during this time of ferment. This brought them into ever deeper disagreement with the higher echelons of the ILP. In October 1936 the Marxist Group decided to start their own journal, *Fight*, and in November CLR abruptly led the Marxist Group out of the ILP. It was a classic Trotskyist-party story: endless splits over points of genuine principle, leading to an array of tiny parties, all convinced they had the purest political analysis but largely impotent in the face of the great events around them.

And the great event of the time was clearly Spain. That October the International Brigades were launched. This was a Communist International-led initiative, with Stalin at the head, to mobilise leftists from all over Europe to come to the aid of the Spanish Republic, and not just by sending money but by travelling there to join the Republican Army and quite literally fighting against fascism.

There was no way the ILP or the Trotskyist Marxist Group were going to join in a Communist Party initiative. CLR had spent far too much time denouncing Stalin's crimes to do that. Instead the Marxist Group, through *Fight*, lent its support to the anti-Stalinist communist grouping POUM,* while making it clear that this was 'critical support'.

* The Workers' Party of Marxist Unification (in Spanish: Partido Obrero de Unificación Marxista).

In Spain as in London, the Marxist Group's firm belief in the superiority of its own political analysis meant that it was continually disappointed by its natural allies.

Nevertheless CLR, in later life, told friends that he had wanted to go to Spain to fight, but was once again persuaded that he was more useful as a live polemicist in London than a dead volunteer in Catalonia. And so he laid out the Trotskyist line on the war: in essence, that the workers should make no alliance with the liberals – or 'capitalists' – who formed part of the Popular Front, but demand a workers' state right there and then.

There's something tragic and poignant, from this remove, in the fact that Western communists and Trotskyists, so alike in their belief in a better, fairer world, were so far apart, even on such a basic question as fighting fascism. It's telling that CLR's downstairs neighbours, a young communist couple called George and Nan Green, both went to Spain – George in January 1937 to fight, Nan a few months later as a medic.* George died in fighting the day before he was due to come home. What seems startling now is that the Greens and CLR appear to have been utterly oblivious of each other despite living in the same building, so strong was the tribalism of politics.

On the top floor of 9 Heathcote Street, literary production was the order of the day. CLR and his comrades were still working on *World Revolution* – a Herculean task given that CLR was also writing reams of copy for *Fight* – and the book was only completed when CLR took himself off to Brighton for a few months, furiously turning the mass of research into a 150,000-word book.

Remarkably, this wasn't the only book to emerge from the flat that summer. Ernest Borneman, only just turned twenty, had been busy writing what would become one of the century's enduring cult novels. This was a brilliantly tricky murder mystery within a murder mystery called *The Face on the Cutting-Room Floor* and credited to one Cameron McCabe, who was also a character in the novel. Heathcote Street

* Leaving their two young children to be sent to the progressive boarding school Summerhill, paid for by the previous tenant John Lehmann's brother-in-law.

appears as a setting and there's a minor character – a sports reporter with a strong interest in the Abyssinian War – who is more than likely a riff on CLR.

By an odd quirk of fate, *The Face on the Cutting-Room Floor* appeared in May 1937 from the communist-aligned Victor Gollancz, the very same month that *World Revolution* by CLR James appeared from the increasingly Trotskyist-aligned Secker & Warburg.

If *The Face on the Cutting-Room Floor* was a revolutionary take on a traditional format – the detective story – *World Revolution* tried to take a revolutionary situation and make it comprehensible to the general reader. As a plug for *World Revolution* in *Fight* put it, 'this book is written in a language which any worker can understand', then adding the important proviso that 'although the price is prohibitive for the average worker, every comrade should endeavour to obtain a copy in the local library'.

Harry Wicks went further in a review in the same issue, saying that 'it is a book that every socialist should read and every revolutionary possess'. Though this is hardly surprising, given the degree of input Wicks had into the book. It was help that CLR freely acknowledged, giving Wicks a personal thanks in the preface, as well as making the collegiate statement that:

> My task has been chiefly one of selection and co-ordination. Yet in so wide and complicated a survey, differences of opinion and emphasis are bound to arise. Therefore, while the book owes so much to others as to justify the use of the term 'we', the ultimate responsibility must remain my own.[15]

Dedicated to the Marxist Group, *World Revolution* is for the most part a systematic attack on Stalinism, full of detailed research, facts and figures. Finally, having done his best to persuade the reader to let go of the comforting illusion that Russia under Stalin was a workers' paradise, CLR argues that a new radical politics needed to be formed. The focus for that, he argues, should be the Fourth International. He acknowledges that, as of the time of writing, it is organisationally 'pitifully weak'. But he still has faith that ultimately 'the huge fabrication of lies and slander against Trotsky and Trotskyism in Russia will tumble to the ground, and Stalin and Stalinism will face the masses inside and outside Russia naked'.

World Revolution was a limited success. Fenner Brockway gave it a very balanced review in the ILP paper, the *New Leader*. He praised the dismantling of Stalinism, but reasonably enough decried the incessant factionalism of Trotskyists: 'It is no accident that in every country they become a negative and destroying force. They cannot relate their intensities to the whole situation. To them communists become as hateful as fascists.' And, indeed, much of the response to *World Revolution* was to use it as ammunition in the lopsided war between Stalinists and Trotskyists. The *New Statesman* predicted that 'this is a book which is unique of its kind, very badly needed and likely to excite more anger than anything yet published this year', and it wasn't far wrong.

CLR later recalled that 'it created a sensation',[16] which may be overstating its impact outside the sectarian world of the left. But it was undeniably a powerfully evidenced attack on Stalinism, and it's surely relevant that one of its supporters was George Orwell, who described it as 'a very able book' and was soon to make sure that anti-Stalinism would no longer be a fringe position.[17]

Final word may have to go to the long-suffering publisher,* who later commented that '*World Revolution* sold moderately well, if you apply low enough standards of sale to it.' It was at least enough to prompt Warburg to commission another book from CLR. This was to be the magnum opus, the book he had been planning for years: the life of Toussaint Louverture.

* Warburg looked back on the book's actual content with some cynicism, commenting on CLR's hopes for a workers' uprising in Russia that 'fortunately James' prophecies remained unfulfilled since otherwise it can hardly be doubted that Nazi Germany would have won the war'. (*An Occupation for Gentlemen*.)

Chapter Ten

CLR's workload in the summer of 1937 is something to contemplate. On the Trotskyist side of things, he was one of a small group putting out a densely packed monthly journal, *Fight*, as well as addressing meetings. On the Pan-African side he was still very involved with the group that had come together to support Abyssinia. On top of all that, he had his book on Toussaint Louverture to write and that was going to necessitate further trips to the archives in Paris, not to mention the time needed to actually write the book. And on top of this he had to earn a living.

For the past couple of years he had got by on the small advances paid to him by Secker & Warburg, plus regular handouts from a Trotskyist sympathiser, a young Indian called B. K. Gupta, who was a student at London University. CLR later described him as one of the 'most attractive men I have ever met' and credited him with his education in Marxism in the early days of their friendship.[1] He was particularly taken with Gupta's ability to have read all the newspapers by ten in the morning and be ready to dissect them for political bias.

He also talks about Gupta's skill at charming young English women. It is not the only place in CLR's memoirs, written much later in life, in which it seems as if he is really writing about himself rather than his ostensible subject. Certainly CLR's girlfriend of the time, Louise Cripps, remembered things very differently:

> For some reason James thought Gupta was fascinating to English women. I never found him so nor knew of any of my friends that did. He certainly had no competition with James. When the women fell in love, it was with CLR.[2]

Cripps describes a 'tall, somewhat plump, ivory-faced man, very genial. I was told by James that his father had a very large export business of jute in India and was a very wealthy man; that Gupta had a large allowance.'

The friendship with Gupta clearly echoed that with Alfie Mendes years before: two men with a common passion, one from a wealthy background and the other not. But while Gupta helped James out, he certainly didn't support him. So CLR must have been delighted when he got the offer of a weekly column in the *Glasgow Herald*, rounding up the main cricket stories of the moment. And so he added yet another writing job to his already punishing load.

It's fascinating to look at CLR's cricket pieces from this revolutionary year and compare them with his writing elsewhere. It's hard to believe they were written by the same person.

On 12 May he tells his Scottish readers that 'Things look better and better, though the weather conspires to prevent players finding their feet. If only we have a decent summer then 1937 is sure to be a fascinating year.' Three weeks later and he is more bullish yet, announcing that 'The big week is over and not a single thing is wrong with cricket after 150 years. The financial question remains but as a spectacle, as exhilarating competition, demanding physical fitness, skill, and judgement, pleasing alike to players and watchers, the game is in a flourishing condition.'

This satisfaction with the status quo contrasts quite starkly with his political analysis, which suggests that pretty much everything has to change. That same month he had told readers of *Fight*: 'It is the duty of every revolutionary to be out in both Mayday marches. The streets are the battlegrounds of the class struggle.' And in the next issue he goes further: 'The workers are demanding unity for action. They will soon sweep the reformists and Stalinists from their path. When once a fighting unity is achieved, capitalism will not have long to live.'

CLR's workload could only have been managed by someone utterly driven. The socialist feminist Ethel Mannin offered a neat comic account of what it was like to meet him in those times in her satirical novel of the pre-war left, *Comrade O Comrade.** In a chapter entitled 'Trotskyists at Tea', her protagonist Mary announces that 'I have an eminent Trotskyist coming to tea.' She is hoping for a discussion. 'An extremely handsome young Negro' duly arrives with two friends but there is nothing you might call a discussion – 'The Trotskyists arrived promptly at four and they left punctually at five, and in that hour Mary uttered exactly twelve words.'

For an hour the CLR character monologues on the political situation, while working his way through afternoon tea:

> 'Blum . . . Daladier . . . Popular Front . . . French workers . . . Stalinist bureaucracy . . .'
>
> She settled herself to listen.
>
> When she saw his cup was empty she reached for it. 'More tea?'
>
> He nodded. She filled his cup and the cups of the other two, who never took their eyes off him, hypnotised by the strong flow of his words. In another fifteen minutes he had reached Spain . . .
>
> At a quarter to five he was dealing with Abyssinia and 'the real nature of imperialism'.
>
> At five o'clock he glanced up at the sun-ray clock over the door and compared it with the time as recorded on his wrist watch and jumped up.
>
> 'We must go,' he said . . .
>
> It was then Mary said her twelfth and last word.
>
> 'Goodbye,' she said.

There was one element in CLR's life that couldn't be controlled by his rhetorical powers. This was his relationship with Louise Cripps, which had now been going on for two years. There had been talk of them marrying. She was ready to divorce her husband. He told her about his previous marriage:

* CLR clearly took this mickey-taking in good spirit: he kept a copy of the relevant passage in his papers.

He had been married in Trinidad to a half-Chinese wife. He spoke of her very tenderly. I asked him why he had not brought her with him. He said this, 'She just would not have fitted into my life here.' However, he had been in touch with her. They had been separated a sufficient time, and she was ready to set him free.[3]

So the way was clear for CLR and Louise. 'After some months I asked her to marry me,' he recalled. 'She said she would go to the south of France and spend a week thinking it over.'[4]

Louise decided against it, largely on practical grounds. She would be giving up a comfortable house with servants to live in a Bloomsbury bedsit with an indigent revolutionary. When push came to shove, she couldn't make the commitment. CLR wasn't entirely surprised that she decided not to leave her husband: 'He bought a house in the country for her, a new car, a lot of clothes, and was very, very patient with her during the time that she and I were intimate.' Still they carried on their relationship, until life intervened for Louise:

Our love affair continued with the question of marriage unresolved. Then a new and dramatic event made us again review the whole situation. I found I was pregnant.[5]

CLR was initially less than delighted. His life was already impossibly over-committed:

I think he felt in some way that a child would not fit into his lifestyle, in the same way as his Trinidadian wife would not fit into his present goals. It was not that he was hard-hearted; it merely meant he had set his mind on a certain path of which he was sure he was giving wholly of himself and that he should not let anything obstruct. He was dedicating that life to a cause; and lesser things or even people that did not fit into his main plan were, therefore, to be regretfully discarded.

Louise, however, did want the baby, and CLR clearly loved her, so they tried to find a way forward:

> I would have been very happy to have James's child. However, again, there were the practical matters. I saw no possibility of our bringing up a child in his one room. A flat of our own became essential ... James felt that his cricket reporting and his books would provide some money. But it would obviously not be sufficient for the three of us ... We discussed it and we discussed it and we discussed it. He wanted me to marry him and be by his side always. But what were we to do? I was in a state of anguish. Finally, it was decided between us, but woefully by me, that I must have an abortion.

This was no simple matter in London in the thirties. Abortions were illegal and dangerous. Gupta came up with an address, 'a back street in one of the less desirable areas of London'. The abortion itself was a terrible business:

> This was a desperate back-alley affair. The man was supposed to be a doctor. He had credentials in his one-room office but evidently made his living by doing abortions. I think he had possibly been a doctor but had been disbarred. I got home in a taxi and soon started haemorrhaging. Luckily, I had the guest room, and I tried, as far as possible, to stem the tide of blood myself. I thought I probably should have had medical attention, but as it was, I managed at first on my own.
>
> In the end, it was necessary to call our local doctor. He knew what had happened but did not report it as he was supposed to do. Over some days and nights I hovered between life and death. Nello was upset that I had gone through such suffering and was frustrated that he could not visit me. When I next saw him, James said in real agony: 'If I knew you were to be so hurt, I would have drowned myself in Regent's Park Lake if it would have saved you.' Yet for his part, I thought he could have taken extra precautions. I had taken those that were then available to me.

This he clearly failed to do as, after a brief period of separation the lovers resumed their affair, with the same consequence:

> Then I became pregnant again: it seemed incredible. We had used contraceptives, but in those days, they were not 100 per cent effective, as they usually are today. It was always hit-and-miss. Once I realized I was pregnant, I had the second abortion very quickly, in less than six weeks. Someone had recommended a doctor of integrity . . .
>
> I had a little money of my own, saved from my days of journalism, from which I was able to pay for both abortions. Nello could not pay for them. I could not ask my husband for the money. I would not let Gupta pay for them.

This time, probably towards the end of 1937, Louise did go back to her husband and in short order got pregnant again and this time was able to have the baby. CLR was deeply hurt: 'I was sick for a year at losing her,' he would later write.[6]

CLR's great project for the rest of 1937, going into 1938, was to write *The Black Jacobins*. On one level it might have seemed a curious project to take on with the world on a precipice, but for CLR the story of the Haitian Revolution had both relevance and urgency.

As he saw it, Europe's capitalist nations were getting ready to tear each other apart. That would create opportunities for their colonial subjects to break free. If the great nations of Europe were caught up in a war, then what better time for India and Africa and the Caribbean to rise up and throw off the shackles of imperialism? All the colonial subjects lacked, in CLR's view, was self-belief. They had been brought up on the version of history in which the Black people of the world were dumb victims, to be enslaved or freed at the white man's whim.

The abolition of slavery, for instance, was always presented as a triumph of Western democracy. Slaves themselves were portrayed as having been utterly powerless. There was no mention of the countless slave rebellions, let alone a true history of the one slave rebellion that had fully succeeded. CLR intended his account of the Haitian Revolution to be both a history and a blueprint for revolutions of the future.

He was still heavily involved in the anticolonial struggle in London. The IAFA, formed to protest the Italian invasion of Abyssinia, had disintegrated following Italy's military success and Emperor Haile Selassie fleeing to London (where he won few friends by denying that his people were 'Negroes', insisting instead that they were 'a mixed Hamito-Semitic people').[7] However, the key participants continued to agitate for African liberation. George Padmore formed an organisation that came to be known as the Pan-African Federation, along with the likes of Chris Braithwaite, Jomo Kenyatta and Ras Makonnen.

In 1937 the group reconstituted itself once more as the International African Service Bureau,* with the addition of the Sierra Leonean Isaac Wallace-Johnson as general secretary and CLR James as editorial director. His principal task would be to launch a newspaper for the new group – as if he hadn't already taken on enough writing work.

In later times, being simultaneously part of a (mostly white) Trotskyist group and a (mostly Black) anticolonial group might have been resented by either or both sides. In this time and place, though, CLR remembered that no one saw the two causes as mutually exclusive:

> When I hear people arguing about Marxism versus the nationalist or racialist struggle, I am very confused. Because in England I edited the Trotskyist paper and I edited the nationalist, pro-African paper of George Padmore, and nobody quarrelled. The Trotskyists read and sold the African paper and the African nationalists attended each other's meetings and there were nationalists who read and sold the Trotskyist paper. I moved among them, we attended each other's meetings and there was no problem because we had the same aim in general: freedom by the revolution.[8]

For all the formality of its name, the IASB was a fairly loose and informal organisation of thirty or so people, whose main activity in

* If that wasn't unwieldy enough, the full name was the International African Service Bureau for the Defence of Africans and People of African Descent.

the summer of 1937 was to address the public on Sunday afternoons at Speakers' Corner. Ras Makonnen gives an entertaining picture of how they operated in his autobiography:

> We organised a rota of speakers for Hyde Park. That was an interesting set-up. I made use of this chap Monolulu* to help draw in the crowds. He was a tall outstanding Negro, a race-course tipster, but a big draw for the crowd because he had a kind of Rasputian tone. He was crude in all his references, but knew the British psychology, and traded in subtle vulgarity of a high order. I would let him start off. So he would set up his platform with his two flags, one Jewish and the other the Union Jack, and then he would begin his funny talk; 'God bless Lyons Corner Shop: two veg and roast beef . . . When I came to England forty years ago, the English woman was something to look at; she was built for speed and comfort. She had a powerful roast beef and two veg. But look at them now! They are all just speed and you've got to run like hell, like a gazelle to keep up with them . . .'
>
> As soon as he was through and this huge crowd was around I would disassociate myself from this buffoon and try to present a different type of Negro. 'We, unlike those of you who are praying for peace, are praying for war.' Then after stirring them up for an hour, we would end with 'Now you know it is against the law to sell papers or ask for aid, but all the things we have just been talking about and much more, all right here in our paper *International African Opinion*.' So sometimes I would clear more than £20 worth in a single meeting.[9]

Makonnen's memoir gives a good sense of the hand-to-mouth nature of being an African radical in London, always scuffling for cash. He, Padmore and Kenyatta would share rooms to save money. To build up the profile of the IASB, Makonnen says that in the newspaper they

* For a while there was a pub in Fitzrovia named the Prince Monolulu after this extraordinary character.

'would sometimes concoct letters purporting to come from the Congo and many other places, or Nancy Cunard would write in, to show that there was a branch of the bureau here and there in Africa'.

Their best source of funds was a stash of two thousand copies of George Padmore's pamphlet 'The Life and Struggles of Negro Toilers', which the Communist Party threw out once Padmore had become *persona non grata*. These they would sell at protest meetings wherever and whenever – 'often people would give sometimes 10 shillings or more – especially if you are well-dressed. George always was. Spic and span like a Senator, and his shoes shone so you could see your face in them; his trouser creases could shave you.'[10]

This was the world CLR operated in: one in which the gap between the lofty ambitions and the workaday reality was so immense that any man with less than complete confidence in himself might well have given up. Fortunately CLR in the late thirties was a man of quite extraordinary self-confidence allied to an equally extraordinary work ethic.

During late 1937 and early 1938 CLR worked intensely on *The Black Jacobins*. He must have been researching as he wrote, as he made several trips to France over this time to visit the assorted archives. His companion on some of these visits was a young man called Eric Eustace Williams.

Eric Williams was a fellow Black Trinidadian. He had been a student of CLR's at Queen's Royal College and went on to win an Island Scholarship in 1932. He studied history at Oxford University, writing his thesis on the economics of slavery. CLR had advised him throughout. Williams had visited the older man in Nelson and had stayed with him at 9 Heathcote Street. In a memoir, CLR described Williams's fondness for a pub crawl: outings on which CLR, never a big drinker, would tag along but bring a book to read, while Williams and his friends caroused.

A serious historian in his own right, Williams was the ideal research assistant:

> We went to the Archives and went to the Bibliotheque nationale, and I would take Williams with me and we would go through the work and he would help me a great deal. He covered a lot of work for me, he is a wonderful man at research, collecting information and putting it in some sort of order.
>
> We would go to Versailles and visit, see France, do a lot of eating and have a very good time, and he helped me a great deal. And there are certain pages in *The Black Jacobins* where most of the material and all the footnotes are the things that Williams gave to me.[11]

On another of CLR's visits to Paris he was accompanied by Harry Spencer, the man whose generosity had allowed CLR to start out on this project in the first place. Much of their time was spent in the company of Ghita Luchaire. Any worries he had that Harry might be a fish out of water were soon dispelled:

> The visit was a great success. It was many years since Harry had been in Paris but he knew the city pretty well and we not only sat and talked a great deal, but we went about looking at things. Above all Harry was a maestro in the restaurants. We learnt that when we went somewhere to eat we ought to leave it to him to order from the menu. Somewhat to my surprise Harry turned out to be a fluent conversationalist and a ladies' gentleman in the attention he always paid to Ghita's personal needs. So it went the three of us enjoying ourselves immensely, and once or twice Ghita's husband came along.

Somehow, amid the Parisian researching and the wining and dining, CLR managed to fit in side research trips to Bordeaux and Nantes, and to attend a Pan-Africanist conference in Paris along with Ras Makonnen. It was called the Rassemblement Coloniale and was held in the Latin Quarter. The delegates were mostly Francophone, including CLR's old friend Léon-Gontran Damas and a couple of people who were to become highly influential pan-Africanists, Tiemoko Garan Kouyaté from French Sudan and Aimé Césaire from Martinique.

The research complete, CLR repeated his pattern of the previous year. Then, he had taken himself off to Brighton to write *World Revolution* in a furious burst of activity. He did the same again in late 1937, staying in a guest house in the suburb of Portslade, and once again emerged with a finished book. He duly delivered *The Black Jacobins* to Fred Warburg, who pronounced it excellent and readied it for publication in the summer of 1938.

The Black Jacobins is an extraordinary book – a truly ground-breaking achievement. CLR had set himself the task of writing of the Haitian Revolution as Trotsky had written of the Russian Revolution: to show it as the product of a great social movement, underpinned by class and economics, rather than the traditional British-style history in which a great man does great things because he's a great man.

And yet CLR was also well aware that great events do require great leaders, if the opportunities provided by an historical moment are to be successfully realised. As he says in his preface: 'Great men make history, but only such history as it is possible for them to make.' So *The Black Jacobins* is at one and the same time a study of a revolution that erupts spontaneously from below and a portrait of one extraordinary man. CLR's pioneering achievement is to make clear the dialectic relation between the Haitian slaves and their leader, summed up in this neat formulation: 'Toussaint did not make the revolution. It was the revolution that made Toussaint.'

The early parts of the book have great visceral power as CLR deftly sets out the history of the island country then known as Saint-Domingue, and the development of a slavery-based economy there. He offers an unflinchingly gruesome account of the depravities of that trade, through the Atlantic crossing and on the Haitian plantations. Then he goes on to delineate the power structure of the island, before forensically piecing together the roots of the revolution, the gathering forces that called Toussaint Louverture into being.

It's these opening sections that likely stay clearest in most readers' minds. As the revolution develops, with its complex twists and turns, huge cast of characters and constantly shifting allegiances, the reader is no longer guided solely by moral outrage, but has to get to grips with the difficult business of working out how you follow through on revolution.

The second half of the book is not an easy read – it would likely have benefited from CLR having had longer to work on it – but steadily the bigger picture emerges. The Haitian Revolution is indelibly linked to the French Revolution and vice versa. CLR makes incontrovertible the case that the one can only be understood with reference to the other. That the idealists of France should, in the end, be the self-same people as tricked and betrayed Toussaint is the grimmest of ironies.

Finally it's a book that, as CLR intended, was not just a study of a revolution, but also an investigation into how a revolution can succeed, what it needs in leadership and political vision. It's both a study of the past and a road map for the future. All it needed was an audience ready to learn its lessons.

CLR might very reasonably have eased up a bit after this remarkable achievement – synthesising all this material, almost entirely written in French, into a great readable work of revolutionary history – but not a bit of it. No sooner had he finished the book than Raymond Postgate got in touch to ask him to write another, albeit a much shorter one.

Postgate* was a former CP member, now an influential left-wing journalist. He had started publishing a serial magazine called *FACT*. Each issue consisted of one long article by a well-known left-wing writer, such as a report by Ernest Hemingway from the Spanish Civil War. Now Postgate wanted to devote an issue to Black revolt. He asked George Padmore first. Padmore said he was too busy and suggested (the not at all busy!) James. CLR of course agreed, and within a month he produced a twenty-thousand-word booklet entitled 'A History of Negro Revolt'.

Aided by Padmore, and doubtless making use of the material he had already written for countless articles and speeches, the booklet featured

* Later a crime novelist and the founder of the Good Food Guide, also the father of the children's television auteur Oliver Postgate.

concise accounts of historic Black rebellions in the US, Africa and, of course, Haiti. Bringing his essay up to date, he gives an account of the career so far of Marcus Garvey, plus a survey of nascent Black rebellions around the world – from the Trinidad oil workers to the Rhodesian copper miners.

The struggle of the Rhodesian miners was one that had particularly engaged CLR. So much so that he ended the manuscript of *The Black Jacobins* by expressing his hope that Toussaint's mantle would be taken up by them. He finished his *History of Negro Revolt* the same way. Africa was where he expected the anticolonial movement to catch fire.

He handed in the manuscript in April 1938, and promptly went back to covering cricket for the *Glasgow Herald*. Not content with that, he also took full charge of the IASB journal, widening its remit to include culture and news from America.

On top of all this, he took on another commission for Fred Warburg. This was to translate Boris Souvarine's biography of Stalin from French into English. This was a huge book that systematically revealed Stalin as the tyrant he was. It would have been a big job even for a professional translator to take on, but nevertheless CLR agreed to do it, proposing to deliver by the end of the year.

Just as the cricket season ended in September, both of CLR's two new publications came out. *A History of Negro Revolt* wasn't widely reviewed, being somewhere between pamphlet and book, but it was widely distributed. CLR later said that it 'could be seen on all bookshops and railway stalls'.[12] Very likely it was his most commonly read offering at the time.

Secker & Warburg had higher ambitions for *The Black Jacobins*. In newspaper ads they trumpeted that 'the romance of a great career and the drama of revolutionary history combined in CLR James's magnificent biography'. CLR returned their enthusiasm by presenting Warburg's wife Pamela with a copy of the book that he had had specially bound in black Morocco leather.

Unfortunately, their hopes were roundly dashed. *The Black Jacobins* was all but ignored by the British press. There were no reviews in the broadsheets. It found some favour in the magazines. *The Listener* said that it 'has all the excitement of a first-rate documentary film', while, bizarrely, the high-society magazine *Queen* proclaimed that 'lovers of the struggle for freedom will prize this book'.

The left-wing magazines paid limited attention to it – or, in one notorious case, damned it. The CLR James scholar Christian Høgsbjerg sums up the situation neatly:

> Flora Grierson in the *New Statesman* famously dismissed *The Black Jacobins* because of its 'bias', noting James was 'a Communist and wants us to see the worst'. Leaving aside the question of quite which 'best' bits of the slave-experience Grierson had hoped to see James highlight, the awful truth was that if he had actually been a Communist with a capital C, the work would have received greater attention on publication.[13]

Indeed James's reputation as a Trotskyist meant that the book was rejected out of hand by an intelligentsia still dominated by the Communist Party. CLR was always very good at seeing success where others saw failure, but he must surely have been dispirited by this lack of reaction. Here was the project he had laboured on for nearly a decade; an epic and original mix of history and revolutionary manifesto and it was not even attacked, just ignored.

The lack of response to *The Black Jacobins* must have weighed on CLR's mind as he decided whether to take up an offer that had been made to him the previous month. There had been organisational changes in James's Marxist Group. Earlier in the year, the group had merged with their closest comrades, Harry Wicks's Marxist League, to form the Revolutionary Socialist League (RSL).

However, that had still left Britain with four competing – and tiny – Trotskyist groups. This displeased both Trotsky himself and the rather bigger American Trotskyist party, the Socialist Workers Party. Trotsky encouraged the SWP's leaders, James P. Cannon and Max Shachtman, to make a trip to London in August 1938 and attempt to broker a merger between the British parties. This was a partial success. The

Militant Group and the Revolutionary Socialist Party agreed to come under the umbrella of the Revolutionary Socialist League, with James at the head, but the Workers' International League refused to join.

Around the same time Cannon invited CLR to come to the US on a speaking tour. This was obviously a tempting offer, especially as *The Black Jacobins* was due to be published in New York that November. But some suspected that the US trip was a gambit to get CLR out of the way, so that Denzil Dean Harber,* a more biddable character, could take over the leadership of British Trotskyism.

Nevertheless, CLR was seriously considering taking up the invitation, but first he had to attempt to finish the Souvarine translation. He travelled to Paris one more time to work on the book, and to attend the founding conference of the Fourth International.

He was accompanied to the conference by a Scottish comrade, Willie Tait, who he had met on his frequent speaking visits to Glasgow. James was elected to the International Executive Committee of the Fourth International along with the Americans, Cannon and Shachtman,

In his translation work CLR was aided by Eric Williams and 'a girl, an English girl who had an extraordinary knowledge of French'.[14] Her name was Marjorie Froggatt and she would go on to work in Trinidad during the war.† Elsewhere he elaborated a little, saying that 'I knew a girl in Rouen who came over every morning at 9, helped me in the translation. We had lunch and dinner and walked in the woods. I took her to the bus at 9, and went back and read Maupassant until I fell asleep.'[15]

CLR returned to England utterly exhausted and ill, and with a decision to make. Should he stay in London and devote his energies to the Revolutionary Socialist League, or should he go to America? From what he told friends, it was the unsurprising breakdown in his health, after the relentless pace of the last few years, that made up his mind.

* Later a prominent British ornithologist.

† She wrote to CLR from Kent nearly forty years later, after he'd appeared on TV, 'if you ever come this way it would be fun to meet you again. I don't suppose you would recognise me either! Au revoir, peut être?'

He would take the boat to New York and recuperate on the way. He would be in America in time for the publication of *The Black Jacobins*. He would see old friends from Trinidad there. And, of course, he would be transported away from a Europe on the brink of a terrible war. A war that, as a Trotskyist, he was completely opposed to. The fight between liberal capitalism and fascism was not one he wanted to give his life to.

So, within a week or two of returning to London from France, CLR was off to the USA. His passage was booked on a boat leaving Liverpool on 8 October. Just as when he left Trinidad six years earlier, he made his decision and acted on it immediately, telling as few people as possible. According to James Cannon, the man who had invited him to the US, he even failed to inform any of his comrades in the RSL: 'For weeks after his arrival here we kept receiving letters as to his whereabouts and stating that he had left without authorisation or notice.'[16]

However, he did make one exception. Before he left, perhaps even en route to Liverpool, he went to Nelson to say to say goodbye to Learie Constantine. The two men had stayed close through all CLR's political changes. At the end of August they had both played together in a charity match for the Nelson mayor, the last time CLR would ever play cricket at any serious level.

CLR describes their parting in *Beyond a Boundary*:

> I turn up in Nelson to say goodbye before I leave for the United States. I am dressed in my literary-political grey flannels and sports jacket. Constantine takes one look at me and says 'You cannot go to the United States that way.' I protest in vain. 'I know the United States. It wouldn't do.' He is in his dressing gown, but he runs upstairs, dresses and comes down. 'Come on with me to the Co-op.' There he stocks me out so that I do not know myself. When I am finally dressed to leave he takes an approving look at me, but is not satisfied. 'Wait,' he says, and he runs upstairs and comes back with a most expensive camera in a Newmarket case and straps. I can do as little with a camera as with an aeroplane. No use. He puts it across my shoulder and is at last satisfied.

PART THREE

America

Chapter Eleven

CLR made the Atlantic crossing on a Cunard liner, the *Laconia*, a state-of the-art vessel that carried around two thousand people and was the first ship to conduct a round-the-world cruise.* The journey took around a week and CLR, a man from a maritime island, enjoyed the trip, spending time with a Polish family who were apparently much impressed by his command of Marxism.

On arrival in New York, CLR hit the ground running, just as he had in London six years earlier. And, as before, it was his old QRC connections to whom he turned first. A former pupil of his, now a doctor, Cecil Marques, put him up at his apartment at 125 West 121st Street in Harlem.

He clearly wasted no time making friends, as two weeks later he was writing to Alfie Mendes explaining that he had tracked him down thanks to Harold Jackman, and suggesting that the three of them have lunch. Harold Jackman was a man right at the heart of things uptown. Known as the most handsome man in Harlem, he was a teacher and art collector, and also at the heart of Harlem's gay scene, along with the painter Bruce Nugent and the man reputed to be his lover, the poet Countee Cullen. Jackman was the inspiration for characters in two of the key novels of the Harlem Renaissance, Wallace Thurman's hilarious *roman-à-clef Infants of the Spring* and Carl Van Vechten's infamous *Nigger Heaven*.†

It's an intriguing friendship as, once CLR became settled in the US, there's very little trace of him having much to do with the writers of the Harlem Renaissance – people like Langston Hughes, Claude

* The *Laconia* would come to an untimely end four years later, when it was torpedoed in the Atlantic in September 1942, with the loss of 1621 lives.

† Infamous not so much for the content but simply for the title, an audacious but thoroughly ill-advised one for a white writer to use, even a white writer as deeply connected to Harlem as the enigmatic Van Vechten.

Mackay and Zora Neale Hurston. He was certainly aware of their work from the twenties, when he was a would-be novelist himself, but the face he chose to show the world by the late thirties was that of a hard-line Trotskyist activist with no time for literature. A few years earlier, Alfie Mendes had sent him a copy of his second novel, *Black Fauns*. CLR had responded with a rather aloof letter, which he concluded by saying 'Let me hear from you again, though I am afraid my interests are now almost entirely political.'*[1]

And yet here he is exploring the city with Harold Jackman. The two of them must have made quite an impression. Both were photographed in the forties by Carl Van Vechten and could easily be mistaken for very elegant brothers. It could easily have been Jackman that introduced CLR to Carlo, as he was known. CLR's only other documented interaction with the Harlem Renaissance comes in Van Vechten's correspondence with Langston Hughes. Hughes comments simply that CLR was 'Said to be very brilliant. But he did not seem to have much of a sense of humor . . .'[2]

What may well have come between CLR and Langston Hughes, two men who had much in common – not least that they had both written plays about the Haitian Revolution† – was their rival political allegiance. Hughes was a communist sympathiser,‡ while CLR was of course a Trotskyist.

And it was Trotskyism that quickly became the focus of his activity in New York. CLR made regular visits to the SWP's downtown headquarters and familiarised himself with its leaders, starting with Cannon and Shachtman, who he had met before. He talked to the rank and file members too, but professed himself disappointed with the level of understanding of Marxist theory: 'I was much struck at their ignorance and lack of understanding.'[3]

* The letter ends with a classic query between writers: 'Did you make any money by the books?'

† Hughes's play, *The Emperor of Haiti*, focusing on Dessalines rather than Toussaint, was also first performed in 1936.

‡ He had, for example, supported Stalin's purges in 1938. Like many others, though, he would break with communism following the Hitler-Stalin pact of 1939.

For all their lack of theoretical rigour, CLR had decided that these were now his people: 'For the most part I dealt with the New York members for the first few months of my stay. They were extremely glad to see me, very hospitable, they invited me out to dinner . . .'

Looking back on this era from the mid-seventies, CLR offered a rueful summary of the mindset of the Trotskyist movement:

> You fought for the correct line of the party however small you were; you fought against those who were not prepared to accept your line, and through your success, along these rather narrow and limiting efforts, you would in time rise to the position of being the dominant political party and lead the hundreds of millions of people in the United States to success. It may seem now that I am speaking about it with irony. But I had more or less the same idea and rather more than less. All of us had it at the time.[4]

So CLR started attending meetings, speaking at some of them and preparing to give a full-scale lecture on 30 November, on the political situation in Britain and Europe. He quickly became aware of the extent to which the imminent war in Europe was pulling the American Trotskyist movement apart.

The Socialist Workers Party, which had invited him over, was the only substantial Trotskyist party, formed just a year earlier after previously being a faction in the Socialist Party (broadly parallel to the way the British Trotskyists had split from the ILP). They had perhaps two thousand members, hardly a huge number but far more than any of the British or international groups.

However, it was always, in practice, an uneasy coalition, split from the start into two factions around the two leaders. James Cannon was in his late forties, of Irish stock, a stern figure steeped in Labour politics. Max Shachtman was younger, in his early thirties, a New York Jew who had arrived from Poland when he was ten years old and came from a journalistic, intellectual background. He'd been Trotsky's secretary for a while in the early thirties.

The big area of disagreement was over their attitude to Stalin's Russia. Cannon, like Trotsky, still believed that the Soviet Union had to be supported, even under Stalin. Shachtman, though, was coming to believe that the Soviet Union was effectively beyond redemption, its revolution utterly betrayed.

CLR, expecting to return to London soon, declined to take sides. He focused on preparing for his speech. He was uncharacteristically nervous about it. 'It is my first here and it takes every moment of my time,' he wrote to Alfie Mendes. 'When it is over we shall meet.'[5]

In the event, it was a great success. As ever he spoke without notes and exhibited his extraordinary memory for facts, figures and quotes. Suddenly it was clear to the Americans just why CLR had risen so fast in Britain. A young Trotskyist called Martin Glaberman, later an important collaborator of CLR's, was there:

> He was an honoured visitor, a fabulous speaker . . . I remember the first time I ever saw him – it was a lecture at a hotel ballroom in New York, where he spoke for about three hours on the British Empire, walking back and forth across the stage without notes or anything else.[6]

The SWP quickly realised they had a new star. Not only was he an extraordinary speaker, but one of very few Black Trotskyists. Trotskyism had made precious little headway with the Black population, far less than the communists had managed. CLR James, they hoped, might be the man to change all that.

They promptly arranged a speaking tour of the US, to begin in early 1939. Meanwhile *The Black Jacobins* was published by the Dial Press in December 1938. It had a rather more enthusiastic reception than in the UK. *Time* magazine described it as 'an impassioned account of Toussaint Louverture and the Santo Domingo revolution, written from the Marxist point of view by a young British Negro'. Better still, the *New York Times* said that 'his detailed, richly documented and dramatically written book holds a deep and lasting interest'.

CLR had a little time to enjoy literary New York before heading off to preach revolution. He socialised some more with Alfie Mendes, whom CLR invited to a party in Greenwich Village with the pioneering doctor and advocate of socialised medicine Paul Luttinger. They spent time together at Mendes's place in Long Beach, along with their old friend, Sonny Carpenter. Mendes was living there with his new wife Ellen, their baby son and his son from his first marriage, also called Alfred. Alfie Senior was still writing novel after novel but never showing them to anyone, despite having a coterie of literary friends, among them Benjamin Appel and Malcolm Lowry.*

CLR's speaking tour took him all over the US, generally meeting small but enthusiastic audiences. A particular highlight was an event at the University of Chicago on 1 February, a debate between CLR and the grand old man of British philosophy, Bertrand Russell, who had reluctantly taken up a post at the university at the time. The debate was on the question 'Can democracy be defended?' Bertrand Russell defended it. CLR argued that liberal democracies were inevitably sliding into fascism. CLR later claimed that 'I rolled him around in the dust' and won the public vote comfortably.[7] It's a memory backed up by an audience member:

> Mr Russell maintained his usual manner in this debate, and was virtually cut to pieces rhetorically by his opponent. This is to say, [he] brought an enormous passion to his argument which Russell did not match.[8]

The two men had a very cordial chat afterwards, however: 'We spoke together as two Britishers who were in the United States,' remembered CLR.

CLR's tour finally ended in Los Angeles, where he met several people who were to be enormously important to him in the years to come. First came the Gogols. Dr Louis Gogol and his Russian emigrée wife Bessie would become close friends. They lived in a fabulous

* Lowry, years before *Under the Volcano*, would show up, get drunk and 'pick up his guitar … and in a soft voice sing obscene ditties for hours on end, the accompaniment impeccable'.

modernist house in Los Feliz, looking over the city. CLR would stay with them whenever in LA.

There was clearly an effort made to showcase CLR to Black communities, as one of his LA events was held in a Black church. The church was packed out by a mix of Black churchgoers and white radicals. One of the latter was an eighteen-year-old called Constance Webb. CLR made a particular impression on her:

> The black minister made an introduction and then from the wings strode a six-foot-three-inch tall, brown-skinned handsome man. His back was ramrod straight, his neck rather long, and he held his head slightly back, with chin lifted. There was elegance and grace in his stance, and he looked like a prince or a king . . . James looked out into the audience and then at his wristwatch. He said, 'It is now 11 a.m., and I shall speak for exactly forty-five minutes.'[9]

CLR was as good as his word. Constance Webb was enthralled, not least by 'the beauty of his voice'. A few nights later she heard the voice again. She was lying in bed at the time, in the house she shared with her equally young husband and fellow SWP member, Norman Henderson. CLR had stopped by with his driver, a cartoonist called Carlo, after addressing a meeting in Pasadena. Constance got up to greet the honoured guest, but soon went back to bed.

CLR, however, was obviously just as taken with her as she was with him. A few days later he arranged for another party member, the distinguished violinist Sol Babitz,* to call Constance and invite her to meet for 'a small conference'.

Constance later claimed not to have seen anything especially odd about a senior party figure inviting a strikingly pretty young rank-and-file member to a private meeting. And her account of the

* Sol Babitz may well be the only man to have made music with both Jelly Roll Morton, who he jammed with in South Central LA, and Igor Stravinsky, who was a regular visitor to the Los Angeles house where CLR had arranged to meet Constance. His daughter is the writer and sixties LA it girl Eve Babitz.

'conference' describes an entirely proper discussion in which she shared with CLR her reservations about the SWP, and in particular its lack of any real engagement with Black people. In the LA region, 'there were only one or two black men, they might come to our socials not to meetings, and they did not join'. CLR responded, as was his wont, by suggesting a reading list: in this case featuring the communist historian Herbert Aptheker, and, interestingly, the Black conservative columnist George Schuyler. He went on to suggest that she formed a discussion group, and said that he planned to lobby the party to set up a bureau devoted to 'Negro Affairs'. Furthermore, he told her he was about to travel to Mexico to debate this very question – the relation of Black Americans to a vanguard party – with the Old Man himself.

The meeting with Trotsky had been loosely set up for early April, but was put in jeopardy as CLR's time on the road had led him to a physical collapse. Word of this reached Trotsky himself, who wrote to offer his advice:

> It is my opinion . . . you should devote the next months exclusively to the care of your health, if necessary, even postponing the projected book on the Negro question. As I understand it, you suffer from a stomach ulcer. In this condition, your trip to Mexico represents – I say it with the deepest regret – a direct danger . . . Everyone, even those who have sound stomachs, suffers from stomach trouble here; and those who have it abroad suffer doubly and triply in Mexico City. I know it from my own experience and from the experience of several friends. That is why, if you have the choice, you should cure your stomach before making the trip here, and even in this case it would be advisable not to live in Mexico City.* Your ideas for the Negro organization and the Negro paper are very interesting and important, but the first condition is the reestablishment of your health.[10]

* Presumably CLR had entertained the idea of coming to live there!

CLR, though, was not going to let a stomach ulcer stand between him and the opportunity to meet his political hero, and he set out for Mexico in early April. He didn't see Constance again before he left, but he began her education, sending her a letter with several newspaper articles enclosed, including a piece by George Schuyler and a report on the Scottsboro Boys trial. He also sent her a sheet of British reviews for *The Black Jacobins*.

A Spanish-speaking comrade called Charles Curtiss was on hand to escort CLR to meet the Old Man on 4 April 1939. Trotsky was living in the Mexico City suburb of Coyoacán, in La Casa Azul, Frida Kahlo's home since childhood. It had been turned into a fortress due to the very real threat of assassination by agents of Moscow. Bessie Gogol's sister, Raya Dunayevskaya, had been Trotsky's secretary in the previous year and later recalled her first impression of the house. She remembered floodlights that gave the house 'the appearance of a Hollywood movie theatre', an impression undercut by a sentry box, steep walls, windows and doors with bars, and a complex alarm system. Less a theatre, then, than a 'well-nigh impregnable fortress'.[11]

All this security was courtesy of the Mexican government. Inside the fortress, though, there was a further line of defence 'composed of Trotsky's devoted and unflinching revolutionary followers.'

By the time CLR arrived, however, it was also a household in some turmoil. Trotsky and his wife Natalia were in the midst of moving out. Frida Kahlo and her husband Diego Rivera had been Trotsky's main sponsors on his arrival to seek asylum in Mexico in January 1937. But it had become a complex relationship. Trotsky and Kahlo soon embarked on an affair. She called him Piochitas (little goatee), referring to his white beard, or, less affectionately *el viejo*, as he was twice her age at the time – fifty-seven years to her twenty-nine. Ironic too, given that Trotsky's nickname to his admirers was the Old Man. Oddly, it wasn't the affair that caused the Trotskys to move out – it had come to an end when their respective spouses discovered it. It wasn't even Frida Kahlo giving Trotsky a self-portrait for his birthday, and him hanging it above his desk in his study. Instead it was

Rivera and Kahlo's move towards Stalinism. That was a betrayal that could not be ignored.

Given the circumstances, it's remarkable how focused Trotsky was in his discussions with his latest visitor. But then Trotsky's life had been lived in extraordinary circumstances for decades, and while the threat of assassination was real, it was hardly new.

CLR was very struck by finally meeting Trotsky. This man, whose writing had transformed him from would-be bourgeois novelist to ardent revolutionary, turned out to be something of a surprise.

> His manner and style were those of a European nobleman of the 19th century. There is nothing proletarian or Bolshevik in the crude sense about him at all. Furthermore he had a great gift of languages. He would speak in English if necessary, when he was in trouble for a word he would use the French word, pick up the English word. His wife was very handsome, very gay, very stylish and the whole household worked extremely well, centring around him and his activity. They were a really striking pair and very different from what I'd expected a leader of the Russian Revolution to be.[12]

The two men spent several days together, debating, in particular, the 'Negro question'. Trotsky was already convinced that this was an area in which the SWP were failing to make headway. CLR had prepared well, writing a document detailing his thoughts on the matter.

It's a remarkable piece of work, coming from a man who'd been in the US for barely six months. He'd evidently spent his time in Harlem productively, getting to understand the Black American mindset – one very different from that of the Black Trinidadian, let alone the Black Africans he'd met in London.

Black Trinidadians like CLR had grown up under the colonial yoke, but they lived in a majority Black culture, without formal segregation. Black Americans, on the other hand, in many ways felt themselves to be an oppressed nation within a nation. The successful Black protest movements had capitalised on that feeling. Marcus Garvey had offered a crude Black nationalism with a promised land over the ocean.

The white radical left only offered sympathy and the promise that if you join and help make a socialist revolution then you will be free. 'Black and White Unite and Fight' was a slogan leftists liked, but in practice Black Americans weren't listening.

CLR had thought hard about this and formed a radical plan. He argued that Black Americans, thanks to the oppression they faced, represented potentially the most revolutionary section of the population. He didn't believe that Black Americans would happily join a white socialist organisation, however noble its aims. Black Americans needed a Black-led movement, one that would work alongside the SWP, but couldn't simply be a puppet body controlled by senior white theoreticians.*

This was a brave submission. Trotsky, and Lenin before him, believed in the key role of the vanguard party. The masses needed clear-eyed leadership from above to take them to the socialist uplands, in which they would in time come to political maturity. To offer a section of the proletariat, in this case Black Americans, this degree of self-determination was frankly unheard of. Much to his surprise, though, CLR found the Old Man to be in almost complete agreement.

> Trotsky accepted the idea, we discussed it for three or four days and there was very little difference between him and me. We ended with the idea that the thing we had to do was to urge and in every way do what we can to create a black movement that would fight for its democratic rights.[13]

And so the bones of a plan were laid out. The SWP would form a Negro Bureau to consider policy. Members would be encouraged to familiarise themselves with Black history and culture, and, somehow or other, they should help to encourage an autonomous Black

* There's an intriguing observation buried within this document – 'The question, however, is pertinently asked: Why is it that intelligent Negroes with political understanding never attempt to lead Negroes but always leave them to men like Garvey?' – which is worth keeping in mind as CLR's career progresses.

revolutionary movement that would fight for civil rights first and socialism second.

That decided, the two men went on to other less fruitful discussions. Trotsky disagreed with much of CLR's thinking as expressed in *World Revolution*. CLR disagreed with his disagreement. The Old Man may have had the air of a European aristocrat, but CLR was not to be intimidated. Trotsky was evidently impressed by his visitor, as revealed in a letter to James Cannon:

> We have already had some discussions with Comrade James. The two most important were on the Negro question. He presented an important and very good statement. I do not accept his categorical rejection of self-determination (an independent state) for the American Negro* ... The rest of his statement is very good. The party cannot postpone this extremely important question any longer. James's sojourn in the States is very important for the serious and energetic beginning of this work.[14]

The discussions finished, CLR spent at least ten more days in Mexico City, though once again laid a little low by his stomach and a slight fever. Nevertheless, he greatly admired Diego Rivera's mural in the Government Palace and addressed a couple of meetings, talking in French translated into Spanish. The city as a whole he found 'a most fascinating place: charming, pleasant, kindly people, and yet not at all servile. Poor and dirty, with some tawdry finery, but full of life and colour and vitality.'[15]

He decided to take a scenic route back to New York. He would take a boat to New Orleans and then ride to New York on the bus, giving him a chance to see the South for himself. He travelled overnight to the port of Veracruz and caught the SS *Tegucigalpa* the following evening. This was a fruit freighter which carried just a few passengers to the US, for fifty dollars one way.

* This is odd. Trotsky seems to have conceived of Black Americans as a geographic minority, like Catalans in Spain, who could somehow achieve physical independence.

While on board CLR wrote to Constance Webb, describing the journey. It's an extraordinary letter, revealing a side of CLR that had remained hidden from public view. Far from the humourless politico that others, from Ethel Mannin to Langston Hughes, described, this is a funny self-deprecating man who delights in all the comedy of life. Perhaps his meeting with the Trotskys and finding them so far from the humourless Bolsheviks he'd imagined, had set something free in him.

He tells her about his one and only fellow passenger, 'a Mexican tenor' heading indirectly to Rio de Janeiro, where he had an engagement, and the steward, another musician who, despite being English, plays Spanish songs on the guitar:

> So now he and the tenor and I sang during lunch – and after lunch Mr Steward brings out his guitar and – Mr James chiefly audience – the two of them sing and play till 5 to 3. As I write, the steward is trying some of the chords the tenor has taught him, the tenor is looking at a book and all the time singing away, chiefly snatches and I am scribbling away. We are in the little stateroom, six tables only and if I wore a top hat and stood up suddenly it would get crushed. Through the door and the port-holes is the sun on the sea, and the ship taking everything in its stride. You know how it is on a ship. You are sick, well, happy, miserable, tired of it, the ship does not care. It just goes on.[16]

CLR goes on too. He tells Constance of his dreams, remembers a ghost story he heard in Trinidad from 'an East Indian girl, wife of an old, old friend of mine, a clergyman'. He tells her how much fun it would be if only she was there too, and he tells her about his bath:

> I rose at 7 and looked out of the port-hole till 7.20 waiting for the steward. There is no shower and he has to put water into the bath. I got up and went into the bathroom for my own purposes and there was some water in the bath, towels, etc. My dear, had you been there you would have been proud of your Nello. I did not hesitate. For

> about two minutes I pondered. Was this bath mine or not? I weighed up both sides and then decided I didn't know ... Then I remembered I was a Bolshevik ... Without a trace of Menshevism with nothing that might even be construed as Lovestoneism (centrism) this hero (darling it is the *only* word; forgive me if I sound boastful, but I *must* be true to myself), this HERO took the bath.

Was this CLR always there? Yes and no, perhaps. None of the letters he wrote to Juanita or Louise survive, but it seems likely that the CLR of these letters is one that existed only in relation to Constance. Juanita and Louise were similar in age and experience to him. Not Constance. She was a very beautiful eighteen-year-old who had just written to him in Mexico to tell him that she had separated from her husband. He is wanting to impress and to seduce but he is also keenly aware that she is half his age, a pure ingénue. He wants to educate her in political culture and he wants to make her laugh.

It's difficult, at this remove at least, to feel entirely comfortable with the imbalance of age and power in this correspondence, but it is undeniably revealing of its author.

CLR had gone to New Orleans so that he could experience the South and its racial politics for himself. It didn't take long to reveal itself to him – in fact, it damn near knocked him down.

> One day I stood up at the side of the road and put up my hand to stop a taxi. He passed within a foot of me and paid no attention to me. A black boy came up to me and told me do not stand in the road to stop them, he will run you over as easily as he would run over a dog. They are not going to stop for you.[17]

His saviour then showed him around for the next few days, till he was ready for the series of bus rides up to New York. On the first leg he came up against the Jim Crow system at its most blatant. As a Black man he had to sit in one of the three back rows. CLR took the front-most and started spreading out his newspapers and the book by Hegel he was reading. But then the white section filled up and a white man indicated that he wanted CLR's seat. CLR moved back a row, feeling angry. Then it happened again at the next stop and he had to move to the very back, by which time he was furious. The cumulative pettiness of the humiliations built an uncharacteristic rage in him. This was a racism so flagrant, and so institutional, that it was impossible for him to simply ignore it – normally his preferred option.

And so his journey went on, stopping off here and there to meet fellow radicals: sometimes Trotskyists, sometimes Black leftists. As he moved further north he was able to sit where he wanted, but at restaurants he would still have to eat in the kitchen with the cooks, while the white passengers sat in the dining room. Eventually he arrived in Washington DC, where Raya Dunayevskaya was waiting to meet him. She had been Trotsky's secretary the year before. Now she wrote to the Old Man in advance of CLR's visit, making it clear that even the nation's capital was no place for a Black radical:

> We are finally getting James to speak here and even so routine a matter as arranging a meeting for him is, in this Jim Crow town, a problem as the Negroes will not have him because he is a 'Red' and the whites will not have him because he is a Negro and of course, also 'Red'. I am so fed up with this town.[18]

In fact, the only place the Black and white SWP comrades could freely meet in Washington DC was a Black funeral parlour with a sympathetic owner. CLR had already developed an intellectual analysis of the situation of Black people in the USA. By the time he got back to New York he felt it in his gut.

Chapter Twelve

CLR James arrived back in New York riding high. He was ready and willing to become the SWP's leader in regard to the 'Negro question'. Trotsky's words had paved the way – 'James's sojourn in the States is very important for the serious and energetic beginning of this work.'[1]

His position would be formally ratified at the SWP conference in July. Meanwhile, he was busy getting to know the people whose cause he was championing. In Harlem he went to political meetings and storefront churches. Everything he saw, everyone he spoke to, confirmed his instincts. Black people were ready to revolt all right. But what they wanted to revolt against was the oppression they experienced in their daily lives. The oppression that denied them access to decent jobs; that even in New York barred them from most restaurants; that kept them poor and hungry in the ghetto, harassed by police if they came downtown.

CLR's own position was anomalous. As a Black man in New York, he had to get used to the fact that most restaurants, for instance, wouldn't serve him. This wasn't the Deep South, but it was still a profoundly racist society. However, he was also an outsider, a West Indian intellectual at ease in a white world and who was indeed already a key member of a mostly white organisation. It took him a while to understand how racial matters worked in New York. He brought some of his white comrades to a Black church and was struck by the hostility of the congregation. He realised then that there was no sense in telling people that their real oppressor was the capitalist system when, as far as they were concerned, their oppressors were right there in front of them: the white cops and politicians, the white shopkeepers and club-owners.

CLR didn't only see the oppression, though – he also began to experience the extraordinary vibrancy of Harlem's nightlife. He started visiting the Apollo Theatre, just a few blocks from Cecil Marques's place. It was a wonderful time for jazz, and CLR saw Ella Fitzgerald, Benny Goodman, Jimmy Lunceford, Artie Shaw et al. He was struck by the way that the Harlem audience didn't mind a band with a white bandleader, as long as they swung.

Best of all, in his eyes, were two of the great individual voices of Black American music: Louis Armstrong and Billie Holiday. Armstrong, he noted, was an absolute master of the stage: 'The impression of absolute ease and absolute control of himself as a public performer was something beyond belief.'[2]

With Holiday too, the thing that really fascinated CLR was not the singing so much as her absolute self-possession, an extraordinary quality in a world that treated Black people as it did.

> Billie Holiday is one of the most graceful women as a public performer I have ever seen. It was astonishing the way she used to walk onto the stage. The centre of the stage, begin to sing, and remain there. There was a finish, a style, a style in the sense of an inner grace that I have never seen in anybody.

The July conference of the SWP, as expected, confirmed CLR's new status. He was made head of the Negro Bureau and given a weekly column in the party newspaper, *Socialist Appeal*, under the banner 'The Negro Question'. He was also given a party name to operate – and write – under. The use of party names was common practice in US revolutionary groups. The idea was to offer some protection from harassment by the authorities. For CLR there was the added benefit of helping him to hide from the immigration authorities. He was nearing the end of an extension to his visitor's visa. From now on his name would be J. R. 'Jimmy' Johnson. New friends would know him as Jimmy; just a few old friends and new intimates would call him Nello.

CLR went to work in his very own 'hen coop' of an office, writing his column, addressing meetings, trying to attract Black members to the party. He was also very active in enthusing the party's youth, many of whom had passed through their junior branch, the Young People's Socialist League. CLR still looked a decade younger than his true age (thirty-eight), and was an exotic character, a Black man who spoke as they imagined an English aristocrat to speak. That made him rather more of a draw than someone like James Cannon, a dour American Irishman who spoke with a pint of milk at his side to help with his stomach ulcers.

Meanwhile, CLR kept in touch with a couple of contrasting protégés. He continued to correspond with Constance, his ardour slackening a little in the face of the news that she had fallen in love with another young comrade, but his letters were still both educational and flirtatious. The other protégé was his former student Eric Williams, who had completed his doctorate at Oxford in 1938 and just arrived in New York, prior to taking up a post at Howard University in Washington.

As ever with CLR, even this level of activity was not enough. Dissatisfied with becoming the SWP's leader on all things race-related, he was determined to further advance his formal studies of Marxism. He had bought a copy of *Das Kapital* in Mexico City and, somewhat to his embarrassment, as he confided to Constance, he was now engaged in reading it for the first time. That and Hegel's dialectics had him enraptured.

Most of his SWP comrades were more interested in the nuts and bolts of political organisation than the frankly abstract theoretical side, but it wasn't long before CLR found a real kindred spirit, an equally intellectually driven comrade. This was Raya Dunayevskaya, who he'd first met in Washington a few months earlier.

Dunayevskaya was twenty-nine years old, a brilliant, self-educated activist; small, dark and intense. She had been in Mexico* for a year, had been there when the Trotskys learnt of the murder of their son by Stalin's agents in Paris. She saw them closet themselves for a week, lost in grief, before emerging ready to fight again – Trotsky with the

* There's a wonderful photograph of her in Mexico with Natalia Trotsky. Raya is staring straight into the camera, while Natalia looks at her quizzically.

handwritten manuscript of his tribute to his son. This was the kind of Bolshevik spirit that Dunayevskaya treasured. She'd once asked Trotsky how he dealt with living in exile, having to worry about money, rather than leading a great nation. He told her that 'it was the tide of history and we had to know how to swim against the current as well as with it'.[3] Words she would live by.

She had been forced to return to the US in the spring of 1938 following the sudden deaths of both her father and brother. She was working closely with Max Shachtman and living unhappily in Washington DC when she'd first met CLR back in May. She had been immediately impressed: 'He is an excellent speaker and completely wins the confidence of the Negroes,' she told Trotsky.[4] Across the summer the two of them started to work together, both on the Negro question and on a systematic study of Marxism, with a particular view to analysing the Soviet system.

CLR's visa had been renewed for six months in March but was unlikely to be further extended. If he was going to stay beyond the summer then he would have to take the risks involved in being illegal, not least the inability to get a regular job. It was Raya who persuaded him to stay:

> If it hadn't been for Raya Dunayevskaya I would have come back to Britain, where I had a movement, where I had people, where I had a paper and where I was known, because I was writing cricket for the *Manchester Guardian*. So I thought that I ought to go back to where the boys were speaking against the war. But Raya Dunayevskaya had come to the conclusion that I was the man to remain in the United States, a black man who was automatically the leader of the black movement, but whose education was such that he could be head of the Trotskyist movement as a whole. I was in doubt whether to go or stay. Raya was insistent that I stay, and then I said that I had no money to live on she said, 'Don't worry about money'. For months she got money for me. She had friends and was well established, and that is why I stayed in the United States.[5]

He made his choice. He decided to stay in the US and study Marx and Lenin in new depth with Raya. As a result of this decision the name CLR James vanished from public view for over a decade. Jimmy Johnson had taken over.

There's a curious omission in CLR's account of his reasons for staying in the US. That's the fact that Europe was moving steadily towards a war. CLR, having been persuaded not to fight in two wars he believed in, in Ethiopia and Spain, would hardly have been enthusiastic at the prospect of being conscripted into a war he very much did not believe in.

In August Stalin and Hitler entered into their infamous pact, immediately throwing communist parties around the world into a state of confusion. This was rapidly followed by the German invasion of Poland, and then Britain and France declaring war on Germany on 3 September.

The SWP did their best to make sense of this. Trotsky ruled that the Soviet Union had to be supported, even under Stalin, even after making a tactical alliance with Hitler, because it was still ultimately a workers' state, albeit 'degenerated', and so it had to be defended above all else. James Cannon went along with this. The Jewish Max Shachtman found it difficult to stomach. CLR, for his part, wrote a propagandising pamphlet entitled 'Why Negroes Should Oppose the War', putting forward the line this was essentially an imperialist war between different types of capitalism. And anyway, Black Americans knew what their real enemy was – the discrimination they found at home.

Meanwhile he and Raya, who had now moved to New York, worked on the project to analyse Soviet society. If they could prove that Russia was no longer a workers' state, then it was logical to oppose it as just another warmonger.

When Russia invaded Finland in November 1939, launching the Winter War, tensions within the SWP started to boil over. There were now two acknowledged factions within the party: the 'majority' led by Cannon and the 'minority' led by Shachtman.

Throughout this time CLR continued to write to Constance, regularly revealing the inner man. He wrote to her from Washington while he was working with Raya there, telling her how hard a road it was, the revolutionary one. He told her he had 'discarded all my hopes of writing anything else except that which strictly concerns the revolution'. In September, as war began, he summed up his decision to stay in the US working undercover:

> I shall work inside but I may have to come out openly, according as the situation develops. I don't mind going to prison here or in England. But my nightmare is that I will be deported to the W. Indies and be out of everything.[6]

In October he expressed his frustration at the party split, offered Constance a reading list on the Negro question, and repeatedly asked her to send photographs. He also complained of bouts of illness. Throughout the year he had repeatedly been laid low by stomach trouble, which he put down to a duodenal ulcer that he believed to be sensitive to stress and not watching his diet.

It can't have helped that he was living a peripatetic life. He was working at the SWP's new headquarters at 118 University Place in Greenwich Village. They had the top three stories of a red-brick building to house their leadership, their publishing arm and a meeting hall. He was staying here and there in New York and often visiting Washington DC, where Eric Williams was now teaching, at weekends. In December he told Constance to write to him care of Dwight Macdonald at an address in the Village.

Macdonald was another star recruit to the SWP, and an obvious friend for CLR to make. He was in his early thirties, a brilliant Yale-educated journalist who for a time was something of an American equivalent to George Orwell (with whom he corresponded at length). Like CLR he was a man of wide cultural interests, but unlike CLR he was unprepared to drop everything in the cause of revolution. In his memoirs he gives a vivid account of the looming split in the SWP and the contrasting characters of the two opposing leaders, plus his new friend:

> Both Shachtman and Cannon were great speakers ... Shachtman spoke with New York Jewish slang and Yiddish references. He was witty and inexhaustible. A three-hour talk was nothing to Shachtman. Cannon spoke in the old Wobbly* style. He sounded patriarchal, Lincolnesque, and honest ... He was slower, but probably more impressive.
>
> Then there was CLR James, whom we called Nello ... James was the greatest speaker of them all. He used the entire range of vocal qualities.[7]

As the war progressed into 1940 it became obvious that the SWP were heading for an imminent split. CLR was reluctantly forced to choose sides and, along with Macdonald, he threw in his lot with Shachtman's minority. A delighted Shachtman promptly sent CLR out on a speaking tour around the regional branches, looking to build support.

James Cannon responded by sending an extraordinarily vituperative letter to Charles Curtiss, the man who had facilitated CLR's visit to Trotsky. Headlined 'Concerning Johnson', it paints CLR as a man incapable of following orders, who walked out on his comrades in London and was now doing the same in the US:

> I hear that Johnson is in California ... I hope the comrades who value the unity of the party will give him a suitable reception. Here is a first-class example of an irresponsible adventurer within our party who deserves to be handled without gloves.
>
> Johnson, who wants to give us lessons in organisation methods never organised twenty workers in his whole life. His chief contribution to his own section [i.e. the Trotskyist movement in the UK] was light minded splits. We hoped by bringing him to America and letting him see a real functioning party at work, giving him every possible encouragement and aid, making it possible for him to visit

* The 'Wobblies' were members of the revolutionary trade union the Industrial Workers of the World, who had their heyday in the early part of the century, before being brutally suppressed by the government.

> Trotsky ... to cure him of some of his petty bourgeois prejudices and his irresponsible attitude towards organisation. He now undertakes to repay us by making himself the agent of a petty bourgeois faction whose design is to disrupt our movement by a split ... Johnson represents nothing and nobody but himself.[8]

Given that the political line the Shachtmanites were taking was directly in disagreement with Trotsky's own views on the Russian question, it's unsurprising that the Old Man, too, took a dim view of CLR's dissension. In a letter to another SWP figure, Farrell Dobbs, Trotsky dismissed CLR as a 'freelance bohemian'.

CLR, however, was by now confident enough of his own abilities not to be swayed by these criticisms (in part, at least, because they had an element of truth – he was not a man who took well to following orders). He stuck with Shachtman and, at the party conference in April 1940, matters came swiftly to a head. They debated the Russian question.* The Shachtmanite minority left the party, taking around 40 per cent of the membership, including almost all the leading intellectuals and most of the youth group. They promptly founded their own group, to be called, quite simply, the Workers' Party.

For the next seven years, the Workers' Party would be CLR's life. As a party dominated by intellectuals and enthusiastic youth, and light on old-style bureaucratic leftists, it gave CLR the framework in which he could follow his own political enthusiasms – without having to wait

* James Cannon's take on the Russian invasion of Finland is worth quoting at length, just to give a sense of how insanely grandiose the thinking of this tiny party was: 'We don't support Stalin's invasion only because he doesn't come for revolutionary purposes. He doesn't come at the call of Finnish workers whose confidence he has forfeited. That is the only reason we are against it. The "borders" have nothing to do with it. "Defence" in war also means attack. Do you think we will respect frontiers when we make our revolution? If an enemy army lands troops at Quebec, for example, do you think we will wait placidly at the Canadian border for their attack? No, if we are genuine revolutionists and not pacifist muddleheads we will cross the border and meet them at the point of landing. And if our defence requires the seizure of Quebec, we will seize it as the Red Army of Lenin seized Georgia and tried to take Warsaw.'

for the latest instructions from Mexico. He also finally had a place of his own to live, an apartment at 520 West 150th Street in Sugar Hill, the most desirable part of Harlem. He wrote to Constance to tell her how much he was enjoying the novelty of having something resembling an actual home for the first time since he left married life in Trinidad:

> I have an apartment. I am stocking it myself – I buy icebox, Babbitts,* dust-pan, soap, toilet-paper, eggs, sheets, old chairs. I wash up the plates and wash down the Frigidaire. I defrosted it yesterday. Hell of a mess. I clean forgot that ice becomes water that must be disposed of. And Christ, I nearly forgot, I'll tell you if I haven't before. One of my secret desires has long been to own (no socialism business, private property), to own Beethoven's last quartets, 5 of them; to own all. They are without a shadow of a doubt, the greatest music ever written.[9]

And lo and behold, a fellow party member turned out to possess them and promptly lent them to him, much to his delight: 'I have, my dear, acquired enormous confidence in the future. What I want, I'll get. God is with me and history.'

He hadn't been in Harlem long when he had a visitor from the past, one that he didn't mention in his letters to Constance. Louise Cripps had decided to take the chance of a passage to America for women and children to escape what looked like an imminent German invasion of the UK. She arrived in New York in June 1940, along with her young son, and soon went to visit CLR:

> He rushed towards me. We fell against each other. The strong ties between us had only lain buried and we made love almost immediately. I heard very little of what he was doing or of what was happening with him in the New York group.
>
> I made a second visit too. Again he made the same proposition to me that he had made in London; that I would stay with him and

* Soap powder for washing clothes.

> that the American group would support us both. 'As my wife, they would have to do so,' he said. I reminded him that I now had a child. He said: 'Well, I think that could be taken care of too.' But my child now was the centre of my life. I was not going to sacrifice him to any politics. I knew in that milieu, my little boy would be left on the fringe as far as care. I knew that it was stupid to start again with a love affair with James. Again I had to do the walking away.[10]

The Workers' Party had taken the SWP's theoretical journal, the *New International*, with it. CLR's first post-split piece for the May 1940 issue of the magazine was unusual for him, in that it was about a novel, and a novel written by a communist at that, though his primary focus remained the 'Negro question'. The book was Richard Wright's *Native Son*. Wright's classic novel of Black rage and anguish was an instant hit on publication that March. CLR admired it greatly and saw within it justification for his belief that Black Americans needed their own racial movement. He notes that the Black protagonist, Bigger Thomas, is helped by white communists, but he cautions Wright to beware the influence of Stalinism.

The dangers of Stalinism were given clear form for CLR just three months later, when a Russian agent murdered Trotsky at his home in Mexico. What made this all the more shattering was the fact that the assassin had used the SWP to get into Trotsky's inner sanctum.

Ironically, the SWP had been too busy tearing itself apart to realise that it had been infiltrated by Stalinist agents. Cannon's long-time secretary Sylvia Caldwell was a Stalinist agent who passed information back to her handlers. Another agent, Robert Sheldon Harte, managed to join Trotsky's bodyguard, which was provided by the SWP, but bungled his assassination attempt in April 1940. Finally, Ramón Mercader seduced an SWP member and went with her to Mexico in August. He inveigled his way into Trotsky's house and eventually got the Old Man alone, at which point he killed him with an ice-pick.*

* Years later, in 1947, Shachtman uncovered the name of the spy in Cannon's office and told his former colleague. Cannon sacked Caldwell but hushed up the whole affair.

CLR was devastated. 'Now this morning the awful news,' he wrote to Constance. 'It is the greatest blow we have ever received. One by one they have struck down all our best people and now the old man himself.'[11]

Perhaps not entirely coincidentally, it was around the same time that CLR's health problems started to worsen. Over the next two years he would be regularly incapacitated by ulcer attacks. In October 1940 he wrote to Constance to tell her he was going into hospital to be operated on. In the end the doctors decided not to go ahead, and so CLR struggled on in a stop-start way. Stomach ulcers were not well understood at the time. These days it is understood that a bacterial infection (*H. pylori*) is generally to blame, and they can easily be treated.

Still, he managed to keep up a flow of articles during this time, mostly on 'Negro issues' – jobs and civil rights – as well as a steady stream of anti-war pieces. He condemned the conflict in a pamphlet aimed at Black Americans called 'A Fireside Chat About the War'. This was a deliberate riff on President Roosevelt's folksy addresses to the nation; except that where Roosevelt was pressing for war against Germany, CLR was exhorting Black Americans to resist the call, and to fight for justice at home.

At the same time, he continued to work hard on the Russia question. At the 1941 party conference both he and Raya Dunayevskaya submitted papers arguing that Russia was a state capitalist country. They determined to start a study group within the party, dedicated to Marxist analysis.

Max Shachtman likely disapproved of this, seeing the potential emergence of a party within a party. He was doubtless aware that CLR had form in this respect. And furthermore, in CLR he had the man acknowledged to be the finest political speaker around. Surely it made sense for him to be out making converts, rather than poring over obscure Marxist texts. So from late 1941 onwards CLR was sent out on the road again, addressing Black and white workers, pressing the party line against the war, even as Pearl Harbor came and went and Roosevelt finally decided to enter the fray.

* * *

This activity culminated in an extended stay in Missouri in the summer of 1942. The St Louis branch of the Workers' Party had made contact with the radical Black sharecroppers in the Bootheel, the flatlands near the Mississippi River in the south-east of the state.

The sharecroppers of the region, both Black and white, had come to national prominence three years earlier, when they had staged a successful protest in the face of flooding and starvation wages. Led by a local Black pastor, Owen Whitfield, they had set up a kind of roadside refugee camp which had attracted national attention and ultimately led to the federal government building a series of small model communities – the Delmo Labor Homes – which gave decent housing to at least some of the sharecroppers.

Emboldened by this success, they were now threatening to strike in protest at the pitiful wages they were receiving. They received little support from their union, the United Cannery, Agricultural, Packing and Allied Workers of America. This was because the union was under the sway of the communists, who had committed to the war effort and didn't want to be seen to be encouraging strikes. So the opening was there for the anti-war Workers' Party to get involved.

CLR's role was to talk to the sharecroppers and produce agitprop materials. This he duly did. Calling himself Brother Williams, he went down to the Delmo Labor Homes community just outside Lilbourn. There, in the simple but smart new white-painted wooden houses of Liberty Street, he talked to the community leaders and the farm labourers and produced a pamphlet called 'Down With Starvation Wages in Southeast Missouri', which was widely distributed around the Black community, and helped encourage the Black sharecroppers to lead a strike action in May 1942.

The strike lasted eleven weeks and then the bosses caved in, scared that they would lose their crops completely. Wages were more or less doubled and CLR was able to return to New York with a new understanding of what a labour struggle felt like on the ground, and with renewed conviction that Black people acting autonomously could provide a revolutionary vanguard.

* * *

This sojourn in Missouri would be the one and only time CLR got directly involved in hands-on political struggle in the US. There are several explanations for this. Firstly, his health, on returning to New York, took a further turn for the worse. Secondly, his interest in Marxist theory was becoming ever more consuming. Thirdly, it may well have to do with a bitter rivalry that had sprung up between CLR and the only other senior Black figure in the Workers' Party, Ernest Rice McKinney.

By this time – 1942 – Ernest McKinney was in his late fifties, considerably older than CLR and a time-served veteran of political struggles since the early years of the century. Like CLR, he was the son of a schoolteacher. McKinney's father was a one-time Appalachian coal miner who had made his way into the Black middle class via a career in education. McKinney himself had been to college, and had been close to W. E. B. Du Bois in the formative years of the NAACP. He had served in the First World War. He had organised the unemployed in Pittsburgh during the Depression. He had been a prolific columnist in Black newspapers. He joined the Communist Party early and left it early too. He had basically been there and done that.

And along the way he had formed the definite belief that the future for Black Americans was in seeing themselves as part of the class struggle. He believed that they needed to make common cause with white workers and together fight for their rights, mostly through the vehicle of trade unions, but also through the Trotskyist parties. To have such a man in the Workers' Party was a considerable coup, and he had the key role of trade union secretary.

In this role he had been down to Missouri the year before CLR and laid much of the groundwork. Indeed, it is reasonable to figure that Shachtman sending CLR to Missouri was a test as to whether the two men could work together. As such, it failed. They took completely opposite messages from the strike. For CLR it confirmed the necessity of Black radical autonomy. For McKinney it showed that workers' solidarity across the races was the key to winning.

It wasn't just politics that divided the two men, though. McKinney saw CLR as an opportunist, a freelance bohemian if you like. Privately he referred to him as Sportin' Life – after the amoral pimp from *Porgy and Bess*. He may well have resented CLR's still-youthful good looks, the many women he had flocking around him, his obvious intellectual brilliance and his fancy British accent. There had long been a certain amount of rub between West Indian Blacks in America and African Americans. The West Indians who had grown up in predominantly Black environments, who had not had to suffer Jim Crow, could easily be characterised as arrogant.

It was a power struggle that McKinney effectively won. From here on the Workers' Party policies on the Negro question would be essentially McKinney's. CLR returned his energies to political theory. With Raya Dunayevskaya he focused his attention on studying Marx and, increasingly, Hegel, whose concept of dialectics had hit him hard, seeming to offer a way of understanding the world that allowed for the complexities of the world.

To others, however, this turn towards philosophy while the world was at war seemed baffling. Dwight Macdonald, for instance:

> Personally, I think he was a bit nuts. He read Hegel and it changed his entire life. I once told him I couldn't understand Hegel. CLR told me that if you don't understand Hegel you'll never be a genuine revolutionary. Hegel, he said, is our kindergarten.[12]

By then Macdonald, like many of the intellectual fellow travellers – Saul Bellow perhaps the most notable of them – who had initially been drawn to the Workers' Party, had moved on. Macdonald offers an elegant summary of his own reasons why. He could no longer reconcile the grandiloquence of their thinking with their lack of impact on the wider world:

> We behaved as if . . . great issues hinged on what we did, or rather what we said and wrote . . . It was all rather like engraving the Lord's Prayer on the head of a pin. The problems we were concerned with were so vast that we couldn't do much about them. We were really engaged not in politics but in meta-politics.

Cynical though Macdonald may have become, he cannot disavow the intellectual appeal of these hot-housed debates: 'In cheap meeting rooms off Third Avenue, in arguments around the cafeteria tables of Fourteenth Street. I have not before or since lived in such an atmosphere of passionate, if somewhat scholastic, intellection.'

Dwight Macdonald might have had enough of living in such a world, but for CLR it was very heaven. He would refer to this period time and again in the years to come as the best of his life. In studying the dialectic he found something strangely close to rapture:

> When a group of people . . . find something new, it is as if they have been living on a level with everybody else but by some chance they happen to get up to a great height. When you get to a certain height above the others it is as if you have discovered a new field, a new prairie, a new landscape, and all you have to have is the energy and drive to go on and you immediately begin to pick up a whole lot of new things which others on the level below don't see, it never crosses their mind.[13]

Chapter Thirteen

In August 1943, a year after his return from Missouri and subsequent immersion in the world of the Hegelian dialectic, CLR wrote to Constance Webb for the first time in almost three years. His letter begins dramatically:

> At last I am able to write to you. [I] am now out of town, living alone by the sea, absolutely alone . . . I have not written because I could not write – just that literally. It is a long story, I'll tell it to you.[1]

The story he told her was largely one of sickness. The stomach trouble that had flared up intermittently through 1940 and 1941 had come back with a vengeance on his return to New York in August 1941: 'I was in bed and out until December 1942 when I fell ill in the street, was lifted home and operated on that very night. My ulcer had perforated. The operation was completely successful. I made a marvellous recovery.'

Alongside the ulcer, he tells her he was also suffering from 'nervousness of the fingers' – the ailment he previously referred to as 'writer's cramp', which caused his hands to shake so badly that his handwriting was more or less illegible, hopeless for any serious writing, even of letters. 'It was very trying because I have never had so much to say as during the last few years . . . I dictate most of my work now.' This, he said, was why he hadn't written. A cynic might note that their correspondence had fizzled out when Constance had married for a second time and started up again when that marriage ended as quickly as the previous one.

CLR actually makes few bones about it: 'Are you still as beautiful as ever?' he asks (before adding, with rather less gallantry, 'You know your single weakness – the possibility of weight').

For the next few years CLR wrote to Constance, well, constantly.

Mr. C. L. R. James, law student and writer, is a member of The League of Coloured Peoples

CLR arrives in the UK as a deceptively youthful thirty-two-year-old.
(© British Library Board. All Rights Reserved/Bridgeman Images)

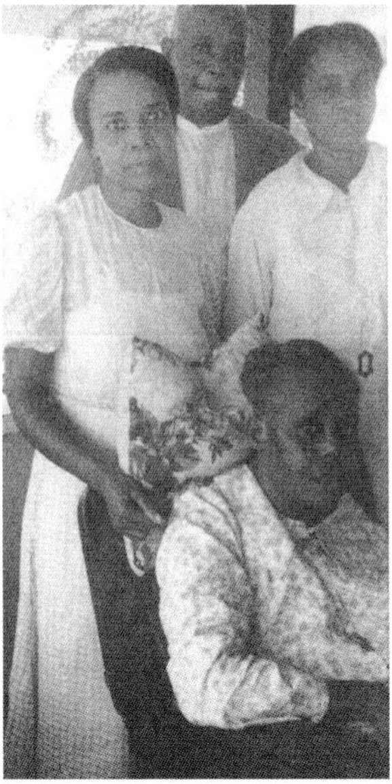

The only surviving picture of CLR's family. His long-suffering sister Olive on the left, his father Robert at the back and beloved Aunt Judith to the right. His mother Bessie is at the front, recovering from a stroke.

The Queen's Park Savannah where the young CLR lived with his father in the schoolhouse. *(Alma Jordan Library/ University of the West Indies)*

Queen's Royal College, where CLR studied and later taught. *(Alma Jordan Library/ University of the West Indies)*

Alfie Mendes in New York, 1936, with his third wife, Ellen, on the right and her sister-in-law Lea on the left.

Learie Constantine at the height of his British fame, early 1930s.
(Trinity Mirror/Mirrorpix/Alamy Stock Photo)

CLR addresses a rally on Ethiopia, 1935. No microphone.
(Keystone France/Getty Images)

Paul Robeson on stage in London as Toussaint Louverture, the title role in CLR's 1936 play, performed by the Stage Society.
(© British Library Board. All Rights Reserved/Bridgeman Images)

Ernest Borneman and his wife listening to records in the Hermitage, the house at 9 Heathcote Street, Bloomsbury, that he shared with CLR. *(Private collection)*

Louise Cripps, CLR's lover and collaborator in the late 1930s, pictured in later life. *(Private collection)*

CLR on arrival in the US aged thirty-seven, still looking implausibly young. *(Courtesy of the Constantine Collection)*

Raya Dunayevskaya and Natalia Trotsky in Mexico City, 1938. *(Walter P. Reuther Library/Wayne State University)*

CLR flanked by his two co-leaders in the Johnson-Forest Tendency: Grace Lee Boggs on the left, Raya Dunayevskaya on the right. *(Columbia University)*

Lyman and Freddy Paine. Lyman subsidised CLR's income for decades. His wife, Freddy, was one of CLR's closest confidantes. *(Columbia University)*

Constance Webb around the time she met CLR in 1939, aged nineteen.

Constance Webb and CLR, late 1940s. *(Columbia University)*

CLR, Constance, the Paines and friends, late 1940s. *(Columbia University)*

CLR, Constance and baby Nobbie, 1949. *(Columbia University)*

He pledged his love for her again and again, but also educated her, instructed her about art and politics and theatre, and most surprisingly, he told her about the little things of his life.

Since he'd last seen her, Constance had studied acting at the Actors' Lab in Hollywood and become part of a troupe performing for the armed forces, alongside the likes of Lee J. Cobb, Lloyd Bridges and Boris Karloff. She'd even appeared with Marlene Dietrich in a fund-raising show. Later in 1943, Constance would move to New York to try her luck as a model with the Conover agency. She didn't come to be with CLR. She claimed to see him as a father figure, not a romantic possibility, and she had a string of New York lovers, among them the actor Jack Gilford.

The CLR she found in New York was a man in intellectual clover. The state capitalist discussion group he had begun with Raya Dunayevskaya was now a fully fledged party within a party – called the Johnson-Forest Tendency after CLR and Raya's party names (Raya's being Freddie Forest).

The Johnson-Forest Tendency started out as a tiny discussion group of eight to ten people and gradually grew to a membership of around seventy, mostly young and intellectually questing. They tended to be referred to by the wider party as the Johnsonites because CLR was so clearly the dominant personality. But as far as the actual intellectual work went, there was not one leader but rather a triumvirate. There was CLR, of course. There was Raya, who had recently married a Boston Brahmin called Bernard Adams and taken up residence in possibly New York's fanciest residential neighbourhood, Sutton Place.* And now there was a new collaborator, Grace Lee.

Grace Lee was a young Chinese American woman whose father owned a chain of very successful Chinese restaurants, including a huge

* How this unlikely turn of events came about I have absolutely no idea. According to Constance Webb, Adams was handsome, brilliant, distinguished and unassuming, with a senior role as an economist for the US government. The apartment itself was apparently modest.

dining and dancing establishment called Chin Lee's on Broadway. A brilliant student, she had completed a PhD in philosophy at Bryn Mawr a couple of years earlier, at the age of twenty-five. Then she had moved to Chicago, where she joined the Workers' Party under the influence of one of its senior figures, Marty Abern. However, it was only when CLR James came to town that she started to see how her philosophical training could link up with her radical politics:

> CLR was everything that the Chicago branch was not. He was bursting with enthusiasm about the potential for an American revolution inherent in the emergence of the labor movement and the escalating militancy of blacks. When together with another comrade I met him at the train station, he was carrying two thick books, volume 1 of Marx's *Capital* and Hegel's *Science of Logic*, both heavily underlined. When he discovered that I had studied Hegel and knew German, we withdrew to my basement room where we spent hours sitting on my old red couch comparing passages in Marx and Hegel, checking the English against the original German.[2]

CLR was likewise delighted to find a comrade with such ability. Soon she was living back in New York, working in her father's restaurants and entering into the fevered philosophical research that CLR was leading.

> CLR, Raya, and I were inseparable. In today's New York the sight of us together – a tall, handsome black man flanked by two women, one a somewhat stooped and scholarly Jew and the other a round-faced Asian – might not attract much attention. But in the 1940s a lot of people must have wondered where we came from and what we were about, especially as we entered and left Raya's swank Sutton Place apartment where we often worked ... Our energy was fantastic. We would spend a morning or afternoon writing, talking, and eating and then go home and write voluminous letters to one another extending or enlarging on what we had discussed, sending these around to other members of our tendency in barely legible carbon copies.

There's a famous photo of the three of them together and they are indeed a striking grouping, so different from every other picture of left-wing intellectuals of the time. It was still a very macho world, as Grace Lee remembered:

> One of CLR's great gifts was that he could detect the special abilities and interests of individuals and encourage them to use these to enrich the movement and at the same time enlarge themselves. In those days most radical women worked at secretarial jobs so that their men could be full-time party functionaries. We were proud that in our tendency Raya Dunayevskaya was a co-leader with CLR. I was sometimes considered the third leader of the tendency because I did so much of the research, wrote some of the documents, and typed even more of them, but I saw myself as a junior and a learner, and both CLR and Raya treated me as such.

Of particular importance to CLR were two translations made by Grace and Raya. Grace translated Marx's *Economic and Philosophic Manuscripts*, then Raya found Lenin's *Notes on Hegel*, which CLR saw as vitally important in understanding the revolutionary process.

The Johnson-Forest Tendency soon gathered further key members. There was Marty Glaberman, the organisational pivot. And then there were Lyman and Freddy Paine.

Lyman Paine was another Boston Brahmin, a representative of America's ruling class, and a direct descendent of Robert Treat Paine, one of the signatories to the Declaration of Independence.* He was a tall aristocratic figure, a man who had grown up playing with the Rockefeller children, but had since embraced Trotskyism. Freddy was his second wife. They had met in the movement. She was a working-class Jewish woman, tough and funny, a sometime waitress, dancer and artist's model.

The Paines had a lot to offer the Johnsonites. For starters, they had an apartment in Greenwich Village, at 629 Hudson Street, which the group

* Just like Raya's husband's ancestor John Adams. What are the odds!

used to congregate in. There was also a summer house in Northport on Long Island, and the Paine family also had their own private island up in Maine, the perfect upper-class bohemian summer retreat.

CLR became extremely close to the Paines. According to Grace, he practically lived in their apartment. Freddy was the one person he confided in about his private life, asking her advice as he pursued Constance. Lyman was like a brother to him – Grace speculated that for Lyman CLR replaced the brother he'd lost in the war – and Lyman had such faith in his new friend's genius that he undertook to underwrite CLR's living costs to the tune of $75 a month. This was not a fortune, but allowed CLR a basic standard of living while he concentrated on changing the world.

After his hospitalisation with the stomach ulcer, the Paines had let CLR use their Northport place to convalesce – and it was from there that he wrote to Constance in the autumn of 1943. In the first long letter he wrote to her, after telling her about his illness, he related what he'd been doing with his leisure time. It turned out that even as he was furiously reading Hegel, Marx and Lenin, he was simultaneously immersing himself in American popular culture:

> During the last two years, illness and other difficulties have caused me to spend a certain amount of time at the pictures. I rather despised them – Hollywood I mean. I don't any more. The rubbish I look at would astonish you. I can sit through almost anything. When it is very bad I see why it is bad. I have, on the other hand, seen *Now, Voyager* six times and will see it if necessary six times more. The reason? I work at home. At times I must stop. The only thing that keeps me quiet is the movies.[3]

He goes on to explain what he's learnt from his movie-going habit:

> The movies, even the most absurd Hollywood movies are an expression of life, and being made for the people, who pay their money, they express what the people need – that is what they miss in their own lives ... Like all art, but more than most, the movies are not

> merely a reflection, but an extension of the actual, along the lines which people feel are lacking and possible in the actual. That, my dear, is the complete secret of Hegelian dialectic.

It's a beautifully simple yet deep formulation: what people want, what they glimpse in the movies, is what is 'lacking and possible'. He is thinking of revolution, no doubt. But no doubt he is also thinking of Constance Webb, the girl from Hollywood.

While CLR read, wrote and went to the movies, his fellow comrades were encouraged to take part in 'proletarianisation'. The Workers' Party were uncomfortably aware that they were rather lacking in actual workers. So their cohort of young intellectuals were encouraged to take jobs in factories and plants. Such positions were plentiful during the wartime manufacturing boom and they were newly available to women and Black people, now that a large section of the workforce had gone to war. Grace Lee was one of those who took the leap into factory work, and she found it a revelation:

> Americans of all ethnic groups worked side by side in the defence plants. Women left their kitchens and offices to work on the assembly lines. Radicals and intellectuals seized the opportunity to become 'proletarianized' ... People from different backgrounds exchanged stories of where they had come from and how they viewed their lives, lent each other books, went bowling and drinking after work. The plant was like one big school. This was the first time in US history that racial, educational, sex, class, and age barriers had ever been broken down to such a degree.
>
> The workers who wired and soldered electrical parts with me in the plant were mainly young black women. Before the war most of them had only done domestic work. Now they came into work every day laughing and joking, not only because they were looking forward to the security of a check at the end of the week but because it was exciting to work with modern machinery and to be producing goods that you felt would help your country win the war ... Life in New

> York and all over the United States was exhilarating during World War II. It was a transcending time. The insecurity and despair of the Depression years had been replaced by full employment and a sense of common purpose and hope for a better future.[4]

Racial barriers were being broken down outside the factories too. Black people's social lives had been almost entirely confined to Harlem before the war. Now there were places opening up downtown. Barney Josephson was the pioneer. He had opened Café Society, the first racially integrated nightclub in the US, in Sheridan Square in 1938. A year later it was there that Billie Holiday sang 'Strange Fruit' for the first time in public.* Then, in 1943, a Black Trinidadian woman called Connie Williams opened a restaurant and nightclub called the Calypso in a basement on MacDougal Street, just off Washington Square.

The Calypso – always known as Connie's – became CLR's regular haunt. There's no mention of it in his writings but it must have been enormously frustrating for a man as sociable as CLR to be so restricted in the places he was allowed entrance. The arrival of Connie's was a godsend. It was the ideal place for him to socialise with whomever he wanted, Black or white. In particular, it was a place where a Black man could be seen with a white woman – something that could easily get you lynched in many parts of the US.

The part-time dishwasher at Connie's was a young white merchant seafarer called Stan Weir, who had recently joined the Workers' Party and been introduced to CLR:

> Early in the war, I was taken to his cold-water tenement room in uptown Manhattan to be introduced to him. He was surrounded by piles of newspapers and magazines from around the world and was involved in reading and annotating articles from them as we entered. He was ill, but had just finished a draft of an article on the national liberation movement in Western Europe. Just feet away, Grace Lee Boggs was in the process of typing it at high speed.[5]

* Constance's sometime boyfriend Jack Gilford had been the MC there at the time.

Weir, who would be a lifetime radical, and came from a working-class background, was struck by the way that CLR genuinely believed in the power of workers to lead radical action rather than needing to be led:

> James was the first and only leader in the entire Trotskyist movement, or any socialist movement, from whom I heard discussion of the special form of workers' control which develops in every workplace naturally and informally. He knew of the existence of informal cultures and felt they were the basis from which to broach the entire question of workers' control.

The irony here, of course, is that CLR himself never worked in the factories. Instead he listened to the people who did, comrades like Grace Lee and Marty Glaberman, and took his lessons from their experiences. But Stan Weir didn't just see the CLR of the book-stuffed room, he also saw the night-time CLR who haunted Connie's:

> It wasn't all just politics. In my early twenties, CLR was (and remains) one of the most attractive personalities I had ever met. In fact, in the 1940s he was one of the few leaders that I knew in any movement who from childhood had experienced real social adjustment. A teenage star in cricket, the major sport of Trinidad at the time, he had early developed an ease which allowed him to relate without difficulty in almost any social stratum. I particularly appreciated the enthusiasm with which he ate good food and drank good booze, his eagerness and insight when evaluating moving pictures, and, at a time when we were both single, his ability to initiate discussions with attractive women without formal introduction.
>
> To mind springs a late supper in the Village at Connie's Calypso Restaurant after seeing *The Glass Key* starring Alan Ladd. Our table companions had never heard cinema analysis used so effectively to relate the depths of alienation in our society, but I knew as I switched attention momentarily from them, to myself, and back to James, neither had I.

A regular companion of CLR's at Connie's was Richard Wright. *Native Son* had established Wright as the voice of Black anger in American literature. It had also, as CLR had noted, been written while Wright was still tied to the Communist Party. *Native Son* had crossed over to the mainstream in a way no novel by a Black writer had done before – all the more remarkable given how hard-hitting a book it was. It was a Book of the Month selection, selling two thousand copies a day. Orson Welles had adapted it for the Broadway stage, where it had a successful run in 1941. When CLR met Wright, he was working on his new book, an autobiographical account of his harsh upbringing in the Black South. When it was eventually published, as *Black Boy*, in 1945, it would sell over half a million copies.

Wright was in his mid-thirties, a man who'd come up the hard way in Mississippi and Memphis and Chicago. His success must have impressed on CLR the idea that there wasn't necessarily a complete dichotomy between literature and politics. *Native Son* demonstrated that a novel could be both a work of art and a vehicle of protest. And, of course, its author could make a handsome bourgeois living.

In early 1944 CLR himself was inspired to start work on his first creative writing project in years, a play based on the life of the great Black opponent of slavery Harriet Tubman. He wanted the singer and actress Ethel Waters, who he admired enormously, to star in it. He wrote up a synopsis and Carl Van Vechten got him a meeting with a possible producer, but the producer, unsurprisingly, wanted an actual play script, not just a synopsis, before he would commission it, and the project faded away.

In November he had his first really in-depth talk with Richard Wright, once he heard he had finally broken with the CP. CLR told Constance about it:

> For years I have wanted to talk to him more than to anyone else in America (political and literary) because from his books I felt that he understood the Negro question ... It was a wonderful meeting.[6]

They were in complete agreement, he reported:

> Briefly, the idea is this, that the Negro is 'nationalist' to the heart and perfectly right to be so. His racism, his nationalism, are a necessary means of giving him strength, self-respect and organisation *in order to fight for integration into American society*. It is a perfect example of dialectical contradiction.

This must have been a considerable relief to CLR, as he was at the same time fighting a losing battle with Ernest McKinney to change the line of the Workers' Party.

Through Wright, CLR got to meet an upcoming generation of Black writers looking to make their own mark in Wright's wake, a young Ralph Ellison and the reformed jewel thief Chester Himes among them. They discussed producing a magazine for new Black voices, or getting writers together to create an anthology. A group of them met at Wright's place to discuss it. Once again though the same old disagreements about 'Black nationalism' versus integration slowed progress, and none of these plans ever came to anything. This was largely because Wright's own career was going so well that he had little time to devote to outside projects. He was also getting more and more angry as he discovered that, for all his success, he was still confronted by racism wherever he looked.

He wanted to move from Brooklyn to Greenwich Village with his white Jewish wife Ellen and their daughter Julia. He identified a house to buy, but discovered that he would only be allowed to do it if the deal was done in the name of their white lawyer. He was livid but reluctantly agreed. Once the deal was finally done CLR would meet Wright at his new house, or around the corner at the Calypso. Sometimes he would bring Constance Webb to the Calypso. He was still determinedly wooing her, though with no visible success as she was moving from boyfriend to boyfriend with abandon, while telling CLR he was a father figure.

Connie's saw a remarkable variety of important Black patrons. Richard Wright brought Black American intellectuals and writers there. CLR would bring Pan-Africanists, like the young Kwame Nkrumah or Eric Williams. By then Williams had expanded his thesis, with CLR's help, into a book that was about to be published – the groundbreaking study *Capitalism and Slavery*, a book that made the highly influential argument that it was the slave trade and slavery that actually drove the development of industrial capitalism.

And if all that intellectual ferment wasn't enough, what no one realised was that there was one more remarkable talent in the room, working as a waiter: the nineteen-year-old James Baldwin (or 'the outcast little Negro switch', as CLR called him in a letter to Constance).

It's worth taking stock of CLR's life once more, as it was in 1944 and 1945, the end of the war years: where he lived, what his political activity was, and what was happening in his private life.

First his living quarters: in the summer of 1944 he left Harlem (which had become a more difficult place to live, or at least to invite white friends to, following the riots of summer 1943). For the next six months or so his address was given as Sutton Place, presumably Raya Dunayevskaya's apartment. Raya's husband Bernard was a man CLR admired, both for his character – 'a man of *exceptional* ability'[7] – and for the way in which he supported Raya's work without agreeing with her politics. Some time early in 1945 CLR moved out to the Bronx, to an apartment on Chisholm Street which offered more space than his previous homes, and was in a racially mixed neighbourhood.

His political activity next. Aside from the abortive plans with Richard Wright, he was still essentially taken up with the Johnson-Forest Tendency and the Workers' Party. He was writing a weekly column in the party's popular newspaper, *Labour Action*, and regular longer pieces for the *New International*. The Johnson-Forest group was his real focus. Though they were still small in number, they were becoming ever more excited by their political work, as Grace Lee remembered:

> We were not discouraged by the smallness of our group. Energized by our contact with the workers in the plant and the ideas that we were absorbing from our studies of Marx, Hegel, Lenin, and past revolutions, we moved about as if we had discovered the secret of the universe. In any gathering you could tell us by the stars in our eyes.[8]

The mainstream of the party, however, were increasingly critical of the Johnsonites. CLR, in particular, was attacked for his sweeping historical generalisations and grandiose political claims. On occasion it's easy to see their point, especially in the pieces he contributed during the course of the war. He persisted in arguing that the European carnage was fertile ground for revolutionary activity, leading him to make morally bankrupt statements like this:

> To say that Hitler has hurled society back, in any sense except the purely agitational, is wrong. He has so contributed to the ruin of bourgeois society in Europe as to bring the socialist revolution immeasurably nearer.[9]

His fellow party intellectual Albert Glotzer (yet another former secretary of Trotsky) justly ridiculed him for such foolishness. Such criticism failed to dent the belief of the Johnsonites, though. Grace Lee again:

> We were convinced that by being in tune with what the American workers were thinking and doing we had become part of the continuing historical movement of those at the bottom of society to take control over their own lives. The workers, CLR used to insist, didn't need an organization to organize them. They would organize themselves. In *Notes on Dialectics* CLR took this idea of spontaneity to the extreme limit. 'The task is to abolish organization,' he wrote. 'The task is to call for, to teach, to illustrate, to develop spontaneity – the free creative activity of the proletariat.'[10]

This is utopian thinking, of course. It's a dream of politics as it should be, not really a reflection of the reality of America towards the end of the Second World War. It's the kind of thinking that would come into its own a generation later, as the dreamers came briefly to the fore in the sixties. It's no wonder that the hidebound Shachtmanites scoffed. This wasn't a rally or a strike, not conventional political activity, this was a dozen young intellectuals sitting around in an apartment in Greenwich Village.

Ernest McKinney, in particular, was implacably opposed to CLR. According to Constance Webb, he used to do an impersonation of CLR. He would wrap a scarf around his head and have his colleagues sit round him in a circle, mimicking CLR's adoring acolytes. CLR attempted to start an independent Negro Bureau within the Workers' Party. McKinney shot him down. It was starting to become clear that the Johnsonites' time within the party was limited.

CLR's personal life was also building towards a crisis. He was never wanting for female company, and had affairs with some of the women in the Johnson-Forest circle. He had a longer relationship with a woman he only identifies, in a memoir, as a married member of the Black middle class. This was very likely Gloria Ramsey Marques, the wife of his friend Dr Cecil Marques.* According to CLR, she was a pragmatist happy to have an affair but unwilling to commit any further.

CLR wanted more than that. And so his attention was ever more fixed on the woman he'd been chasing for years. Rarely can anyone have been pursued quite as single-mindedly as CLR pursued Constance Webb through the summer of 1944. Although she was in New York and they would meet up in person regularly, he wrote to her constantly. Even in an edited collection, his letters to her from that year alone stretch to at least sixty thousand words – the length of a short novel.

He writes to her about Shakespeare and acting, about poetry from Spender to Mayakovsky, and about Marxism; he calls her 'the most amazing creature I have ever met in my life' and compares her to, of all people, Lillie Langtry, Edward VII's mistress.[11] She sends him poems and he critiques them, admires them excessively, and sends her a poem by Shelley to learn from. Intriguingly, he also suggests that 'in European literature there is one man worth your while. He is Burns.' In July he reads *Moby-Dick* and is overwhelmed by it.

* Evidence for this claim comes from the fact that the woman in question is identified by Constance Webb as being the wife of a Harlem doctor, and much later CLR listed a 'Gloria' as the important woman in his life at that time. Gloria Marques fits the bill very neatly.

He writes about sensual love, how it is unappreciated in the modern world, except perhaps by some young Americans and D. H. Lawrence ('the French are interested in love too, but there is an atmosphere of "gallantry" with an undercurrent of "vice" which is repulsive'). CLR suggests that the old pagan sensuality will come back to the world again. And, unsurprisingly, he has identified in Constance a great capacity for sensuality!

In the midst of all this he sends her a long letter headed 'Autobiography of a Man by Him'. He starts with a jokey introduction – 'The author wishes his identity to be kept secret. He therefore regrets that everybody knows who he is' and so on – before launching into an account of his childhood. It's his first attempt at autobiography and probably his most honest. The most striking revelation is as follows:

> I didn't love my parents. I loved nobody. I didn't hate them. I had no grievances. I just didn't feel to them as I was supposed to. Once when my mother was near death I cried because everyone was crying and I thought I ought to cry. But I knew I was faking.

There's an awful irony in this, as just a few months later he wrote Constance another letter, this time headlined 'Portrait (Partial of a Man)'.* For the first while he talks about how tired he is after a long day spent wrestling with Kant's *Critique of Pure Reason*, then watching Hazel Scott play at the Roxy before a showing of a new movie, the classic film noir *Laura*. It's only at the end that he adds this postscript: 'You know I heard this afternoon that my mother died and was buried a few days ago.' And it turns out that he loved her more than he realised:

> I had always looked forward to going back and seeing her once more. I was her eldest son, wayward, but people always talked to me about her and she loved me very much. I have not cried and I shall go about my business as usual – but something in me has gone. A hope I cherished and a little, a tiny flame … In these few hours I have discovered

* In *Special Delivery* the letter is incorrectly dated as 1945. The true date can be identified by the fact that Hazel Scott only appeared on a bill with the film *Laura* in October 1944.

> something. Life is so hard. It batters you into shape, toughens you. When your mother dies it's bad for you. Another tie to the ordinary things of life goes. Take care of yourself and you write your mother often.

By November, in the wake of this bereavement, even CLR is tiring a little of this so far fruitless courtship. 'I am tired in my bones,' he writes and even allows that he knows there is madness in this one-sided passion – 'At my age, a serious man, shaken up and torn from my tranquillity by a slip of a girl.'

In 1945 the pace of the letters slows but their emotional range is greater. Early in the year Constance tells him that he needs to accept the futility of his quest, she doesn't want to hurt him. CLR writes back with a humorous broadside:

> No more of this 'You will be hurt' business. Take it to its logical conclusion. Constance (solemnly): 'Nello, you will be hurt.' Nello: 'What! Hurt *badly*!!' Constance: 'Very very badly.' Nello: 'My God, if that is so, if I am going to be *really* hurt, then I had better retreat and save my precious hide.' Constance: 'You are very wise, my dear *dear* Nello. I feel so relieved.'

By that summer, though, he has tired of the joking and puts his cards firmly on the table. The war is approaching its apocalyptic end in Japan and a new chapter for the world is evidently about to begin. During this time Constance has been through several men, she has modelled with some success, and joined a repertory company in upstate New York, where she is acting in several shows. CLR had come to see her and had been less than impressed. He had thought her poems had promise. Her acting makes him fear that he has wasted his attentions on just another vain, pretty girl, 'a frivolous, thoughtless, irresponsible young fool' he calls her at one point. Her last letter has infuriated him: 'Don't scribble inanities.' In his next letter, written a few days later, he goes further:

> You stood on that stage amid the other performers, forlorn, lonely and miserable. I am on the whole a poor psychologist, but you, you

are my washpot, to use a phrase of [Arnold] Bennett. I see through you, not everything, but plenty . . . Now you have to get out of all that and the first thing . . . is to get out of your attitude to me . . . If you cannot do that, for your own benefit, then we will soon be episodes in each other's past.

The irony here is that while one might suppose that the author of all these amorous outpourings was a lonely pining figure, that was far from the truth. He even tells Constance as much in one long angry letter: 'It's time I stopped philandering around and dreaming dreams of you and seriously begin to think of someone else.'

In other letters he tells her about Louise Cripps and his estranged wife Juanita. He even tells her about his attempt to go out with Lyman Paine's widowed sister-in-law, in a less than gentlemanly passage:

She needs to go to a hairdresser and get a good hair-do to begin with. She is snobbish too, but she is a solid person – and could be very attractive. I talked to her the other day for two or three hours then asked her to go out with me. She thought it over and then in the cool direct way I admire her type for – she said 'No. You are slick and insidious. You put across your ideas and I find myself agreeing without knowing.'

Come October 1945, the correspondence picked up something of its old rhythm, with a series of long pedagogic letters. But by the new year, February 1946, he is making his intentions towards Constance about as clear as can be:

You playfully said the other day that I had pursued you. I laughed inside. I have not 'pursued' you. I have for all sorts of deep internal reason not pursued you. If you will allow the remark I am a skilful, resourceful, incredibly successful pursuer. But always such folks come to a bad end. You make me feel . . . I want to be good and get rid of falseness and superficiality and be good – be honest and have a fine life.

He follows this by discussing a poem they have both recently read, Walter Benton's *This is My Beloved*, which had caused a storm with its frank eroticism. He uses it as a springboard to lay out his own thoughts on sex, in fairly graphic detail.

This direct approach struck home. Constance started to dwell on what her real feelings for CLR were. Why had she resisted his approaches for so long? Before she could come to a conclusion, another letter arrived, this time with a very different approach:

> Now to me and you. First me. Look at me,
>
> I am 45.
>
> I am not a healthy person.
>
> My hands shake.
>
> My beard is terribly grey. I can very often look my age.
>
> I don't know when I will be yanked up from here and told to get out with no possibility of ever coming back again.
>
> I am a Negro, which means that an association with me will be tough for anyone.
>
> My life with women in the past has not been good for me, I am just beginning to understand.

This cut to the core. Constance was finally forced to admit that her great reservation was simply that CLR was Black – and not because of what the world thought, but because of what she herself thought. She was horrified at the realisation, and steeled herself to tell him when they met for dinner at Connie's:

> We left the restaurant and walked slowly through Washington Square and still I couldn't tell him about my dreadful discovery. We were nearly out of the park when I forced myself to turn back and ask that we sit down for a while on one of the benches. Taking a deep breath I told him what I had discovered, that I was resisting him because he was black. It took so much strength to get the words out I thought I would choke. When I finished my story, Nello began to laugh … 'Listen sugar pie, do you think I didn't know how you felt?'[12]

And that was that. Within days they were at last lovers.

Chapter Fourteen

At first it was all CLR had wanted, all he had spent nearly eight years wishing into being. He could now write letters addressed like this – 'To the loveliest girl in the world. No Stamp. No address needed' – letters that sing with his at last requited love.[1]

In a month or so Constance moved into the apartment in the Bronx. She describes it in detail in her autobiography: a one-bedroom place on the top floor of a purpose-built apartment building, once smart but now fading. CLR was the only Black tenant in the building, but the neighbourhood as a whole was mixed.

'He was inordinately proud of his home,' she noted.[2] He told her that he had acquired a mop and broom (for his acolytes to use rather than himself, but still). Like all CLR's living spaces it was sparse and spartan except in the matter of books and papers. The couch was just a mattress on the floor plus cushions, but there was a phonograph and a collection of mostly classical records, plus a few calypso sides. There was a typewriter – again for his acolytes to use – and there was always rum and Angostura bitters.

Once she moved in, she was immediately aware that CLR came with an entourage. Members of the Johnson-Forest Tendency were liable to appear at any time of day or night. She managed to persuade him that they should have some time to themselves, and so he organised a two-week holiday from politics. This was idyllic:

> Nello occasionally called Raya to see if there was news but otherwise we spent the time alone. He played calypso music and taught me the dance. We listened to music for hours on end. We sat or laid on the mattress, holding hands and just being quietly content. He talked about cricket, said he had been a good bowler but not very good as a batsman. We went to the opera to see and hear Don

Giovanni, and once to the New York Symphony. Nello would want to make a real evening of these events so we would have dinner out in a restaurant, almost always Chinese places because other places would not serve blacks.

At home they would drink rum and bitters over crushed ice and CLR would cook steak, or fish and rice and callaloo. In this honeymoon period Constance even learnt to make CLR's preferred breakfast, a mix of blackened bacalao with bread, Bisquick, milk and butter. She also began to adjust to the fact that whenever they went out together they would be stared at, mostly with hostility. CLR dealt with this everyday racism imperiously:

He simply raised his head higher than ever – it was always high – tilted his chin upward and became engrossed in his own thoughts. Nello claimed that he was not aware of the hostile reactions of many people to our presence, even when their faces reddened and the skin, particularly around the neck, swelled like that of a turkey gobbler.[3]

To Constance he offered some advice, notable for its lack of bitterness, and a very clear illustration of his instinctive reluctance to give racism the time of day:

'People are interested, not always angry, at the sight of us. We are two distinguished-looking citizens, appear dramatic, and' (he would pause and lift a finger) 'they are burning up to know what we are about! Watch the women especially,' he advised. 'Most of them are jealous of you. Not just for your beauty which is, Lord help us, enough, but you are a woman in charge of her life. You are obviously living the way you want to live, ready to tell anyone who interferes "go to hell".'

Once the fortnight's holiday was up, CLR was off to work from ten in the morning to ten at night, with Raya and Grace or the Paines. Then came another routine: CLR's bath-time dinner.

> While he undressed and drew his bath water, I prepared a tray with Italian or Jewish salami in thin slices, Italian or French bread, a bottle of Guinness Stout, and a glass. I would then sit on the lid of the toilet and hand him in turn, a slice of bread and salami and then the stout. After a few bites and sips of stout he would tell me what he had accomplished during the day.[4]

None of the comrades took easily to Constance. She felt that they saw her as an airheaded model who was distracting their leader from his great work. This was a view not untinged with jealousy. Both Raya and Grace were on some level in love with CLR, while Constance suspected that Lyman's generosity to CLR came from a latent crush.

Raya was the most friendly:

> At least Raya was able to hide her disapproval because she was essentially a warm, passionate woman. I think she was also somewhat like a Jewish mother, and loving Nello as she did, she wanted him to be happy.

Grace, however, was another matter. 'Grace Lee hated me and having to hide her feelings must have been torment,' wrote Constance in her autobiography. She goes on to describe Grace in such vindictive terms that it quite clear the feeling was mutual: she calls her 'deluded and egotistical and desperate to imprint herself on history'.

It was soon clear to Constance that she had walked in on a set of relationships which were a lot more akin to a cult than any regular political group:

> Raya and Grace were Nello's handmaidens. He liked to be waited on, lying on his back on the couch, propped up on pillows. They brought him his slippers, took off his shoes, made him eggnogs, and cleaned the apartment, including the toilet.

When another member of the group, Ike Blackman, came to the apartment, Constance was disconcerted to see the visitor talking to CLR as he lay in the bath, and then scrubbing his back for him.

Worse yet were the reminders that CLR had scarcely been living a monk-like existence while wooing Constance. They had only been living together for a couple of weeks when a woman came knocking on the door at half past two in the morning. CLR let her in and talked to her in the living room while Constance lay in bed. Afterwards he explained that she was one of two sisters he'd been sexually involved with, and she'd come to see him because she was having trouble with her husband and needed advice. This was probably Gloria Ramsey Marques, as he told Constance that she was 'married to a well-known Harlem doctor'.[5]

The absolute worst of it, however, was CLR's approach to these problems. 'He simply ignored whatever he did not want to deal with. There was no way that one could get him to talk; he became a stone wall.'

Constance, still only twenty-six, soon tired of this life, stuck out in the Bronx on her own with a lover who worked all hours and refused to talk about the things that bothered her. 'My isolation soon became unbearable, particularly when Nello went into his withdrawal stages. After several months of silent treatment, my frustration grew so strong I had to get away.'

Over the next few months she would go away on her own. She would visit the Paines' Long Island house or take solo trips up the coast. Each time, CLR would write and tell how much he missed her and go back to being the eloquent lover he was on paper (at one point he even tells that 'you are my personal proletariat' – surely words to gladden any young woman's heart!).[6]

And then she would come back and it would be the same as ever. After a while she persuaded CLR that they should move into Manhattan. Grace and her brother had adjoining apartments on Orchard Street. Constance and CLR agreed to swap apartments for a time with Grace's brother and his wife. This was an improvement inasmuch as CLR spent more time at home, but the Lower East Side neighbourhood was dilapidated and borderline dangerous, and having Grace next door was a very mixed blessing.

They did have their own circle of friends outside the group. There were the Wrights, Dick and Ellen; Ralph Ellison and his wife Rose;

Meyer Shapiro; CLR's old protégé Eric Williams; and his old London friend Ernest Borneman* among them. Constance was particularly close to a bohemian couple called the Raskins. She'd met Eugene Raskin, a professor of architecture at Columbia, while she was acting in summer stock, and he'd introduced her to his wife, Francesca.†

Meanwhile, the Johnsonites were preparing to split from the Workers' Party. The reason this time was that Shachtman failed to share CLR's belief that America was on the brink of revolution.

While CLR's pursuit of Constance had been coming to its resolution through late 1945 and 1946, there had been seismic events in the world. The war had ended with the bombing of Hiroshima and Nagasaki and the horrors of the German concentration camps had been revealed. For many on the left, especially Jewish leftists like Shachtman, these were devastating developments. They had still held on to the hope that the end of the war and the return of the soldiers would lead to a socialist uprising, but nothing of the kind transpired. CLR, however, a man who had paid oddly little attention to either the Bomb or the Holocaust, still believed that radical change was imminent.

Shachtman, by contrast, had noted that while the end of the war had failed to inspire an immediate worldwide revolution, it had, for example, led to the election victory of the Labour Party in the UK. His new, pragmatic analysis was that the best bet for radicals was to work with bourgeois socialist parties.

CLR and his comrades were enraged. With Raya and Grace he was preparing an alternative manifesto – 'The Invading Socialist Society'. Meanwhile, their erstwhile adversary James P. Cannon had just made a speech to the SWP convention on 'The Coming American

* Ironically, despite being an exile from Nazi Germany, when the war broke out Borneman was deported to a detention camp in Canada as an enemy alien. He was released after a little while and started working in film in Canada and New York.

† The Raskins are an interesting couple. Gene taught architecture but together they were a folk-singing duo, featuring Gene's songs. His most popular number, 'Those Were the Days', was covered by Mary Hopkin and became a huge worldwide hit in 1969.

Revolution'. The Johnsonites started to make clandestine negotiations to return to the SWP.

To help this process along, CLR went on a national tour in early 1947, looking to persuade party members to join him in this reverse breakaway. As he travelled around – mostly by plane this time – he wrote to Constance on a more or less daily basis. Again distance allowed him to express his feelings, and acknowledge his failings. 'Over and over again I feel an emotion for you, to say I love you, or you look wonderful, or that was profound, or clever – I feel it. I don't say it . . . I end by shutting my mouth and going on with my business. That's me.'[7]

On 21 April, writing from Cleveland, he made his biggest commitment yet:

> We should get married. You know why I hesitate? Because I'm terrified that after a little while you'll feel trapped again. That I don't make you happy, that I mean well but haven't got it in me. For my part I'd be the happiest man in the world to be Mr Constance Webb tomorrow.

Exactly a month later, on 21 May 1947,* the two of them took a bus to Fort Lee, New Jersey, to marry.† They told no one about their plans and the ceremony itself was less than romantic:

> Our witnesses were two policemen who could barely control their rage and consternation at this black and white union. They swelled at the neck of their uniforms and their faces were red throughout the short ceremony. At the end of the brief rite we kissed hurriedly – on my part, in defiance – and left the ominous atmosphere as fast as we could.[8]

* Constance Webb give the date as May 1946 in her autobiography and this has been generally accepted, However, the New Jersey records revealed that the actual date was a year later.

† CLR had by now obtained a 'mail order' divorce from Juanita.

Afterwards they went to visit Richard and Ellen Wright at their flat in Greenwich Village. They drank champagne, and Ellen had made a cake. Then the newlyweds went to a French restaurant in the Village. This was a risk – there were no other non-white people there – and CLR went into his shell, refusing to speak at all.

It was a pointer towards what was to come. Marriage failed to work any magic for CLR. Again and again he would retreat into silence. Soon things came to a head. At the end of a weekend in which CLR had spoken not a single word to her, Constance started playing Billie Holiday's 'Love Me or Leave Me', loudly singing along. Still CLR refused to react. The only result was that their sex life came to an abrupt end:

> We'd been living together not quite a year and quite suddenly Nello became impotent. Being a child in many respects, and never, ever having experienced such an event, I believed it was my fault, some lack, or that he had lost interest. He, being the strange withdrawn man that he is, would not even touch me. (Obviously, he was panicky and worried and brooding. It was a new experience for him too.) One night I tried to comfort him by actually placing his arms around me, he remained frozen and pulled away. He wouldn't talk. It was agonising and I shouted at him, trying to make him answer. At last, he got out of bed and went into his study down the hall. After a moment I followed. He sat rigid, staring into space utterly deadpan. I sat on his lap, put my arms around him and sobbed until my body trembled. He still did not touch me, just sat like a stone. It was one of the worst moments in my life.[9]

Soon Constance had had enough and moved out for a while. She went to stay with two party comrades, Hank and Cuppy. This was a poor idea. A few days later Cuppy got a call, telling her that CLR needed some typing assistance:

> She did not return until about eight in the evening, when she bounced into my room and said she had been in bed with Nello . . .

> I'll never forget her first words: 'I threw my panties in his face to tease him!'[10]

This, unsurprisingly, was more than Constance could stand. It was clear that New York was CLR's town, peopled with his devoted followers – and plenty of them were dying to take Constance's place at his side. So when an old friend from California, Lionel Steinberg, invited her to come back out west, she immediately agreed, letting CLR know that she wanted a divorce, just three months after they married.

While Constance was in California, touring Lionel Steinberg's vineyards and swimming in his pool, CLR was frantically trying to discover her whereabouts. No one in the party knew, unsurprisingly enough, but it took CLR a while to think of trying her non-party friends. Eventually he called Francesca Raskin. She gave CLR the address in California and advised him 'to forget all the politics and treat [her] like a woman'.[11]

He immediately sent Constance a long telegram, beginning with the words 'After a hard year I understand myself and so can understand you.' He goes on to tell her he will come out to Los Angeles in two weeks' time, and begs her to hold back on the divorce, as it would potentially impact on his immigration status:*

> All that you wanted to hear I want to say. All that you wanted me to do I want to do . . . I have missed you and have suffered just like any petty-bourgeois existentialist while I maintained a front outside. I have never really loved you until now.[12]

CLR flew to Los Angeles in early October, called Constance from the airport, and they agreed to see each other the following day at the Gogols' house, where he would be staying.

That night CLR wrote down an extraordinary stream of consciousness in which he tried to prepare himself for seeing Constance by

* An unfortunate effect of getting married had been to remind the immigration authorities of his existence.

absolutely baring his soul.[13] It's a remarkable piece for a man like CLR to write. Or perhaps not remarkable at all – CLR, by now, knew his weakness, knew that he might find it impossible to say the things he felt out loud. So he decided to set them down on paper.

The document begins like this – 'Terrified I was too old for you. You *cried* when we slept together' – then it travels through sexual rapture and apologies for the Orchard Street apartment to self-recrimination – 'English gentleman / James is against gentleness' – and on to sexual dysfunction – 'Sexual fear / I never had it / You are . . . / *Terrified I was too old for you / Financial worry . . . / The old me was destroyed and there were sometimes antagonisms passions hates / My sexual life went to pieces . . . My political life was threatened.*'

Then there's the marriage.

He swerves from self-confidence – 'I know how powerful I am. I know that once you feel secure you will sacrifice everything' – to, in the following lines, absolute abjection:

> No friends
> I was badly beaten as little boy. Father fierce Puritan
> Women I never trusted
> Never wanted to be leader
> worthwhile . . . wherever I went always a leader.
> Never spoken to anyone. I have changed.*

The next morning, they met and talked. The day after that they went for a drive and talked some more. CLR, as he suspected he might, failed to open up. But he did give Constance an envelope that contained both a new theoretical piece he had been working on, on the theory of state capitalism, and also the notes he had written for her, baring his soul.

Unsurprisingly, it was the notes rather than the theory that won Constance back. She came to stay with him at the Gogols' and then

* The most intriguing part of the screed is the very end, in which he suggests Constance write to Pamela, Fredric Warburg's wife, because she 'saw through me': 'tell her that the shell is broken and the man below has appeared'.

they went to San Francisco visit two young comrades, Filomena Daddario, a working-class girl from New York with a great love of popular music, and her husband Willie Gorman. Gorman was emerging as CLR's protégé, a brilliant young man with a club foot, the son and grandson of Talmudic scholars. He was perhaps the only person who CLR would regularly defer to, whose intellect he believed equal to, if not superior to, his own.

Unfortunately, Willie was also mentally unstable and they lived in a whites-only neighbourhood, so the stay was uncomfortable. Before long the newly reunited lovers went back to Los Angeles, where Constance discovered that yet another of her comrades, this time a close friend, had slept with CLR during their time apart. Nevertheless, Constance decided to let it lie and she returned to New York with CLR. They moved back into the apartment in the Bronx and set about remaking their marriage.

Just as he was trying to get his marriage back, CLR was busy with the political split. That summer the Johnson-Forest Tendency left the Workers' Party. They spent a few months as an independent entity before moving en masse into the SWP. During the period of independence that autumn, they produced several key documents.

The first is what they called a 'Balance Sheet' summing up their grievances with the Workers' Party and their enthusiasm for the SWP. There was also a pamphlet called *The American Worker*, produced by an auto worker called Phil Singer (using the pseudonym Paul Romano) with help from Grace Lee; and then a kind of political manifesto called *The Invading Socialist Society*, which concluded with this rousing call to arms:

> Never was the proletariat so ready for the revolutionary struggle, never was the need for it so great, never was it more certain that the proletarian upheaval, however long delayed, will only the more certainly take humanity forward in the greatest leap forward it has hitherto made . . . hundreds of millions of people are crying out for an expression which only the socialist revolution can give. There is no power on earth that can suppress them. They will not be suppressed.

It is *The American Worker* that holds the most enduring interest, for all that it's a far less ambitious work. CLR had encouraged Romano to write a diary of his working life. The result is a quietly devastating portrait of the alienation and violence of factory work. It made little impression in the US at the time, but the following summer Grace went to Paris as a representative of the Johnson-Forest Tendency at the Second World Congress of the Fourth International (such invitations were a perk of once more being part of the largest Trotskyist party in the US).

While there she made contact with a brilliant young Greek intellectual called Cornelius Castoriadis (party name Pierre Chaulieu), who was living in Paris. He was working as an economist for the OECD and had devised his own critique of the Soviet Union as a bureaucratic capitalist state. He had founded a group called Socialisme ou Barbarie, whose politics were very much in line with the Johnson-Forests. He was particularly interested in *The American Worker* and his group would translate it into French (and subsequently into Italian). Grace thoroughly enjoyed the trip:

> I spent a wonderful four months in Paris, mostly socializing with Chaulieu and the members of his group. I spoke French poorly but I could read and understand it fairly well, and it was a pleasure to hear discussions about political and philosophical ideas in French. In fact, I enjoyed these comrades so much that when Richard Wright invited me to spend a day with him and his wife visiting the flea market, I declined because I was looking forward to an afternoon with Chaulieu's group. I have always felt more comfortable around rank and filers than around celebrities.[14]

Doubtless CLR would have relished the chance to revisit Paris, but he had a new and urgent problem to deal with – the renewed attention of the immigration authorities. He had been arrested in Los Angeles and was on bail in New York while his case was investigated. He hoped that his marriage to an American would keep him safe, but now the FBI had a file on him as a potential subversive it wasn't going to be easy. By April he was under surveillance.

Around this time CLR and Constance decided they wanted to have a baby. No sooner was Constance pregnant, though, than there was bad news on the immigration front. The US authorities refused to accept that CLR and Constance were legally married, as the mail-order divorce he'd obtained to end his marriage to Juanita was inadmissible.

They were advised that CLR would have to divorce Juanita properly, and then he and Constance should remarry immediately. However, getting a quick divorce wasn't going to be easy. The best option seemed to be for CLR to travel to Reno, where a divorce could be obtained after six weeks. To make matters worse, Constance couldn't go with him, as interracial marriage was illegal in Nevada. She would have to stay in New York, pregnant and alone.

CLR arrived in Nevada on 2 August 1948. Reno is in effect Las Vegas's little sibling. Back then it was a hick town with a few casinos and a sideline in quickie divorces. It was also a hard-core Jim Crow town. After asking around, CLR found a room in a Black parson's house, and a local woman who would cook his meals for him.

He was in a poor state, mentally and physically. He wrote to Constance most days and at first confessed he was unable to write or read seriously. Instead, he was reading the stories in *True Romance* magazines in bed. Naturally, being the man he was, he was fascinated by them, finding them more interesting than the stories in literary magazines:

> Here it seems the proletariat scores heavily on the petty bourgeoisie. People sleep before marriage, wives leave husbands, etc., live, come back; psychoanalysis is rampant; they are by no means literature but they are very very indicative. They are a curious grasping at the real problems . . .[15]

After a day or two spent exploring Reno and meeting some local Black people who took him for a drive around a nearby lake, stopping now and then to drink whisky and tell dirty jokes, he found a sympathetic lawyer, Charlotte Hunter,* who agreed to handle his case. She suggested they have lunch in the whites-only Trocadero, confident that no one would dare throw her out, but CLR was keen to avoid drawing attention to himself and took her to the one Black restaurant in town, a café-cum-nightspot-cum-gambling parlour called Club Harlem.

Charlotte Hunter asked CLR if he wanted to work while he was in Reno. Perhaps he could give some lectures? CLR told her that he would be happy to work but he definitely didn't want to draw attention by giving lectures. Hunter made some calls and found him both a job and a place to live.

Which is how CLR James came to spend three months living at the Pyramid Dude Ranch, thirty miles north of Reno, next to a lovely lake in the middle of an Indian reservation.

The owner, a sometime rodeo rider, a buckin' bronco man called Drackert, agreed to hire CLR as a handyman despite his reservations about the usefulness of overeducated employees. He would receive board and lodging and a small wage. CLR told Constance about his new responsibilities:

> I am gardener. I clean the yard – leaves and paper. I see after the water jets, for irrigation keeps the whole place alive. I mow the lawns and clean up the mess. I help put portmanteaux on the station wagon. I am a handy man. I eat in the kitchen with the cook, the cowboy, two waitresses, the pantry-man and the house-maid. The food is good. I dry dishes twice a day ... I am out in the sun and the dust for hours. I am very stiff sometimes – bending down constantly. *But it is good for me.*[16]

It was certainly quite a change for a man used to having his acolytes scrub his floors and his back alike. But for these first few weeks it was a change he relished:

* The daughter of Ukrainian Jews, Charlotte Hunter was one of the first female attorneys in Nevada. An instinctive liberal, she represented those who needed help at flexible rates. Clearly a character, she said of her first husband, Max, 'He was a saxophone-player, what more can I say?' Later, CLR would recommend her to Eric Williams, and she handled his divorce too.

> Down here I am in the open, sun and the lake and physical exercise and dirt and sweat and fatigue. God! If you knew what the afternoon shower is like. I haven't had that feeling for fifteen years. And we have not had it. We haven't been anywhere, walked on beaches. Somehow sweetie, I have to live a more active life. I'll be better in myself and better for you ... I know how different things would be for us if we could live together every now and then as I am living here.

He also enjoyed being in a place where no one knew who he was, where he was just another hired hand, albeit a rather unusual one. He wrote to Constance about the various characters he worked with. Budd, the Indian cowboy; Joe, the Filipino chef; Ramona and Mary the waitresses – evidently watching their lives with avid curiosity. In these letters you can again see the man who wrote *Minty Alley*, the bookish fly on the wall in the midst of the turbulent dramas of regular working people.

As the season came to a close in September, so too did his yard-work. Drackert said he could stay on as a paying guest for $40 a week. CLR was happy to take the offer, but somewhat challenged when it came to paying for it. He had bought some money with him and had earned a little from his work, but before long he was writing to Lyman Paine, asking for funds.

When he received the money he wrote Lyman a long letter explaining, among other things, the reason why he came to be in such dire need of cash. It turned out that it was a common enough reason for visitors to Nevada:

> Whenever possible I rush into Reno, for this place is absolutely isolated ... And I play the machine and lose. I am a gambler now. I needed jeans, clothes, shoes and extra expenses, legal ... all this makes a nice mess. To be quite frank, I could have bought many things with the money I played in the slot machine, but there you have the whole messy, sordid, Zola-esque details.[17]

Back at the ranch, though, CLR was writing feverishly. He was still wrestling with understanding Hegel, and out there in the desert he felt he had finally cracked the secrets of the dialectic. So he started work on a series of epic letters that would add up to a book-length elucidation of Hegel's dialectic with reference to the political thinking of Lenin and Trotsky. As soon as he finished each section, he would send it off to his comrades back in New York. He wrote at a furious pace, as he told Lyman:

> I found that . . . I could work here as I have not worked for some dozen years. I don't know what the reasons all are, but the work has amazed me. I could do 10,000 words a day without stopping to put a comma.

He didn't stop going to Reno and gambling, though. He wrote to Constance a week later:

> As I told you, I went gambling, hoping to make a lot of money. It is not as stupid as it sounds. But I made an awful fool of myself. After some heavy losses at the start, over and over again, three or four times running, I have won between $25 and $40 and if there had been a train I would have gone home. But there wasn't, there was nowhere I could go, and I just played and played and lost every penny back.[18]

In the same letter, clearly written immediately after a desperate phone call, he acknowledged that this was not the behaviour of a man in balance. 'I am going through something,' he tells her, before explaining himself in terms that owe much more to his Trinidadian childhood than Hegel or Lenin:

> In many ways I think I have crossed a great milestone in my own life down here. I knew for years something was wrong somewhere. The evil spirit, the demon, fought to hold me in the old groove. I know now exactly what the writers in Scripture wrote about, they and their demons.

Being out in Nevada gave him time to reflect on his life in New York. Even as he worked on the dialectic, trying to tame it for his comrades' better understanding, he was wondering if they weren't wasting their time. To Lyman he wrote that, 'There is a terrible discrepancy between the range, the boldness, the philosophical basis, the concreteness of our ideas, and the miserable little places we do hold, both as a group and individually.'[19] He reiterated these thoughts to Constance: 'Our ideas and plans and perspectives are so big, our work, and our concrete sphere is so small.'[20]

His stay in Nevada was extended from six weeks to three months because of delays in getting divorce papers served to Juanita in Trinidad. CLR kept on grappling with the dialectic but still struggled to find his equilibrium. He was evidently receiving letters from Constance asking that he change, become a better, more present husband, and these demands were causing him to look deep into himself. He had always had – and would continue to have – a loathing of psychoanalysis, but in the throes of what seems to have been both a marital and midlife crisis he wrote the following:

> I remember a picture with Ingrid B and Gregory P [he's referring to Hitchcock's *Spellbound*] in which it was made clear that G.P. would be angry with the woman who was forcing him to dig down into the buried past, but that was the only way . . . I know now why people go to psychiatrists (which does not in the least lessen my desire to stick a long pin into the whole tribe).

Finally, in early November, he had his divorce and could return to New York. He told Constance to make arrangements for a second wedding as soon as possible. After that, he told her to investigate a resort called Bear Mountain where they could have a honeymoon together in the country air. But even as he wrote, he knew he was not out of the woods:

> I wonder when I return, how it will be. The demon is waiting for me. I am preparing, As long as I am nervous I know something is

> wrong . . . You should know the long, long solitary hours I have spent, reading – reading – reading, thinking, writing. Since I was about four years old. It is the ingrained pattern of a lifetime. You must talk to me . . . For our sake, for your sake and for my own, or I shall sit there, apparently doing my business, but strained and tense and frightened inside. And my sex life too. I feel that it will get itself right, the more we break down, or rather tear away all the barriers, the restraints, the nervousness, the doubts and fears.

He finishes off with a quotation (actually a paraphrase) from a D. H. Lawrence poem describing the kind of man he fears that, down deep, he is: 'See that British bourgeois, washed and clean and strong. But put him in a situation where a little human understanding and feeling are required. He is a good for nothing.'

Chapter Fifteen

Before he left Nevada, CLR wrote to Lyman Paine, expressing his awareness of the responsibility Constance and he were taking on, and how hard it promised to be:

> My wife is still something of a stranger among us. Marrying me she married into a doubly difficult environment, the movement, my personal status here, and my race. We all, me included, are apt to forget that I am a Negro. Our child will be half-a-Negro. As long as I am around, we can manage. One must plan. Large insurances, etc., are for the time being beyond me. But that child will be a special responsibility. I am going to do my best to meet it.[1]

A week later he was back in New York. A week after that, on 24 November, CLR and Constance married for the second time, in White Plains, New York. They did not get to go on honeymoon, as it turned out the resort CLR had suggested did not admit Black people. Within the magic circle of the Johnson-Forest it might have been possible for CLR to forget he was Black. In the wider world, there were regular reminders.

Immediately before leaving for Nevada, CLR had submitted a paper called 'The Revolutionary Answer to the Negro Problem in the United States' to the SWP's annual conference. This was a refinement of his earlier work on the same issue, arguably his definitive statement on the subject, and would be reprinted regularly over the decades to come, its relevance sadly undimmed by history.*

Essentially, he argues once again that the Black people of the US are

* As I write this, the US is in flames. The murder of George Floyd has caused the world to notice systemic racism once again.

its most revolutionary group, inevitably cynical about the benefits of bourgeois democracy:

> On the question of what is called the democratic process, the Negroes do not believe that grievances, difficulties of sections of the population, are solved by discussions, by voting, by telegrams to Congress, by what is known as the 'American way'.[2]

More controversially, as far as his immediate audience was concerned, he still insists that Black Americans do not need a Marxist vanguard to lead them. The task of the SWP, according to CLR, was to act as a bridge between the Black struggle and the organised workers' struggle, with the Black struggle very much at the forefront:

> Let us not forget that in the Negro people, there sleep and are now awakening, passions of a violence exceeding perhaps, as far as these things can be compared, anything among the tremendous forces that capitalism has created ... although their social force may not be able to compare with the social force of a corresponding number of organized workers, the hatred of bourgeois society and the readiness to destroy it when the opportunity should present itself, rests among them to a degree greater than in any other section of the population in the United States.

This was urgent, rousing stuff, and very much what the SWP had hoped for in bringing in CLR and his group. There was rather less enthusiasm for the tablets CLR had sent – the series of long letters – from Nevada. These were the notes on Hegel's dialectic.

His intimates, Raya and Grace and Marty Glaberman, were thrilled with them. CLR, in these letters, seemed to be offering a philosophical explanation of why Trotskyist politics weren't working, why the revolutionary wave that was meant to follow the Second World War had failed to arrive. Passages like this were both a challenge and an inspiration:

> Organization as we have known it is at an end. The task is to abolish organization. The task today is to call for, to teach, to illustrate, to develop spontaneity – the free creative activity of the proletariat.[3]

This, of course, pretty much did away with the Trotskyist/Leninist notion of the vanguard party. CLR had already outflanked that policy with his notes on the Negro question; now he was encouraging his followers to challenge it head-on.

Which was in some ways a strange position for them to take, given that they had recently joined a Trotskyist party. Certainly the SWP cadres were less than impressed by the philosophical bent of its new, largely youthful members. Ridicule was poured on these 'barely literate kids touting copies of Hegel's philosophy of mind'.

It's probably fair to say that at this point CLR James – or Jimmy Johnson – was starting to cross the line from conventional Trotskyist leader to something close to a guru. It was no longer just a handful of close associates who revered him. Young members, many of them female, were starting to cluster around him. Years later one of these acolytes, Evelyn Sell, commented that there was 'a cult in the party which regarded Jimmy Johnson as a sort of god'.[4]

On 4 April 1949, CLR's son was born. As Constance went into labour, Eric Williams was visiting. It's a sign of how close they all were that, for a while, Williams held one of Constance's hands and CLR the other. The birth itself was extremely difficult and Constance took a while to recover physically.

CLR arranged for a nurse and she stayed with them for six weeks. Throughout Constance's pregnancy they had referred to the imminent baby as 'Nobbie' or 'Nob', after the way his head bumped through her stomach, and CLR kept up the habit now he was born. And Nobbie would remain his family nickname, but his given name was exactly the same as his father's: Cyril Lionel Robert James.* Quite a legacy to bestow.

Constance remembered how delighted CLR was with his son:

> Every evening Nello held Nobbie in his arms and talked to him in baby talk, cooing at him. When Nobbie was ten days old he

* It is perhaps worth noting that Alfie Mendes, whose example CLR often followed, had also called his first son by his own name.

cooed back at his father and Nello declared we had a genius on our hands.[5]

The idyll didn't last long. Once Constance was fit again CLR was back to his old routines – out working all hours with his comrades, saying little at home. Raya and Grace, however, did take an interest in the baby. Raya even bought Constance a couple of Claire McCardell dresses.* After a few months, CLR determined that Constance needed an afternoon off a week. He would look after the baby. This seemed to go remarkably smoothly, although, after a while, Constance realised that this was because either Raya or Grace would show up after she left, to do the actual childcare while CLR carried on working.

Having a wife and child to support was a huge challenge for CLR. He had been used to scraping by as a single man, supported by the generosity of patrons like B. K. Gupta or Lyman Paine. But even Paine wasn't going to support an entire family. CLR needed to earn a proper living again. Which wasn't an easy task for a Black intellectual with uncertain immigration status. The strain was terrible. In the summer of 1949 he was convinced he was suffering from heart failure. He was cleared by the doctor, but still found it hard to work. Raya and Grace collaborated with him on a book that would be called *State Capitalism and World Revolution* – the most thoroughly worked-out statement so far of the Johnson-Forest political philosophy, bringing together their state capitalism theory with the new dialectical insights – but that was not the kind of literary endeavour that was ever going to make money.

He took on a job for his friend, the French Trotskyist Daniel Guérin. Guérin had written a new study of the French Revolution, which CLR much admired. CLR offered to translate it so that it might find a US publisher. Guérin, a wealthy man, agreed to pay CLR an advance

* McCardell effectively invented a new look for American working women in the wartime and post-war era, practical but chic. Her signatures were the wrap dress and the remodelling of ballet shoes as street wear for women.

to do the work. Feeling sick and depressed, however, CLR failed to deliver on time and instead wrote Guérin a long apology, laying bare just how hard he was finding life:*

> I don't know if you have ever asked yourself how I live. I live literally how I can. I do some ghost-writing here, a little research there, a little lecturing on the quiet there, friends who I assist in their literary work help me. This illness and various other factors brought on a crisis that I had been holding off. Perhaps you have experience of this perhaps you have not. I simply had to spend most of my time trying to raise some money. My friends stood by me but I have been having a hard time, loans for a few weeks, more loans to cover those and so on.[6]

And then he explains that he is working on a new project, one with the potential to get him out of his financial hole:

> I have been for years preparing to write a book on the civilization of the U.S. As a last resort for putting my hand on some substantial sum to get my affairs in order I set out on the task of writing at great speed some sort of rough presentation of it.

This was something completely new for him: an analysis of contemporary American culture and politics, intended for a wider readership than just the Trotskyist movement.

American Civilization is a remarkably ambitious survey of the landscape of his adoptive country, one that strove to incorporate both his political reading and his endless nights spent watching Hollywood movies. Briefly summed up, it moves from discussing the great American writers of the nineteenth century – Whitman and Melville, primarily – to a remarkably un-elitist look at popular culture from radio soaps to detective novels, before shifting to sociology as he asks

* At the end of the letter he urged Guérin to destroy it after reading so word wouldn't get around as to just how fragile the great Jimmy Johnson really was.

'What is it that people want?' and finally to the specific situation of women and Black people in the America of the day.

Its ambition is summed up in this sentence from the introduction:

> In observing the content and form of the popular arts in America today, with their international success, it is possible to deduce the social and political needs, sufferings, aspirations and rejections of modern civilization to an astonishing degree.

It's a sentiment that may be commonplace in the modern age of cultural studies, but it was literally revolutionary in the context of the left-wing political world of the time, which tended to take the 'opium of the people' line towards popular culture.

There's no denying the brilliance of many of the insights (though as with much of CLR's work it's worth bearing in mind that this was always a collaborative project, and some of these insights are very likely the work of Willie Gorman or Grace Lee*), but it is an unfinished work. Some parts are really no more than notes.

It's hard to see why a mainstream publisher would have been interested, given that CLR was far from being a household name. This unfortunate fact was soon borne in to CLR after he sent off a copy of the manuscript to Constance's friend Eugene Raskin – precisely the sort of smart metropolitan intellectual that CLR hoped the book would appeal to. Raskin got back to CLR to say that he liked the insights and the 'sharp, almost remorselessly vivid style', but felt there was a major problem:

> I feel that what the book lacks is a clearly stated subject and a clearly drawn plan. I would not recommend that you show it to a publisher until this lack has been remedied. To get his point of view just try to imagine what kind of an advertisement or blurb he might write.[7]

* Much later, in a letter to Robert Hill, Grace Lee noted that 'I detect Willie Gorman's hand in the sections on the Abolitionists and the Civil War. I recall writing some of the paragraphs on Whitman et al.'

It's a valid criticism. As it stands, *American Civilization* has the bones of maybe three or four different books embedded in it. CLR himself soon saw that and his next book would indeed be an expansion of one part of *American Civilization*. The book as a whole, though, would not see the light of day until after his death.

It certainly didn't provide a magic solution to his money problems. He didn't do much more work on the manuscript, just set it aside. Domestic life was difficult. Constance found him more aloof than ever. He was again starting to lose interest in sex. Only special events – a visit from Richard Wright, over from Paris, or a trip to the opera to see *The Magic Flute* – seemed to raise his spirits.

Come summertime, CLR, along with Raya and Grace, had finished *State Capitalism and World Revolution*, which would be published by the SWP that September, as a formidably dense eighty-page pamphlet or 'discussion bulletin'.

Before that the SWP held its annual residential summer camp in New Jersey, a party-bonding affair with a mix of lectures and entertainment. CLR was one of the lecturers. Constance and Nobbie came too, with disastrous consequences. First, as part of the entertainment programme, there was a play based on Al Capp's *Li'l Abner* comic strip. Constance was asked to play the part of Daisy Mae, a blonde sexpot. CLR disapproved. 'It was unseemly,' he told her.[8] Constance went ahead anyway. Later she observed that:

> My behaviour the week we were at the camp was disgraceful. I acted the role of Daisy Mae in the camp play, wearing a very revealing costume; went to camp dances leaving Nello to look after Nobbie; and had a brief affair with the son of a senior Trotskyist leader. Although I thought we'd been discreet, in a close and ingrown circle, there is no way to keep such a scandal secret. Nello was embarrassed and humiliated. These actions were indeed cruel. Not only were they a blow to Nello's pride and dignity but worse, he was in a situation where he could not make a scene or take any action at all. In the enemy camp, as it were, his wife was consorting with his foes.[9]

Unsurprisingly, when they returned home to the Bronx things went from bad to worse. CLR dealt with the crisis in his relationship in typical fashion by ignoring it and burying himself in work. The *State Capitalism* booklet was duly published in September. However, it didn't have the effect the Johnson-Forests were hoping for. It was largely ignored by their comrades. At the subsequent SWP convention they complained about the lack of debate. It's clear that the Johnson-Forests were becoming an ever more marginal group within the wider party.

That winter, Constance moved out of the apartment in the Bronx and found a place of her own with Nobbie on East 13th Street, close to the SWP headquarters in Greenwich Village. Before long she was having an affair with another SWP intellectual, Jules Geller. The two of them had been set up by an SWP member called Evelyn Novak, whose husband George was one of CLR's ideological rivals in the party.

CLR kept on working, writing for the various party magazines and planning the group's next moves. And with Constance gone he was soon back to his womanising habits. He concentrated his attentions on the group's young female recruits. One of these was Isa-Kae Meksin, now one of the last survivors. She had joined the SWP's youth wing as a teenager, excited by the newness, the modern politics of the Johnsonites:

> For me as an adolescent during a very difficult time for girls this was so liberating, not so much the politics as a group which saw the world so differently, racial integration and so on . . .[10]

She followed the Johnson-Forest group through the moves into the Workers' Party and back into the SWP, but she too saw how the reverence of the followers was affecting the leader. 'We spoiled him,' she says. The extent of this spoiling became all too clear when she was one of the many young women – always young women – selected to act as his secretary:

> A bunch of us typed up his correspondence – Ceil, Selma, Fil, Freddy etc. I can only see him for the human aspect. This man always needed a woman and his behaviour would not be acceptable nowadays. One time I was typing for him and he just put his hand on my breast – I said 'What are you doing!' and pushed him away. But he had his entitlements . . .

Isa-Kae went on to point out that such behaviour from men was far from unusual at the time, but still that scarcely excuses it. And it seems especially disturbing coming from a man like CLR, who liked to present himself as a pillar of moral rectitude.

Early in 1951 CLR went out on another long lecture tour, eventually arriving in Los Angeles, where he stayed with the Gogols again. While he was there he began an affair with another young recruit. This was Selma Weinstein (née Deitch). At the time she was twenty years old, married with a young son. CLR had just turned fifty and was also married, though separated, with a young son.

Selma had grown up in Brooklyn's Jewish community and joined the SWP's youth group when she was fifteen, in 1945. It was the bombing of Hiroshima that inspired her to make the move. Her sister Ceil was CLR's secretary at the time and she had introduced the young Selma to the party leader. Selma remembers CLR asking her what she was studying in school. When she told him she was studying French, he picked up a French book and asked her to read something. When she did so he simply told her 'your accent is not very good', which didn't impress her greatly.[11]

She didn't see him again for about a year and a half, when she was sixteen and started listening to his speeches. What really interested Selma was his concept of the dialectic, as explained in a private seminar. This stunned her. The dialectic, as explained by CLR, gave her a way of understanding the world which went beyond Stalinism or Trotskyism.

At seventeen she'd left home to marry another young comrade, Norman Weinstein, and had a baby son, Sam, a year later. They had headed out west to take up factory work as part of the Johnson-Forest proletarianisation programme.

By 1951 Selma was an impressive young woman, a committed revolutionary whose experience of both motherhood and factory work meant she was connected to 'the people' in ways that CLR wasn't. He was fascinated to hear her accounts of life in the factory and opinions about the ordinary lives of the working-class women she knew.

When she'd come to New York a few months earlier, she'd had lunch with CLR and talked to him at length. He told her that the group needed to take on 'the woman question' that would engage the great mass of ordinary women. In that moment Selma realised that she did indeed have something to say. She told him about a woman she knew who was selling her children's clothes because she was so desperate to have some money of her own.

He encouraged her to write a pamphlet on the subject, and when she didn't write it immediately he called her to ask why:

> I said, 'Because I don't know how to write a pamphlet.' 'The way to do it,' he said, 'is to take a shoe box and make a slit at the top; then whenever you have an idea jot it down and slip the piece of paper into the shoe box. After a while, you open the box, put all these sentences in order and you have a draft.'
>
> Looking back later, I realised that the advice CLR gave me as a person with no writing experience says a lot about him and indicates what a great organizer he was. I suspect he invented the shoe box method on the spot.[12]

CLR's intellectual and political commitment to feminism and women's equality generally is clear and well ahead of his time. Though whether he also used those same power relations that oppress women to work in his own sexual favour is at least a question that bears consideration.

While in California, he corresponded with Constance, who was entertaining ideas of returning to showbusiness, culminating in his writing her two extraordinarily harsh letters. He evidently no longer saw her as the poetic genius and instinctive representative of American womanhood of his earlier letters. Instead he sums up his feelings as follows:

> I have done all I could. I have tried to change my life. I am not going to do it any more. It is up to you. But if you are not prepared to accept the conditions as I place them before you, then that's up to you. I can live very well without you. In fact, I regret the whole business from 1939 to the present minute. It is the most catastrophic blunder of my life – my association with you. In fact the only serious one ... However, there is Nob, and a tangled situation personally, politically etc. Under the circumstances, I am prepared to make some sort of life with you but on the condition that you put an end to all this blasted nonsense of 'living with meaning' by getting a job at Billy Rose's nightclub; your intolerable selfishness and greed, your refusal to do anything serious in any sphere whatsoever, and your hatred and jealousy of all I am doing and my close associations.[13]

Both CLR and Constance, for all their respective selfish sides, did realise that it was in Nobbie's interests that they at least made an effort to patch up their marriage. In a subsequent letter, CLR refers to him as 'that doubly, trebly unfortunate little boy whom sometimes I cannot bear to think of'.[14]

Matters came to a head when he returned to New York. Constance was starting to contemplate making a life with Jules Geller. She was disconcerted, though, when the SWP's overall leader, James P. Cannon himself, came to see her, essentially to plead that she divorce CLR and marry Jules instead: 'Cannon urged me to leave CLR, saying that marriage to a black man was too difficult and no one would hold anything against me if I could not stand the strain.'[15] This strong-arming, which Constance believed to have been instigated by Evelyn Novak, was counter-productive. She told some other Johnson-Forest members what had happened, and word quickly got back to CLR.

CLR was outraged by Cannon and Novak's behaviour and impressed that Constance had not gone along with it. And the chance to see his son again gave him a spur to try to mend their relationship, as he wrote to Lyman and Freddy Paine:

> Nob recognised me at once. He looked up and said 'Dada'. Then he was bashful and then came and played. He spends every second he can playing with me and he woke in the middle of the night screaming 'Daddie Daddie Daddie'.[16]

Gradually, Constance and he came up with a reconciliation plan. After the SWP convention in August, CLR would take a year off to write a book. They would live together in California. He had a project for Constance as well. She would work with a new comrade, a Black Detroit auto worker called Si Owens, to write a book about his life and experiences. Constance wavered – 'I was being asked to break with Jules in such a cruel manner, a good man who loved me, who had treated me with such tenderness' – but finally agreed.[17]

Meanwhile, CLR planned his revenge on the SWP. With his close comrades he prepared for the future. The first outward manifestation of their thinking was a document called 'The Balance Sheet Completed: Ten Years of American Trotskyism'. They delivered it at the SWP convention, and from the very first sentences it was a declaration of war:

> 'Johnson-Forest' has now made its final and complete break with what the Fourth International of today stands for. We are leaving behind forever the ideas of those who today represent Trotskyism, their unsocialist, anti-proletarian practice and organizational life.

The document went on to detail their grievances. They disapproved of the SWP's (albeit limited) support for Tito's Yugoslavia, which the Johnson-Forest group dismissed as essentially Stalinist. They complained the SWP had failed to engage with their theory of state capitalism as an analysis of Stalin's Russia. They claimed that the SWP as a whole had nothing to say to Black people, women, or youth. They said that they themselves could speak to those elements in a way traditional Trotskyists simply couldn't. This, in particular, was a powerful argument. It's only in the final section, 'Bolshevism and Personality', that there's a hint of a personal agenda lurking beneath the political one.

> The more sensitive of the leadership know that the party was attracting elements who could not possibly be called revolutionary. This was particularly so in New York ... One of the most striking of these types, distinguished by great energy in the ersatz political activity of the party, was at the same time distinguished by a vulgarity and corruption of character which repelled even those who depended on her and those like her for the success of party activities.

It's clearly Evelyn Novak that he has in mind here, the woman who tried to engineer the end of his marriage. It was this passage that caused Raya's new husband John Dwyer later to claim that: 'So anxious were we – and rightly to be done with Trotskyism – that, in 1951, J [James] was allowed to get away with the basis of the break – a personal situation in which he found himself.'[18]

The document finished with the horribly overblown suggestion that life in the SWP for the Johnson-Forests was like being in a 'political gas chamber'.[19] And once the paper had been delivered, the Johnson-Forest Tendency collectively got up and left both the convention and the party in one coordinated movement.

Two years later, an evidently still very angry James P. Cannon reflected that he had never seen anything like it:

> I will admit that I lived sixty years in this world before I stumbled over the fact that there are such things as political cults. I began rubbing my eyes when I saw the Johnsonites operating in our party.

> I saw a cult bound to a single person, a sort of Messiah. And I thought, 'I'll be damned. You're never too old to learn something new.'
>
> In order for a cult to exist, it is not enough for a leader to have personal followers – every leader has personal influence more or less – but a cult leader has to be a cultist himself. He has to be a megalomaniac who gets revelations outside the realm of reality ... That is what happened with the Johnsonites. The cult followed Johnson, not simply for his theory of the Soviet Union – other people have that theory; a lot of people in the world have that theory about 'state capitalism'. The Johnsonites were personal cultist followers of Johnson as a Messiah; and when he finally gave the signal for them to jump out of this party for reasons known only to himself, but allegedly because of some personal grievance he imagined ... they all left the party at the same hour, Eastern Standard Time. That is a cult.[20]

Cult or not, the Johnson-Forests came out of the SWP with an evident sense of liberation. They chose a new name – the Correspondence Publishing Committee – which both reflected their intention to concentrate on written work of various sorts, and also referenced the radical committees of correspondence active in the American independence struggle.

Their first key decision was to choose a new base, choosing between the small number of cities in which they had active branches. They settled on Detroit, where the workers were, as opposed to New York, where the intellectuals were.

Several of the leading Johnson-Forest members, including Raya Dunayevskaya and Marty Glaberman, had already decamped to Detroit. Marty had taken a factory job and they were starting to make inroads in interesting auto workers in their political approach. So the city was the obvious choice for their initial conference in October 1951. To demonstrate the newness of their approach, a whole session was given over to discussing the woman question. CLR was increasingly convinced that women's role in society was neglected in conventional left-wing politics, and determined to redress the balance. Selma Weinstein was the keynote speaker.

Meanwhile, Constance was working with Si Owens, recording two weeks' worth of interviews with him that they could use as the basis for his book to be published by the Correspondence Publishing Committee as soon as possible. This would represent the new outfit's initial statement on Negro rights. The Detroit branch would publish *Punching Out* by Marty Glaberman, which would deal with workers' rights. The Los Angeles branch would be responsible for Selma Weinstein's pamphlet, to be called *A Woman's Place*. The New York branch would produce a pamphlet called *Artie Cuts Out*, dealing with juvenile delinquency.

All of which made quite a coherent programme. This new, decentralised party would foreground the struggles of Black people, women, industrial workers and youth. As soon as possible, they would also start producing a regular newspaper, one that would be accessible to precisely those groups, and which would be called *Correspondence*.

In order to get ready to produce such a paper, the leadership decided they needed a radical rethinking of how their new party would operate. They did not want to be a party in which a small group of leading intellectuals instructed their followers in what to think. They wanted to be one in which those groups – the potential spearheads of change – would set the agenda. To do this they came up with the idea of third-layer schools, as Grace Lee explains:

> We organized a school where members of the four groups identified as the new revolutionary social forces would be the teachers and the older members and intellectuals would be the students, ready with 'full fountain pens' to write down the views of our 'teachers'. We called it the Third Layer School, based on Lenin's efforts in 1921 to mobilize a 'third layer' of workers and peasants because the first layer of Bolshevik leaders and the second layer of trade unionists had not been sufficient to keep state capitalism from overtaking the fledgling workers' state. The school was held in New York in the fall of 1952. Among the third layer comrades who came

> to the school were James Boggs from Detroit and Selma Weinstein . . . from Los Angeles.[21]

This innovation showed just how far the party's leaders – CLR, Raya and Grace – had come. It was a radical break with the top-down structures of Trotskyism, opening the way for a new form of politics that drew from anarchist traditions as well as communist.

But while this new group, as a whole, had a coherent and inspiring programme, CLR's own contribution was enigmatic, to put it mildly. At this crucial moment he doubly surprised his followers. First, he announced that he was ill with exhaustion and needed to take a year off to get well. He would move to Los Angeles with Constance and Nobbie, and work on a book.

The second surprise was the nature of that book. Up to this point all the collective intellectual effort had been focused on the great minds of revolutionary thought – Hegel, Marx, Lenin. Now CLR told his followers that he planned to write a study of *Moby-Dick*. Herman Melville, he declared, was second only to Marx as a theoretician of the modern world. So a study of his masterwork from a radical perspective would be a truly revolutionary work. Not only was he going to work on this project, but he detailed Grace and Constance to start studying Melville as well, so they could provide him with notes and insights.

It's a measure of the extent to which CLR was indeed something of a cult leader at the time that no one queried what seems in retrospect to be a baffling sideways move for a revolutionary leftist.

In the last months of 1951, CLR and Constance headed for LA to give their troubled marriage one more chance. They found a small two-bedroom house in Compton, still a mixed area back then. There was a friendly Black couple on one side and an unfriendly white family on the other. They bought a beaten-up Chevrolet and found a nursery school for Nobbie. They worked on their respective books and took Nobbie to the beach some afternoons – outings fraught with worry due to the regular attentions of the cops, who hated to see an interracial couple together.

CLR took a little time out of domesticity in February to do a brief lecture tour, talking about Melville. He clearly had the idea that he might be able to start a parallel career as a public intellectual alongside his revolutionary activity. So he got Grace Lee's partner Saul Blackman to act as his manager and booking agent. The highlights were the talks he gave at the Institute of Arts and Sciences at Columbia University. Afterwards the director, Russell Potter, wrote to him to say that in twenty years of presenting lectures, 'Never have I heard one that surpassed yours in content, organisation and presentation.'[22]

The possibility of a dual career must have felt tantalisingly within reach at this point. The book itself, however, was proving hard to wrestle into shape. In a letter to Lyman Paine dated 2 June 1952, he wrote to Lyman to tell him that he was struggling to work effectively:

> I am working badly ... It is one long grind most of the time. Strangely enough last October–December ... Three times more a week I would sit and write five or 6000 words ... Now if with Benzedrine I do 5000 I feel I have achieved – a piece of shit if ever there was. I have a horrible feeling that ... I am way behind.[23]

It's a letter notable for containing probably the only swearword to appear in millions of written words from CLR, and also for the first mention of his use of Benzedrine as a writing aid. Benzedrine was a freely available amphetamine. Initially sold as a nasal decongestant, the American public had soon recognised its capacity for keeping the user awake and alert. Writers were great devotees – Kerouac famously used Benzedrine to write *On the Road* in three weeks.* CLR had been used to churning out a phenomenal amount of writing. Now, in his early fifties, it's not surprising he needed a little help, whatever its attendant risks.

Within a few weeks, however, CLR would find himself with a rather greater obstacle to his writing. He was arrested by the

* That was the story he liked to tell anyway. More likely he just typed out the final draft in three weeks.

immigration authorities, who had finally decided to reject his application for citizenship. He had put forward his need to support his American wife and child but they decided, after consulting with the FBI, that, in these McCarthy years, his revolutionary sympathies trumped all else. So he was sent to New York's Ellis Island to await deportation. His comrades immediately mobilised lawyers to file an appeal.

From the 1890s up to the Second World War, Ellis Island had been the great entry station for immigrants to the US. Twelve million and more had come through its doors. Since the war, it had been converted to a detention centre for those threatened with deportation. It was expensive to maintain, however, and by the time CLR arrived, around June 1952, there were only thirty or forty detainees there.

Apart from the cruelty and injustice of his situation, CLR was immediately struck by the irony that in the midst of writing about a great novel concerned with a group of men confined to a whaling ship, he was now on an island likewise outside of society: 'It was as if destiny had taken a hand to give me a unique opportunity to test my ideas of this great American writer.'[24]

He was placed in a room set aside for political prisoners. The other five inmates were all communists. At first this worried CLR, given their mutual ideological antipathy. But he came quickly to admire their effective leader, a man he referred to as M, who looked out for the rights of his fellow prisoners, especially the most vulnerable, with unerring care.*

What really did for CLR on Ellis Island was the terrible food. His ulcer problems had lately been under control – in fact, recent domesticity had seen him weigh in at over 14 stone, a lifetime high – but now they started to flare up badly. Before long he was in the infirmary with terrible stomach pains, unable to eat anything. In the memoir that serves as the final chapter of his Melville book, he goes into great

* In an unworthy passage from *Mariners, Renegades and Castaways*, doubtless inserted into the account to prove his anti-communism, CLR says that for all his kindness and principle, M was really as mad as Ahab.

detail about all this, also mentioning his dependence on sleeping pills, which would become another long-term problem. Overall, he describes his suffering as 'an unpardonable crime'.[25]

Eventually, he was taken to the Marine Hospital in Stapleton, where he spent two months making a partial recovery and working on his book. He was transferred back to Ellis Island in early October 1953, just before his lawyer finally persuaded a court to give him bail, four months or so after his initial incarceration.

Once released, CLR decided to stay in New York, apart from time spent in Long Island working on what would become *Mariners, Renegades and Castaways*. To get the book finished he asked Grace to help him with the literary theory, and Selma to come out from California and help him give it a populist touch. The three of them worked together intensely on writing the book. And while there would be only one name on the cover, the book was something of a collective effort – the text regularly refers to 'we'. CLR acknowledged Selma's contribution in particular, in a letter to Raya:

> [she] has an instinct for the problems that the intellectual has to solve. She was responsible for the final structure and form of *Mariners*, not only in general, but in important chapters.[26]

While they were working together so closely, CLR and Selma resumed a relationship that had begun the year before in Los Angeles. She remembers the writing process:

> The *Mariners* process was that I had to read everything he wrote before Grace typed it, or I typed it, and I had to okay it. They had already changed the nature of the book because while I was in Los Angeles, and he was in Ellis Island, I had put together some notes . . . He came to the conclusion that what I wanted was a story. That shaped the book, telling the story rather than being only analytical, and that was because of my comments. It was what he thought a popular audience, which I represented, would like to read. So that was an interesting experience. I hadn't read *Moby Dick*, but I was

very interested in the theory, and that was my first experience of literary criticism, which I really liked a lot.[27]

Constance, meanwhile, had wanted to come out to New York as soon as CLR was released, but she was also ill. She was diagnosed with fibroids on her uterus and had to have surgery. While she was recovering in Los Angeles, she had a call from Norman Weinstein, Selma's husband. He told her that his wife was having an affair with CLR. He was angry and betrayed. 'My God,' he said to Constance, 'the man is almost old enough to be her grandfather.'[28] He exaggerated, but there was a significant age gap between them: CLR was fifty-two years old, Selma twenty-three.

When Constance told Bessie Gogol what she had learned, Bessie was dismissive, unable to see the problem with the revolutionary leader exercising something suspiciously like *droit de seigneur*. She told Constance that 'with what Jimmy has been through I would line up every woman in the group and let him take his pick or take all of them'.[29]

The book was finished by the end of November. There had been a plan to find a major publisher, but that was always a long shot, and anyway time was of the essence, with the threat of deportation still imminent, so the Correspondence Publishing Committee themselves would publish it early in 1954. CLR persuaded his comrades to print twenty thousand copies of the book, in a dime-store paperback format that would appeal to the legions of workers eager to read a Marxist reassessment of *Moby-Dick*.

It's a short, curious book. The first forty thousand words offer a continually interesting, sometimes eccentric assessment of Melville's great work, one that attempts to draw out lessons for contemporary politics. CLR sees Melville as having anticipated all the great upheavals of the world since – capitalism, communism, Stalinism and fascism. He takes in other work of Melville's too; *Pierre* is analysed in some detail as is the extraordinary short story 'Bartleby, the Scrivener'. Finally, he uses the example of Melville to belabour modern day novelists, who he characterises as neurotic, guilty and hopeless:

> How light in the scales is the contemporary mountain of self-examination and self-pity against the warmth, the humour, the sanity, the anonymous but unfailing humanity of the renegades and castaways and savages of the *Pequod*, rooted in the whole historical past of man, doing what they have to do, facing what they have to face.[30]

The autobiographical last chapter, though, is quite different. After his first-person account of his stay on Ellis Island, he makes a plea for acceptance in America. He attempts to persuade the reader that the rest of the book is proof that he is a harmless literary man of letters, rather than an ardent revolutionary. It even ends with an appeal for readers to write to CLR at his then home address to request further copies at a dollar apiece.

It's an awkward combination, this deeply thought analysis of Melville and the journalistic campaign on behalf of the author. Of the twenty thousand copies printed, eight thousand were given away. Copies were sent, for instance, to every single senator and congressman, as well as literary critics, political sympathisers, or anyone at all who might conceivably be able to help CLR's case. Correspondence even spent $500 on taking out an advert for the book in the Sunday *New York Times*.

It was an extravagant gesture, and an unsuccessful one.* The book fell on deaf ears. There were no reviews and the few personal replies from literary critics were mostly politely baffled. It had succeeded neither as a way of making his fortune, nor of gaining his reprieve.

* Raya's husband John Dwyer offered this baleful assessment of the book's publication a couple of years later: 'Actual sales of the book amounted to less than two thousand copies. Whenever a person would send in money for one copy he got eight or ten copies from the author, who handled all these matters personally and pocketed all cash receipts. The response from workers, to who the book was presumably addressed, was nil. The financial cost to the organisation was tremendous. The political and social gains were nil.'

What lingers in the mind, though, is the simple and moving dedication, as written in the first edition:

> For my son, Nob, who will be 21 years old in 1970 by which time I hope he and his generation will have left behind them forever all the problems of nationality.*

Constance had arrived in New York as the book was finished. CLR came back to her and not a word was said about his affair with Selma. For the first month or so they lived at that bohemian landmark, the Chelsea Hotel, sometime home to his fellow Trotskyist writer James T. Farrell.

This time, though, there was barely even a honeymoon period to their reunion. CLR worked and stayed silent. They moved into an apartment near the Chelsea, where there were at least friendly neighbours with a son for Nobbie to play with. But at Christmas CLR failed to buy a present for her or Nobbie, while apparently deputising Grace to buy a skirt for Selma. And it wasn't long before Constance discovered that the relationship with Selma wasn't just a passing affair but something more serious. She knew he was receiving airmail letters from Los Angeles, so one night while he was in the bath she went through his wallet and found a love letter from Selma.

Understandably furious, she waited for CLR to come out of the bath, then asked him if he wanted a divorce. He denied he did. Was he having an affair? He denied that too. This was the last straw for Constance. CLR had always claimed to abhor dishonesty and now this: 'My dear Victorian husband had lied to me – a crushing fact as we had always been open and honest with each other.'[31]

That was the end. CLR moved out, published his book, gave another series of lectures at Columbia,† and come summer, facing the

* I wonder if CLR's friend John Berger had this at the back of his mind when he titled a film script 'Jonah who will be 25 in the year 2000'.

† Two of these were recorded and are available to listen to in the archives at Columbia. Unfortunately, the sound quality is challenging but they do give a sense of CLR's oratorical command.

fact that publication of *Mariners* had failed to turn the tide in his favour, he took legal advice which suggested that if he voluntarily left the country he would at least be able to come back in a few years' time, if the political climate changed. Selma, it was agreed, could follow him to England once they had both concluded their divorces. On the other hand, if he was deported, he might never be able to return. He decided to take the lesser of two evils. In July 1953 he sailed back to England.

PART FOUR

England and Trinidad

Chapter Sixteen

The Britain CLR returned to in July 1953 was a very different country from the one he had left in 1938. It was broke and battered, struggling to remake itself after the trauma of war. And CLR himself was a forgotten name, this pre-war Trotskyist who vanished when the going got tough.

He had been warned. While he was on Ellis Island, CLR and his friends had sent out an appeal for funds to help his case. It had some success in America, but rather less in Britain. George Padmore, in particular, wrote CLR a stern letter upbraiding him for having been out of touch for years, warning him that the cost of living was high and suggesting he'd be better off continuing to enjoy the American way of life.

At first CLR managed to put on a brave face. He was interviewed by the police on arrival in Plymouth, the authorities having been told to expect some kind of communist. The interviewing officer, however, was clearly impressed by the new arrival:

> His description is – aged 52 years; Ht 6' 2"; very well built; short black curly hair; brown eyes; clean shaven; slightly upturned nose. A man of colour. Wears horn-rimmed glasses and is very well spoken. Dress – grey double-breasted suit; white shirt and collar; brown shoes; brown trilby hat. Of very good appearance.[1]

CLR had $1600 with him, most likely courtesy of Lyman Paine. Within a few weeks he had found a place to live, a flat on King Henry's Road, near Primrose Hill in north London.

And he had been to see his first cricket matches in years. He saw England play Australia at the Oval. And, quite the novelty, he was able to watch the Leeds Test on television. He was particularly impressed by the quality of the TV commentary ('splendid, if somewhat on the cautious side').[2]

In August he wrote to Grace to tell her that 'My good health, spirits and energy really amaze me. I sleep like a top. I walk all over Central London and am not tired when I get home,' before asking her to make sure to see Nobbie and tell him that 'his daddy always asks after him'.[3]

Nobbie was very much on his mind. Before he left New York, he had agreed with Constance that she should write once a week telling him everything that was going on, both good and bad, and he would write to her and also to Nobbie, for whom he would write stories, just like the ones he used to make up for him at bedtime. He was as good as his word and, over the next few years, there would be a steady stream of short stories sent across the Atlantic, featuring the adventures of two boys called Good Boongko and Bad Boo-boo-loo, and a cast of characters including talking fleas, a lion, assorted fish and birds, and a man called Nicholas the Worker. The stories would roam to Rome or Greece, gently trying to educate Nobbie as well as to entertain him. There's a playfulness, a revelling in absurdist humour, that sees CLR expressing an often-concealed side of his nature.

For the next few months, CLR did his best to perform a complex balancing act, effectively living two lives at once. He was simultaneously trying to lead the Johnson-Forest group by remote control, through the means of a torrent of very long letters, and also trying to regain his footing in London's political and literary worlds.

Both projects were challenging in their own way. That October, the Publishing Committee finally published the first issue of their fortnightly newspaper *Correspondence*. This should have been a great moment for CLR – the launch of an entirely new sort of political newspaper, one that saw the lives and interests of Black people, women and youth as central, not peripheral – but it was put together in Detroit, not London, and while he might have been the project's architect, he wasn't there doing the day-to-day work.

The paper itself was a modest triumph. Edited by Johnny Zupan, it combined hard news, political comment and personal pieces. Selma

Weinstein had her own column, 'A Woman's Place'. There was a cynical cartoon, 'The Needle', and reviews of films and music. It belongs to a different, more modern world than the rival Trotskyist papers, which were all stuck in a pre-war rut of dour earnestness.

CLR's frustration is palpable in the letters he sends to the group, full of suggestions about what should have gone where, how much space should have been allotted to this or to that. He did his best to micromanage, but much as the group still revered their leader, in practice they were having to get used to making their own decisions.

CLR did his best to rekindle his old friendships. He talked to George Padmore, clearing the air. He reported back to the US comrades that George 'holds himself steady, because he is rooted in the colonial question, more particularly the question of Africa'.[4] He corresponded with Harry Spencer in Nelson. He talked to Learie Constantine about writing a new biography of his old friend. Constantine was agreeable and suggested CLR also talk to the great batsman George Headley. CLR duly contacted Neville Cardus, who put him on to the *Guardian*'s new sports editor, Larry Montague. CLR went to Manchester to meet him and was commissioned to write a piece on returning to cricket after fifteen years without seeing a game.

He also contacted Fred Warburg, who invited him to lunch on 14 October. CLR had high hopes for this meeting, anticipating a serious advance that would allow him to concentrate on writing. So he presented his former publisher with a whole slate of books he proposed to write. First, he wanted Secker & Warburg to publish a British edition of *Mariners, Renegades and Castaways*, then he would write a full-length version of *American Civilization,* and then the twin cricket biographies of Constantine and Headley.

Warburg responded with limited enthusiasm. He suggested that a new edition of *Mariners* might be possible, but CLR would have to remove the final chapter and beef up the literary criticism aspect. He thought *American Civilization* might have some potential, but CLR would need to finish writing it before selling it. That was not at all what he wanted to hear. Then he pitched the cricket books. The response was interesting:

> Warburg tells me after I explained to him my ideas on cricket that it would be better if I wrote on cricket altogether, that is to say on cricket per se and not on Constantine. There is a tremendous vogue here for writing books on the game. They are all feeling for something. But they don't know what it is . . .[5]

At once, CLR sees the book he could write. One that would revolutionise the establishment view of the game:

> The God damned English writers with their elms and their green lawns and church steeples and eleven men playing cricket and the Englishness of it etc, etc, are all going to be thrown in the dustbin. They have to explain why in India, in Ceylon, in the W.I. and in places where there are no elms and there are no church steeples but mosques and tom toms the game is played with more fanaticism than in England.

He came away from the lunch with no advance, but a burning idea. Before he could act on any of his plans, though, he needed a solid base: a flat big enough to work in, and some secretarial help. Still in his dynamic mode, he found both in short order.

First came the secretary, a Jamaican law student called Mavis Watts. She took on the considerable task of typing up CLR's streams of dictation. A radical herself, she introduced CLR to a Kenyan revolutionary called Mbiyu Koinange. And after a few days of working for him, she helped CLR move into the new flat he'd found, a two-bedroom place on Tanza Road, near Hampstead Heath.

Once settled, CLR wrote Lyman Paine a long letter describing his new circumstances. It's worth quoting from at length as one of the few times CLR stopped to detail his daily life. He describes the flat: two rooms on one floor, a bathroom with plentiful hot water and a fully equipped kitchen. He has his own television and, in the room upstairs, a lodger. This is a young woman called Lorna Painter who works at the British Museum and whose brother George has translated André Gide for Secker & Warburg. He's interested by her and he's pleased with his secretary:

> She has been busy organising all my correspondence – letters that come, copies of letters that go, clippings every morning and the multitudinous pamphlets and periodicals which I am accumulating. Perhaps for the first time that I can remember I have the assistance I want . . . the work done in my moving and getting settled here was done with the devotion of a countrywoman and a highly capable person.[6]

Helpful though Mavis had been, she was shortly to move on. Fortunately CLR had found someone else who would greatly aid his daily life. This was his formidable charlady, Mrs Walls. Not only did Mrs Walls clean but she also assisted in buying his food and cooking his meals. And she turned out to be a woman with surprising depths, a spiritualist and devotee of Krishnamurti and Berdyaev:

> For years she has lectured on this topic all over England and she still does it occasionally. She was pleased to say that she felt I have a strong spiritual quality. And she took the enormous pains that she takes with me (for which no money could possibly pay) because she could see that I need seeing after. And she wanted to do work which had something to it more than the mere money . . . I was considerably sobered and made to reflect a great deal when she explained to me why she was doing what she did.

The neighbourhood too was thoroughly to his liking. If he walked one way he arrived at 'a shopping centre which serves the Hampstead intellectuals'. Walk the other way and he was in a working-class shopping street, Mansfield Road. 'I have discovered this last recently and I went shopping there last week and making acquaintance of the people. When I have time I shall go to the pub over there.'

Next he told Lyman about his punishing working schedule:

> The schedule is something like this – up in the morning at about 8 or 8.30 and I go out for breakfast. Five or six days a week, unless I am too tired. I do that to get out in the open. I then come back and

> am busy with clippings, correspondence, dictation of letters, dictation of memoranda etc., despatch and receipt of books, until 5 o'clock. Then I stop. I always eat in except under compulsion. Somewhere about 8 or 9 I start again, when everything is quiet, and I write until 12. On weekends I write letters to you all, for about 18 or 20 hours in all.

Later on, though, he does admit to going out two or three times a week, to see a film perhaps. Finally, it emerges that such expeditions were made in the company of a young woman, his landlady's daughter. He doesn't name her, but this is Martina Thomson, a German Jew who had made it out of Germany with her family in 1938. When she met CLR she was acting in television and radio, under the stage name Martina Mayne.* CLR describes her to Lyman:

> The young lady herself is a trained professional actress. She does a lot of work for the BBC. She is in her middle twenties, over medium height and one of the most elegant and graceful persons you could think of.

CLR was evidently smitten, and they were clearly spending a lot of time together in London, as well as taking a trip to seaside Margate. Martina was a woman who moved in glamorous circles:

> We go out and see movies together and she is ready to get me to meet all sorts of BBC people. The fact is however I just haven't the time. She took me to a party the other night where I met Arthur Koestler. He had read Chapter 7.[7] He was tired and a cynical, embittered man. There too I met a young fellow who reviews for the *New Statesman*. The other evening I was at the girl's apartment and Gilbert Harding the most popular broadcaster and journalist in the country was with some friends and called to tell her to come over.

* You can find her on YouTube, appearing in an episode of the Sherlock Holmes series from the mid-fifties.

She asked me whether we should go or not and we finally decided not to.

CLR's relationship with Martina was far from conventional. She was already involved with David Thomson, the BBC producer she would eventually marry. CLR himself was waiting for the two divorces to be sorted out – his from Constance and Selma's from Norman – in the expectation that Selma would then join him in London. Nevertheless, it was a strong, deeply affectionate relationship that would continue in one form or another for the rest of his life.

As Christmas approached, CLR was running out of money once again. The $1600 he arrived with was gone, spent on rent and secretaries and the business of living. He was full of grand plans for books, but yet to sell any of them to an actual publisher. On 20 December he wrote a long letter to his American comrades explaining his situation and asking for further support.[8]

He tells them about the work he's doing, the various writing projects, the trip to Paris to see comrades there, the party he gave in London to renew old friendships, the libraries and societies he's joined, and the accounts he set up with booksellers in Oxford and Cambridge. He says he had hoped to secure an advance that would have let him write and also, somewhat surprisingly, visit the West Indies – 'to see my father and sister and renew myself'. This was an admission, perhaps, that his expulsion from the USA had left him adrift and hankering for the family he had long seemed to have left behind without a backward glance.

Then he explains that he has just two secretaries and a charwoman to help him in his work: 'I am alone, I have to see about everything ... If [I need] a book or magazine or beef for the weekend, or pillowcases or anthracite, I personally have to do it.'

After a while he lets down the grandiosity a little to admit that it's a harder struggle than he expected, re-establishing himself in London. The war, he has realised, has changed everything. His old friends, those that have survived, had been through a huge drama, while he had been in New York, and presumed to have been living the life of Riley:

> I have no moral status here. I was away during the war. I was deported – I would have stayed in the US, but I was forced to leave. I cannot speak from experience of the great common effort and suffering during the war; or of the Labour Government experience. Padmore can. I can't. The workers by and large will not mind as long as I am not overbearing . . . I have to knit myself once more into the fabric, be once more in as many spheres as possible one of the British people. Not only in their eyes, but for myself too.[9]

It's an uncharacteristically humble, and obviously sincere, statement. England, though he had only spent six years there against fifteen in the US, was still a place that felt like home. An interesting omission from any of CLR's letters around this time is any mention of racism – something we have come to expect from first-person accounts of West Indians in London in the fifties. Perhaps it's because after America the racism was less blatant, or perhaps because CLR, this distinguished academic gentleman in his fifties, was a long way from the rambunctious young men who made their way to Bayswater and Brixton. And of course it was still early in the post-war immigration curve, just a couple of years after his countryman Lord Kitchener had written the calypso 'London is the Place for Me'. West Indian immigrants were more of a novelty than a threat, easily stereotyped as happy-go-lucky calypso-singing cricket players.

One of the new arrivals, a Barbadian writer called George Lamming, based his second novel, *The Emigrants* (1954), on his experience in London at just this time. And for him too racism is more background noise than daily ordeal. Things would change as the fifties wore on, immigrant numbers increased and nativist resentment rose in turn, but for now CLR had more urgent problems to deal with, starting with a hardy perennial: his lack of money.

CLR was very clear as to what he expected from his American comrades. In effect, he wanted complete financial support. And the fact he needed it was in itself proof of their failure: 'I must have relief from what you all have been doing to me . . . The way in which I've had to beg for things shows me the mess you are in. The financial mess I am in shows me the mess you are in.'[10]

What he needs, he tells them, is a financial reserve. And why should they – in practice Lyman – fund him? Because once again CLR had divined that they were at a moment of revolutionary potential – 'The depth of the crisis is only equalled by the scale of the opportunity.'

The vehicle which will take the Correspondence Publishing Committee to the forefront of change will be their written works – the fortnightly newspaper and the books CLR and Raya are working on. Their ideas, untrammelled by a conventional party apparatus, will be enough: 'We will be the first who start not with a theory but the results of a theory ... Make the paper a success, write our books and the hungry, drifting people will cluster round something that has new ideas and works.'

Simple, really. But in order to put this plan in action, the comrades needed to send him a helper:

> I would like to have a worker, a woman, a young person who knows the US workers, and the organisation and can move around here among workers, particularly the young people, who would take over the office ... the result would be seen in a week.

New Year 1954 began with a further blow to CLR's fragile equilibrium. He received divorce papers from Constance, who was now in a relationship with a friend of his, a Black Trinidadian from a prominent family called Wilbur McShine. CLR was eager to get the divorce too, so he could bring Selma over, but he was horrified to discover that the grounds cited were fraud. Constance was alleging that CLR had tricked her into marriage, despite being unable or unwilling to support her and their son. She would claim later that this approach had been suggested by her lawyer as the quickest way of obtaining a divorce – as opposed to alleging infidelity and then having to provide proof – but CLR was outraged at the suggestion of dishonesty, and worried that word would spread if he conceded. He wrote furious letters back to New York. Constance, who was still a part of the Correspondence group, was hauled in front of a political committee to explain herself. She walked out feeling angry and humiliated, and the divorce proceedings stalled.

The crisis postponed, CLR went back to demanding a helper. Ideally, he wanted Grace to come; failing her, then Filomena Daddario would do. Selma couldn't come until her divorce was finalised. He was petrified that his health would collapse, particularly the shaking of his hands. His handwriting had been noticeably better than during his last few years in the States, but now it was starting to deteriorate again, as he wrote to the comrades:

> The tum is splendid, the hands terrible. I am scared stiff they will go back on me altogether. A secretary cannot substitute, only a friend can. Mozart's wife sat at table next to him and cut his meat for him. I know why. He needed his hands for playing and for writing music. They had to be ready whenever he was ready.[11]

He arranged to see a doctor, a specialist recommended by Learie Constantine. The doctor failed to find anything physically wrong with CLR, diagnosing instead 'excessive nervous strain and tension'. He told him he needed to relax and improve his diet. He suggested hypnosis, which horrified CLR, and yoga which he was sceptical about but agreed to try.

He was as busy as ever. He flew to Paris for a few days to meet old friends, including Daniel Guérin, whose book he had still failed to finish translating, and Ghita Luchaire, who he invited to come see him in London (and help him complete the translation). Once back home he had a commission to write about the British literary scene for an American magazine, the *Saturday Review*.

For the piece, James talked to three key literary figures of the time. Two were Stephen Spender, who he admired and who he hoped might ask him to write for *Encounter*, the magazine he edited, and John Lehmann, editor of the *London Magazine* (and former resident of 9 Heathcote Place). The third man was the one he was particularly interested in meeting. This was F. R. Leavis, the most influential literary theorist of his day. He went to meet Leavis in Cambridge and was clearly impressed with his 'high and severe standards' and his willingness to go against the cultural orthodoxies of the time:

> He is no academician. He believes that great literature is rooted in a community. But the old English community life, of which even a writer as recent as D. H. Lawrence wrote, has been destroyed. The old cultural tradition, rooted in that community, had but one remaining link with the present world: literature. And he believes that this tie too has been severed.[12]

He wrote Grace long letters talking about Shakespeare and literary theory, before coming to cricket, that heartbeat of 'old English community life': 'I am ready to launch a sociological re-evaluation of the game that is as radical as our ideas on society and literature.'[13]

In February the cavalry arrived as ordered. First came Filomena Daddario and then Grace Lee. Filomena had recently split up with Willie Gorman, CLR's brilliant but unstable and – it transpired – violent protégé. CLR sympathised and wrote to the American comrades to insist that Willie was monitored and kept away from female members of the group. According to Constance, he also started sleeping with Filomena (Martina was most likely in France with David Thomson, which may also have fed into the dip in CLR's spirits over Christmas and the new year).

Certainly Filomena's arrival immediately cheered him up. 'Everything has turned out wonderful,' he wrote to Lyman.[14] When Grace Lee arrived a few days later, however, she gave a rather more sober assessment of the situation: 'I think we arrived just in time,' she wrote to Raya.[15] She felt that CLR had visibly aged since she last saw him, and while initially the shaking wasn't as bad as she expected, after a few days he had a relapse.

Grace was staggered by the amount of work going on, and by the evident hard work of the various secretaries: 'Manila folders for everything, all his multifarious activities separated onto different tables and desks and bookshelves. But every morning a pile of some fifteen papers arrives. We didn't take care of them the first week at all and by Sunday they had piled up so much that it took almost a day just to sort without reading.'

The first thing Grace had to help CLR with was finding a bigger place to live, one that could more easily accommodate all this industry. They found a flat around the corner on Parliament Hill and Grace supervised the move. The flat was in a handsome red-brick house, just yards from Hampstead Heath, with fine views over London. George Orwell had lived in the house opposite in the thirties, while he was writing *Keep the Aspidistra Flying*.

The move completed, Grace was given a task of her own: to work with the Kenyan radical Mbiyu Koinange on a pamphlet about his country's resistance movement – the Mau Mau campaign against the British colonial power. She found this fascinating politically, though she found Koinange himself 'a somewhat pedestrian type, not at all charismatic', who 'hated living in England'.[16]

When Grace's report on CLR's health was received in the US, the comrades decided that what he needed was a holiday. He and Filomena went off to Paris for a few days while Grace was given the task of trying to figure out a workable schedule for all CLR's multifarious projects to actually get done.

The holiday didn't do much good. On CLR's return Grace was alarmed to note that there was a sluggishness about him she hadn't seen before, a disconnect between whirring mind and labouring body. She wondered whether it had to do with the medication his doctor had given him – tonics, pills and sleeping tablets.

> The physical tone of his body appears to be good on the surface. But when he walks, he will stumble . . . Since he has been taking all this medicine, he will be lying down, listening to something on the phonograph, to which he is very much interested, and before you know it, he has dozed off . . . I have never seen that happen before . . . To write an ordinary letter seems to be more than he can summon up the energy to do. He has been preparing an article on sports for the last week. He scribbles bits and pieces of it on sheets of paper, so small you can scarcely see them. To write the recent long letters he had to take Benzedrine.[17]

It was clearly very difficult for CLR himself, or for those close to him, to assess the extent of his health problems. In particular, to decide whether they were signs of serious illness – as CLR often felt they were – or whether they were the external signs of an overstressed lifestyle, exacerbated by an increasing dependence on pills to help him sleep and Benzedrine to help him work. It's tempting to speculate that there may be an element of what used to be popularly referred to as manic depression in his swinging between an urgent belief that his ideas were about to sweep the world and a sense of utter futility.

And it's certainly telling that what pulled CLR out of his lethargy, at least for a while, was a phone call from Larry Montague at the *Guardian* that April, asking him if he would like to do daily cricket match reports for the paper. In a letter written soon afterwards Grace reminded him of the effect of the call: 'The whole room brightened up, not just people but even the furnishings, that afternoon, and you got dressed and sat on the edge of the bed looking like a different man.'[18]

Cricket seemed to soothe CLR: Grace saw it as 'something familiar where your organism feels at home. That is what the cricket was in May. I could see it in the way you walked round Lord's and called in your reports.'

It was only a partial panacea, though. Grace headed back to Detroit in June, where she would marry Jimmy Boggs, the Black auto worker and activist, somewhat to CLR's disapproval. Before she left she sent another bulletin on CLR's health to Raya:

> The situation is very serious . . . after some months what seems to me to be taking place is that he is living purely on his nerves and his will, and that this is undermining his fundamental stocks of organic functioning . . . it is painful to watch.[19]

She describes the effort it took CLR to drink a cup of tea, his hands shaking madly, pouring half the tea into the saucer to cool it down, then pouring it back, and looking like a man who'd just run a hundred-yard sprint by the time he'd finished.

With Grace back in the US and Filomena visiting family in Italy before heading back to America herself, CLR carried on reporting on the cricket, turning in his reports from the beginning of May till the end of July. He also persuaded the *Guardian* to run extracts from the George Headley book he had been working on. By the end of his stint, though, he was on his knees and writing to Lyman again, telling him he needed a break, three months at least.

Lyman came up trumps once more and that August CLR headed off to Europe for an extended stay. He had hoped that Selma might be able to come over to Europe to join him, but his divorce was still dragging on. He wrote to Constance, who had now broken up with an increasingly violent Wilbur, asking her to speed things up, and promising not to make trouble. He invoked Nobbie's interests, suggesting that she might be able to bring him over to London for a visit:

> The situation is unfortunate but it is not unusual, and in all bad situations, the thing to do is to turn the evil into good. He is a brilliant child. Give him the security of constant and friendly contact with both his parents. From early on he can gain wide experience of the world, United States, England, France, West Indies. This that can hurt him can be made into something that will help him. You can make it or you can break it.*[20]

And so CLR embarked on a three-month tour of Europe. He went to Paris, to Florence and Rome and on to Athens, and evidently had a wonderful time. He wrote to Grace from Athens full of ecstatic thoughts about the genius of Michelangelo, as seen in Italy, and now the anonymous sculptors of ancient Olympia. Being in the country itself had taken his longstanding interest in Greek history and philosophy to a new level. He saw transitions everywhere: from Greek

* It clearly cost him a lot to keep up this positive tone to Constance The very same day he wrote to his lawyer that 'my wife is a person who has no principles or shame whatever, and is governed solely by what she can get away with'.

sculpture to drama, Olympia to Aeschylus and from Michelangelo to Shakespeare. All of it, CLR thought, was a product of 'the drive of the popular democracy for a new form of expression'. Even his beloved Melville could now be properly situated in history:

> Now I think I know where Melville stands – he is in literature what this Olympian fellow and Michelangelo are in sculpture. He takes the traditional mode of expression and carries it to the utmost limit – different civilizations are held together in *Moby-Dick* as they are in the Olympian man and Michelangelo.[21]

He also tells her that his health is much improved, his hands have stopped shaking and he has quit smoking cigarettes (though he is still smoking six small cigars and six pipes a day!).

On his way back from Greece he stopped off in the South of France at Rustique Olivette, a villa owned by Daniel Guérin and used as a small artists' colony, a place writers and painters stayed for free with meals cooked for them by a Madame Reita.* A decade later Chester Himes would begin writing his autobiography there. It was up in the hills just above the communist-leaning port town of La Ciotat.

This was very much CLR's ideal environment, but while staying there he grew fretful at the prospect of his return to 'dark, gloomy' London.[22] Martina came to see him for lunch one day. She had indeed been with David Thomson in France, but she was now in the midst of an affair with an artist and en route to Italy. CLR cannot have been pleased about this, as his next letter to Lyman sees him once more demanding assistance back in London. He has decided he wants Selma to come, divorce or no divorce.

CLR finally arrived back in London on 24 November 1954. Six weeks later, at the beginning of the new year, Selma and her son would finally join him there.

* CLR would appear to have been there at the same time as the poet Paul Celan.

Chapter Seventeen

Selma and Sam arrived in London in early January, right in the teeth of winter. CLR had done his best to prepare for their arrival. He'd installed a gas stove and had a vast amount of shelving erected. He wrote to Lyman telling him that he had a acquired a local reputation for 'American-ness' – expecting things to be done straight away. It had all been a considerable operation, though one he seems to have largely supervised from his bed. Mrs Walls had been a tower of strength, as had Geoffrey Bagot, an old friend from his first days in London twenty years earlier.

It was they who were deputised to meet Selma and Sam on arrival and bring them to Hampstead. A few days later Selma wrote to the Paines to tell them they had settled in quickly and Sam was already at school. They were getting used to England and had developed a stable routine.

This stability, however, was soon to be interrupted by a crisis in the Correspondence Publishing Committee. The past year had seen relations between CLR and Raya steadily deteriorate. Raya was still deep into her investigation of Marx and Hegel. She had written long letters to CLR and Grace Lee, developing her understanding of Hegel's 'absolute idea'. CLR had barely responded, wrapped up in his new interests: Melville and Shakespeare and the lessons of great literature for political philosophy. Once he finally did read some of Raya's work, he suggested that Selma should rewrite it, to make it more comprehensible to the workers. This added insult to injury, as Raya was already dubious about CLR's championing of Selma.

Ultimately it was probably the simple fact of CLR being in London, while Raya was in Detroit, that prevented them from patching up their differences. Instead Raya's unhappiness with what she saw as CLR's dictatorial style festered to the point at which she decided to split the group.

In the last week of March 1955 Raya and her followers, probably a little over half the party, removed files, typewriters and mailing lists from the Correspondence office in Detroit. They took copies of *Indignant Heart*,* but left behind *Mariners, Renegades and Castaways*. Martin Glaberman, CLR's man on the spot, managed to secure the bank account, but the split was a fact. After fourteen years of working hand in glove, calling each other Brother and Sister in their letters, Johnson and Forest, CLR and Raya, would go their separate political ways.

CLR took the split hard. As the rupture took place, unfolding in a series of letters from the US, he became ever more depressed. Selma bore the brunt of it. Each day's mail was fraught with danger for her. She told Freddy Paine that she lived in terror of CLR receiving bad news. He would get ill, or walk around the house like a ghost for days on end, only brightening when Sam came back from school.

It was a heavy blow to an already embattled organisation. CLR had always argued and believed that a small organisation with the right policies was more valuable than a larger one – like the SWP – with outdated ideas, but Correspondence, now, was tiny. There were perhaps twenty-five members remaining, in New York, Detroit and Los Angeles. Their flagship paper – the effective reason for their existence – was losing a fortune. They were printing five thousand copies of each edition, despite having no more than a hundred or so subscriptions, according to Marty Glaberman. It was losing around $2000 a month. Lyman Paine was underwriting this. In a letter Glaberman acknowledges $20,000 worth of loans from him at this time (around $200,000 in today's terms). Lyman was also subsidising two households: Constance and Nobbie in New York; CLR, Selma and Sam in London.

This was hardly a sustainable basis for a revolutionary movement, but nevertheless they battled on. *Correspondence* continued to appear, if less regularly. It was now edited by Jimmy Boggs. They continued also

* The autobiography of Si Owens (party name Charles Denby) that Constance had put together.

to put out pamphlets on particular subjects. First Marty Glaberman wrote one on wildcat strikes, then CLR set himself to write an essay on Athenian democracy and its relevance to modern-day radicals.

Entitled *Every Cook Can Govern*, this justly celebrated essay saw CLR arguing that nothing had ever surpassed the Athenian approach to politics.

To further simplify an already fairly broad-brush argument, CLR writes that in ancient Athens, around the fifth century BC, the city-state was governed by constantly revolving committees of fifty, elected by drawing lots, so that laws and policies were made by ordinary men (not women – there were limits to the Athenian virtues) serving for a short, fixed time:

> The vast majority of Greek officials were chosen by a method which amounted to putting names into a hat and appointing the ones whose names came out. Now the average CIO bureaucrat or Labour Member of Parliament in Britain would fall in a fit if it was suggested to him that any worker selected at random could do the work that he is doing, but that was precisely the guiding principle of Greek Democracy. And this form of government is the government under which flourished the greatest civilization the world has ever known.[1]

CLR's reverence for Athens is all-encompassing. *Every Cook Can Govern* hymns its qualities – not just its rigorous approach to democracy but its achievements in arts, philosophy, science, mathematics, drama. And yet the uncomfortable truth is that Athens was also a slave society. How could a man, whose own family history followed on so swiftly from slavery, come to look so favourably on this world?

To answer that, it's worth considering the ways in which, when writing about ancient Greece, CLR is actually also writing about Trinidad. Both are compact societies with a significant, effectively disenfranchised element – in the Trinidad of CLR's youth the Indians or 'coolies' were still clambering out of indentured labour status – and keen intellectual ferment. When CLR put on plays at the Pamphyllian

High School or sat outside QRC following his own curriculum, was he seeing himself in the footsteps of the Athenians? Were CLR and Mendes and the rest of their circle all aspiring to those same essential qualities?

Part of CLR's great contribution to modern thought lies in his ability to extract the positive, useful lessons from past models, be they Athenian democracy or the novels of Herman Melville, while effectively discarding the more problematic areas: slavery in Athens; religion in Melville.

Every Cook Can Govern remains one of CLR's most enduringly influential theses, as it combines a clear lesson with clear prose and finds surprising parallels with the modern world. Thus he finds a quotation from Pericles,* whose relevance to the changing Britain he lives in, with its new immigrants, is obvious:

> And, just as our political life is free and open, so is our day-to-day life in our relations with each other. We do not get into a state with our next-door neighbour if he enjoys himself in his own way, nor do we give him the kind of black looks which, though they do no real harm, still do hurt people's feelings. We are free and tolerant in our private lives; but in public affairs we keep to the law. This is because it commands our deep respect.

How much racism CLR experienced in London at this time, now that he had a racially mixed family there, is hard to gauge. Living in Hampstead rather than one of the immigrant hotspots like Notting Hill or Brixton must have helped. Neither CLR nor Selma mention any racism in their letters to friends. Instead Selma writes to Freddy Paine that she did encounter some prejudice, not against her for having a Black partner but because she was an American.

Selma found an unusual way of countering that prejudice. Within just six months she became a serious cricket fan. CLR would play cricket on the Heath with Sam and other local boys, including their

* Or, at least, from Thucydides' account of what Pericles said.

landlord's son Oliver, and as a family they went to watch matches. CLR was thoroughly enjoying getting to know Sam and teaching him the rudiments of cricket ('the infant Samuel is a phenomenon,' he wrote to Lyman, sounding every inch the Victorian patriarch).[2]

Sam, like his mother and stepfather a lifetime political activist, remembers finding the move to London surprisingly easy. He remembers CLR – or 'Jimmy' as he called him – as a fine father substitute. He took enthusiastically to cricket and even mastered the arcane art of bowling a googly. CLR refused to believe him at first, then Sam took him out on to the Heath and bowled him with one.

Selma too developed a passion for cricket. She told Freddy that she could happily spend all day watching a game. And how amazed the locals were when they saw this young American queuing up at seven in the morning to buy Lord's Test Match tickets (CLR himself turned up rather later).

CLR was starting to develop his ideas for a book on the game. To his great satisfaction he gave a lecture on the subject at Lord's itself: 'The reception astonished even me,' he declared.[3] Better yet, he went on to discuss his ideas with C. B. Fry. Fry, who he had encountered as a reporter back in the thirties, was one of the men who had personified the great English game in the Edwardian era:

> A few days ago, I went to see C. B. Fry, the greatest athlete of his generation and a great authority, theoretical and practical, on sport of every kind. He is also, by the way, a classical scholar of Latin and Greek and has been all his life. He took a brilliant degree in both at Oxford. I spoke to him about the Olympic games of Greece and also what I call the aesthetics of cricket. He asked me to come back to see him again. He said he had never seen the subject treated anywhere.

Quite what his American comrades made of this news, imparted in a letter and followed by an obscure attempt to link cricket to Detroit union militancy, is hard to say. Certainly the gulf between CLR's life in London and that of his comrades back in Detroit was starting to loom very large.

Selma knew this better than anyone. She had taken on an enormous challenge, coming from LA to London in the middle of winter with her six-year-old son, there to make a life with her much older, and highly preoccupied, partner. But, writing at the time, she was remarkably positive about her adopted country. She thought London beautiful and her newly assembled family a great success, though they all missed Nobbie's presence.

By this time CLR had given her Dorothy Bennett's biography of Arnold Bennett (he had also given Constance a copy years before). CLR's love of Bennett's work, especially the novel *Lord Raingo*, had endured from his early years. He also identified with the man himself to a surprising extent, and never more so than in Dorothy Bennett's memoir of her husband. His intention, in giving Constance and Selma copies of the book, seems to have been to prepare his partner for the reality of life with him. Selma found it particularly illuminating. She told Freddy she had never been so affected by a book. And it's not hard to see why. Take this passage for instance:

> It was almost a justification of his squandered powers of energy and his high-pressure existence that he was able to enjoy life so vitally at so many facets of consciousness. That is to say, in the intervals when he was not suffering from neuralgia or over-fatigue, and all the internal or muscular ills that this habitual general strain engendered, he enjoyed it.
>
> These bodily ills were the outcome of his high concert-pitch of nerves and sensibility, so that they were often dissipated by fresh contacts with brilliant and interesting people, even when peace and quiet would have better conserved his powers and energy.

All of this could easily apply to CLR too: the endless ailments and the exhaustion, alternating with an absolute zest for life and insatiable intellectual curiosity.

One other respect in which CLR resembled Bennett was in his constant worrying about money. Bennett did actually have money, while CLR was heavily dependent on Lyman Paine, but the result was the same – stress and sleeplessness. Again and again CLR's letters to Lyman offer an uncomfortable mixture of political ideas and pleas for financial help. He even asks him to read the Dorothy Bennett book, to show that he is both needing of and deserving of help.

Just what a low ebb CLR was at is brought home by the impression he made on George Lamming, who he ran into in central London:

> We met by chance on the Charing Cross Road in London. He had recognised me from a photograph on the jacket of a book of mine which he had read.* He introduced himself. To my innocent eye he had the air of a vagrant. Lean and frail.[4]

Nor was Lamming much reassured when they sat down to talk:

> When he said, 'Lamming,' and I said, 'Yes,' I was very excited and a little shocked when he told me who he was. I would not have known who he was just by seeing him, and I said, 'Let us go and have some coffee.' We went into this coffee shop and what I noticed was the shaking of his hands. I mean he couldn't hold the cup of coffee with one hand. He had to take his head down to the cup. I don't know what he was doing on Charing Cross Road. I didn't pursue that then, but later what I discovered was that Charing Cross Road had these pinball games ... Apparently he was very fascinated with this and would quite often visit these pinball machine places where he played and betted. I think he was also there book-hunting.

So concerned were the American comrades as to CLR's physical and mental health that Lyman Paine came to visit in December. Before he arrived CLR wrote to him to ask him to bring a Royal Deluxe Stetson from New York, size 7⅝, colour brown. This would be CLR's trademark hat for years to come. He also mentions that he has a swelling on the neck. Nothing too serious, he is fairly sure.

* *In the Castle of My Skin*, Lamming's first novel, which made quite an impression on literary London when it appeared in 1953.

Lyman's visit went well enough. The two old friends were glad to see one another and they celebrated Christmas and CLR's birthday together – the latter with the aid of a bottle of Bols gin.

However, Lyman had been hoping to persuade CLR that his eccentric course of study – all this cricket and Shakespeare – was of little use to the comrades in America. He wanted a change of tack and was frustrated to find CLR unwilling to listen. As Grace Lee wrote years later: 'Upon his return he reported that the visit had been a disaster; CLR simply would not listen to anything that did not confirm his own views.'[5]

Eric Williams was also in London at that time and he asked CLR to join him to discuss his plans for a radical new party, to be called the People's National Movement (PNM). The Trinidadian people were tiring of their laissez-faire colonial government, led by another old friend of CLR's, Albert Gomes, still something of a cultural radical – a great champion of carnival and calypsonians – but these days definitely a political conservative. Williams, who had spent the past decade working for the Caribbean Research Council, believed the people were ready for independence, probably as part of a Federation of West Indian Islands. They just needed a party to lead them. He realised he needed help in formulating a plan, so he called on his old friends: CLR for political philosophy, George Padmore for practical liberation politics and Arthur Lewis for economic advice. All three made their contributions and Eric Williams went back to Trinidad, ready to get to work.

The year of 1956 was a difficult one for CLR. After Lyman's return to the US his health broke down again. He wanted to work on his cricket book but struggled to get down to the actual writing. The financial woes continued. In March he wrote to the comrades demanding that they provide the sum of £110 a month for his family's upkeep. He clearly hoped that the organisation as a whole would raise funds to keep him afloat and writing. In practice, though, it was only Lyman who responded.

By the spring his health had declined to the extent that he had to go to hospital to have the growth on his neck removed. Fortunately, it turned out to be benign. To make matters worse Selma also spent time in hospital that spring.

On a happier note, the divorce from Constance finally came through. The way was now clear for CLR and Selma to get married, which would have the additional benefit of allowing her to get a job in the UK. Before they were married, though, Constance came over with Nobbie for an extended visit. They arrived in June; Constance stayed for a couple of weeks, then left Nobbie to stay with his father for two months before returning to the US in September.

It was three years since he'd seen his son. Throughout that time he'd done whatever he could to keep the relationship alive, writing letters and stories, sometimes even recording them on tape or vinyl. Constance wrote to him with news and CLR did his best to advise her. Self-centred as he may have been in many ways, CLR's devotion to his son is absolutely plain in his letters: 'I love you 873217314256891234023456789 million billion times. And that's a fact, Nob. That isn't only a lot of figures, that's a fact.'[6]

Nobbie was seven years old, a very bright but troubled child. He was a precocious reader, but found it difficult to get on with other kids or listen to his teachers. One of them suggested Constance take Nobbie to see a psychiatrist – an idea that CLR was vehemently opposed to. Objectively, of course, Nobbie's situation as a mixed-race boy being brought up on precious little money by his white single mother, in a place and time in which all that was highly unusual, was never likely to be easy.

The visit to London was a success. Father and son were delighted to see one another, and the two boys got on reasonably well, after a few initial difficulties, both of them being used to being only children. Selma wrote to Freddy Paine to express her delight at having Nobbie there. She comments on how like his father he was, how brilliant and beautiful.

Nobbie wrote to his mother after a few weeks and also showed every sign of having a good time. He tells her that he is going to get a badge for his blazer from 'our cricket club'. He tells her that they saw the Australians play: 'Benaud is an Australian and he hit one over the boundary for six'; and they visited the Tower of London – 'Boy we had a smashing time there!'[7]

Nobbie left for New York in early September, accompanied on his journey by CLR's old flatmate from 9 Heathcote Place, the German schoolteacher Ernst Perl. Shortly afterwards, on 16 September, CLR and Selma were finally married at the Hampstead Register Office. The best man was their friend, the West Indian doctor and activist David Pitt (for years he was also effectively CLR's private physician). They celebrated with a two-week honeymoon in Rome, paid for, inevitably, by Lyman.

Back in London the struggle to write and keep financially afloat continued. CLR's spirits were raised in October, however, with the advent of the short-lived Hungarian Revolution. CLR saw this uprising against Soviet communism, led by workers' councils, as a validation of everything he'd been saying for the past decade or more. He saw it as proof positive that the people not the party would be the engine of any progressive revolution. Despite its ultimate defeat by the Russian tanks, CLR saw events in Hungary as a beacon and a model. Here he is, writing a year later in a short book called *Facing Reality*, co-authored with Grace Lee and Cornelius Castoriadis:

> One of the greatest achievements of the Hungarian Revolution was to destroy once and for all the legend that the working class cannot act successfully except under the leadership of a political party. It did all that it did precisely because it was not under the leadership of a political party. If a political party had existed to lead the revolution, that political party would have led the revolution to disaster, as it has led every revolution to disaster during the last thirty years. There was leadership on all sides, but there was no party leading it. No party in the world would have dared to lead the country into a counter-attack in the face of thousands of Russian tanks. Nothing but an organization in close contact with the working-class population in the factory, and which therefore knew and felt the strength of the population at every stage, could have dared to begin the

> battle a second time. Still later, after the military battle had been lost, no organization except Workers' Councils would have dared to start a general strike and carry it on for five weeks, unquestionably the most astonishing event in the whole history of revolutionary struggles.

For years CLR and his group had been struggling against the tide, up against a prosperous and complacent post-war America. But now, as 1956 turned into 1957, change was in the air. Snuffed out for the moment in Eastern Europe, but alive in Africa and alive in the American South.

In Africa, the Gold Coast was leading the way to independence for Britain's former colonies. After ten years of struggle, and now led by the charismatic Kwame Nkrumah, the people had voted overwhelmingly for independence. And the British, resigned to the steady diminution of the empire, had agreed to let them go. On 6 March 1957 the Gold Coast was to become an independent country with a new name, Ghana. And Kwame Nkrumah would be the first president. The standard-bearer of a liberated Africa.

In the American South, the civil rights movement was starting to emerge as a real power. The murder of Emmett Till in 1955 had provoked outraged horror across the nation. At the end of the same year Rosa Parks began the Montgomery Bus Boycott. A year later, on 20 December 1956, the city caved in and desegregated its buses. By which time the movement had found its own charismatic leader, the young Reverend Dr Martin Luther King.

Even in CLR's home country, the traditionally sleepy backwater that was Trinidad, change was afoot. Eric Williams was now the new chief minister, sweeping the election after attracting huge crowds to hear him speak in the open-air 'University of Woodford Square'.*

CLR's influence on Williams was plain to see, but only if you were one of the tiny handful of people who'd read *Every Cook Can Govern.*

* Woodford Square, a big open space in the centre of Port of Spain, had long been a place where speakers could address crowds.

Williams's use of Woodford Square was a completely conscious echo of CLR's idealised Athenian agora; he even concluded one of his speeches with a reading from Pericles' funeral oration, CLR's favourite.

The only problem was that over here were these momentous world events, and over there was the Correspondence Publishing Committee, a couple of dozen people spread across Detroit, Los Angeles, New York and London. The oppressed people of the world were rising up spontaneously, just as CLR had predicted, but without the remotest notion of his – or his organisation's – existence. It was only their leaders who knew the name of CLR James.

Then, in early February, came a letter from Accra. One of these leaders, Kwame Nkrumah himself, was inviting CLR to take part in the independence celebrations. And crucially, given his straitened circumstances, travel would be paid for by the Ghanaian government. Thanks to the good offices of his friend George Padmore,*[8] CLR would be back at the high table of politics.

Lyman Paine, of course, was delighted – and helped out with expenses. Selma, too, was thrilled. At last her sombre, worried husband had something to look forward to. He flew out to Accra on 23 February. Selma wrote to Freddy that day to tell her how proud of him she felt, when she saw him off at the airport, and how richly he deserved this day in the sun.

* The Jameses had invited the Padmores for Christmas dinner a couple of months earlier, an invitation the notoriously antisocial Padmore had been reluctant to accept, according to his partner Dorothy: 'He does moan so at having to go out. I can envisage us growing old and becoming hermits in our own house, because he will neither go out nor have people home!'

Chapter Eighteen

CLR stayed two weeks in Africa, arriving in a colony called the Gold Coast and departing from a proud new nation called Ghana. He made the most of his time there. He made several speeches, travelled around the country meeting a range of Ghanaians, including opposition voices, and spent time talking to the man who had led his country into independence, Kwame Nkrumah.

CLR had first met Francis Nkrumah, as he was then known, in New York in 1945. Raya Dunayevskaya had met Nkrumah in a Harlem library, at a talk by W. E. B. Du Bois, and arranged for him to talk to CLR at the Paines' apartment on Hudson Street.* At the time Nkrumah had just left Lincoln University, where he'd written a Pan-African manifesto called *Towards Colonial Freedom*. He was preparing to travel to London, now that the war was over, so CLR wrote him a letter of introduction to give to George Padmore. In words he would come to regret, CLR told Padmore that Nkrumah was 'not very bright, but nevertheless he is determined to throw the imperialists out of Africa'.[†1]

The Nkrumah he met in Ghana twelve years later was clearly a formidable political leader and one who retained a strong belief in the importance of political ideology. His ambition was to be recognised as the originator of a distinctly African political philosophy; to be the equivalent of Lenin in Russia or Mao in China. He was also bright

* He also met Grace Lee, with whom he was clearly very taken. Here's her account: 'I invited him to a party that some friends who worked with me in the plant were giving that night. Subsequently, he wrote me a number of letters from England, and after he returned to the Gold Coast ... he wrote to ask me to come to Africa and marry him.' (*Living for Change.*)

† In subsequent years CLR would explain that what he really meant was that Nkrumah was not yet that well educated in political theory.

enough to know that he needed help in the venture. He had recently published an autobiography, but that was hardly a philosophical work and had been largely ghost-written by his English secretary, Erica Powell. CLR saw an opportunity beckoning:

> Nkrumah told me that his autobiography told the story but nobody had yet 'philosophized it'. All he had been able to do was the narrative. He practically asked me to do it and I told him I would . . . [he] says that he wants his story 'philosophised' 'Put into principles'. Who else can do it but we?[2]

The obvious answer to this question might have been George Padmore, who was far closer to Nkrumah and a prolific writer on Africa. But, according to CLR, Nkrumah had decided Padmore was not up to the job. He reported the conversation back to Lyman: 'GP has been left behind. It is very sad. N wants more than GP can give. He may be bitter and fight us.'[3]

It's worth noting here that while CLR was personally friendly with Padmore, they were frequently at odds in their approach to politics. CLR clearly saw himself as the greater intellect. Padmore, for his part, thought CLR had his head in the clouds. A year or two earlier, in a letter to Richard Wright, he let on that 'Nello is still in his Ivory Tower, planning the American revolution. What a dreamer!'[4] And while they were in Ghana together, Dorothy Padmore* had written to Ellen Wright, describing CLR as a 'poseur'.[5]

In other letters to the US comrades CLR talks about how well received his speeches were by the masses and by his fellow delegates. It's clear that he was thoroughly reinvigorated by his experience, the move from a political byway to the very heart of change. He had been surrounded by delegates from all over the world and found a ready audience for his ideas: 'Believe me, I do not talk much, but when I talk, they listen.'[6]

* Though she was not actually married to George, his partner Dorothy Pizer was generally known as Dorothy Padmore.

CLR's diary of his trip gives a rather more balanced view of Ghana. In particular, he notes the beginnings of a personality cult around Nkrumah. However, in his public writings, and even his letters to his comrades, he chose to ignore his doubts, preferring instead to add to the adulation Nkrumah was receiving from all sides: 'He could tomorrow become a Prime Minster in Great Britain ... an exceptional man.'[7]

CLR stopped off in Paris on his way back from Accra to talk to Cornelius Castoriadis, who he wanted to collaborate with him on a pamphlet dealing with the implications of the Hungarian Revolution.

Back in London, on 12 March, he managed to switch concerns in a way only he could. He led a debate at the Cricket Society on a topic he'd chosen: 'Neither Toss, Weather nor Wicket were Decisive Elements in the Defeat of Australia Last Season'. Without missing a beat he managed to move from Nkrumah and revolution to the English spinners Laker and Lock, and the Australian fast bowlers Lindwall and Miller. His opposite number in the debate was a former Hampshire policeman turned poetry producer turned cricket commentator, John Arlott. Arlott was a quiet revolutionary. As a poetry producer at the BBC he'd championed the likes of Dylan Thomas. And as a commentator he'd shown the immensely stuffy BBC that it was possible to have a regional accent and still be knowledgeable, erudite and enormously popular with the listening public. CLR and John Arlott would be friends from here onwards.

Two weeks later, though, CLR was entertaining not a British institution but a man on the cusp of becoming one of the great figures of his century, the Reverend Martin Luther King, Jr.

Although CLR hadn't met him there, King had also been in Ghana for the independence celebrations, accompanied by a whole raft of civil rights luminaries, not to mention the vice-president of the United States, Richard Nixon. King had taken the opportunity to talk to Nixon and had been invited to Washington DC. Nixon, however, had refused to come down to the South to see for himself what was going on.

From Ghana, King had spent a few days travelling through Europe before arriving in London on 21 March. He spent the following day seeing the sights: Buckingham Palace, Westminster Abbey, the Houses of Parliament. A month later he would reflect on this visit – the beauties of London and the ugliness of colonialism – in a sermon he gave back in Montgomery.

That evening, 22 March, there was a dinner, to which CLR was invited. Afterwards he spoke to King and evidently made an impression as he ended up inviting him to lunch at Parliament Hill on the 24th. King and his wife Coretta accepted the invitation and duly arrived at half past twelve. The other guests were George Lamming and Dr David Pitt.

The lunch was a great success. The Kings stayed until 5 p.m., when they had to leave to catch an overnight flight to New York. Selma served the guests fish and was struck at the time by King's humility:

> He was extremely modest in 1957. The story of his work was told by Coretta, not him. He just listened for long periods and bowed his head. He was quiet. You could see that he could be angry, but he kept it in check.[8]

CLR was enormously impressed by his visitor. He wrote a long letter to the comrades describing the Kings' account of the Montgomery Bus Boycott. 'It was one of the most astonishing events of endurance by a whole population that I have ever heard of,' he wrote.[9]

While this is obviously true, it's a little puzzling that CLR seems only then to have woken up to the significance of what had been happening in the civil rights movement. Being based in London, and immersed in his literary/philosophical project, not to mention watching the cricket, he seems to have let it pass him by. The visit to Ghana, though, had reset his political compass. Once again he was seeing specifically Black liberation movements in Africa and the West Indies and the US South as at the vanguard of revolutionary change.

CLR was bursting with ideas. He wanted to write a book about Ghana, somehow incorporating what was happening in the US. As ever he was optimistic about its commercial potential ('I can see the possibility of selling 10,000 copies in Britain alone'[10]). He wanted to continue with his book about cricket. And he wanted to write his collaborative pamphlet on the Hungarian Revolution and the importance of workers' councils and the English shop steward movement.

Much of CLR's knowledge of English working-class politics had come from an old Trotskyist comrade from the pre-war days called Alan Christianson. It was Christianson who persuaded CLR of the revolutionary character of the British trade union shop stewards. CLR fell out with the volatile Christianson early in 1957, but no matter: he was able to get the inside track on British factory life from rather closer to home.

Now that she had legal status in the UK, Selma was working in a west London factory. For her it was a welcome change. In LA she had always worked in factories and CLR's Hampstead intellectual world was deeply foreign to her. She started work near Gypsy Corner, in a television factory, wiring and soldering. It was the same sort of work that she had done in California. She enjoyed meeting regular Londoners, West Indian immigrants among them, and started to garner a deeper understanding of her adopted city.

In a letter to Freddy she described her fellow workers. The young men were imitation Americans while the women seemed amazingly sure of themselves: more so than she had ever seen anywhere else. CLR told her this was 'British self-reliance', where the crucial thing was to avoid self-pity. Selma appreciated the lack of respect for authority, but struggled to adapt to a culture in which it was considered rude to pay her fellow workers compliments on their clothes, or to ask personal questions.

As for popular culture, Selma told Freddy that everything in London was rock and roll – all the young people at work loved it, and hearing the stuffy British radio presenters announce a rock'n'roll number particularly amused her. She went on to say that she hadn't found any opportunity to go out dancing. It's a reminder of the thirty-year age gap between her and her husband, the sacrifices she'd made to live with him in London.

The strain of working on three books at once quickly began to show. Selma quit work at the factory to assist and soon CLR was writing to the US comrades demanding that Grace come over and help. Sure enough, in late April, she took a boat across the Atlantic, bearing with her a trunk full of items as requested by CLR, including a pressure cooker, a stack of yellow lined writing pads, two Paper Mate pens, a wall-mounted can opener, some metal drinking cups and a whole Virginia ham – for 'personal enjoyment, which is not to be disregarded'.[11]

Grace arrived at the end of the month and was quickly incorporated into a relentless daily schedule, as detailed by CLR in a letter to Lyman. 'It is a good schedule,' he announced, 'and I am proud to say that I am entirely responsible for both its organisation and its administration.'[12]

It began at 8 with an egg and grapefruit juice and a shot of Vitamin B ('administered by Dr Selma Weinstein') and ended with the TV news at 10.45. The rest of the time was spent working, with breaks for meals, a bath, a walk and an hour's cricket on the Heath with Sam. The TV was a novelty hired for the cricket season: 'only 50 bob a month, for four months'.

The main focus of the work was the Ghana book. Selma was busy turning CLR's notes into the first section of the book, while Grace and CLR worked on a political reinterpretation of Nkrumah's autobiography. She describes how CLR went about it:

> [He] tells, for example, how Nkrumah arrives in Ghana in 1947 after a sea trip, during which he has been very cautious, almost hiding, afraid that he will not be admitted. He is met by an official, an African, who asks him his name and takes him aside. N is sure that the game is up and he will be deported. Instead, out of earshot, the African says that the people have been waiting for him day after day, shakes his hand enthusiastically and tells him not to worry about his papers. He will take care of them ... It only takes one paragraph ... but after J has devoted two paragraphs to it in the book, it becomes a guide to all who are seeking to find a way to draw strength from the people themselves, and who want to learn how to act.[13]

Little more than a month after Grace arrived, she got the chance to meet Nkrumah again in person. He was in London for the Commonwealth Prime Ministers' Conference. A whole group of them – CLR, Selma and Grace, plus George Padmore and Eric Williams – all went to visit Nkrumah at the Dorchester Hotel.

This meeting must have dashed CLR's hopes that he was to become Nkrumah's resident advisor. George Padmore was, after all, to take that role. Padmore had stayed on in Ghana for two months after the celebrations, working on detailed plans for the new society Nkrumah was building. He was focusing on infrastructure, water depots, electricity generators, roads. Later in the year he would be returning to Ghana to live, with his own government department and the title of Advisor to the Prime Minister on African Affairs.

This news would appear to have put the brakes on the Ghana book project. Attention swung back to the political manifesto, Hungary et al. Grace dutifully switched her attentions to this new task. Her husband, Jimmy Boggs, came over to London on vacation from his job in the Chrysler auto plant (a place whose routines were doubtless a tad more arduous than CLR's Hampstead schedule). It was Boggs who gave the project the name, one that was both perceptive and ironic: they would be Facing Reality, this tiny cadre of revolutionaries with huge ambitions and minuscule resources.

Boggs, whose relationship with CLR was always guarded, soon went back to Detroit. Grace followed in September, leaving CLR (and an uncredited Selma) to finish the work on the manifesto, and chivvy Castoriadis to produce his contribution.*

After the euphoria of the early months of the year, the last months were a dreadful comedown. All the expenses of the summer had been predicated at least partly on the promise of contracts for potentially

* Ultimately, *Facing Reality* would appear credited to CLR, Grace Lee and Cornelius Castoriadis. However, Castoriadis felt that he hadn't properly signed off on the project, and that would be the end of their collaboration. Castoriadis's politics of radical autonomy later inspired the British radical group Solidarity. He would eventually become a psychoanalyst – which must surely have horrified CLR.

bestselling books But there was nothing ready to sell, just a half-written book on Ghana to go alongside the half-written book on cricket, the half-written book on American civilisation, the half-written book on George Headley, et cetera, et cetera. The only thing that was more or less completed was a manifesto advising them to Face Reality.

Well, CLR was about to have to do that. He put forward a publishing plan that would allow him time to finish all these various books and thus lead to huge sales. He just needed the US comrades to send him $7500. He was very clear that he didn't expect Lyman to fork out. Instead it should be the collective responsibility of the organisation. That's to say, the assorted factory workers who made up their membership should somehow find this very substantial sum – roughly $70,000 in today's terms – and send it to London so that the guru could carry on his life of the mind.

Lyman finally snapped. He told CLR that there was no money left. He had had to go cap in hand to his own father to provide the last monies and that was that. As for the membership, they did indeed scrape together a few dollars here and there, but hundreds not thousands.

On receiving this news CLR started to unravel. He wrote a series of hysterical letters to Lyman and Freddy that contained an unpleasant mixture of begging and threatening, shot through with the odd flash of self-knowledge. Again and again in the letters from this period he would include the line 'Don't psychologise me'. On one level that's a statement of political belief, but the constant repetition of the phrase suggests a man deeply worried about his own mental health.

Of course, there were simple practical reasons for his distress. Lack of money is always profoundly destabilising and CLR was unable to pay the rent, or support his family, without regular money coming from the US. Here is a little of what he wrote to Lyman on 29 November 1957:

> Send me $3000 and finish up with it for good and all . . . Can you send it or not? My credit here is at zero. In fact less than zero. I have thrown away or neglected every single opportunity that was

> presented to me . . . And behind it all is the fact that I can make my own way here. There is no problem about that. But I have to publish my books. I must have something to go on and people are getting very tired of me and my promises to produce manuscripts which I do not produce.[14]

Lyman cracked and sent another $1000. CLR responded by writing to Freddy, a strange rambling letter in which he wished any naysayers among the US comrades 'a horrible Christmas and a worse New Year'.[15] A week later he wrote again to say that they would be subletting the Parliament Hill place.

CLR and Selma had decided to cut their losses. CLR would finish work on *Facing Reality* over Christmas 1957 and send it off to the US, and then they would go to Algeciras in southern Spain where the climate was closer to the California Selma missed, the living was cheap and CLR could work on the one project that he could honestly see having some commercial viability: his cricket book.

He had written the opening chapters and already sent them to a Mr Boroughs at the BBC in the hope that they might be the basis for series of radio broadcasts, to run perhaps in tandem with the upcoming opening of the new West Indian Federal Parliament. The BBC were interested, but unsure what to do with the material. CLR wrote to David Thomson, who worked there, to express his frustration:

> I have heard that the Light Programme thinks that the material is more suitable for the overseas program. That is a load of nonsense. The overseas people know more or less what I'm writing about. It is people in England who don't.[16]

The Jameses arrived in Spain in mid-January 1958. Algeciras was a poor and dusty port town, mostly used to take ferries to Tangiers. It had a limited number of tourist places, doubtless all very cheap. They settled in a bungalow at the Hotel Solimar. Neither of them were well, both buffeted by the strains of the rows within the organisation and their money troubles. And yet CLR was mysteriously able to write

– 'Despite every obstacle the book is going marvellously,' he told Lyman.[17]

Indeed it was nearly complete when, a year after the Ghana independence celebrations, he received another invitation to a significant event in the colonial liberation struggle, this time in a place he knew very well.

CLR had been hoping Eric Williams might invite him to Trinidad for the inauguration of the West Indies Federal Parliament, which was taking place in Port of Spain on 22 April 1958. The invitation had not come – or at least not with an offer to pay for his travel. But then, in mid-March, CLR received a telegram from the Governor General. He was invited to the ball after all. His initial reaction, though, was decidedly equivocal. This is what he wrote to his US comrades:

> His telegram was cordial, beyond the bounds of duty. The political situation of the Federation internationally, and externally is critical to the last degree and I being who I am, this puts me in the heart of it.
>
> I have for many years wanted to go home. It will I believe add 10 years to my life and take off 10 years, but I view the prospect of mobilising myself for it with a distaste and bitterness of spirit that surprises even myself.[18]

This reluctance may simply have been a matter of health. Not long afterwards he wrote to Lyman to report that they were both suffering: 'Selma collapsed last night, is in bed and will stay there. For weeks I have had a beating and thudding in my head at nights. Have seen doctor.'[19] A few day later he reported again, to say that Selma was feeling better and as for himself, it was just another manifestation of his familiar stress: 'I have seen two doctors now. Nothing organic. Same old story.'[20]

Lyman responded with the same concern, and indeed love, for CLR that he and Freddy had consistently shown for nearly two decades:

> Only a relatively short time ago this trip home would have meant a great solace and caress to one a long time away from the mother roots. It is a terrible indictment of us that we have permitted or compelled such a strain upon you that now to go carries with it further difficulties in place of ease and freedom . . . it strikes me as far more imperative that you find the way to make the trip one of joy and reward rather than sheer duty . . . other things can wait.[21]

Long experience also led Lyman to suspect that there might be a financial component in CLR's reluctance to go. Even if his fare was paid, he would still need living expenses:

> [If] it is a matter solely or mainly of finances then I beg you to present at least a few of us with a blunt yet clear statement of the facts so that appropriate solutions can be found.

That did the trick. CLR left Spain on 15 April. A few days later he flew to Port of Spain. After twenty-six years, he was coming home.

Chapter Nineteen

There is a newspaper photo of CLR James on his arrival at Trinidad's Piarco airport. It was the first time in a long while that the press had taken sufficient interest in any of his doings to send a photographer. There are three men in the picture: the tall CLR is flanked by two shorter figures, his brother Eric and his old friend, the library chief Carlton Comma. CLR himself looks thin but animated, in a light-coloured suit and his Royal Deluxe Stetson.

The reason for the interest was essentially curiosity. The vast majority of Trinidadians knew nothing of CLR James. Those who knew most about him were his contemporaries, for whom he was an enigma – the brightest boy in Trinidad, who had belatedly gone to London and published books, as he was destined to, but had then all but vanished. There were rumours as to what had happened. He had gone to America. He was a communist, an outlaw.

The rumours weren't the reason for the newspaper photographer, though. The important thing wasn't that CLR had returned home after a quarter of a century, it was the matter of the man who'd invited him back. He had come at the invitation of the new chief minister, Eric Williams, aka the Doctor, the man who was going to lead Trinidad to independence. Word had it that this CLR James had taught the Doctor at QRC. Apparently, he had helped him with his big book, *Capitalism and Slavery*. He was the *éminence grise* come home to advise his protégé. So that's why the photographer was there: to see what an *éminence grise* looked like.

CLR had arrived with plenty of plans to talk to Eric Williams about. But he wanted to start by seeing his family for the first time in decades. His brother was the only exception: they had met up a few times in the fifties, in New York and London. Eric James was a significant figure in Trinidad, both the chief accountant of the Trinidad railways (a job for which he had already received an MBE from the Queen*) and secretary of the Trinidad Football Association.

Even though it was late in the evening, Eric took his brother straight to their father's house in Tunapuna. CLR described the reunion in a letter to Lyman soon afterwards:

> We went down to the old man that night and reached there at about 2 o'clock. He was very glad to see me and I was glad to see him. He said, 'well, it's a long time' and he practically said that he didn't think that he would see me. But there I was. We had a big meal. He had a bottle of champagne. And it is very difficult for him to be up so late.[1]

Perhaps a surprise, perhaps not, was his discovery that Robert James, the original Old Man, was still working:

> He lives in a good house, a house he built when he retired. He has a school of some nearly 60 pupils to whom he gives commercial lessons, and they sit for the English examination and pass. They come to him from all parts of the neighbourhood, some of them 20 miles away. He has to turn some back. He is, however quite old. He was 81 on July 15 and the strain on him is very great. But he can't help it. He must continue with the school because that's what he lives by.

There are obvious resemblances between father and son. Like CLR, Robert seems to go up and down in mood and health and, like CLR, he had a much younger female helper:

> He took a turn towards real old age about a year or two ago and when he goes out now, he has to go with a stick. But his mind is still as lively as ever. He talks by the yard to me telling me all the old stories and a whole heap of new ones. The other day he picked up

* In the 1956 Birthday Honours.

himself and went off to the races with his assistant. She is a young woman of about 30 whom he taught and she became an assistant after she passed her examinations. She has been with him for 14 years.

The other person who had been with Robert since his wife Bessie died, also fourteen years earlier, was CLR's sister Olive. CLR was quickly aware that, of the three siblings, she had drawn the short straw:

> Olive is a wonderful person. She is 56 and her life has been spent first of all nursing my mother when she was struck down with the stroke and afterwards taking care of my father. She is an old maid but she has very few of the characteristics of an old maid. She dresses herself very well and she has a good, good head. You will pardon me if I quote someone as saying that Olive has the James brain. When I left here, she took little interest in politics. Now she's as acute in analysis and as capable in gathering up information about the general political situation and the situation in her own neighbourhood as anybody I have met. She and my father, I regret to say, are reactionaries both. They are on the opposite party, though they deny it. I could win over Olive without a doubt because she has always believed that I was the most wonderful brother in the world and now I have come back, we start off exactly where we left off.
>
> But the essential thing about Olive is that she's a good woman, a fine person, recognised as such by anybody who knows her. There is nothing mean or cheap about her and her general responses to things and the sentiments are practically always fine. That is despite the hard life that she has lived. I hope to goodness that I should be able to give her a trip to England. My father says that he will give her the money to go any time. But of course he says that but he will be very put out if Olive left him, although he makes a great show. And I'm afraid he persecutes Olive quite a lot. That, however, is by the way. At 81, he is entitled to his idiosyncrasies.

When Selma arrived in Trinidad a little later, it was very clear to her as well that Olive had had a rough deal. Olive told Selma that taking care of her mother had been a pleasure: 'When I went to the movies she didn't resent it, when I came home she would ask me to tell her the whole story.' She had planned to finally leave home when her mother died, but by then her father was also going downhill and she was stuck. CLR gave her some money from time to time and Selma paid her for making her some clothes, but Olive's was a hard life.

CLR found a place to stay, Miss Stollmeyer's Guest House overlooking the Savannah. It was an eccentric establishment ('a century out of date,' according to another visitor of the time)[2] and run by a formidable old lady – a stout personage from one of the island's most prominent white families. CLR immediately set to giving lectures. And, clearly inspired by reconnecting with his family, he arranged for Nobbie to come to stay with him.

Nine-year-old Nobbie arrived with his best friend, Martin Slaughter, the son of Constance's erstwhile landlady in Greenwich Village. CLR evidently had no idea what he was letting himself in for. The two boys ran wild. Miss Stollmeyer told him off for letting them clamber over the building's rickety roof. He worried about them playing in the Dry River amid the snakes. He deputised his nephew, Eric's son Heno, to babysit the boys. They went into town and bought sheath knives, which he rapidly confiscated. Undeterred, they managed to buy a pair of cutlasses from some labourers. CLR confiscated these as well. However, the main activity of the trip – introducing Nobbie to his father's family – went well:

> I have to say that my father, my sister, his aunt and everybody else looked at him and after one or two glances, said emphatically: He is a James, and they must have seen from his colour that his mother was white.[3]

Nobbie even got to meet his godfather Eric Williams. The chief minister, who of course had been present at Nobbie's birth, took them all out for lunch and did not complain when the boys fooled about throughout, taking photographs with their new camera. One day CLR took Nobbie to the beach on his own and found him a much calmer boy when alone. The point at which he really felt a kinship with his son, though, was when they went to the cinema:

> All of us went to the theatre to see *The 10 Commandments*. Nob sat down through it for four hours. When it was finished he was ready to see it for four hours again. His father's own child. I couldn't go with him the next day but he went off and sat through the four hour picture again. He is a strange boy.[4]

CLR used his time well. Eric Williams seemed delighted to have him back in Trinidad and was constantly asking for his advice. The socialist parties across the West Indian islands had organised themselves into the West Indies Federal Labour Party (WIFLP). Williams's People's National Movement refused to define itself as socialist but was allowed in on the grounds that it was progressive. Williams used his influence to have CLR made secretary of the WIFLP. In this new role, CLR started to pay visits to the various other West Indian territories. He began with the one non-island territory, British Guiana.

He spent three weeks there. The highlight was making a speech at Georgetown's very own Queen's College. It was a wide-ranging talk, moving from Caribbean literature to the Federation and also discussing the issue – key in both British Guiana and Trinidad – of encouraging solidarity between Black and Indian citizens.

Selma joined CLR in British Guiana, having made arrangements for Sam to stay with his father in California. The two of them travelled together to Trinidad on 7 July. They found temporary lodgings in a bungalow at the Bergerac Hotel, in a leafy northern suburb of Port of Spain.

CLR immediately took Selma on a tour, showing her all the places he had been writing about in his autobiographical cricket book. They began with the little house opposite the Tunapuna recreation ground where he lived as a boy with his much loved but now deceased aunt Judith. Judith's daughters were there, greeted them and brought out the family portrait of their mother. Selma was overwhelmed by the experience of coming to the place where her husband's story had effectively begun, this little house that had been in the James family from before the abolition of slavery.

Next stop was Robert and Olive's home, a little further up the hill in Tunapuna. Robert greeted Selma with, 'How do you do, Madam, welcome to Trinidad,' and shook her hand. Olive said, 'But she is so small' and gave her a hug. Selma described her as having the James eyes, and well-dressed in modern clothes, rather than the long flowing dresses and tight corsets of CLR's reminiscences.

From there they went to the hotel where they were visited by CLR's niece and nephew, Eric's children Heno and Erica, known as Sis. Heno she described as open, friendly and funny, a would-be RAF pilot with a Harry Belafonte walk. Sis was a tall teenager, her father's favourite and the one planning to carry on the family profession of teaching. Her mother, Alys, was a teacher too.

Selma was right about that: Sis – Erica James – is now approaching eighty, but still helps runs a nursery school in Brooklyn, New York. She started it with her mother, Alys, and now shares responsibility with her own daughter. The teaching ethos of the James family runs deep. Her brother Heno lives close by and remains just as funny as Selma suggests. Erica well remembers her grandfather's house in Tunapuna. From her Trinidadian perspective, it was no ordinary middle-class existence that Robert James lived:

> They lived a very upper-middle-class black life. We went there every Sunday with my father. My grandfather was a very bright man. He loved to tell a story. He played the piano beautifully. And the way he dressed! He was very British, he was always in a three-piece suit. His daughter Olive was there. Olive never worked. She played the piano. She was a very bright lady. She lived with her father and her mother, and when her mother died she remained there. She had her garden, a most beautiful rose garden. They had servants. Olive had a gardener. When you went there you had to sit for dinner.[5]

The whole clan gathered on 15 July for Robert's eighty-first birthday. CLR reported to Lyman Paine:

> Selma and I and one of his grandsons, Eric's son, went up to the house and we carried presents for him, a fancy silk tie and cufflinks and a tie clip. He was vastly pleased. When Selma came he had a bottle of champagne, and he talks to Selma all the time and is very gallant, makes complimentary remarks and jokes, et cetera, and he obviously accepts her as a member of the family.[6]

CLR was much interested in making sense of his father, seeing this towering figure through adult eyes and after so long apart:

> In many respects he is a very cantankerous old man and at times he behaves very badly, particularly to my sister Olive. But it will take a whole lot of things on his part to make me quarrel with him or even be angry with him. Whatever he does, I say, okay old man, and I think he's beginning to lean on me now because he has had a quarrel with my brother.
>
> By the way the young ladies who come for lessons, and some of them are very handsome, very charming and very fashionable ladies, like him a great deal. He is a fine teacher and after they leave the school and get jobs or get married, most of them come back to see him and talk to him and he is very pleased.

Looking back, however, Selma gives a rather bleaker portrait of CLR's father. She remembers him as a grumpy old man, and saw little love lost between father and son. CLR always called him 'Sir', not 'Dad' or 'Father'. She didn't even see them as alike but clashing. They didn't quarrel, there was just an obvious distance between them. A clear sign of this was that while most of the family had come to hear CLR speak in public – Erica was particularly impressed* – his father did not make the effort.

> He hasn't come to hear me speak. It's too much of a bother, especially as it is at night. But when I send clippings to my sister from

* 'I saw him at Queen's College several times. Everybody was flabbergasted because he had no notes. People were listening to him but they were thinking – is this possible?'

> British Guiana, as soon as she shows them to him, he grabs them up and goes off into the school, which he runs in the house, and shows them to all the pupils.[7]

CLR's relationship with Eric was perhaps the trickiest. Eric had grown up in the shadow of his brilliant brother, but it was him who had made the successful career, had a good job and income and social status, who had an MBE. And while on a personal level he might have been happy to see his big brother return, on a professional level it was worrying. He knew more than most of his brother's revolutionary politics and was concerned that sooner or later he would say something that would cause trouble.

For the moment, though, those fears were in abeyance. CLR was obviously close to Eric Williams, and Eric James, the first Black general manager of the Trinidad Railways, simply had to put up with being patronised, as Heno remembers:

> CLR used to tease him. He'd say, 'Oh, I respect the General Manager of Affairs!' And my father would look at him! I remember one day someone came to the house and they brought CLR a beautiful pair of shoes, not Clarks – better than that, and CLR took off his shoes and put them on right away. My father says aren't you going to pay for them CLR says, 'No, he gave me a gift!' My father said, 'That's not a gift.' CLR looked at my mother – she loved him, he'd been her teacher at the teacher training college – and he said, 'The General Manager of Affairs does not want me to have these shoes. But I love them.' And he was walking around like a model in these shoes – brown, like brogues – teasing him. My father was so angry – 'How can you take something from somebody and you're not paying?' Of course, CLR never had any money. But if he had anything and you wanted it, he'd just give it to you, he was that type of person.[8]

Selma remembers the two brothers together as two very different men, but ones who got on well together. CLR liked to hear about

Eric's work, with the Railways and then organising the Trinidad football team. Eric, she notes, was a womaniser.

As well as seeing his family, CLR also caught up with old friends. Alfred Mendes was back in Trinidad. He'd left New York in 1940, burning seven unpublished novels before his departure, and had settled down to a regular career in Port of Spain, rising to become general manager of the Port of Trinidad. Albert Gomes had stayed in Trinidad all along, growing exponentially in both girth and power. But the rise of Eric Williams had marked the end of the road for both of them. The Black majority had finally taken power and the Portuguese middle class could no longer crowd into the top jobs.

Selma saw this process up close. In a letter from the time she describes the old friends as members of the middle class who have lived way beyond the rest of the population because of the corruption of the old regime. She saw them as clustering about CLR, hoping that his return might enable them to find a way back into the island's political mainstream.

The one who was most affected by this changing of the guard was, of course, Albert Gomes. In the wake of his downfall he was stereotyped as a corrupt colonialist lickspittle. This is to underestimate the man considerably. There's an interesting portrait of him from a decade earlier, when he was in his pomp, written by the American travel writer and novelist Wenzell Brown. Brown first encounters Gomes addressing the crowd in Woodford Square (for Eric Williams was not the first to use it as a pulpit):

> A huge man weighing some 350 pounds was addressing the audience. 'There is only one reason for passing the flogging bill,' he shouted. 'That is to satisfy the sadistic tendencies of the legislature. This is the one unforgivable sex perversion – the desire to cause pain, the pleasure which comes from another suffering. Man suffers too much already.'[9]

Brown soon became well acquainted with both Gomes and Alfred Mendes, whose writing he much admired. But Gomes was the personality he was most taken with. He saw him as the most idealistic and unselfish of the Caribbean leaders, and also the most likeable and the most entertaining, a pragmatist with no inclination towards demagoguery. Brown correctly anticipated that this would be Gomes' undoing, and quotes the big man as saying 'Normal man may find that there is no place for him in a world that is being formed by fanatics.'

Most interesting, perhaps, is Gomes's relationship to the island's popular culture. Brown describes him as the idol of the calypsonians* and 'the champion of those who seek to form a Trinidadian cultural pattern out of the interests, traditions, music, mockery, laughter, bright colours, speech, and art of the common people'. He goes on to quote Gomes on calypso: '[It] is the most effective political weapon in Trinidad. The singers – all of them – are men reared in poverty and oppression, and they sing of the life they know.'

Gomes was surely not the only person to promote the charms of contemporary calypso to CLR on his return to Trinidad, but he may well have been the one who most clearly saw its significance. However, it was clear to both CLR and Gomes himself, that his old friend's time was up.

In October, Eric Williams offered CLR a job as the editor of the PNM's weekly newspaper. It came with smart accommodation by the sea to the west of the city in Point Cumana and a salary of $600 a month. There was one condition: CLR would have to subordinate his own political opinions to the party line. He could not use his post to advance his own politics, only those of the PNM.

CLR accepted the conditions and took the job. He was, after all, in broad sympathy with the PNM's programme and willing to accept that a governing party needed discipline. Meanwhile, the relief at finally having some financial stability for the first time since he left Trinidad twenty-six years earlier must have been immense. He and Selma made arrangements for Sam to join them, and on 1 November they started work on the newspaper.

Working as a team, they renamed the paper *The Nation* and remade

* Gomes even appears in a calypso by Lion, which includes the lines 'Oh what an awful thing / To see Gomes in a lion skin' – referring to Gomes's carnival costume.

it as a radical general-interest newspaper, clearly influenced by *Correspondence*, rather than simply a party propaganda sheet. There was coverage of arts and literature and, of course, cricket and carnival alongside articles on the key issues of the day – Federation, the US base in Chaguaramas,* etc.

CLR's hand was obvious everywhere. In a carefully judged display of political moderation, he devoted a good part of one issue to a celebration of Abraham Lincoln, a popular figure in the Caribbean thanks to his role in the US abolition of slavery, but scarcely a Trotskyist.

In December he decided to run a Christmas literary special, a clear sign that the return to Trinidad had also reignited his sense of himself as a literary man. In the new wave of writers from the West Indies, he saw art that was also political. These new writers – his friend George Lamming, plus two Trinidadians in V. S. Naipaul and Sam Selvon – were giving the West Indies a new sense of cultural self-worth. The Christmas special featured an extract from Lamming's *In the Castle of My Skin* and a provocative essay from Naipaul on 'The Dilemma of West Indian Writers: To Stay Abroad or Come Home'. Alongside these new voices, clearly not wanting to be outshone, CLR decided to reprint an extract from his own novel, written nearly thirty years earlier and rarely acknowledged by him since, *Minty Alley*. A few weeks later, he would follow that up by reprinting his short story 'Triumph' in full.†

Eric Williams was evidently also happy with this cultural emphasis. In January 1959 he wrote a piece for the newspaper, responding to Naipaul's doubts about the viability of the Caribbean as a cultural environment by announcing plans for a Congress of West Indian Writers and Artists, to take place in Port of Spain. This was an idea that had been floated by George Lamming a year earlier, but for some reason Williams credits it to CLR and John Lehmann.

The planned programme sounds terrific: plenty of Caribbean writers, from Aimé Césaire to George Lamming, V. S. Naipaul to the young

* Eric Williams wanted the US to leave their base there.

† It appeared with the somewhat bathetic billing 'Listed in the best short stories of the year (London and New York) 1929'.

poet Derek Walcott. There would be arts and music from Geoffrey Holder, Pearl Primus, Hazel Scott and even the popular pianist Winifred Atwell.

Guests from abroad would include John Lehmann, Stephen Spender, François Mauriac and, intriguingly, another former resident of 9 Heathcote Street, CLR's old friend Ernest Borneman.* The star attraction would be none other than Jean-Paul Sartre. It's a wonderfully optimistic cultural vision, though one that sadly never came to be. After the initial announcement, nothing more was heard of the planned convention.

Alongside the newspaper, CLR was also busy with Federation business. The goal of an independent federation was starting to look imperilled. Both the two major players, Trinidad† and Jamaica, had leaders who, while personally in favour, were unsure whether their home populations were equally enthusiastic. In the recent federal election, all of the small islands had voted in favour, but in both Trinidad and Jamaica the anti-federation parties had narrow majorities. CLR was particularly concerned that Jamaica, led by an old acquaintance, the patrician liberal Norman Manley, might be in danger of going its own way.

Manley was sixty-five years old, part of the island's light-skinned elite. He had been an outstanding athlete, a Rhodes scholar at Oxford, a lawyer and a decorated First World War hero, before turning to politics in the thirties and starting the People's National Party, championing the workers and opposing colonial power.

CLR admired him, and the two men conducted a lively correspondence over the next few years, both of them writing with the formality of a bygone age – 'My dear Manley', 'My dear James'. After some initial mutual wariness, their friendship was established once CLR and Selma went to stay with the Manleys in Jamaica in April 1959.

* Ernest Borneman had spent the intervening twenty years writing popular novels and making films. His magnum opus, an anthropological history of jazz, failed to find a publisher, however, despite Richard Wright writing an introduction and CLR saying he thought it a more important work than Eric Williams's *Capitalism and Slavery*.

† Apologies to the beautiful island of Tobago for generally referring to the country as 'Trinidad' rather than the full 'Trinidad & Tobago'.

The Manleys' nine-year-old granddaughter Rachel lived with them (her father, the future Jamaican prime minister Michael Manley, was in England) and she got to know all the key political figures of the West Indies. CLR, however, was her favourite, and he evidently took to her. He reprinted a story she told him in *The Nation* – an early encouragement for a girl who grew up to be a writer. In her autobiography she remembers how struck her grandfather, who she calls Pardi, was by CLR:

> James was a man of ideas and his ideas were often quoted by Pardi to those he thought deserved to hear them like Mardi and my father ... I noticed that James ... became one of the rare people Pardi kept in mind. He would say 'I must tell' or 'I must show CLR' or 'CLR told me ...'[10]

The next time CLR would meet Norman Manley was on 4 July, and the occasion was the plainest statement yet of CLR's new status in Trinidad. This was a celebration dinner given for him at the Hotel Normandie. It was hosted by Learie Constantine, who had made his own decision to come back to Trinidad, and was now the PNM's party chairman and Minister of Communications, Works and Utilities. All the major politicians were invited. Eric Williams made a speech in CLR's honour and they worked their way through a five-course dinner, all the way from *huîtres* native cocktail to pudding Victoria, taking in snapper, chicken and *salade* Trinidad along the way, washed down with Bordeaux red and Graves white.

The *éminence grise* was having his moment in the spotlight. There were those in the know, who believed that CLR had the chief minister's ear to the extent that he was the second most powerful man in the country, if not actually the most influential. Constance Webb came to visit that summer, along with her new husband Ed Pearlstien, and later recalled that 'Eric was sending his chauffeur nearly every night to pick up Nello or receive or deliver messages. He was utterly dependent on him. This could be at any hour, midnight, 1 or 2 am etc.'[11]

But CLR would soon discover was that such access to the levers of power breeds jealousy and resentment.

Chapter Twenty

The celebration dinner marked the end of the honeymoon period. Troubles with the Federation began to heat up. In August CLR had to write to Eric Williams to tell him that the other Caribbean leaders suspected him, Eric, of plotting to depose the current leader of the Federation, Barbados's Grantley Adams.

By September the strain was definitely starting to tell on CLR. He wrote a letter to a Trinidadian abroad, only identified only as 'B', asking him to come to Port of Spain to help with *The Nation* and then take over when CLR leaves. And he makes it clear that he did intend to leave in the reasonably near future. CLR was never happy to serve under a leader for long, be they James P. Cannon or Eric Williams:

> As long as I am editing a PNM paper or working with the PNM, I subordinate my own political ideas to the politics of the PNM. Now what you and others are asking me to do is to continue to do this for the rest of my life. In other words I am just to abandon the political ideas and the practical policies which flow from what I have arrived at after 25 years, I am just to abandon them and become a PNMite. Not only would all my colleagues and associates of many years consider me a renegade and rightly so. Inevitably the very people who are telling me to do this would rapidly and in spite of themselves treat with contempt the ideas which I would have so lightly abandoned.[1]

That's to say, his heart was still with the rigorous political theorising of the Correspondence group. He still hankered after what George Padmore had called his ivory tower.

Padmore himself was busy in Ghana, working with Nkrumah. However, that September he was taken ill and had to return to London to be treated for cirrhosis of the liver. A few days later, on 23 September, he was dead of liver failure.

It was a loss that struck CLR hard. For all their differences of politics and personality, they had been comrades for decades and friends for longer still. CLR devoted large swathes of *The Nation* to a series of pieces he wrote on the life of Padmore, the man who'd given his life to the Pan-African cause, and had died just as his efforts were finally coming to fruition, first in Ghana and now in Trinidad.

Ironically, it was only a few months after Padmore's death that CLR found a political campaign he could get behind, and one that also had genuine popular appeal. This was the matter of choosing the West Indies cricket captain for the upcoming tour of Australia.

At first sight it's a trivial matter, the selection of a cricket team. But for at least two reasons, in this particular place and time, it was anything but. Firstly, the West Indies cricket team had never had a Black captain. In the pre-war days this went without saying: it reflected the colonial state of the West Indies; Black men did the hard work, while white men were in charge. In the post-war era, though, with the British Empire collapsing, it was ever more anachronistic.

Earlier in the fifties there had at least been white players whose cricketing prowess had given them a decent claim to the job – Trinidad's opening batsman Jeff Stollmeyer and then the Bajan all-rounder Denis Atkinson. After Atkinson, though, there was a lack of any obvious white successor. A former captain, John Goddard, was brought back for one disastrous series. Meanwhile, there were three great Black batsmen playing in the middle order. These were the 'Three Ws': Frank Worrell, Clyde Walcott and Everton Weekes. Worrell was an obvious captain, intelligent, articulate, dignified, a fine tactician and a great batsman. He was finally offered the captaincy for the upcoming tour of Pakistan in the spring of 1959. However, he was unable to accept as he was committed to studying in England at the time. The suspicion in the West Indies was that the selectors knew this in advance, a suspicion confirmed when the captaincy was next offered not to Walcott or Weekes, but to a white wicketkeeper with an indifferent record, Gerry Alexander.

Alexander had remained captain for three more series, but against England, the great enemies, he was under more pressure than ever to prove his worth. The flashpoint came in the second Test match, at Port of Spain in January 1960. A record crowd of thirty thousand piled into the stadium. The atmosphere was febrile and got worse as England took control of the game. They scored a patient 382 in their first innings and, late on the Saturday afternoon, had reduced the West Indies to 84–8 when frustrations boiled over. Bottles were thrown onto the pitch and a mini riot followed. Play was called off for the day.

CLR was shocked at the desecration of a cricket ground, but understood his countrymen's anger. When play resumed on the Monday the match was duly lost. In the following edition of *The Nation* CLR wrote a whole series of articles. One of them attacked the Queen's Park Cricket Club for their neglect of the paying audience. But then he moved on to the team itself, and he was adamant he knew what the problem was. They had the wrong captain. Frank Worrell was back from England and playing in the team. How on earth was Gerry Alexander still captain?

CLR did not express the question in racial terms. Instead he laid out a strictly cricketing rationale for Alexander's removal. But everyone knew that the reason Alexander had been chosen was racial. He had, in many ways, risen to the occasion, but like Albert Gomes in politics, Gerry Alexander was a symbol of a bygone era. Looking back on the affair a little later, CLR reflected that 'It was hard on Alexander . . . I put my scruples away and I think that for the first, and I hope the last, time in reporting cricket I was not fair. But I was determined to rub in the faces of everybody that Frank Worrell, the last of the Three Ws, was being discriminated against.'[2]

The hidebound West Indies cricket administration did not cave in immediately. But CLR was relentless. For week after week he cranked out editorials demanding that Worrell be made captain for the coming tour of Australia.

> It is the duty of the Selection Committee and the Board of Control to explain why they asked Worrell twice, when he was not available,

CLR and seven-year-old Nobbie reunited in London, 1956.
(Columbia University)

Cricket lesson: CLR, Nobbie and Selma.
(Columbia University)

In his teens Nobbie took to music, first the guitar and then the flute.
(Columbia University)

Martina Thomson in her acting days (as Martina Mayne).

Dr Eric Williams in his heyday, admirably turning his hearing aid into a signature look. *(BNA Photographic/Alamy Stock Photo)*

Albert Gomes in the last years of colonial rule in Trinidad. *(Rege Burkett/Getty Images)*

The prodigal returns: CLR at the Trinidad airport, welcomed by his brother Eric on the left and old friend Carlton Comma on the right.

A family reunion in Trinidad. Sam Weinstein, Selma, CLR, Nobbie, Constance and her husband Ed Pearlstien. *(Columbia University)*

CLR with the greatest of cricket commentators, John Arlott. *(© BBC Photo Library)*

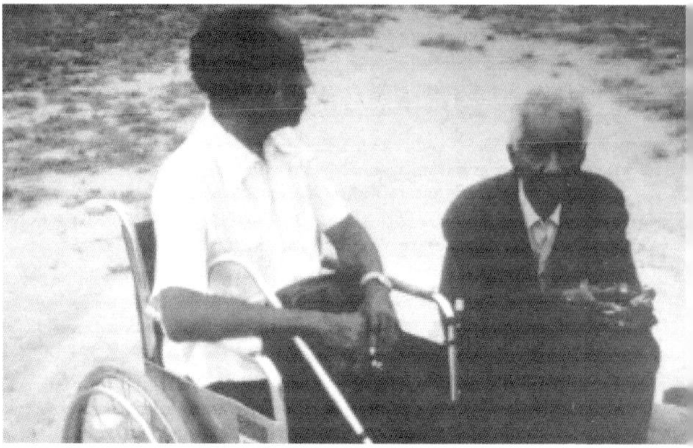

CLR with his one-time batting partner, the West Indies international Clifford Roach. The two men reunited for the BBC documentary based on *Beyond a Boundary*. *(Mike Dibb)*

CLR's sixty-seventh birthday party in Havana, with Aimé Césaire on the left.

CLR at Speakers' Corner, late 1960s. *(Roy Milligan/Stringer/Getty Images)*

CLR with the revolutionary Caribbean poet Léon-Gontran Damas at the 2nd Congress of African People, San Diego, 1972.

CLR at home in Washington DC, his lifestyle increasingly bed based. *(Columbia University)*

CLR in DC, Stetson in place. *(Columbia University)*

Darcus Howe *(left)* and Leila Hassan Howe *(below)* at work in the Race Today offices, and Leila today. *(left, United News/Popperfoto/Getty Images; below, PA Images/Alamy Stock Photo)*

(above) Margaret Busby: pioneering publisher and the woman responsible for bringing CLR's work back into print from the late 1970s onwards. *(Evening Standard/Stringer/Getty Images)*

(right) CLR upstairs at Railton Road, wrapped up against the London cold and surrounded by his books, teetering on shelves improvised by Jim Murray. *(Columbia University)*

Sharply dressed to the end. *(Columbia University)*

At home with Anna Grimshaw, secretary to his final years. *(Columbia University)*

A final portrait. The eyes have it. *(© Val Wilmer)*

> and now when he is available turn him down for a man so obviously his inferior and unfitted for the post? ... This fooling with the West Indies captaincy has gone on too long. It has to stop and the time to stop is now.[3]

By 4 March, as the Test series ground on with a series of attritional draws, CLR upped the ante again: 'The Board should know that the eyes of the world are upon them. Yes, the eyes of the world. Not to select Worrell would be an act of war.'[4]

The military metaphor might seem over the top, but it points to the other reason why the captaincy controversy was so important. The West Indies cricket team was Federation in action. It was the one organisation that really linked Trinidadian with Jamaican, Bajan with Antiguan. The success of the team, both on and off the field, inevitably impacted on how people felt about the idea of a political federation. Having a white man at the helm was completely the wrong message.

CLR's campaign dragged the issue into the public arena. And while the great and good tried to ignore it, there was no doubt which side the mass of the people were on. At the end of the England tour, which had finished as a one–nil victory to the visitors, the Board of Control bowed to the inevitable and Frank Worrell was appointed captain for the Australian tour. This would turn out to be a classic series, one that revitalised interest in Test cricket across the world. Worrell himself would be knighted following the 1963 tour of England, and universally revered as one of the game's great captains.

Whether Worrell's captaincy would have happened without CLR's intervention is moot. Surely the tide of history meant it was only a matter of time. But what CLR indubitably did was to make it a political issue and not just a cricketing one. On that level it was a great personal success.

It was the sort of personal success, however, that immediately attracted jealousy from within the PNM. Many of the senior figures had been unhappy about CLR's sudden rise, seeing him as a glory-seeking interloper who had arrived in Trinidad only after the hard work had been done.

Matters came to a head that March, at the Fourth Annual Convention of the PNM. This went well for CLR at first. Eric Williams made a speech lauding the achievements of *The Nation* as a party newspaper like no other.

CLR summed up what he had achieved:

> In all my experience I have never known or heard of any paper, least of all an official organ, which in editorial range and point, production, advertisements, circulation, starting with a grossly incompetent accountant, a disloyal assistant, an office boy, a borrowed typewriter, one filing cabinet and one desk, all in a room twelve foot square, has reached where *The Nation* has in fifteen months, with the political and other journalistic prestige of the paper on an international scale, a staff of over fifty people, a printing plant and office equipment . . . a circulation of 12,000 and the respect and confidence of a large majority of the population.[5]

He announced that he was ready to start putting the paper out twice a week. On the last day of the Convention, however, his rivals struck. Some of those opposed to CLR, including Lynne Beckles and Gil Thomson, put though a resolution to set up a committee whose duty was to investigate the finances of *The Nation*. As CLR saw it, this committee was going 'to investigate *The Nation* as though it had committed a series of crimes'.

It was a terrible blow and seemed, to CLR at least, to have come out of nowhere. Selma resigned on the following Monday morning, and immediately left for the US. CLR wrote an anguished public response to what had happened, stressing the commitment both he and Selma had shown to party discipline:

> My wife and I have suppressed ourselves and accommodated ourselves to PNM until our original selves almost disappeared. My wife is an able, energetic and effective political . . . and a most accomplished speaker . . . I have completely suppressed a large part of all my training, all my personality, in order that we should not inadvertently disrupt even the psychological atmosphere of PNM

and the country. I know what Dr Williams means to this country and the bloody shambles he and no one else in sight may be able to save it from. I have gone around quoting 'Dr Williams' 'Dr Williams' as if he were my master and I a pupil – it is years and years since I have ceased being a pupil to anybody ... My wife found the political restraint harder. But otherwise she has become almost West Indian, she's already wise on Calypso and West Indian food, went in the streets on Carnival looking for bands and jumped up. And if both she and I have unhesitatingly denounced slackness and irresponsibility in work, we know its causes, we speak about it openly, and strive to inculcate a different approach and different habits.[6]

CLR did not resign, but asked for a leave of absence. He based this request on the return of his ulcer attacks and general overwork:

Since my marriage for five years I have never had an ulcer attack. These last weeks I have had the worst attacks I've had in 10 years and I cannot get over it. I've seen my wife 12 pounds underweight for over a year and night after night drop on the bed in her clothes, fall asleep and have to be awakened to get ready for bed.

However, it seems likely that this collapse was not only to do with outrage at the way *The Nation* was being treated, but also a more personal matter: the death of his father. Typically, he said very little to anyone about the passing of Robert Alexander James. There's just this brief mention in *Beyond a Boundary*:

I walked behind my father's hearse with my sister. My mother had been paralysed for thirteen years. My sister had tended her without complaint. She had smoothed my father's last years. When his coffin was about to be lifted from the house she shed two or three quick tears. During the service she sat while one hymn was being sung. That was all.

★ ★ ★

CLR's leave of absence in the spring of 1960 saw him travel to the US. This was a careful, low-key trip. He was uncertain whether he would be allowed in, but in the event the visit was trouble-free and he got to see his old comrades, many of them for the first time in seven years.

On his return to Trinidad, Constance arranged for Nobbie to fly out on his own and spend some more time with his father. This was a partial success. Constance later reported that Nobbie had benefited from seeing CLR and from being in a mostly Black environment as opposed to the white one he struggled with in New York. On the other hand, he had been hurt when, at short notice, CLR and Selma decided to go to Ghana, leaving Nobbie with Eric's family. He wrote a 'brave but forlorn' letter to his mother,[7] telling her what had happened, and she wrote an understandably hurt and annoyed one to CLR by return.

The Ghana trip was in order to join in the celebrations marking the final stage of the country's journey to independence. As of 1 July 1960, Ghana would be a republic and Kwame Nkrumah its first president.

CLR thoroughly enjoyed the celebrations, seizing the chance to spend time with old friends and acquaintances. He offered an unusually gossipy account of the affair to the readers of *The Nation*. Among the guests were George Padmore's de facto widow Dorothy and Mbiyu Koinange from Kenya, and even the grand old man of Black politics, W. E. B. Du Bois. CLR was particularly pleased to spend time with Nkrumah's right-hand woman Erica Powell, and to have lunch with the pianist Philippa Schuyler, who would be giving a recital that night.

She was the daughter of his old friend, the Black American journalist George Schuyler. Philippa, his mixed-race daughter, had been consciously raised to be a prodigy – living proof of the benefits of racial intermarriage. She could read and write aged two, play the piano at four and compose music aged five. CLR had last seen her as a twelve-year-old phenomenon. Now she was in her late twenties and trying to forge a career as a foreign correspondent alongside her music. She had just performed at the chaotic inauguration of Patrice Lumumba in the Congo, and was relieved to find herself at a much better organised affair in Ghana. CLR reports that they gossiped all the way through lunch and she was looking stunning in a Chinese dress she'd bought in Hong Kong. In other news, he revealed that the Duke of Edinburgh had danced with Mrs Nkrumah.

On a more serious note, CLR gave a long thoughtful speech about the difficulties of establishing socialism in an underdeveloped country. He discussed the systematic depredations of colonialism, the economic exploitation that was not remotely made up for by so-called aid. He referred to his own premier's work on capitalism and slavery. He stressed how hard a road the Ghanaian people were embarked on, clearly informed by his experiences in Trinidad. But he was confident that socialism would allow the people to show the leaders the way forward.

CLR was very proud of the speech, as he made clear to a party of Johnson-Forest comrades – including Grace and Jimmy Boggs, plus the anthropologist Kathleen Gough – who had arrived in Trinidad just before he got back from Ghana. Grace remembers what happened on his return:

> CLR's behaviour was so weird that I was ashamed for him, especially since Kathleen was meeting him for the first time. He and Selma were returning from a visit to Ghana; Kathleen, Jimmy, and I, together with Conrad Lynn and his wife Yolanda, had come from the United States and were waiting on the patio of their home in Port of Spain for them to come from the airport. CLR was well known for his graciousness on meeting people for the first time or after a long separation, asking you questions about your work and family and listening avidly to your response. Imagine our surprise, therefore, when immediately upon their arrival, CLR barely exchanged greetings, demanding instead that Selma fetch a tape recorder so that we could all listen to the speech he had made in Ghana! From then on it was all downhill. We spent our time exploring Trinidad, keeping our distance from CLR and the house.[8]

To be fair to CLR, he had a lot on his mind. In the midst of the speech in Accra, he had enthusiastically referenced the prospect of a United States of Africa. Back in Trinidad, though, he could see his federal West Indies starting to unravel. He had been exchanging letters with Norman Manley throughout the year. CLR was worried, with good reason, that Manley was going cold on the project. Manley was focused on the threat to his government in Jamaica. The opposition, led by his cousin Alexander Bustamante, were making gains by exploiting anti-Federation feeling.

CLR offered advice but steadily Manley pulled rank. In one letter, from late May, he wrote: 'I usually agree with half or three-quarters of what you say. This time I disagree, word for word, line by line, totally and absolutely.'*[9] The next letter, a month or so later, ends on an even more damning note: 'I do not think much of your judgment, political or otherwise.' Manley says he will go his own way. 'All I ask is to be left alone to fight it out.'[10]

CLR could see that his time at the heart of Trinidadian politics was coming to an end. The dream of federation was slipping away. Eric Williams had failed to support him over the investigation into *The Nation*. Grace Boggs saw that CLR's influence was visibly waning: 'It was painful to watch CLR persist in sending directives several times a day to Bill Williams† in the Prime Minister's office, despite the lack of response.'[11]

Rather than wait for the axe to fall, he decided to withdraw. He resigned from *The Nation* on his return from Ghana. The last pieces he wrote were a series of reminiscences of his family, no doubt provoked by his father's death. His rivals, however, saw such articles as mere self-indulgence.

Soon afterwards he tried to resign his other formal post, as secretary to the West Indies Federal Labour Party. In the end he agreed to stay on until the new year, but was notably less engaged than before. Instead

* The letter ends, though, on a personal note, as Manley lets CLR know that 'I have just read *Minty Alley* . . . What a human heart you had – or have? I read it all in one sitting.'

† Eric Williams's nickname was Bill.

he decided to focus on his writing. His book on cricket, tentatively titled *Who Only Cricket Know*, had been more or less finished during his time in Spain in early 1958, but following his return to Trinidad he decided to write a couple more chapters dealing with his new experiences.

In order to make money he persuaded Carlton Comma to commission him to deliver six lectures at the Trinidad Public library. They would be delivered on Mondays and Thursdays for three weeks in August 1960, and the subject would be 'Modern Politics'.

These lectures must have been astonishing to witness. Speaking as ever without notes or written text, CLR offered a succinct and brilliant summary of his political thinking as it had developed over the past four decades. The first two lectures spanned the history of radical ideas from ancient Greece to Marx; the third took on the first half of the twentieth century from Lenin to Hitler; while the fourth addressed the post-war world, all the way up to the Hungarian Revolution. The fifth lecture addressed what he saw as the key problems of the modern world – 'Our masters exploit these fundamental relations in society: sex, race and class' – and the sixth and final lecture dealt with literature and art,* psychology and science.

Along the way he offers one of his key insights into the kind of revolution of everyday life that would allow people to achieve real happiness:

> So you see the good life demands a feeling that you are moving, you and your children. You must have a sense of movement and of overcoming difficulties within your organism; and if you are doing that, it does not matter what your wages are as long as you have a certain elementary level of material welfare. You must have a sense of

* Including his decidedly controversial assessment of D.W. Griffith's overtly racist *Birth of a Nation* as a high point of cinematic culture: 'Griffith is a very great artist and should not be judged too hastily. Lenin saw this picture, and he wrote a letter to Griffith in his personal handwriting, asking him to come to Russia and take charge of the Russian movie industry. He did not mind that Griffith had shown prejudice against the Negro. Lenin knew that this could be overcome.'

movement, the sense of activity, the sense of being able to use or on the way towards understanding and controlling what makes your life. I do not mean gadgets the way the Americans play with things; I mean things that really matter.

You go to a country like Ghana where the general level is even lower than what it is here, but you look at the people, you listen to them, you see what they are doing; you get a sense of movement and activity; they are going somewhere. They will have troubles of course; that does not matter. The Greeks had plenty of troubles.

An American woman told me once that she forgot herself and told an audience of white women in the United States – she was a Negro woman – speaking to them she said, 'When I look at you all, I am sorry for you because although whites are oppressing us and giving us trouble, I am actively on the move; every morning I am doing something, but you all are just sitting down there watching.' It is not the complete truth, but it is a great part of the truth. This is some idea of what I mean by what is the good life – the individual in relation to society. It is not, it never has been, merely a question of what the vulgarians call 'raising the standard of living'. Men are not pigs to be fattened.[12]

The six lectures were recorded and transcribed, then published as a book in Trinidad, simply titled *Modern Politics*. It's a testimony to CLR's extraordinary oratorical ability that it reads absolutely as if very carefully and elegantly written. Among the least known of his works, it actually provides a thoroughly accessible introduction to his world-view. That he managed to deliver these lectures at such a turbulent time in his life is remarkable, and no doubt goes to explain why he had so little time for Grace et al. during their visit.

The lectures delivered, though, CLR found himself back in an all-too-familiar position. Full of ideas, multiple book projects on the go, but no money coming in.* He sent Fred Warburg another of his letters

* Confusingly, one or two of his letters suggest he may have made a quick trip to New York and London during October in order to meet publishers, though it's hard to see how he could have afforded it.

listing a bewildering number of projects – among them, intriguingly, the promise of an updated version of *Minty Alley*. Perhaps Norman Manley's praise had had its effect. He also wondered if Secker might re-publish *The Black Jacobins*. He felt that here was a book whose time had come. George Lamming had told him that it was very popular in Haiti itself – much to CLR's delight, it transpired that the Haitian radicals Lamming met there on a recent visit were amazed to discover it had been written by a Black West Indian. Finally, he suggested that Warburg might be interested in his cricket book.

Warburg replied with the slightly baffled tone that such letters generally elicited from him, but it was clear that the cricket book was the project he was most interested in. CLR decided it was time to start sending out copies of the manuscript. Presumably one went to Warburg but sadly there is no record of the response, though he certainly didn't agree to publish it.

Another copy went to Jack Fingleton, the Australian batsman turned cricket writer, whose work CLR admired. He was positive in his response, but unable to help. John Arlott too was sent a copy. Arlott was enormously impressed and took it to a publisher friend, getting CLR's hopes up considerably. Unfortunately, in December 1960 Arlott wrote back to say that the publishers couldn't see it as a commercial prospect. CLR sent a dignified but obviously hurt response.

However, there was at last some good news. He had sent *The Black Jacobins* to several New York editors. One of them, Morris Philipson at Vintage Books, part of Random House, wrote back in November to say that they would indeed be interested in reissuing the book. This was a welcome boost, but not an especially lucrative one. Come December, CLR was writing letters to the same Conrad Lynn that he had largely ignored on his visit to Trinidad, asking for a $1000 loan.

At Christmas there were more visitors from the US, Filomena Daddario and Isa-Kae Meksin. Isa-Kae was immediately impressed by the James's lodgings – 'It was a marvellous place with servants, there was turkey and chicken and fresh fruit'[13] – but it was a short-lived experience for the visitors. Now that CLR no longer had a formal position in the PNM, the family had to move to a smaller place in the suburb of

Mount Lambert. Isa-Kae, like Grace a few months earlier, was struck by CLR's self-absorption: 'During that period, in the middle of all this stressful packing, CLR just wanted someone to bring him a certain record by Sparrow. It was indicative of the treatment he expected.'[14]

CLR could see there was no future for him in Trinidad. He had no role in government, and he was too far away from the London publishing world. He and Selma planned to return to England in April. Before that, the PNM brought charges against him for financial misconduct. All disinterested onlookers saw it as a ruse, a final step towards discrediting a courtier who had overreached. CLR didn't deign to appear before the committee but wrote a well-documented refutation.

Then came the final blow. On 22 March 1961, Eric Williams gave perhaps the most famous speech of his career. It was called 'Massa Day Done' and celebrated the triumph of the Trinidadian people over their white 'massas'. It's actually an odd sort of revolutionary speech. In amongst the anti-colonialism is a paean to Winston Churchill and a promise to invite the Queen to visit the new parliament. In the midst of it all, though, there's a brief but brutal attack on CLR:

> C. L. R. James's case has been sent to our Disciplinary Committee for action; when, it is no longer *sub judice* I shall deal with it fully and publicly, and with all those who seek to use him in their struggle to defeat the PNM and to destroy me.[15]

There was nothing left. His old friend and protégé had cast his teacher aside. Massa CLR's day was done too. CLR and Selma packed up. They would stop off in Jamaica for CLR to deliver a series of lectures and from there return to the UK. At least that was the plan.

CLR and Selma did indeed make it to Jamaica, but while they were there, on 28 April, they were in a terrible car accident, when a bus crashed into them. Selma remembers that the driver they had been given was at fault, just a terrible driver.

Selma was knocked unconscious by the collision but otherwise got off relatively lightly. CLR, however, received a fractured skull. For the next week he was in and out of consciousness at the University Hospital in Mona, just outside Kingston. Selma was relieved to find that the doctor treating him was a man called Harry Annamunthodo, the brother of their Trinidad friend Walter Annamunthodo.

Norman Manley made sure that all the care was covered. Selma gave the comrades a graphic report on CLR's state ten days after the accident. She described him as physically improved but mentally shaken – talking constantly but not always making sense, unaware that he was in Jamaica and occasionally calling Selma 'Olive'. Most alarmingly, when talking about politics, he lacked his customary internal censor and said exactly what he thought about assorted Caribbean notables.

CLR's recovery was slow. His memory and eyesight took a while to get back to normal. You can't rush head injuries, was the message. The Jameses would have to stay in Jamaica for several months. Yet in the midst of this disaster there was significant good news.

On 29 May Robert Lusty, from the London publisher Hutchinson & Co, wrote to CLR. Lusty had published George Lamming's *In the Castle of my Skin*, and the two men had remained friends. When Lamming heard that CLR was having trouble finding a publisher for *Who Only Cricket Know*, which he had read in manuscript and much admired, he personally recommended it to Lusty over lunch. And now Lusty was saying that he would like to make an offer for the rights to publish the book. It's a very English letter, managing to inject a note of hesitancy from the very beginning:

> I would like most warmly to congratulate you on the achievement of your book for it is a memorable one and our only doubt is whether it could expect to achieve the widespread circulation which it certainly merits.[16]

Lusty worries as to whether there might be too much about politics for cricket fans and too much cricket for politicos, before finally getting down to brass tacks: 'I'm afraid we cannot offer particularly attractive terms and I would suggest an advance payable on publication of £100.'

The advance was indeed meagre, around £2000 today. CLR would almost certainly have benefited from having a literary agent to do his negotiating, but nevertheless this was wonderful news. For the first time in over twenty years he would have a new book brought out by a commercial publisher.

CLR wrote back immediately to accept the offer. He let Lusty know that he was still under doctor's orders – this was 12 June, six weeks after the accident. He suggested too that he might write a final chapter, dealing with the Frank Worrell captaincy affair.

The only real outstanding matter was the question of the title. Lusty didn't like *Who Only Cricket Know*. That came from the book's epigraph – 'What do they know of cricket, who only cricket know?' – which is in turn a riff on Kipling's question 'What do they know of England, who only England know?' For a while the title was *The Cricket Crusaders*, before George Lamming came up with a better alternative: *Beyond the Boundary*. Somehow, for no known reason, that would have one final tweak and when the book came to publication, nearly two years later, it would be under the title *Beyond a Boundary*.

While recuperating in Jamaica, CLR started to contemplate a follow-up book. That would be an account, based on his own recent experiences, of the state of the West Indies. He thought he might call it *My Own, My Native Land*. The idea may have owed something to V. S. Naipaul, who had returned to Trinidad from London in late 1960 as the recipient of a scholarship from Eric Williams so that he might write about the West Indies. CLR had met Naipaul at Lloyd Best's house and got on very well with the younger man. But he must have been well aware that Naipaul's politics were very different from his own. Both of them were critical of the state of Trinidad, but for very different reasons.

CLR outlined his ideas for *My Native Land* in a long letter to his close comrades, written only six weeks after his accident. It's a feverish document, equal parts hope and disillusion. He could see that Eric

Williams was planning to come to an arrangement with the US over the military base at Chaguaramas, a significant climbdown in itself, but also an indication that under Williams, Trinidad was in danger of swapping a colonial master – Britain – for an economic master – the USA. CLR objects to this both in principle and because he sees it as leaving Trinidad more than ever without cultural roots:

> The leading people take it for granted that we are attached to the US (i.e. Kennedy). Whatever he says, we say. That is a disaster. We will have no WI history, no native language, no past of independence, are forever slaves unless we get some view of the world, i.e. of history, that is our own; gives us a sense of the past which leads to our present and the future. The absence of all this is crushing us. No nation was ever made without it.[17]

CLR believes that the only solution is education:

> The degradation from standards of social and political conduct in the WI appals me, horrifies me for the first time in my political life. We have to lift the mentality of the people . . . Beethoven, Melville, Twain, Tolstoy, Dostoevsky, et cetera. I can do it . . . We shall buy some cheap copies of the books, for public sale. We shall open up minds . . . Our young people must have a sense of the past, a past. Otherwise a union is only something whereby you demand more money, a party something by which you gain power and place.

His stream of consciousness becomes ever more frustrated:

> We are a special people, colonials who have been deprived of everything except what we have been taught and what we have learnt. We, the WI, are the best example of what Europe (and the US) means to the future of the colonial and Negro peoples. We are Western and yet tied to Africa, et cetera. We have something to say.
>
> We must be independent. We are not joining up with anybody. We are not with the US. We're not with Russia. We want now after

> 300 years to go our own way. British, French, Spanish, African, Oriental – we have everything, we are attached to everything.
>
> But independence, as a satellite of the US, is a degradation, a defeat. It is nothing compared to what we want – all of us, me, Olive, Alys, Heno, Sis. All the culture and discoveries of the world have been pouring on us for centuries – we have taken what we could and made such contributions as we were permitted – we are tired of this subordination.

He finishes with some ideas for a chapter outline for the proposed book: a mix of politics, sociology and cultural criticism not dissimilar to his *American Civilization* project.

CLR's recuperation was dragging on. He and Selma remained in Jamaica till the beginning of October, just long enough to see the dream of federation effectively crushed by the Jamaican referendum. Manley had decided that the only way to get his island behind the cause was to give the people the chance to vote on it first. The people duly rejected the idea by 54 per cent to 46 per cent. This was the end of the line. Without Jamaica, it was just Trinidad and a group of small islands, with the economic burden falling heavily on Trinidad. CLR knew that Eric Williams's lukewarm support for the idea would not survive that. Williams was a canny politician and he would learn from the Jamaican lesson. The loss of the referendum meant the end of Norman Manley's career. When Jamaica came to independence the following year it would be his cousin, Alexander Bustamante, who would be the country's first prime minister.

Later in October the Jameses decamped to Barbados, staying at the Paradise Beach Club. CLR's health was still poor. Selma reported to the US comrades that he was tiring easily, lacking energy. He was going for a sea bath twice a day, and once managed to walk five blocks to a bookshop, but it's easy to sense her worry and frustration.

To make matters much worse, while they were there yet another crisis began. This time it was the Correspondence group. Just a few months earlier Selma had written to the comrades telling them how happy CLR and her were to be free of their PNM responsibilities and ready to work full time for Correspondence. What they failed to understand was just how far things had moved on in their absence.

Grace and Jimmy Boggs were at the heart of things. Grace was editor of the newspaper; Jimmy was the party leader. Jointly they had decided they no longer believed in many of the precepts by which they had lived for so long. They no longer saw the American workers as on the brink of revolution. Instead they felt what was happening in the civil rights movement and the nascent counterculture was indicative of the way the party needed to go. Grace wrote a long article for the newspaper that demonstrated that she had not just rejected Trotskyism but Marxism itself, in favour of a new politics.

CLR read the piece. He was implacably opposed to what he saw as a betrayal of Marxist principle. In his weakened state he felt it as a personal blow as much as a political one, a feeling that shines through in the letter he proceeded to write to Grace: 'This is a terrible blow to me personally,' he told her. 'First Rae [i.e. Raya]. Next you. The Organisation has been the centre of my life for over 20 years.'[18]

The sign-off is especially poignant:

> Yours, the same person as always, Jimmie.

Grace wrote back accepting that she should have consulted before printing the piece, but not apologising for the content. She, in turn, was evidently hurt by the suggestion of a personal betrayal.

CLR made a token offer to debate the issues and, for a short while, both he and Selma thought the split had been averted. But then CLR received a letter from Freddy Paine. In a screed full of sorrow and disappointment, she told CLR that she agreed with Grace. CLR had been away from the US for too long and she and others no longer implicitly trusted his judgement. They saw what was happening on the ground. He didn't. A final split was now only a matter of time.

The political crisis did nothing for CLR's health. The doctors in Barbados recommended he travel to Trinidad where he could get further, better treatment. So the family moved once again. This time they settled at the James family home, the house on Ward Street in Tunapuna that Robert and Olive had shared and was now Olive's alone. It was a handsome wood-framed house on a slight hill to the north of the town centre.*

They stayed there for six months. CLR spent the time working on his Trinidad book. Perhaps because of his lack of energy, he didn't manage anything as ambitious as he had originally planned. What he came up with instead was an odd hodgepodge of a book, which he titled *Party Politics in the West Indies*, though its focus was almost entirely on Trinidad.

The first half simply consisted of old pieces he had written about the PNM before, during and after his time at *The Nation*. The second part of the book, written in Tunapuna and titled 'West Indies 1962: The State of the Nation', is far more interesting. He focuses on key issues and personalities in Trinidad. There are essays on 'The Mass Party', 'The Middle Classes', 'The East Indian', 'The White People' and 'Eric Williams'.

The essay on the middle classes sums up his worries for Trinidad after independence:

> The West Indian middle classes have a high standard of formal education. They are uneducated and will have to educate themselves on the stern realities of West Indian economic and social life. Independence will place them face to face with the immense messes the imperialists are leaving behind ... The effects of slavery and colonialism are like a miasma all around choking us. 150 years ago, when the nonconformists told the slaveowners, 'you cannot continue to keep human beings in this condition,' all the slaveowners could reply was, 'you will ruin the economy, and further what can you expect from people like these?' When you try to tell the middle classes of today, 'why not place responsibility for the economy on the people?' their reply is the same as that of the old

* Still standing, just about, but now derelict and abandoned.

slaveowners: 'you will ruin the economy, and further what can you expect from people like these?'

His piece on 'East Indians' deals with an issue little understood from outside – the complex place of the Indian community, nearly half the whole population, in Trinidad. The Indians were historically looked down on by the Black people, but were now increasingly seen as rivals, a fault line relentlessly exploited by the island's two main political parties. CLR does his best to reach across the divide, first by stating the problem:

> This Indian question, like all serious political problems is above all a human situation. No one can live at peace in a country and make balanced political decisions, where a large proportion of your fellow countrymen live with the feeling that a number of their fellows look upon them as inferior and at the same time a threat and a danger.

And then by giving his own take on the role of the Indian population:

> The Indians are somewhat different from the Negroes, it would be a miracle if they were not. Their ancestors came here with their own language, their own religion, their own way of life. They have had a different development. The influence of these remain, but now the present generation above all is West Indian. The Indian girls I see about consistently startle me in comparison with those I remember 35 years ago. Often I have to look twice to see whether they are Indian or not. But, as I say, looking at Indians, talking to them, listening to them, I find them different, as I regularly noted the remarkable differences between Scotsmen and Englishmen and even between people of Lancashire and people of Surrey. But that I'm convinced is not a weakness: for us this is a form of strength. If the Indians were looking elsewhere, and their eyes fixed, for example, on return to India, that would be a very serious matter. But with

their own qualities they are completely West Indian. For one thing they have produced Vidia Naipaul.

There is also an interesting if rambling essay on the great calypsonian, and good friend of CLR's, the Mighty Sparrow, and finally a deliberately minimal essay on racial harmony. Here it is in its entirety: 'In a book by a West Indian intended for West Indians I refuse to waste time disproving that racial harmony exists in the West Indies.'

CLR finished the book in July 1962. He had it privately printed in Port of Spain, just in time for it to be distributed before 22 August, the date on which Trinidad, under Eric Williams, would finally become independent of Britain, not as part of a West Indian Federation but going it alone. This was his farewell message to his native land.

Two weeks before Independence Day, CLR, Selma and Sam set sail for England, with no plans to return.

PART FIVE

The Sixties

Chapter Twenty-One

London had changed considerably while CLR and his family had been away. The clearest sign of this was the difficulty they had in finding a place to live. Landlords were less keen than ever to rent to 'coloureds'. Finally they found a first-floor flat in Willesden, north-west London. The address was 20 Staverton Road and the landlord, a German Jew, was prepared to take them on. In Selma's opinion, the Notting Hill riots of 1958 had caused a sea change in the way the city saw its immigrant communities.

Racism was abroad in the land. Right-wing politicians were once more seeing it as a cause to be exploited. And, in response, an ever-stronger racial consciousness was developing among the Black people of Britain. The night before they moved in to their new flat, CLR lectured to a West Indian student group in Oxford. After this he soon got to know a group of graduates from the University of the West Indies in Jamaica, who were now in London doing postgraduate studies. Some of them had seen him lecture in the West Indies. Among them were the future lawyer Richard Small, the academics Norman Girvan and Kenneth Ramchand, and the Guyanese revolutionary Walter Rodney.

These young men came to visit CLR at his new abode and he soon saw an opportunity to share with this new generation of radicals all that he had learned in thirty-odd years of political struggle. He set up a weekly study group at Staverton Road. One attendee, the St Lucian playwright and engineer Stanley French, remembered the first-floor flat as an archetypal CLR residence, dominated by literature: 'One wall of the room was lined with books on a temporary shelving arrangement, the kind that facilitates dismantling, packing, transportation, unpacking and re-ordering.'[1] Seating arrangements were dominated by a chaise longue, reserved for CLR so he could address his visitors from his preferred reclining position.

CLR would talk about Aeschylus or Shakespeare or Marx or Trinidadian politics and the acolytes would listen, literally at his feet, and they would discuss and then Selma would bring out a selection of literature that they could buy, mostly Correspondence pamphlets.

This was the beginning of CLR's persona as a grand old man, a role he would inhabit for the rest of his life. Consciously or not, it also echoed the school his father had at his house, late in life.

Alongside this new beginning there was a sorrowful closing down. The split within Correspondence was now a fact. Grace and Jimmy Boggs, Lyman and Freddy Paine had left to start their own organisation. They were able to take the name Correspondence with them, as it had been legally registered by Lyman. Following this definitive move Lyman had evidently written CLR a parting letter, apparently accompanied by a cheque – a symbolic redundancy payment from the man who had funded him for most of the past twenty years.

CLR's reply is painful to read. It's clear that this break, both profoundly political and personal, had wounded him terribly.

> Nobody did more for me than you two. I could not go into detail if I tried to. But it was in your house, 629, as I began to work out what became Johnson-ism, my view of *Capital*, in your house and in conversations with you. When I came down there I was at home as I have never been in any house or among any friends. That is first and stands out above everything else. One has to live as I have lived to understand that. I left home at the age of 11 to board out to go to school.
>
> You kept me and the organisation and my family going. Without that I don't know what we would have done, what would have happened to me. I do not mean that I was faced with ruin and you picked me up and helped me to make something of myself. I would not say such nonsense. I have always been able to make my way ... You helped me though, Lyman, with a generosity that could not be surpassed ... You liked me, I know, but I know too that you felt that I was valuable, necessary to what we were doing and you did all that

you could for me. It is one of the great experiences of my life. Of you, Freddy, I have this to say. Lyman was what he was because of you. You are the finest party member and comrade of them all. They don't make them better than you.

Well, Lyman, Freddy, there we are. I have told you what I still think about you, of the good life we lived in the good times we had. But if you think of them as I still do, you will, you must think of them as gone . . . Perhaps I did what was best. I don't know. Nobody can know. Meanwhile know that I mean every word I say here, that I bear no ill will, and though I am pained at how we parted I do not think of that, but remember always what you two have been to me, what I'm sure I was to you.[2]

And then, at the very last, there's the matter of the cheque:

About the cheque, we have it still. You will understand: I couldn't cash it. I simply couldn't, and it would have been gross rudeness to send it back to you. I couldn't do that, Lyman. Let it stay there. I'll find something to do with it, something that will not discredit or degrade the times we have had together.

It's really striking, this letter. CLR was always prone to hyperbole, but there's no exaggeration here. Again and again, through the rest of his life, if he was asked where he was happiest, where he felt he was at his best, he referred back to the time in New York, holding court at 629 Hudson Street. He had found a family there, and now it was over.

Not entirely over, though. Correspondence was gone, both newspaper and name, but CLR was still convinced he was in the right and as long as there were any supporters at all left, then he would carry on. There really were just a handful of them now, left in this grouplet that decided to rename itself after its recent manifesto: Facing Reality. In practice, the only other significant active members, apart from CLR and Selma, were Marty and Jessie Glaberman, Nettie Kravitz and Frank Marino in Detroit, and Constance Webb and Ed Pearlstien in New York. For the time being they were little more than another discussion group, no bigger than the one that met in CLR's living room on Friday evenings.

At the beginning of 1963, CLR's objective situation was decidedly difficult. Just two years earlier he had been at the heart of an independence movement, and the editor of a newspaper. Now he was sixty-two years old, living in a rented flat in an unfashionable part of London with his wife and stepson. He had no job or regular source of income. He had lost the support of his long-time friend and sponsor. He was still struggling to regain his health and energy, nearly two years after the accident.

The change in him was plain to the people who knew him best, the ones who lived with him: Selma and Sam. Both felt CLR was never quite the same after his accident. Selma describes him as grumpy and Sam stresses that he had lost his energy, and above all his humour. The private CLR had been a natural comedian, entertaining them with impressions of Charlie Chaplin or improvised translations of Molière. But no longer.

Typically, CLR reserved what strength he had for the life of the mind, not the life of the family. He started to focus all his energy on Shakespeare. This was no recent preoccupation, of course. He had seen any number of productions over the years, and studied them as carefully as any game of cricket. A decade earlier he and Grace had exchanged letters analysing particular plays, *King Lear* in particular. Shakespeare was a crucial figure in CLR's worldview: the key link between ancient Greek culture and the modern world. In Shakespeare's plays – written for a popular audience – CLR saw the same engagement of the people with the world of ideas as in the Athenian agora or the theatre.

Around this time he wrote to John Arlott, first to let him know that *Beyond a Boundary* would be published in May, and then to share his thoughts on Shakespeare, prompted by hearing Arlott talking about him on the radio:

> I have long thought that Shakespeare was not only profound but has a positive and very advanced view of society and social relations,

> that he was a social moralist in a very realistic way. I firmly believe the great artist is saying something very definite about the world he lives in. I am more than ever convinced of this since my five years in the West Indies. I lectured incessantly on Shakespeare to all types of audiences. Their response was all I could wish for. West Indians are a modern people in an underdeveloped society that is the closest that we have today to the society in which Shakespeare wrote and the people he wrote for. I believe that Shakespeare today has more that matters than any creative writer. He came at a time of transition from one world to a new. We are in the same position today. That is why Hazlitt, Lamb, De Quincy and Coleridge wrote so well about him. They too knew a world moving from the 18th to the new 19th century. The same newness that West Indians bring to cricket they bring to the classic writers.[3]

CLR suggested that Arlott and himself might make some programmes about Shakespeare for the BBC, to be broadcast at home and abroad. In the event, CLR was invited to take on the task alone, and solely for a Caribbean audience. But it was still a project he relished. He proceeded to write a series of five lectures for the BBC's Caribbean service, each focusing on a different play. What comes through very clearly is that CLR, at this point in his life, was both using the plays to illuminate our understanding of the world and to further his own understanding of himself. Don't psychologise me, he loved to say, but when he writes, for instance, about *Othello*, it's hard to resist the notion that this is precisely what he is doing. It's very typical of the man that the only psychologist he would want to be treated by was himself, aided and abetted by Shakespeare.

So when writing about *Othello*, he makes the seemingly perverse assertion that this is not a play about race:

> I say with the fullest confidence, that you could strike out every single reference to Othello's black skin and the play would be essentially the same. Othello's trouble is that he is an outsider. He is not

> a Venetian. He is a military bureaucrat, a technician, hired to fight for Venice, a foreign country. The senate has no consciousness whatsoever of his colour. That is a startling fact but true.[4]

This is a hard claim to agree with, especially in the modern world in which Othello's skin colour has inescapable meaning. Of course its meaning in Shakespeare's world, before the advent of transatlantic slavery, would have been very different, but still, when Iago refers to Othello as a black ram tupping the white ewe that is Desdemona, it's hard to see colour as irrelevant. It's at least arguable that CLR could, on occasion, be too quick to ignore racism rather than confront it, in his eagerness to prioritise class over race.

However, if you consider the possibility that CLR's take on *Othello* was enormously influenced by his recent experiences in Trinidad, then it's suddenly clear why skin colour should be ignored. What happened to CLR at the hands of Eric Williams was not about his skin colour, but his status as an outsider. And this is precisely the point CLR makes about *Othello*. Any doubt that he has Trinidad in mind is dispelled when he comes to consider Iago:

> Here too we must be on guard against getting misled by race. Iago is in the position of a man in an underdeveloped country who sees himself passed over for strangers with modern qualifications and modern ideas: I personally know the type well.

Beyond a Boundary was published on 13 May 1963. At last CLR had a proper publication: a telegram from Robert Lusty on the day, and reviews all over the press.

Beyond a Boundary is a singular book, singular in the image of its author. It could be summed up to sound straightforward – the autobiographical story of a Black West Indian's love affair with cricket, beginning with watching the game as a small child and ending with a tribute to the West Indies' first Black cricket captain. And that would be true as far as it goes, but what makes *Beyond a Boundary* extraordinary is the route CLR takes between these two markers. As he makes his point that there is much more to cricket than the game itself, he takes in a dissection of the Trinidadian pigmentocracy, an appreciation of the novels of Thackeray and the essays of the writer who is in some ways his natural forebear, William Hazlitt. He takes us effortlessly from colonial Trinidad to W. G. Grace's Gloucestershire to Thomas Arnold's Rugby to the theatre of ancient Greece.

Cricket, for CLR, emerges as politics and as art, but always too as itself: a game that produces joy in both player and spectator. CLR shows off his extraordinary eye for detail as he analyses the technique of a great batsman, or the one great shot of a less great batsman. Even if the reader doesn't have the faintest idea what a leg glance is, CLR still evokes its languorous bite with the precision of a Leonardo drawing.

As with all CLR's books, it has flaws. One, which it shares with almost everything he wrote after the thirties, is that it seems to have been written in sections which don't always flow smoothly together. The last pages of the book, in particular, in which he writes about the Worrell affair, are closer to journalism than literature. But against that there is simply so much to admire. Ideas that other writers would use to fuel an entire book are strewn around with abandon. The writing has the seductive power of a great speech or sermon. If one book sums up the multidisciplinary brilliance of its author, while also revealing his heart and soul, it is this one.

Despite the book's obvious quality, CLR had been nervous about the reviews beforehand. On 1 May he sent letters to selected critics such as the literary magus V. S. Pritchett and the cricket authority Keith Altham, telling them about the book and pointing them towards passages that might particularly interest them.

He needn't have worried. The response was tremendous.[5] 'It is quite the best cricket book that I've read for many a long year,' said Leslie Gutteridge of the Cricket Society in a letter. 'What a wonderful book for any man to have written!' wrote John Arlott, enclosing a piece he had written for *Wisden* on the best cricket books of the year, naming *Beyond a Boundary* as the best ever written and inviting CLR to lunch along with his sports editor* at the Feathers, just off Fleet Street: 'We can get a fair bottle of wine.'†

Another writer with a debt to Arnold of Rugby, George MacDonald Fraser, author of the Flashman novels, was likewise impressed against expectation, commenting in his *Glasgow Herald* review that 'it is unusual to find a cricket book in which the author hops quickly from a superb analysis of George Headley's batting to a brief passage on the reorganisation of Marxist ideas'.

Alan Ross, in his *Observer* review, is the one critic to pick up on one of the aspects of the book that CLR held dearest to his heart, its close study of the visual aesthetics of the game:

> The incidental pleasures and fascinating insights of the early West Indian chapters are many. But Mr James's particular merits derive in the first place from his rewarding the close scrutiny of technique, and secondly from his contention that cricket relates equally to social history, personality and significant form ... Mr James, starting with Greek sculpture, and making a rapid survey of aesthetic trends through Michelangelo to Picasso, establishes cricket in its proper visual, as well as literary context. No one has attempted it in such detail before: and no one could hope to succeed without a similar awareness of both the most subtle points of the game and the general history of the last 150 years.[6]

Ross also wrote CLR a personal note – 'I do congratulate you on your book – a tremendous achievement ... come and stay a night or failing that lunch one day in London' – to which CLR responded, 'I do not know a critical approval on what I've tried to do which I shall appreciate more. I remember an article of yours on cricket in *Encounter*‡ which startled me as quite a statement of ideas I had long held.'[7]

* Probably John Samuel from the *Observer*.

† Which was doubtless a considerable understatement, Arlott's appreciation for fine wine rivalling his love of cricket.

‡ Ross wrote an article about the aesthetics of cricket for *Encounter* in the early fifties. This had a big influence on CLR as he started to think about writing what came to be *Beyond a Boundary*.

The one less than wholly favourable review appeared in the *Guardian*, a prickly affair written by CLR's one-time mentor Neville Cardus. First he takes umbrage at CLR's assertion that he, Cardus, would write about cricket in terms of music but never the other way round, before offering the backhanded compliment that 'when he escapes from polemics and aesthetics he writes extremely well, especially of the cricketers of his own habitation'. Then he goes on to credit himself with CLR's major insight: 'Many years ago I put forth the argument that cricket is an organism in an environment: the spirit and economy of an age shapes the great player's style . . . It is pleasant, in 1963, to have one's opinion backed up by a competent authority.'[8]

CLR responded to this pomposity with a wonderfully sarcastic letter to the *Guardian*, starting with the comment that 'Not only to myself does Mr Cardus render great service in pointing out how much the ideas in my book, *Beyond a Boundary*, owe to him,' before pointing out that even in his own autobiography Cardus had stated that he had written of cricket in terms of music but never the other way round.[9]

Ironically, the much more right-wing cricket writer E. W. (Jim) Swanton found his prejudices conquered by the elegance of CLR's argument. He starts out proclaiming that 'I began *Beyond a Boundary* with the strongest possible prejudice against the author. For me he was not only outside the ropes but excluded from the ground' – here he is referring to CLR's campaign to have Frank Worrell made West Indies captain. But then he goes on to say:

> Without forgetting, or quite forgiving, I was however quickly carried away by the lucid beauty of the writing, the author's width of vision as well as his depth of learning, and by the skill with which he weaves his complicated pattern into an integrated whole. This book will draw the public that is always greedy for fine cricket literature . . . But its value as a sociological document should bring it a wider fame. Englishmen who would understand the background and stresses of West Indian life will find themselves no less impressively informed of the evolution of their own society.[10]

The review from the Caribbean press most treasured by James was written by Derek Walcott, who noted that 'What holds it together is the character of its author, its purposefulness as autobiography, for a mind that can relate the grace of Hazlitt to that of Frank Worrell, genuinely believes in cricket as "a way of life".'[11]

Another Caribbean response came from CLR's own sister, Olive:

> My Dear Nello. The book is fine, you have done it this time. I enjoyed reading about the family and the old cricket days – how well I remember the matches with Shannon. We used to go with you and sit under the big tree to see you all play. I was surprised when I read you thought I was like Aunt J, well perhaps it is so.[12]

There's an interesting further note:

> I met many old friends who have read and liked the book and two said to me it only takes a Nello to write those nice things about Learie after the way he treated him. I said nothing but it was the same thing I thought.

It's a reminder that Eric Williams was not the only one who betrayed CLR in Trinidad. Learie Constantine was president of the PNM, but had still allowed the witch hunt to go ahead. It's perhaps fortunate that the bulk of the book had been written before that happened.

Olive's long, chatty letter is one of precious few communications between the James family that survive. Her fondness for her older brother is obvious, especially in the shared gentle ribbing of their younger brother, 'the Manager in General'. However, Olive's letter reveals that where CLR had failed to stay close to power, Eric was quietly rising ever higher: 'Now for a very secret hint I got – the Manager in General is a big favourite with the PM for successor but what will happen is anybody's guess.' Finally she suggests that the people are falling out of love with the PNM post-independence and mourn the departure of CLR: 'All over the country they remember you and are saying all that he said would happen is happening.'

Following publication, there was a flurry of interest in CLR. He made his television debut on *Wednesday Magazine*, talking to John Arlott about his book. *Wednesday Magazine* was an afternoon arts show, angled at women. Sadly no tapes of it remain. The note CLR sent the producer, Sheila Innes, afterwards is particularly charming:

> I saw the telecast but didn't know what exactly to make of it. However I have received expert opinion: last week I stood in Shaftesbury Avenue where it meets Cambridge Circus and looked at books on a cart as I have done any time during the last 30 years. A man came up to me, about 30, good-looking and very bright in his eye, and wearing a white coat. He said to me, 'I never forget a face. You were on television the other day. I saw you. I found it very interesting.' You can imagine my astonishment: I was now wearing an overcoat and hat and glasses. I made my acknowledgements. He told me afterwards that his white coat was a sign of his selling jellied eels which he did regularly on that particular spot. So I now have a television critic. I shall certainly cultivate him.[13]

Soon the publicity died down. CLR spent much of the summer of 1963 watching the touring West Indies cricket team, led once again by Frank Worrell. It was a triumphant series for the West Indies. They won by three Tests to one on the back of consistent performances from their opening batsman Conrad Hunte, and aggressive fast bowling from Wes Hall and Charlie Griffiths* as well as significant contributions from the team's new stars, the Guyanese batsman Rohan Kanhai and the Bajan all-rounder Garfield Sobers.

CLR's local Test match, at Lord's, was both the only draw and the most exciting game of the series. When time ran out, England needed only five more runs to win but they were down to their last two batsmen and one of those, Colin Cowdrey,† had come out with a broken arm to save England from defeat.

* A great bowler whose career was curtailed after he was accused of throwing rather than bowling the ball,

† Cowdrey was a man CLR much admired and corresponded with regularly over the years.

After the series, CLR gave a talk at Lord's reflecting on what he'd seen. Most interesting is the passage he devotes to the crowd rather than the teams:

> I have been looking at this game and I have had in mind what many serious people and many hard-working people seek to achieve ... the integration of West Indians into English life. Now the various clubs that they have, their welfare offices and all that is very good, but I'm certain that at Lord's on one day that I remember, and in those days of the Oval, more integration took place spontaneously than by 20 years of organisations and individual people. It was a tremendous public show. And I will tell you one or two of the things that I noticed. These West Indians are far more noisy and talkative at Lord's or at the Oval than they are in Bridgetown or in Jamaica. That is an absolute fact. They now feel here that they have to do their share also and the best they can do is to talk. The boys on the field will bat and bowl and they will keep it up behind them. They don't do that and haven't done that in Trinidad: I have seen them. Furthermore, they talk a lot more than this a great deal. Make the English people understand more what they are and respect and respond to it and they also change the habits of the English people themselves.[14]

Having shown the English people, and indeed the Caribbean people, how much the West Indian approach to cricket had changed the game, and for the better, in *Beyond a Boundary*, CLR wanted to do the same thing with Shakespeare. Following his series of radio talks, he started work on a book.

Meanwhile, his sessions with the study group were going well. He was delighted to be able to share with them the new paperback edition of *The Black Jacobins*, which had finally been reissued in America, complete with a new afterword relating the Haitian Revolution to the convulsions of the modern world, the Cuban Revolution in particular. He reported on his study group to his Guyanese friend Sydney King,

> I talk around here a bit to the West Indian students and I am glad to say that within the last six months they have made enormous strides forward ... They have come to the conclusion that the political leadership that the WI have had during the last few years is rotten and will lead the WI nowhere.[15]

Much more problematic, unfortunately, than his teaching of these young people was his relationship with his actual son. Just a week after *Beyond a Boundary* was published, Constance wrote to him to tell him that Nobbie was in a terrible state. Now fourteen and tall for his age, he was getting into trouble on the streets, stealing emblems from car bonnets* and disturbing his friends with his erratic moods. Constance said he seemed to crave punishment, either sanctions from her or actual physical beatings in street confrontations. The letter ends on an agonised note:

> The boy is begging for help and he is also begging for physical harm. I'm terrified that he will invite someone to injure him seriously. We do all that we can but when I look at him and see him so troubled and upset my heart tears out of my body ... Nello, his every action lately, even eating or moving is violent. His nerves seem pitched beyond endurance.[16]

Soon afterwards she took Nobbie to a doctor, who said he was having a nervous breakdown and prescribed tranquilisers three times a day. Constance and CLR agreed that Nobbie should go to London, to get away from New York and to be with his father. CLR suggested that part of Nobbie's trouble must be to do with being a Black boy in an America increasingly gripped by racial strife.

Nobbie arrived during the summer holidays and, for a while, everything seemed to be OK. He spent a lot of time riding his bike around

* This was a popular pastime in the early days of hip hop, when rappers would wear Mercedes emblems on chains around their necks. Interesting that it was going on twenty years earlier.

London. In CLR's view, Nobbie's problems could be solved. He felt that they were to do with how bright he was, while at the same time so disinclined to follow rules:

> So I tell you what I think. As far as I know it. Nothing is wrong about Nob. So get that out of the way ... Whatever problem or problems he has or had, he reminds me very much of myself. He is aware of them, that he had them, and, something I admire immensely and I'm glad to see, he made up his mind that America was no good for him at this time and he had someone else to go – his father, and he has made the break, made it clean. I'm glad to know that my son is like that. I know the quality. I look for it in people ... What I find most important is his attitude to me. I very rarely shout at him or tell him anything unkind and he knows that and has shown me that he knows that. And whenever I'm here with him alone, he takes care of me like a nurse. I'm not so active and he is on the alert to know if I want something or he can do something for me.[17]

CLR and Selma arranged for Nob to take an assessment for entry into the best local grammar school. He passed and was all set to start school when CLR was amazed to hear from Constance that Nobbie had written to her saying he was terribly homesick and wanted to come back to New York. Nobbie duly went back to the US, leaving CLR bewildered.

Looking back, Selma offers her take on what went wrong. Again, she sees CLR's debilitated state after his accident as the key. She was determined to do all she could to make Nobbie feel secure but CLR was preoccupied and distant, leaving Nobbie feeling abandoned and hurt.

That autumn there were a couple more visitors from the US. Nettie Kravitz came over from Detroit and then a new associate, a brilliant young historian called George Rawick, arrived with his wife Dianne, to stay in London for several months in late 1963. Rawick relayed his initial impressions of CLR in a letter to Marty Glaberman:

> He is tremendously alive and is publishing regularly in various English journals, particularly in a Lib Lab independent intellectual weekly called the *New Society* . . . We talked about the Negro question in the United States at length and they asked many questions that we were able to deal with. He keeps returning time and time again to the need for Facing Reality to prepare and publish a document on the Negro question.[18]

All of which suggests that by this time CLR was starting to get his mojo back, at least when dealing with the world outside his immediate family. He talked to Rawick about a book he was excited about, Michael Harrington's *The Other America*. Harrington combined hard research with skilful polemic and a cynical, human eye in a coruscating study of American poverty. It had just become a bestseller, following a long piece by CLR's erstwhile friend Dwight Macdonald in the *New Yorker*. CLR liked it immensely, as Rawick reported in a letter to Marty Glaberman: 'James keeps saying that it is a model of the kind of writing we should be doing, bringing material like this before the public.'[19]

Rawick, looking back years later, noted that, like Harrington's, CLR's politics were based in a curiosity about people:

> James constantly asks questions: 'Where are you from?' 'What did your mother and father do?' 'You lived on a farm? How did you milk the cows, by hand or machinery? How many cows a day? What else did you do on the farm? Did your family make much money? Your father had to work at a gas station in order to make ends meet? What does he do today?' 'You work in an automobile factory? What exactly do you do? What are the working conditions like? Are the toilets clean? How many breaks do you get during the day?'[20]

The Rawicks and the Jameses quickly became friendly, helped by the belated realisation that George had been in the same high-school class as Selma, an extraordinary coincidence. Gradually Rawick got to know the private CLR, 'Buying salt-cod and salt-beef in a London West Indian market, joking with the vendors. Playing the slot machines in London pubs. Betting a few shillings on the horse races . . .'

One thing he also noticed was that CLR was alarmingly thin. Selma was worried about this too, and in early January CLR went into hospital for tests, but not before an enjoyable New Year's Eve. Rawick again:

> Nello goes to the hospital tomorrow for 10 days of observation. He seems in good spirits – we had a wonderful New Year's Eve party with them. Richard Wright's widow was there, as was the widow of the old Fabian H. N. Brailsford. George Lamming, the West Indian writer who is a friend of theirs, came in with his wife.[21]

CLR went into hospital on 6 January 1964. Everyone was alarmed when they realised his weight was a mere 136 pounds, but, as CLR reported to the US comrades a couple of weeks later, there was nothing actually wrong with him, physically at least,

> I am now safely out of hospital. I'm happy to say that after extensive examination nothing is wrong with me that the doctors can find. In fact they say that I'm in every way okay. That is very comforting news though have lost thirty pounds in a few months and (this is extremely interesting to me) they say that maybe I have psychological difficulties.[22]

Out of hospital, CLR was eager to get going with the Facing Reality statement on the 'Negro question', as they were still referring to the civil rights movement. Martin Glaberman had been working on a paper with Willie Gorman in Detroit. CLR decided Marty should come over to London and work on it in company with himself, Selma and George Rawick.

Marty agreed and arrived in London along with his wife and fellow Facing Reality comrade Jessie on 2 March. It was as full a caucus as had been seen in some while, and they worked hard on producing a pamphlet that would be called *Negro Americans Take The Lead* when it appeared later in the year.

The job done, the visitors headed home. Rawick, in particular, had benefited hugely from his time with CLR. He had found a research task that would occupy him for years to come:

> In 1964 in London, C. L. R. James told me, I want you to give a lecture here, in [James's] living room, on American history. After the lecture he asked, 'What do we know about the slaves' reaction to slavery?' I told him not a hell of a lot. He asked, 'Is there any material we have?' I told him what little I knew of the slave narratives . . . That began the process of my collecting and publishing *The American Slave*.[23]

Back in the US, Rawick would start work on the epic assignment of compiling the oral testimonies of former slaves, gathered by the Works Progress Administration, into forty volumes that constitute an extraordinary historical resource.*

The Glabermans spent some time in mainland Europe during their trip, and in July Selma followed suit, heading off to Italy with yet another American visitor, Isa-Kae Meksin. Even Sam got in on the act, travelling to Sardinia to stay with his aunt for the summer.

CLR stayed in London, working. He had sent his publishers material for a book on Shakespeare and Lenin. It was an unwieldy combination that failed to attract enthusiasm. He tried replacing Lenin with Abraham Lincoln, with no more success. It's likely that, still weak, he was attempting to recycle somewhat disparate old lectures into book form rather than trying to create something new and fully developed, as he had done with *Beyond a Boundary*.

* The testimonies are fascinating. Often problematic, as it's clear that many of the old former slaves are trying to please their white interviewers, but still compelling in their accumulation of the quotidian experience of slavery. They can now be found online.

It must have been a frustrating time for him. He could see that, in many ways, the West Indies' time had come. As he had hoped and predicted, its writers, musicians and cricketers were making something new out of their colonial experience. He wanted to be at the heart of it, to be recognised as a leader of this renaissance, but he felt tired and alone and, for once, unsure whether he was equal to the task.

His hopes and frustrations come through in his correspondence with V. S. Naipaul over this period. Naipaul had written a thoughtful, positive review of *Beyond a Boundary* in *Encounter* ('*Beyond a Boundary* is one of the finest and most finished books to come out of the West Indies, important to England, important to the West Indies'). CLR responded with a long letter, responding to both the review and a long article on India that Naipaul had just written for the *Sunday Times*.

In the letter he references the appendix he wrote for the new edition of *The Black Jacobins*, which includes an overview of the state of West Indian culture, including some remarks about Naipaul's great novel *A House for Mr Biswas*:

> The West Indian had made a fool of himself imitating American journalism, Shakespeare, T. S. Eliot, Lorca. He had arrived at truth when he wrote about his own West Indian childhood, his West Indian mother and the West Indian landscape. Naipaul is an East Indian. Mr Biswas is an East Indian. But the East Indian problem in the West Indies is a creation of politicians of both races, seeking means to avoid attacking the old colonial system. The East Indian has become as West Indian as all the other expatriates.[24]

He doesn't quote that paragraph in his letter to Naipaul, but this one that sums up his excitement at the possibilities of this West Indian renaissance:

> The West Indian writers have discovered the West Indies and West Indians, a people of the middle of our disturbed century, concerned with the discovery of themselves, determined to discover themselves, but without hatred or malice against the foreign, even the

> bitter imperialist past. To be welcomed into the comity of nations a new nation must bring something new. Otherwise it is a mere administrative convenience or necessity. The West Indians have brought something new.

Then he goes on to both praise Naipaul's article on India, but at the same time to suggest that his famed honesty in his portrayal of underdeveloped countries lacks real value if it fails to recognise the political context of that underdevelopment:

> This article is very fine. But there is one thing I have to say. I do not believe that at this stage of the 20th century we as what we are can say the things we ought to say and can say better than anybody else unless we at the same time all within its context are penetrating into and showing our awareness of the terrible crises of Western civilisation.
>
> Believe me, my dear Vidia, it is with no idea of propagandising you but as a result of my deepest studies and feelings on the situation of the West Indian writer that I believe we have an immense amount to say about Western civilisation which we more than all other writers from the underdeveloped peoples can say. We not only open up ourselves that we open them too . . . I don't believe that there is any profound difference or rather fundamental difference between the stage of civilisation in which India finds itself and the stage in which the Britain and the Europe of Hitler and Stalin find themselves. And I believe that effective as we are in stripping the wrappings from the underdeveloped countries, we will be more effective if . . . we indicate that we are ready to strip or have already stripped the wrappings from Western civilisation itself. I believe this is necessary for us to reach a final height from which we will be able to see and to point out all things.[25]

Finally, he ends the letter with a plea for friendship. In the younger man he recognised another formidable intellect and hopes and believes they can learn from each other:

> I wish I saw you more often. I'm sure I would benefit by it and I don't think that I would either bore or annoy you. Every succeeding day makes me more certain than ever that we have something special to say but that we remain a collection of individuals and therefore are unable to make the best of our individual selves.

Naipaul, however, was not a man who wanted a mentor. He was an ever more arrogant individualist. Decades later he looked back on his friendship with CLR in a curious memoir-cum-novel called *A Way in the World*. CLR is lightly fictionalised, but it's undoubtedly the real relationship between the two men that is at its heart. As Naipaul sees it, the CLR character, LeBrun, wants to take him over. He sees the brilliance of CLR, but decides he doesn't want it in his life.

In real life their friendship carried on for a little while, they went to the cricket together, but it's clear from the letters that CLR is asking for more than Naipaul wants to give. Nonetheless, Naipaul's portrait of CLR at a dinner party around this time is as vivid and finely drawn as one could wish for:

> He was born to talk. It was as though everything he saw and thought and read was automatically processed into talk material . . . I thought his spoken language was like Ruskin's on the printed page, in its fluency and elaborateness, the words wonderfully chosen, often unexpected, bubbling up from some ever-running spring of sensibility . . . I was moved by the fact that such a man came from something like my own background . . . How, considering when he was born, had he become the man he was? How had he preserved his soul through all the discouragements of the colonial time?[26]

By late 1964 Naipaul was well on his way to dissociating himself from his Trinidadian roots, swapping the friendship of Caribbean writers like Andrew Salkey for high-society folk like Antonia Fraser and Anthony Powell. CLR, by contrast, would be returning to the West Indies rather sooner than he had expected.

The Times and the *Observer* both commissioned him to report on the upcoming cricket series between the West Indies and Australia, a series of five Test matches, including two in Port of Spain. He would sail for Jamaica in early January 1965.

Chapter Twenty-Two

CLR took ship on 15 January. Things went wrong almost immediately upon arrival in Jamaica. He went to see Harry Annamunthodo, the surgeon who had looked after him following the car accident. Dr Annamunthodo was horrified, as CLR wrote to John Arlott:

> He did not recognise me at first, I had lost so much weight . . . he examined me and sent me to be x-rayed at once, When the x-rays came back he told me that I was in a very bad way.[1]

Dr Annamunthodo was convinced CLR had a tumour. He would have operated straight away, except he had to be in Trinidad the following day. CLR decided his only option was to return to London, which offered better hospitals and would allow him to convalesce at home. At great expense he booked a flight back, changing planes in New York. On arrival in New York, though, the US immigration authorities refused to allow him to travel on to the UK and sent him back to Jamaica, all at his own expense. He suspected this vindictive behaviour was inspired by the anti-US line he had adopted when he was editor of *The Nation*. It took him another week to get a direct flight back to London and his worried family.

On arrival he went to see another doctor friend, a neurosurgeon called Chris Pallis, who was a leading light in the British Solidarity organisation, allied to Cornelius Castoriadis' Socialisme ou Barbarie. Pallis examined CLR with extreme thoroughness and found absolutely nothing wrong with him. This was obviously good news, but by now CLR was thoroughly exhausted and wrung out by his ordeal. He had been excited by the possibilities of covering the cricket tour and using his experiences as a basis for a follow-up to *Beyond a Boundary*;

now it all felt like too much. He wrote to John Arlott asking for advice. Could he drop out?

Arlott evidently persuaded him to carry on, as he arrived in Trinidad on 12 March, ready for the second Test match, which would start two weeks later. Eighteen hours after his arrival, however, he was placed under house arrest on the orders of Eric Williams, using the excuse that there was a state of emergency in the country following the sugar workers going on strike. It was a matter of no relevance to CLR's visit, but there it was. The immediate question was where he should stay. His brother Eric didn't want to be stuck between his family and the prime minister. Instead, as her niece Erica recalls, Olive came to the rescue:

> She had moved from the family house in Tunapuna to a smaller house in Barataria. She loved Nello and read all his books and she took him in when he was under house arrest, because my father said he wasn't going to do that.[2]

If Williams thought putting CLR under house arrest was going to keep him quiet, then he was much mistaken. It had the opposite effect. CLR had not come to Trinidad for political purposes, simply to report on the cricket and work on his book. Suddenly, though, he was once again a political figure. Back in London Selma was organising a campaign to get him released from the restrictions and, in Trinidad, Olive's house became a focus for all those opposed to Williams's increasingly dictatorial leadership. Erica remembers it being a severe strain on Olive, who was in poor health herself:

> She did not realise what was going to happen. He would just be lying there – he was always, always lying down! He was in the porch, you know, and everyone came. There would be long lines of people waiting to see him and my father felt Olive did not deserve that.

CLR's house arrest only lasted for a couple of weeks, but it was time enough for him to completely rethink the purpose of his return to Trinidad. He abandoned the cricket reporting and the potential book. Instead, he threw himself back into the rough world of local politics.

He had made three important allies: Stephen Maharaj, the radical acting leader of the Indian dominated opposition party, the Democratic Labour Party; George Weekes, the Black leader of the Oilfields Workers' Trade Union; and Jack Kelshall, an old friend, a white socialist and bibliophile. The four men, all coming from very different political backgrounds, decided to form a faction within the DLP, hoping to turn it into a socialist party that could unite Black and Indian workers under one umbrella. The success of the plan depended on the attitude of the DLP's overall leader, Stephen Capildeo, who was soon to return from London. In the meantime, the radical alliance would begin by establishing a paper called *We the People.*

CLR wrote to Selma to tell of his plans. He would be staying in Trinidad, and he wanted her to come and join him for part of the summer.

Selma was horrified at the news, though not entirely surprised. On 4 July she wrote a long, uncharacteristically emotional letter to Marty Glaberman setting out her feelings about the news. She told him that she had been worried about CLR's mental state ever since the car accident, so much so that she had discussed his hostile behaviour towards her with a neurosurgeon (presumably Chris Pallis). The neurosurgeon had discounted the idea of brain damage, instead stressing the physical toll the accident had taken on CLR and suggesting that he was frustrated by the challenges of his daily life. Selma agreed with this and said, for that reason, she had been afraid that he would be seduced by a return to his homeland where he was still a significant public figure.

What really bothered her, though, was that CLR had not simply re-entered politics, but had done so in a way that she saw as ideologically bankrupt; that he had allied himself with unprincipled locals and appeared to be deifying Stephen Maharaj, all rigour gone out the window. He had sent her the first edition of *We the People* and she was dismayed to find that CLR had written it all and yet it seemed objectively bad. By the end of the letter it is clear that Selma is at the end of her tether, her marriage in crisis. The last years, she says, had been hellish. She felt her cherished family was disintegrating and couldn't bear to see how unhappy, confused and blundering CLR had become.

Meanwhile, Capildeo had returned to Trinidad and, after initially supporting the James faction, he quickly changed his mind and denounced them as traitors to the party. They responded by leaving en bloc to form a new party, which would be called the Workers and Farmers Party – code, in part, for Black and Indian. CLR would be the general secretary and editor of the party magazine. Money was raised to buy Selma a ticket to come over to Trinidad.

She arrived in early August and wrote to Marty again on the 13th. CLR was staying in a two-room flat in the centre of town, living on a diet of swizzled eggs. He seemed old and frail, and yet responsible for everything. Outside the work, he was desperately lonely. None of his old friends visited him, not wanting to be associated with his political breakaway. Olive was recovering from major surgery and couldn't visit him. He was staying, she thought, because he felt a duty. He thought that Trinidad was sliding into dictatorship, and he was a man of unsullied reputation who could rally the opposition.

Selma, however, believed he was in no fit state to achieve any such thing. With George Lamming she formulated a plan. Lamming could raise some money for CLR to spend a few months in southern Europe, recuperating and writing his autobiography. CLR rejected the idea. He was determined to stay, much to Selma's frustration: In her view he no longer had any roots there, and his political struggles just seemed painful and joyless. All she could do was try to get rid of people so he could rest, and make sure he ate reasonably well.

A week later she wrote to Lamming again. CLR was still set on his political mission. She was reassured that his associates were decent people, but still saw their venture as desperate and doomed – an attempted combination of workers and small businesspeople that had no ideological coherence.

Selma left Trinidad in early September. Before returning to London she went to the US. She met up with the Glabermans in Detroit and they came up with the idea of a fund for CLR. They would write to all the moneyed friends and associates they could think of and ask them to make financial contributions that would allow CLR to slide gracefully into a semi-retirement of writing and reading. Her final stop was New York, where she saw Nobbie, who appeared to be in much better shape, but she had a fearful row with Constance, who let fly with decades' worth of bitterness.

Selma arrived back in London at the end of October, in time to celebrate Sam's seventeenth birthday and excellent O level results. A month later CLR was writing to Marty Glaberman, asking for a ticket from Trinidad to London, afraid that he didn't have the health or stamina to stay the political course: 'Although politically convinced, I am personally doubtful.'[3]

He returned in November and stayed seven weeks before returning to Trinidad in January 1966, convinced, after all, that he should return to help the Workers and Farmers Party contest the election that November.

While in London, there was a dinner for his sixty-fifth birthday, which served also to launch the fund. An array of luminaries were announced as being members of the committee. They included John Arlott, plus Caribbean writer friends like George Lamming and Andrew Salkey, alongside former comrades including the Canadian Trotskyist turned poet and professor Earle Birney and the civil rights lawyer Conrad Lynn. There were some unexpected names too: the Barbadian American novelist Paule Marshall, for instance, and the folk-song collector Alan Lomax. At the dinner, tributes were made to CLR and Sam Selvon presented him with a selection of works by West Indian writers.

It was not a happy stay, however, as Selma reported to Marty. CLR had come down with the flu on arrival. His mental state, she felt, was incredibly confused. After spending seven weeks with him in this state she was no longer sure that their marriage could survive. He was not happy with her and he was not happy with himself. His financial situation, meanwhile, didn't bear consideration. The whole experience was horribly painful for her.

The irony is that Selma was in many ways going from strength to strength. She was on the committee of a new organisation called CARD – the Campaign against Racial Discrimination. She was now leading the sessions on Marxism at 20 Staverton Road. The group of young West Indians shared her dismay at CLR's plunge into party politics. Stanley French, for instance, felt that 'It was in fundamental contradiction to everything CLR had advanced and stood for.'[4] And rather than continue to depend on CLR's decidedly erratic income, she had started to forge a career for herself, finding relatively well-paid work as a typist transcribing audio tapes for the BBC, often boring but steady work. She was also developing the feminist thinking that would eventually lead to her launching her own campaign, Wages for Housework, in 1972. Selma was no longer simply CLR's wife but an emerging political force in her own right, very much in tune with the new wave of feminism that was starting to arrive.

Back in Trinidad CLR spent the balance of the year campaigning for the Workers and Farmers Party, preparing to stand as a candidate himself in the election. It was a hard year. The party had no money. They could no longer afford to produce the newspaper or to provide accommodation for CLR. After a while he went to live in the house of one of the party activists, Dalip Gopeesingh, in Curepe, east of Port of Spain. Much of his correspondence sees him begging Stephen Maharaj for money for taxis and typists. Norman Girvan, who had been part of the Staverton Road study group, came to Trinidad at the time and was dismayed by what he found:

> My 1966 experience of CLR was to some degree, the loss of illusion. The Trinidadian masses did not respond to James and his political allies. I remember attending a rally at Woodford Square where James and George Weekes and others spoke. I do not believe there were 50 people present. Some people were laughing openly at 'the old man' ... There was also a personal aspect. I once went to visit James where he was staying with the family of a Party member. He was living in near poverty. He was dependent on people who did

> not seem to accord him the respect that he deserved. I did not like to see James in that condition. The whole experience made me very uncomfortable.[5]

It was all, as Selma predicted, a hopeless, depressing business. That March, Olive contacted Selma to tell her that she was worried CLR was dying.

And yet, once again, just as all seemed impossible, CLR's health mysteriously regenerated. When George Lamming saw him briefly in May, he was amazed to find CLR looking better – healthier and younger – than he had done in years. The upcoming election campaign, quixotic though it seemed to his friends, had given him a new burst of energy. By July, though, when Lamming made his next visit, all was despond.

> I saw Nello last week during a short trip to Trinidad. He's in very low spirits. His colleagues have no conception at all of his value. I suggested that he come here for a two-week vacation. This would give him a break from the pigsty of politics in that quarter; and there is nothing like a little sea breeze and some local food to cheer him up. But the financial situation is very, very bad.[6]

Lamming asks Marty whether the CLR birthday fund might be able to help. Unfortunately, it turned out to be high on goodwill but low on actual financial support. CLR did travel to Guyana for a while. Then, at the beginning of September, his friend and fellow WFP activist Walter Annamunthodo was shot and wounded at a campaign rally.

This news inspired CLR to return to Trinidad immediately. It obviously made him believe that the WFP, disorganised though they might be, were a serious threat to the ruling order. A few days later he issued a curious statement addressed 'to the many whom it concerns', alleging that the shooting was a deliberate attempt at political assassination and that he suspected that the next name on the hit list would be his own.

You can almost sense the energy surge this gave him in a brief note he wrote to Selma to update her. For one thing his handwriting is unusually strong and legible. There's even a renewed affection in greeting and sign-off: 'Dearest S' and 'With love N'. He explains that 'I am speaking on the attempt and all day I was preparing a party statement,' before making the oddly childlike statement 'I am very useful'. Finally he tells her, 'Cheer up. Before the end of the year great deeds will be done. Of course great deeds are secondary to good deeds. OK accepted.'[7]

Shortly after this, a large stone was thrown while CLR was making a speech, narrowly missing his head. He was convinced that this was the predicted assassination attempt, part of a programme of intimidation leading up to the election that was to take place on 7 November.

Before the election, CLR made a brief trip to Montréal, on the first weekend in October, to attend the second Conference on West Indian affairs. This was an important gathering of Caribbean intellectuals organised by a number of radical young expats living in Canada, including a young Jamaican historian called Robert Hill, who had attended some of the Staverton Road study group meetings. He had begun corresponding regularly with CLR, but also with Marty Glaberman, so he was aware of how desperate CLR's situation was in Trinidad and was delighted to be able to invite him to Canada.

CLR was due to give the opening speech, on 'The Making of the Caribbean People'. He rose triumphantly to the occasion. In front of an audience of radicals and intellectuals, members of his London study group and his old Facing Reality comrades rather than confused Trinidadian field labourers, he was in his element. The speech took his listeners from the first slave revolts in Barbados in the early seventeenth century, on to Haiti, of course, and then to Castro's Cuba, stressing that slavery had never succeeded in dimming the slaves' own capacity for organised resistance. Marty Glaberman was both thrilled and relieved, as he wrote to Selma afterwards:

> Had a fabulous weekend in Montréal at the WRU conference. Nello looked the best in years. Spent one night with him at the hotel and you know what he ordered to eat – porridge and ham

and eggs for breakfast! He didn't eat it all but he ate a lot. He gave a great opening speech and participated in a panel the following morning ... The overall impact of Nello's speeches, presence, et cetera was tremendous and will have repercussions for some time to come.'[8]

Between them, Robert Hill and Marty Glaberman had succeeded in pulling together the apparently separate threads of CLR's politics: the Marxists and the West Indian radicals. So George Lamming was there and George Rawick, Tim Hector from Antigua and Willie Gorman from Detroit. At last it seemed as if the politics CLR and his small brand of American comrades had worked on, so scrupulously and for so long, might have a real influence on the global changes that were afoot in the white heat of late 1966. Arrangements were made for CLR to return to Canada, to conduct a lecture tour and lead a new study group, as soon as the Trinidad elections were out of the way.

In the event, the election results were perhaps even more disastrous than CLR's friends had feared. The Workers and Farmers Party didn't just fail to win any seats, they lost their deposits everywhere and received a paltry 3 per cent of the popular vote. Eric Williams's PNM were returned to power with 52 per cent of the vote. The DLP came second and even a further DLP breakaway, the Liberal Party, managed 9 per cent of the vote. Afterwards CLR protested that there had been widespread electoral fraud, but really there was no papering over this utter political humiliation. As soon as he was able he took a flight to Canada.

Chapter Twenty-Three

CLR arrived in Montreal in late November 1966 and remained in North America until the following March. He began and ended his stay in Canada, but once he discovered that the US was now prepared to allow him across its border he embarked on a long lecture tour there in January and February.

Montreal was a refuge, a chance to recharge. Instead of the cynicism of electoral politics in Trinidad, he was surrounded by the idealism of young Caribbean revolutionaries studying and planning to change the West Indies for good.

Over the three months he was there, CLR gave a series of lectures: some to open audiences and some to small study groups. Topics ranged from Trinidad and Haiti to Marx and Lenin. There was one on *négritude* that he delivered in French, Montreal's other language.

He also gave a lecture on the subject that was now preoccupying him the most. It was another Shakespeare play, not *Othello* or *Macbeth*, but *King Lear*. Once again, it's hard not to see some personal resonance in the choice. The old man cast out from his home, stoned by his enemies. Typically, though, CLR was adamant that nothing could be further from his mind. As he wrote to Willie Gorman, 'I am absolutely opposed to the concentration of players and critics on the storm scene and Lear's supposed denunciation of the universe.'[1]

CLR announced that he was planning a book on *King Lear*, but how much of it was ever written is unclear. It was certainly never completed. Instead it was becoming increasingly evident that CLR's most important role, now he was in his mid-sixties, was as a speaker and teacher, as an inspiration to the new generation of Black radicals he met in these three months, men and women rallying to the battle cry of Black Power.

The man who had popularised this phrase was a twenty-five-year-old revolutionary called Stokely Carmichael. Stokely was born and initially raised in Trinidad, before moving to Harlem aged eleven. On 24 February 1967, he came to Montreal to give a speech at Sir George Williams University, where most of the young West Indians were studying. CLR was enormously impressed, as he recalled in a speech made a few months later:

> There were about one thousand people present, chiefly white students, about sixty or seventy Negro people, and I was so struck by what he was saying and the way he was saying it (a thing which does not happen to me politically very often) that I sat down immediately and took the unusual step of writing a letter to him, a political letter. After all, he was a young man of twenty-three or twenty-four and I was old enough to be his grandfather and, as I say, I thought I had a few things to tell him which would be of use to him and, through him, the movement he represented.[2]

It's a telling indication of CLR's acceptance of his new role as mentor rather than participant. The WFP debacle had made it brutally clear that he was simply too old to be the face of a revolutionary movement. Stokely, by contrast, was perfect. He had the oratorical firepower of the Harlem preacher, allied to an instinctive grasp of the power of the moment, and similar good looks to those of the young CLR. Black radicalism had lost one leader with the murder of Malcolm X; Stokely Carmichael was the heir apparent. Brilliant though he was, however, he was still only twenty-five years old and CLR could see that what he lacked was a deep understanding of the lessons of the radical struggles of the past. He said as much in his speech:

> I went on further to indicate in the letter that there were grave weaknesses in the whole Negro struggle in the United States; for one, that it lacked a sound historical and theoretical basis. And I suggested to him, that if he did not see his way to initiate this study himself, he should see to it that others take it up and take it up seriously. So large and far-reaching a struggle needed to

know where it was, where it had come from, and where it was going.

Stokely responded appreciatively to CLR's advice, but it was really the Montreal West Indians who had time to listen and fully absorb his lessons. Perhaps the most notable of them, though he was only there briefly, was Walter Rodney, the brilliant young Guyanese historian who had been part of CLR's London study group, and was the first to really make his name, beginning with his work on the African slave trade and continuing with his hugely influential 1972 book, *How Europe Underdeveloped Africa*. Later he would become an opposition leader in Guyana, before being assassinated in 1980.

Several of these acolytes formed the CLR James Study Circle, devoted to both understanding and propagating CLR's political ideas. Among their number was Tim Hector who, the following year, would start the Antigua Caribbean Liberation Movement, explicitly following CLR's ideas. A few years older than the others was Alphonso 'Alfie' Roberts from St Vincent, who had played one Test match for the West Indies, aged just eighteen, before turning to politics. One can only imagine how delighted CLR must have been to have a follower with such a background. The most significant female member of the group was Anne Cools, who would go on to found Canada's first women's refuge, before becoming the country's first Black – and then longest-serving – senator.*

The group's key organiser, and the one CLR would become closest to, was Robert Hill, who would go on to forge a career as a historian and unrivalled authority on the works of Marcus Garvey. He would also become CLR's literary executor, responsible for overseeing the steady re-publication of his work.

Before he left, CLR summed up the course of study ahead: 'I recommend to you *Lear* – Shakespeare in the seventeenth century.

* Her place in radical history has been somewhat compromised by her latter-day devotion to the cause of men's rights and hostility to radical feminism. It's a political position she shares, perhaps significantly, with the English pioneer of women's refuges Erin Pizzey.

Rousseau in the eighteenth century. Marx in the nineteenth century. And Lenin in the twentieth century. Then you have to master and tackle the West Indian problem.'*[3]

CLR's time in Canada and the US was obviously gratifying and restorative, but come March it was time to return to London. He'd been away for two years, barring his one short visit at the end of 1965. Things had changed, both nationally and domestically. London was swinging, the counterculture visible on the streets. Once rarefied concepts – anarchism, Black Power, feminism – were common currency. In many ways this was the vision that the Johnson-Forest Tendency had anticipated decades earlier, but CLR was now sixty-six years old and very much feeling his age.

Changes were apparent at home too. Selma was earning a living from her transcription work. She no longer had much time to type CLR's long letters and works in progress. They still shared a flat and were still comrades in Facing Reality, but their personal relationship was coming apart. CLR's mood cannot have been helped by the news he'd received just before leaving Canada. Olive had died, the last of the Trinidadian family women, who had encouraged and, perhaps, idolised him.†

George Rawick came over from America to help out, along with Dianne and their young son Jules. The Facing Reality group was reconvened at Staverton Road with the Jameses, the Rawicks, the erratic veteran Trotskyist Alan Christianson, the Jamaican law student Richard Small and Ann Cools, over from Canada. The agreed plan was to produce a new manifesto, ready for their fast-changing times. It would be called *The Gathering Forces*.

Life was not easy, though. Soon after arriving back in England CLR had the sad duty of writing Sir Frank Worrell's obituary. The West

* Thanks to Christian Høgsbjerg for extracting this neat quote in his fine essay 'CLR James and the British New Left'.

† Olive's will, full of touching references to small items of jewellery she wished to give to family members, saw her leave her one major asset, the house on Ward Street, Tunapuna, to CLR. However, for doubtless complex reasons it was a very long time before he succeeded in selling it.

Indies' first Black cricket captain had died of leukaemia at the age of forty-two. James, like many others, had had high hopes of Worrell becoming as inspirational a political leader as he had been a cricketing one:

> To us who are concerned he seemed poised for applying his powers to the cohesion and self-realisation of the West Indian people. Not a man who one slapped on the shoulder, he was nevertheless to the West Indian population an authentic national hero ... He had shown the West Indian mastery of what Western civilisation had to teach. His wide experience, reputation, his audacity of perspective and the years which seemed to stretch before him fitted him to be one of those destined to help the West Indies to make their own West Indian way.[4]

Come June 1967, CLR was writing to Marty Glaberman in the lowest of spirits. As with all his bleakest letters, he begins with the protestation that he is in no way asking for money, before going on to do exactly that. He sets out his plans – to write a book on *King Lear*, to produce *The Gathering Forces* in collaboration with the others – but he simply doubts whether he is up to it. He is old and he is poor; his little sister is dead. For all the work he's done, there has been no financial reward, no university paying his tenure, no newspapers rewarding him handsomely for setting down the stray thoughts of a grand old man.

What makes matters worse, he tells Marty, is his sense that his health is failing:

> I have neglected it for years but recently I have seen, or in fact I am seeing, a specialist. He tells me that my intellectual capacity is as good as it ever was. So much I have always known. But he tells me also that while there is nothing organic or pathological wrong with me, my physique is slowly decaying and that much, if I did not know as such, I am quite aware of what he is saying. He has put me under a regime which I am following out with the necessary

confidence . . . You do not allow yourself to drift physically for years, reach the stage that I have reached and then get yourself better in passing, merely as an adjunct to your regular pursuits.[5]

The result was an unwelcome sense of helplessness, especially now that George and Dianne had moved into a flat of their own. There was only Selma with him, and he acknowledged that there was a limit to what he could ask of her:

Selma is paying all the bills of the household. That is a tremendous task . . . But the idea that you will be able to work and to pay the household bills, do what is required in regard to Lear (which is infinitely more than typing) and now embark on the colossal task of doing the technical, intellectual and political needs or necessities of 'October' and still live some sort of personal life, that is a senile absurdity.

Instead he hankers after what he had had for so much of his life, a young and willing female assistant:

What to do . . . I require technical assistance and under present circumstances, as I see it at present, it will have to be paid for. In my early days in the West Indies from even before I was twenty, there were always devoted people, usually but not always, feminine, who were not only devoted to the work but glad to do it. In England it was the same thing and America was beyond degree, in this respect, priceless. But since my return to England in 1953 the situation has not been the same and we have now reached a crisis that demands resolution.

The obvious question was how to fund such a right-hand woman. CLR hoped that the answer lay in the 65th Birthday committee, launched with such fanfare the year before. Unfortunately, it had still failed to produce anything much in the way of hard cash. CLR beseeched Marty to beat the bushes and see if some financial support might come his way. But really he knew he was on his own. He'd lived to sixty-six through his writing and through the beneficence of rich believers. What now?

In other countries, perhaps there would have been support for an important intellectual in his twilight years. In Britain, then and now, there was nothing. It is assumed that to be famous is to be rich. CLR, like many writers, knew the reality. His unlikely hero, Arnold Bennett, had worried about money obsessively despite always earning well. CLR had always been protected by pride and self-belief, but the instinctive optimism that had carried him forward for so long was starting to ebb away.* A month later, in July, he was writing to Marty again, this time to say that he was simply not up to doing any further work on *The Gathering Forces*. He would delegate the work to his comrades instead.

And yet, once again, just as he seemed to be at his lowest, he managed miraculously to revive. Just as he was writing to Marty, he was invited to take part in one of the seminal counterculture events thus far. This was the Dialectics of Liberation, a week-long programme of talks organised by the 'anti-psychiatrist' David Cooper and mostly held at the underground's new town hall, the Roundhouse in Chalk Farm. This was a former train switching yard that had been taken over by the playwright Arnold Wesker as a left-wing theatre space in the early sixties and had, more recently, become freak-zone central with Pink Floyd's all-night rave attracting everyone from Paul McCartney to Michelangelo Antonioni, while the Trinidadian hustler, and self-proclaimed Black Power leader, Michael X ran the security.

Speakers at the Dialectics ranged from philosophers like Herbert Marcuse† and Gregory Bateson to writers like Allen Ginsberg and William Burroughs. George Rawick was particularly interested in hearing R. D. Laing, who was busy shaking up psychiatry. The speaker

* It would be easy and likely reasonable for CLR to have divined a racial aspect to his lack of support, but, typically, he never makes any such suggestion.

† Who corresponded with Raya Dunayevskaya for a while.

who got the most attention, though, was Stokely Carmichael, who whipped up a storm telling the assembled freaks and intellectuals that revolution was 'only coming from the barrel of a gun'. Stokely spoke twice. Once was at a specific Black Power event. The Trinidadian on stage with Stokely, though, wasn't CLR, but Michael X, who was making a career of bridging the gap between the counterculture and the Black revolutionary movements.

The other event was a symposium on revolutionary violence. CLR attended this one. Stokely was at his most incendiary but Tariq Ali, a leading figure on the new revolutionary left, remembers CLR standing up to him on the key issue of the relative importance of race and class: '"Race is decisive," Carmichael had thundered. "No," James had replied with quiet dignity, "it is class."'*[6]

CLR himself spoke a few days later, presumably at a much smaller event, as his name does not appear on the main posters. But despite his general struggle to write, he managed to give a speech that effectively summed up his decades of thinking on the subject of what was now called Black Power and its relation to revolutionary class politics. It was a long way from Stokely's call to arms. Instead it was a measured and thoughtful speech in which he both managed to give his unequivocal support to the new movement for Black liberation and also to place it in historical context.

He took his listeners from Thomas Jefferson's assertion that all men are created equal, through the writings of successive Black leaders, from Booker T. Washington, who accepted the inevitability of Southern segregation, to W. E. B. Du Bois, who believed that 'the talented tenth' could pull Black America forward. He is particularly positive in his rereading of Du Bois's achievements: 'Dr Du Bois took the lead in making the United States and the world recognize that racial prejudice was not a mere matter of Negroes being persecuted but was a

* CLR elaborated on this, talking to Tariq Ali about Stokely a dozen years later: 'I still believe that [class was the ultimate arbiter]. I have not shifted, but it would be a great mistake to ignore the race question or the racial dimension. I am on the side of all those who are using their racial subordination as a means of getting together because in that way they can make as powerful an impact as possible. But for me the class question is still the dominant and crucial one.'

cancer which poisoned the whole civilization of the United States.' Then CLR carried on through Garvey, Padmore and Fanon. And so he arrived at the present day, this time of Black people rioting across America, and pithily made it clear which side he was on:

> If we know the realities of Negro oppression in the USA (and if we don't we should keep our mouths shut until we do), then we should guide ourselves by a West Indian expression which I recommend to you: what he do, he well do. Let me repeat that: what the American Negroes do is, as far as we are concerned, well done. They will take their chances, they will risk their liberty, they risk their lives if need be. The decisions are theirs.[7]

He goes on to say (in words with a particular resonance at the time of this writing) that the real struggle Black people in the US are engaged in is not with white people, but with the state, and in particular its armed wing, the police:

> Racism is on the decline in the United States. Yes, on the decline. Years ago you used to have white people fighting against black people. Not today. Stokely insists and all the violence points to the fact that what is taking place in American city after American city is black people fighting against the police. In other words, they are challenging an ancient enemy which is one wing of the state power. That is not racism. That is revolutionary politics.

Having first provided historical context for, and then given his complete support to, the Black Power movement, he addresses the question of how Black politics relate to classic Marxist revolutionary politics. It was a question, he told his audience, that he had been thinking about for decades:

> I therefore was in a position from the very beginning to state my position and to state it in a discussion that some of us had with Trotsky on the Negro question in 1939. The position was this: the

> independent struggle of the Negro people for their democratic rights and equality with the rest of the American nation not only had to be defended and advocated by the Marxist movement. The Marxist movement had to understand that such independent struggles were a contributory factor to the socialist revolution. Let me restate that as crudely as possible: the American Negroes in fighting for their democratic rights were making an indispensable addition to the struggle for socialism in the US. I have to emphasize this because it was not only a clarification in the darkness of the Trotskyist movement on the Negro struggle in 1938–39. Today, 1967, I find in Britain here a confusion as great as I found in the US in 1938, and nowhere more than among the Marxists.

Finally he tells the Marxists, in effect the British left, both Black and white, that they should place their faith in Stokely Carmichael, quoting one of the less incendiary, more considered, parts of a recent speech as proof of Stokely's new-found political maturity:

> But we do not seek to create communities where, in place of white rulers, black rulers control the lives of black masses and where black money goes into a few black pockets: we want to see it go into the communal pocket. The society we seek to build among black people is not an oppressive capitalist society – for capitalism by its very nature cannot create structures free from exploitation. We are fighting for the redistribution of wealth and for the end of private property inside the United States.

CLR's was a speech that was little noticed at the time. Stokely's furious contribution got the headlines, and when Michael X tried a Stokely impersonation in Reading a week later he became the first man to be arrested under the new law against inciting racial hatred.*

* At his trial Michael attempted to have William Burroughs appear as his 'interpreter'. For much more on the remarkable, misunderstood life of Michael X, see my biography, *Michael X: A Life in Black and White*.

The dramatic rhetoric of Black rebellion overshadowed CLR's subtler message that racial progress inevitably required a socialist society – and vice versa.

In the following months CLR did do some work on *The Gathering Forces*, determined to get it finished in time to mark the fiftieth anniversary of the Russian Revolution, but continued to struggle. He wrote to Willie Gorman, asking him to come to London, and, in October, he arrived. Gorman worked with George Rawick on the manifesto while CLR took a back seat.

Eventually the document was complete and published, to minimal interest, in mimeographed form that November, a month after the anniversary. The full title was *The Gathering Forces: A Statement celebrating the October Revolution and its meaning for workers, peasants, and all those who are involved in the world struggle*. Facing Reality's cadre of intellectuals may have had plenty to say to the new generation, but for the moment there were precious few listening.

But even as CLR's new political work was going unnoticed, his status as an elder statesman of Black revolutionary politics was beginning to rise. The next year would see him making a whole series of foreign trips during which his life and work would be celebrated.

The first of these jaunts was an expedition to Cuba, to attend an international writers' conference called the Congreso Cultural de la Habana at the very beginning of January 1968. CLR's invitation had come out of the Roundhouse events of the previous summer. There had been a celebration of the Cuban Revolution, at which it had been announced that Cuba was planning a translation of *The Black Jacobins*.*

CLR flew out of London on Boxing Day, accompanied by two close friends, the Trinidadian poet and publisher John La Rose† and

* This never actually came to pass. CLR told Tariq Ali it was because the Cubans belatedly realised that there were anti-Russian regime remarks in the text.

† John La Rose was the Trinidad Oil Workers Union's UK representative. In 1966 he'd started the pioneering Black bookshop and publishing imprint New Beacon Books. They were planning to reissue *Minty Alley*.

the Jamaican novelist Andrew Salkey, as well as David Cooper, mastermind of the Dialectics of Liberation.

Andrew Salkey wrote up a diary of the trip as a book for Penguin.[8] Along the way it gives a nice portrait of CLR, frail and ageing but intellectually undimmed. There are some wonderfully telling details: on the long-winded series of flights needed to get from London to Havana in those days, he observes, 'CLR clutching a well-thumbed coffee-table *Michelangelo* which he very rarely leaves behind on long journeys'. Once in Havana he sees CLR 'looking swish and donnish in his three-piece herringbone tweed suit'. At a formal dinner he hears CLR demanding they serve his favourite dish – bacalao – and getting it.

The highlight of the trip was a lunch party held for CLR's sixty-seventh birthday on 4 January, immediately before the official start of the Congress. There were forty guests, among them the apostle of *négritude* Aimé Césaire and CLR's old friend Daniel Guérin (who must by now have finally given up on the prospect of CLR ever translating his book on the French Revolution). Robert Hill was there too, greatly impressing everyone with the quality of his insights. And John La Rose acted as master of ceremonies. Salkey was delighted by the event: 'Agreed with Robert and John that we'd never seen CLR so warmly and respectfully honoured. Short, witty, properly emotional tributes, CLR's reply, provocative, salty and in the tradition of the man of letters.'

CLR stayed in Cuba for several weeks, making speeches and at least one controversial intervention when he argued that intellectuals should be abolished as a force.* After three weeks of Cuban food he suffered a recurrence of the stomach ulcer, but the country's fabled medical system came to his aid and soon he was well enough to be taken on an extended scenic tour around the island, arriving back in London some while after his comrades.

No sooner was he back home, than he was off on his travels again, *Michelangelo* no doubt close at hand. This time his destination was

* This seemingly Maoist point of view was supposed to be followed up by a written piece, but it doesn't appear to have happened.

Ibadan in northern Nigeria. The university there had commissioned a new version of his *Toussaint Louverture* play, that Robeson had starred in three decades before. The director was an expat Trinidadian called Dexter Lyndersay. CLR had handed the initial rewriting job over to an old comrade, Priscilla Allen, now a playwright herself, with further assistance from Willie Gorman. He had then worked on their draft in London with assistance from Clem Maharaj, the son of his former political ally Stephen Maharaj.* The most obvious difference between the new play and the old was the introduction of significant female characters for the first time – most likely Allen's contribution.

CLR had been due to travel out to Ibadan for the play's premiere in December, but the Nigerian Civil War had caused a delay. Still, when he arrived in February, he was delighted to discover that the play had been enthusiastically received and he wrote to tell Marty that he would 'have a tremendous programme, official lectures and any amount of discussions'.[9] He ended up spending a satisfying month in Nigeria.

He arrived back in London shortly before the Tory MP Enoch Powell made a momentous anti-immigration tirade, now infamous as the 'Rivers of Blood' speech. Powell responded to the militancy of Black Power by prophesying a race war unless Britain reversed its immigration policies. The speech caused a huge and immediate outcry. Powell was roundly condemned in the liberal media and by the political establishment,† but there was widespread popular support for his views, not least from sections of the working-class trade union movement who came out in support, particularly the dockers.

CLR didn't have enough public profile to be asked for his six penn'orth, but in a letter to Marty Glaberman he made his views clear:

* There is a considerably more detailed account of this process in Rachel Douglas's valuable book, *Making The Black Jacobins: C. L. R. James and the Drama of History*.

† For instance Edward Heath immediately sacked Powell from the shadow cabinet, while *The Times*'s editorial, which carried real weight back then, unequivocally condemned it: 'This is the first time that a serious British politician has appealed to racial hatred in this direct way in our postwar history.'

> There is as you can understand a tremendous excitement here about the speech of Enoch Powell and, what in my opinion is a very unhealthy sign, a readiness to compare England and the race question to what took place in Germany on the Jewish question leading to the power of Hitler.[10]

He refers Glaberman to his chapter in *World Revolution* on the rise of Hitler, saying that:

> The whole chapter is worth studying so as to get rid of not only the hysteria but what I am certain is the malice of many people against the working class, particularly the dockers. What they are saying is, those workers whom you think about as being socialist – look at the kind of people whom they are. I have seen too much of that not to recognise it.

It's a very clear statement both of CLR's view that important though racial politics are, it is still ultimately class that is at the root of revolutionary politics, and also that there's a danger of overreacting to immediate provocations; that you can end up playing into the hands of the provocateurs.

Meanwhile, CLR was participating in an offshoot of the Dialectics of Liberation. David Cooper helped to set up an 'anti-university' in the East End. CLR was one of the lecturers. It was a heady moment and the atmosphere of incipient revolution became tangible a month or so later when Paris erupted in the student revolt of May 1968. CLR wrote to his American comrades to inform them that 'I am at present doing a course on what is essentially Leninism* at the Anti-University. I am convinced that we are in a revolutionary situation (although, as Lenin always insisted, that does not necessarily produce the revolution).'[11]

CLR wanted to go to France himself, but didn't manage to get there until late July. This was at least in part due to the latest crisis in the life of Nobbie.

* The subject may have been billed as 'Workers' Power'.

Over the past few years, since his abortive move to London, Nobbie, now known as Bob, had finally found a serious interest: playing music. At his new high school he had distinguished himself as a musician, majoring on the flute. Outside school he began playing in bands around Greenwich Village. He was also maturing into an extremely attractive young man and, on leaving school, his regularly changing addresses always saw him living with one young woman or another.

He turned eighteen in April 1967, and soon afterwards found a mission in life, in the shape of the Scientology movement. Scientology specialised in reeling in impressionable, somewhat lost young men like Bob James, with a mix of psychology, pseudoscience and self-improvement.

Before long he was writing to his father to ask for $2000 to pay for training – this kind of enlightenment never comes cheap. CLR naturally didn't have the money, but he and Constance began to keep an anxious correspondence as Bob's involvement deepened. By April 1968 Constance was writing to say that Bob was working a hundred hours a week at the Scientology offices but still had no money for food and rent. So wrapped up in it all was he, that when she told him about the assassination of Martin Luther King, an event that had sent much of the USA into a frenzy of outraged rioting, he knew nothing about it.

Come June, it was decided that Bob and his girlfriend Helen would travel to England, where the Scientology world headquarters and the home of its founding guru, L. Ron Hubbard, had been located in the unlikely surrounds of West Sussex.

On hearing this news CLR wrote to Hubbard himself. It's an odd letter, essentially making it clear that he doesn't approve of Scientology and, if Bob was to come over to the UK and run out of money, then CLR was not going to be held responsible. Perhaps indicative of his own state of mind, his primary concern seems less with his son's well-being than the possibility of financial demands. Hubbard wrote back personally, signing the letter Ron and at least partially alleviating CLR's worries – 'Do find out for yourself who and what we are. You will be surprised and pleased to discover that we do care.'[12]

The letter gives Hubbard's address as Saint Hill Manor, East Grinstead, but in fact the sci-fi author turned cult leader was actually on the high seas at the time. The Scientology movement had recently bought three sea-going boats, the largest of which was a former passenger ferry called the *Royal Scotsman*, a huge vessel. This was now renamed the *Apollo* and was sailing around the Mediterranean with a large crew of Scientologists on board. It was now officially the flagship of the Sea Org, or Sea Organization, a key element in Scientology's increasingly militaristic structure. And it was to join the Sea Org in Spain that Bob James was heading when he called in at Staverton Road.

CLR reported back to Constance on what was evidently a flying visit. He told her that he'd informed Bob that he thought Scientology was a racket, but it was his decision, before adding some more positive fatherly words:

> By the way, he has impressed everybody by his unusual good looks and impressive appearance. He is undoubtedly a remarkable person to look at and he seems to have very good control of himself in relation to people. As far as I could see, he firmly believed in his Scientology but he was not burning up to convince other people or to hold forth upon it, a characteristic that I admired very much.[13]

It was loosely arranged that once Bob and Helen were settled, CLR would come to visit them in Spain. However, there was no word for some weeks and by then Bob was on board the *Apollo*. The only contact allowed was via letters forwarded on from East Grinstead, a situation that alarmed both CLR and Constance. Was their son effectively a prisoner?

Concern for Bob was one factor delaying CLR's departure for Paris. Another less important reason may have been that he was greatly taken up with following the summer's cricket, as a series of letters to Major Rowland Bowen, editor of *Cricket Quarterly*, attest.* Each

* In one of these letters (2 May 1968) he restates his view that seeing Enoch Powell as a potential Hitler is 'a grievous mistake'.

Sunday he would go to Lord's to see the International Cavaliers play. On one occasion he watched Sobers make 70 'with some of the finest strokes it's possible to see'. Come late June, he was riveted by the Ashes: 'The cricket is remarkable. I have been watching every minute on television and listening to it on the radio at the same time.' He was unimpressed by the Australians, with the exception of the young Doug Walters, and was frankly contemptuous of the spinner Gleason: 'two batsmen could finish up with him in 20 minutes'.[14]

When he did finally make it to France, on 26 July, it was only for the weekend. Nevertheless, it had a powerful effect. He managed to travel to both Paris and Marseille. In Marseille he saw Daniel Guérin and in Paris his key contact was with Andre Gorz, who he had met in Cuba. Gorz was a radical theorist and journalist. He had been close to Sartre at one time, and together they had formulated existentialist Marxism, before taking up political lines closer to anarchism with a focus on workers' self-management. Both CLR and Gorz found their world-views confirmed by the spontaneous and from below nature of the 'French Revolution' as CLR called *les evenements*. For Gorz May '68 was a watershed, leading on to radical critiques of work and education, and an early adoption of the politics of ecology. For CLR, meanwhile, it was nothing less than a cataclysm. Immediately on returning to London he wrote to Marty to tell him that

> the strike and the events that led up to it and that have followed it are the greatest revolutionary upheaval Europe has ever known, and way beyond anything even France has experienced.[15]

No sooner had CLR made his French sortie than he was off to Africa again, where he would spend several weeks in Uganda, Kenya and Tanzania, lecturing and fact-finding, visiting farming communes and so forth. Among the intellectuals he met was a young Kenyan writer called Ngũgĩ wa Thiong'o, who was soon to emerge as one of the pre-eminent African novelists of the late twentieth century. He was particularly struck by Tanzania and its new leader Julius Nyerere.

Nyerere had recently issued a manifesto called the Arusha Declaration and CLR was positively smitten by it, seeing further evidence that his political hopes were at last being borne out in practice. He was very taken by Nyerere's vision of a socialist society rooted in cooperative farms called ujamaa. He compared the challenges Nyerere faced in remaking his society with those Lenin faced after the Russian Revolution. And he had hopes that this time the outcome would be better. Writing up his thoughts on Nyerere and the Arusha Declaration he ended with this ringing paragraph:*

> It is sufficient to say that socialist thought has seen nothing like this since the death of Lenin in 1924, and its depth, range and the repercussions which flow from it, go far beyond the Africa which gave it birth. It can fertilise and reawaken the mortuary that is socialist theory and practice in the advanced countries. 'Marxism is a humanism' is the exact reverse of the truth. The African builders of a humanist society show that today all humanism finds itself in close harmony with the original conceptions and names of Marxism.[16]

The great revolutionary moments seem to be coming thick and fast, yet there was the old and tiresome problem of making a living. Back in London life continued in its pattern, with no end of requests for him to talk but still no dependable income. 'Alas,' he wrote to George Rawick, 'I have reached the stage where teaching and other matters are the only things I can genuinely depend on.'[17]

He talked to West Indian organisations in Manchester and London. He was in discussions with Sussex University about some sort of guest lectureship, which offered the prospect of at least a measure of financial stability, but nothing seems to have come of it. A boost to his spirits, however, came when, after a lecture to the Third World Society at York University, he met a young American student called Terisa

* On a more downbeat note, on returning to London he sent a copy to Andre Gorz, calling it 'a most important document from Tanzania and one which involves the whole future of that depressing continent'.

Turner, who would soon become his latest occasional secretary when she moved down to London:

> I was living at the home of Erich Fried, a German* revolutionary and the translator of Shakespeare into German, and I would work regularly with CLR James. I was going to the British Library and reading everything that was about petroleum, which was not that much. And I would discuss it with CLR James, discuss the oil workers of Trinidad. And we would have fun. He early on put me in charge of his social life. I could call up Ronnie Scott's and make reservations so we could go and listen to the best jazz. Any poetry readings, any play, anything progressive or interesting, he was interested to hear it. Even though he was fifty years my senior, he was very keen to go and hang out and find out what young people were thinking and doing. He was always very much attuned to what teenagers thought and wanted, and could do. He would hold court – people would visit him, people from all over the world, journalists, right left and centre, mostly left![18]

October saw CLR returning to Montreal for another big conference. He was to give two speeches on different aspects of the slave trade. On learning this, he contacted George Rawick, who was still working on his own book based on his researches in the archives of oral narratives from former slaves. It's clear that, on this subject, CLR believed that the pupil had outrun the master:

> Now, my dear George, I cannot imagine my speaking on those subjects without some substantial assistance from you. What can you send me . . . which can help me to speak on those subjects with the necessary authority. Please note that I shall take the occasion both in what I say and in my references, to refer to the work you have done on slavery and the work that you are doing, and the fact that that work is going to be the next great advance on the question of

* Actually Austrian.

the background of the Negro movement in the world today. It is an opportunity for all of us . . .[19]

The conference was a great success. Among the attendees was another young Trinidadian who CLR had recently met in London. This was Radford Howe, a second cousin of CLR's, and he would play a significant role in CLR's life in later years, with the adopted name of Darcus. Another new contact was Jimmy Garrett, and he was to have a more immediate effect. Garrett had connections at Federal City College in Washington DC, which was launching a Black studies programme, and he was sure CLR would be the perfect man to teach there.

It took a little over two months, but on 8 January1969, just four days after his sixty-eighth birthday, CLR was finally offered his first academic job. He was to join Federal as a visiting professor on a salary of $20,000 a year (approximately $140,000 in today's money), starting in the spring. Remarkably enough, though, by the time the letter arrived, CLR had also accepted an offer from Northwestern University in Chicago to teach the fall semester. He asked Federal City to allow him to take a term out to honour the arrangement with Northwestern. They agreed and the course was set.

CLR was on the move once again. Back to the USA.

PART SIX

Washington DC

Chapter Twenty-Four

CLR flew out to Washington on 26 March 1969, to take up his teaching role at Federal City College. No doubt he was already aware that this was no ordinary academic institution.

Federal City was in its first year of operation. It had been set up as a result of the 1966 Public Education Act: 'To serve the needs of the community by directing the resources and knowledge gained through education toward the solution to urban problems.' Its roots in DC went back as far as 1851, before the Civil War, and a pioneering educational establishment for African Americans called the Normal School for Colored Girls.

Federal City had come a long way from that. Here was an educational establishment explicitly set up to help poor Black people to get a college education. There were 2400 places available when it opened its doors in 1968. Six thousand prospective students applied, so the places were given out by lottery. Ninety-six per cent of the original intake were Black and its biggest department was the one that specialised in the newly minted area of Black studies. This was where CLR would be teaching.

There were two men responsible for his hiring, and between them they give an idea of just what kind of a place Federal City was. The man who had made the initial connection with CLR was Jimmy Garrett, a twenty-six-year-old who had been right at the heart of the civil rights struggle. A member of the Student Nonviolent Coordinating Committee, he had gone on to be a student leader in San Francisco and was an out and out militant.* Garrett had been found with a gun when the police came to arrest him and had subsequently been banned

* 'We threw a racist professor out of a second story window,' he told interviewer Ibram Rogers. (*Journal of Pan African Studies*, vol. 2, issue 10.)

from the city. His militant rhetoric had continued to make him notorious, though, not least when, in the course of a speech to students at the University of Oregon, he was alleged to have instructed them on how to make firebombs and hand grenades.

It's a measure of the times that this CV allowed Garrett to become head of the Black studies programme at Federal. But while he was the man who recommended CLR, William Couch, the chairman of the Humanities Department, was the one who actually hired him. Couch was another remarkable figure. In his mid-fifties by this time, he had been a notable jazz musician before the Second World War, playing with the likes of Nat King Cole and Cab Calloway, before enlisting and becoming a war hero at Iwo Jima. After the war he had gone to college, emerged with a PhD, and become a pioneering Black educationalist.

Just a few weeks before CLR arrived, Federal City had become the subject of a story in the *Washington Post*. The piece explained that Federal City courses would 'include not only black history and black English but also black physical education and black mathematics. The proposed curriculum would devote the first two years to the "decolonization of the mind", described as the systematic eradication of "white values" held by entering students'.[1]

While this was precisely Jimmy Garrett's vision, other staff members were less happy. David Dickson, the college provost, and a Black man himself, was quoted as saying that 'a well-disciplined and intense cadre of white radicals and black separatists [who] neglect academic principles for revolutionary ends' were taking control of the college.

Concerns were raised that the college was recruiting lecturers without the usual academic qualifications. William Couch, however, was having none of it: 'Isn't it conceivable that activists would have something to offer that PhDs do not?' he enquired. The white faculty chair Joseph Brent added that their student intake might respond better to activist tutors: 'Street education has produced a very sophisticated individual even if he can't write well or add.'

It's doubtful that anyone was thinking of someone like CLR when they talked of activist lecturers, but in fact it was only these new politics that enabled him to take on such a post. In the past any approaches he made for teaching work at universities were liable to founder on the surprising fact that not only did he not have a PhD, he didn't even have a degree.

On the other hand, if anyone expected CLR to teach his new students a diet of Malcolm X and the Black Panthers and little else, they were most definitely mistaken. When he submitted his reading list, there was no Malcolm or even James Baldwin. Instead his students were presented with CLR's now established library of the greats: Aeschylus, *King Lear*, Marx, Melville and Du Bois, plus two books on Frederick Douglass, half a dozen more books on Marxism, and no less than eleven on Abraham Lincoln.

He sent a copy of this reading list to John Bracey, the Black professor who had invited him to teach at Northwestern later in the year. Bracey was delighted:

> I am very much pleased at the breadth of the subject matter you are presenting. It should compel some serious study on the part of our people, many of whom tend to view 'black studies' etc as a chance to escape hard work and the mastering of a scientific approach to the study of history and culture.[2]

In fact, CLR did add Malcom X's autobiography to the Northwestern reading list, compromising a little with the expectations of his students. Challenging or not, CLR was an immediate success on the lecture circuit. Frail though he might have looked offstage, he still had the old charisma and ability to talk without notes. One of those who saw him speak around this time was Paul Buhle, a young leftist academic who was one of the prime movers behind a new magazine called *Radical America*, which had reprinted some of CLR's work. He recalls the contradictory experience of meeting CLR in that era, at the turn of the new decade:

> I heard he had been notoriously charming in his younger years, handsome, athletic. At seventy he looked badly aged. Gaunt and

> tired, he seemed so fragile that I instinctively clasped his arm when we crossed traffic. Palsy in his hands, the result of nerve degeneration, made writing and eating difficult. Yet he had an unmistakeable composure. Sitting across from him at a breakfast of toast, marmalade and tea I felt transported into a Masterpiece Theatre drama. Images deceived me. Once he had begun lecturing, he drew physical powers from somewhere inside himself. He sounded like a revolutionary orator of the old school, mastering his audience through detail and intonation.[3]

Word of his presence in the US soon got around. He'd been at Federal for less than a month when John A. Williams, one of the key Black American novelists to emerge in the sixties, contacted him. Williams was co-editor of a new venture called *Amistad*. This was to be a regular paperback anthology of essays on Black studies, heavily backed by Random House – one more sign of the liberal establishment's sudden enthusiasm for responding to the civil rights upheavals. Williams asked CLR for a twenty-thousand-word piece on 'the economic significance of slavery with regard to the economic development of Europe and the United States'.

CLR accepted the commission and 'The Atlantic Slave Trade' duly appeared in the first edition of *Amistad*. How much of it was written by CLR himself, however, is unclear. The published piece, according to Martin Glaberman, was largely written by Willie Gorman, and certainly the prose doesn't have CLR's particular cadence, while George Rawick commented that if you compared it to some of his own works written around that time, it looked like 'somebody was copying off somebody' before making the crucial point that whoever the actual writer was they were all drawing on ideas 'that it would have been impossible to have without James'.[4] And of course, CLR's cooperative work on the economic importance of the slave trade goes all the way back to the early forties and his mentoring of Eric Williams as he wrote *Capitalism and Slavery*.

Much of CLR's written output around this time was either shorter pieces – book reviews and so forth – or transcribed lectures, generally based on earlier work. One significant exception – and perhaps a guide to where his current interests really lay – was a venture into art criticism intended as a TV lecture. Its title and subject was 'The Olympia Statues, Picasso's *Guernica* and the Frescos of Michelangelo in the Capella Paolina' and it gave him a chance to expand on the three artworks that meant most to him. His analysis of two frescoes by his beloved Michelangelo is particularly telling. As with his work on *King Lear*, it's hard not to see traces of autobiography as CLR identifies a collection of easily overlooked figures in the top right-hand corner of the Sistine fresco depicting the crucifixion of St Paul: 'The man is talking to the woman explaining what is going on. She is listening eagerly to him. Behind them both is an old man who, it is obvious, has been in battles all his life. And to the right of the central figure, eager to get into the fray, the youth of about sixteen or seventeen.'[5]

Is CLR seeing himself in the talking man, the old man or the young rebel – or in all of them? Are these the three ages of the radical life? Or does he still actually identify above all with the man in the centre of the fresco, the ostensible St Peter, who is in fact Michelangelo himself?

CLR's fascination with the central works of European civilisation came as something of a surprise to the enthusiastic proponents of Black studies among whom he now mixed. When he arrived at Northwestern, John Bracey was initially taken aback:

> I can recall a discussion where several comrades and I were railing against Europe and its evils. CLR intervened with 'But my dear Bracey, I am a Black European, that is my training and my outlook'. CLR said this without apology, and without seeking our acceptance. He was merely (merely?) saying that to blindly reject all things originating in or influenced by Europe would mean not only rejecting people like himself, but rejecting a significant part of our own cultural and intellectual baggage.[6]

This complex mixture of Black radicalism combined with an awareness of the European tradition might, on paper, have been a hard sell, but in practice students were fascinated. Over the next couple of years CLR talked constantly at different colleges, including the prestigious likes of Howard, Rutgers and Harvard, as well as at specifically Black initiatives. Just a roll call of some of those names immediately conjures the spirit of the times: the Institute of the Black World in Atlanta, the National Congress of African People Conference (San Diego), the National Association of Black Students, the Black Liberation Front, the Association for the Study of Negro Life and History.

One of his closest relationships was with the Institute of the Black World, thanks to Robert Hill's presence there, along with Vincent Harding, who recalls CLR's impact on students when they arranged for him to speak at a small-town Black college in Mississippi:

> When CLR spoke at Tougaloo College in 1972 it was the only time I've ever seen a speaker here, at whose speech attendance was not required, first of all pack the hall, and secondly, by the time he'd been speaking about five minutes, everyone in the room was taking notes. They knew this was something they didn't want to get away from them.[7]

CLR and Robert Hill became close associates during this time. Hill remembers CLR's time in Washington well:

> Washington DC was a hotbed of black radicalism. One of the organisations very prominent at the time was Drum and Spear Book Shop, and the couple that were spearheading Drum and Spear Press, James lived in a room in their apartment. When I met him in 1970 in Washington DC, that's where he was living . . . James was very loyal to Federal City College. He never wanted to accept an appointment of a permanent kind from anybody else. He felt he owed it to Federal City, which had gone out on a limb to bring him to America and he was very loyal to them. It suited him to a T.[8]

Indeed, CLR only taught the one, autumn 1969, term at Northwestern. From the beginning of 1970 onwards, he was on an annual contract at Federal. Drum and Spear housed him for a while and released a new edition of his 1938 booklet, *A History of Negro Revolt*, now retitled as *A History of Pan-African Revolt*. Before long, though, he found himself an apartment that he would remain in throughout the rest of his time in DC. This was in a massive, formerly grand apartment building called the Chastleton on 16th and R.

Over these years, CLR settled into something unusually like a routine, teaching in autumn and spring and spending the summers on lecture tours or visiting London. This was something he was obliged to do in order to renew his visa. His marriage to Selma, however, was becoming ever more ephemeral.

In the spring of 1970, just as CLR was settling into this new life as a doyen of Black radicalism, his old life as leader of a Marxist group finally ground to a halt. He had had his own radical grouping ever since the thirties, but no longer. In March, Marty Glaberman, the most loyal of lieutenants, moved that Facing Reality should formally disband and cease publishing their occasional newspaper *Speak Out*.

There are any number of reasons for the initiative. Facing Reality had simply gone on beyond its time. The final straw, though, as Marty explained to CLR in a letter, was that Willie Gorman was becoming impossible to deal with and alienating the few remaining members:

> One of the reasons that I am proposing dissolution of the organisation is to avoid the inevitable confrontation in which you (or anyone) will have to choose between William and the organisation ... It is a literal fact that half the membership will not allow William in their homes except as a political obligation or out of deference to you ... He cannot function in an organisation.[9]

Writing to Selma, Marty made the point clearly that the problem was not Facing Reality's ideas but its actual organisation:

> Nello's point that people will degenerate outside of an organisation is neither more nor less true than that people will degenerate

> inside of an organisation. It depends on the organisation. One of the unfortunate contradictions that has plagued us for the last few years is that our organisational problems keep mounting at the same time that our ideas continue to attract people . . . There is no reason why a new start cannot be made in the relatively near future. But the only way that a new start can be made is by cutting ourselves free of the accumulated factionalism, clique ism, routines, et cetera of the past . . . If the discussion begins with the assumption that Facing Reality is a viable organisation, it can only lead to false conclusions – in the same way as if you examine capitalism with the assumption that it is a viable society, you can only reach conclusions which confirm your assumption, but have no relation to the facts.[10]

CLR did not agree. He was still reluctant to let go of the role he had played for so long. But a vote was held and the dissolution upheld. On 27 April Marty made a formal announcement that Facing Reality was no more, ending on a rueful yet upbeat note:

> We are recording a failure, but a failure that we are certain will be but one small pause in the development of a revolutionary theory adequate to these revolutionary times.[11]

Of course the end of Facing Reality, that tiny clique, made little difference to the dissemination of CLR's ideas. Just a month later Paul Buhle's *Radical America* devoted a whole 120-page issue to extracts from CLR's work, chosen for their relevance to the new generation. And the introduction was written by none other than Martin Glaberman. As far as CLR went, it meant he no longer had to concern himself with wrangling over the group's internal problems. Instead he could float above: *éminence grise*, grand old man.

Marty was right in another prediction – that the dissolution of Facing Reality would allow CLR to continue working with Willie Gorman. Willie operated a minimal bookstore in Detroit selling the old Facing Reality material. A local Black activist, Modibo Kadalie, came by one day to shoplift some literature for the revolution, but ended up getting into conversation with him:

> Willie was a dedicated activist. His loyalty to CLR was clear. He was always talking about CLR and what CLR meant to the movement, and he was always wanting us to know ... I would engage, saying, 'You can come by the house all the time.' My wife Michelle [just] thought he was kind of a scruffy white guy.[12]

CLR was next in Detroit the following Christmas, for the release of the last and most unlikely of Facing Reality artefacts: a vinyl album with recordings of his speeches on Melville and Shakespeare. Willie took him to see Kadalie. They clearly made a strange pair, this dishevelled white guy in his forties and the frail old Black man about to turn seventy, both of them smoking like chimneys. Certainly Michelle thought so, as he remembers:

> She knew who Willie was, because Willie had come over there before. So when Willie brings CLR, then he's just bringing a black guy tagging along ... She basically saw CLR and thought Willie was his mentor ... I don't know where she got that from, but I think she just reacted to the fact the guys were smoking all the time. She didn't want the smoke in the house. It was something ...

It's an image of some poignancy: the very end of the Johnson-Forest group, the club-footed son and grandson of Talmudic preachers and the old man who'd once debated the original Old Man, smoking and walking the bitter cold streets of Detroit in December. It's hard not to see them as a kind of revolutionary Don Quixote and Sancho Panza.

A few months earlier, in the summer of 1970, CLR had set off on another US lecture tour. For at least part of the time he was accompanied by a 'a friend', as he wrote to Constance, who he was planning to see when he reached Los Angeles, before adding a handwritten postscript – 'Martina is my "friend". You remember her? We went to see her. She had just married. But even before that we had meant something to each other . . .'[13]

So Martina Thomson was back in his life. It's suggested in a biography of her husband, David, that their relationship had carried on, at least intermittently, during the sixties. But now that CLR's marriage was effectively over they were able to go more or less public. Martina was always less worried about her own marriage, given that she had tolerated her husband's affairs.

Most likely CLR saw her again when he returned to London that summer. Black militancy was starting to gain a foothold in the city. Over in Islington the inveterate hustler Michael X, now calling himself Michael Abdul Malik, had started up an ambitious (though largely unfulfilled) arts and community centre called the Black House. On All Saints Road, in Ladbroke Grove, Frank Crichlow's new restaurant, the Mangrove, had become a more organic meeting place for Black radicals and counterculture types. Both places suffered continuous harassment from the police. CLR was a regular visitor to the Mangrove – 'he used to take over one side of the restaurant, because everybody wants to hear', Crichlow later remembered[14] – and Darcus Howe had started working there on his return from Trinidad.

The Mangrove was raided twelve times in eighteen months. The local community, amongst them the nascent British Black Panthers, had had enough. On 9 August the Panthers led a protest march to the local police station. This was met by a massive show of force, and a small riot kicked off. The police arrested those they saw as the ringleaders, among them Darcus Howe, Frank Crichlow and several of the Panthers, including Altheia Jones-LeCointe and Barbara Beese. According to Frank Crichlow, it was CLR who immediately saw the gravity of the situation and called a meeting at the Metro Youth Club, just around the corner from the Mangrove, at which they planned their response.[15]

CLR had to return to Washington to teach but he was back in London in January 1971, in time for a seventieth-birthday celebration in Ladbroke Grove. His timing was propitious. John La Rose's New Beacon Books were finally ready to publish their long-planned new edition of *Minty Alley*. And meanwhile the Mangrove affair had come to a climax with the Mangrove Nine Trial, which had started in December.* At the birthday event he gave a long, powerful speech summing up his seventy years of activism and culminating in an exhortation to his audience:

> Your future is the future of Great Britain; the future of Great Britain is your future. If you make it, then it means that Britain will be making it. And if you don't make it then the Britain that there is will not be making it, and there will have to be a new Britain, not only for you, but for all the oppressed and poor everywhere.[16]

Part of the speech deals with his recent experience of teaching in the US and shows a new appreciation of Black women as playing a leading role in progressive politics. Previously they had, as a specific group, rarely received much mention in his work. But now he was meeting the likes of Jones Le-Cointe and Beese in London, and any number of young activists in DC, young women who were no longer happy to accept the macho politics of the early Black Power years:

> I am always struck by the black women in the United States. I have known many revolutionary movements and I have known women in them, and those black girls in the movement in the United States may not be strong on Marxist theory, but they are ready to take action, and do all sorts of things. They are astonishing people.

Angela Davis had led the way and now the new world of Black studies courses and Black bookshops was one in which women were making their presence felt. One of these was Cynthia Hamilton. She heard CLR speak at Stanford, where she was an undergraduate. Encouraged by Robert Hill, she deferred going to graduate school in

* The trial – which ended in a sensational acquittal – is the subject of Steve McQueen's film drama *Mangrove*, released just as I finished writing this book.

order to study with CLR, and act as the latest in his long line of secretaries, at his Chastleton apartment, as Robert Hill remembers:

> [Cynthia] helped to maintain some kind of semblance of order, because he would be invited to speak at different campuses, different political events, and between his teaching and speaking and I guess just paying his bills, he couldn't function on his own. He had to have help. And sometimes there would be students who would pitch in. There'd always be someone to take him physically to his classes at Federal City College and then bring him back.[17]

While CLR was continually surrounded now by young people eager to hear him talk, there was still one young Black American he found impossible to reach: his son Nobbie, now Bobby.

Bobby had returned to New York from the Scientology ship in late 1968. He fell out with his supervisor and left Scientology behind, and threw himself back into music. He started playing as a duo with a Canadian singer-songwriter called Tony Kosinec, who had just made an album on Columbia Records. They played together at the Village Gate and in July the pair supported Linda Ronstadt at the Bitter End club. *Cashbox* magazine sent a reviewer along and a positive write-up noted in passing that Tony Kosinec was 'aided on stage by Bobby James who plays brilliant flute, subtle guitar, and pulsating conga'. Fifty years later Tony Kosinec remembers that 'Bobby contributed a beautiful lyric line to one of my songs.' What he also recalled was that 'Bob told me he had "escaped" from the Scientology Sea Org and he was pretty vigilant, looking out for anyone from there'.[18]

Typically, though, Bobby didn't stick with Tony Kosinec, but carried on drifting about, avoiding responsibility wherever possible. His mother and stepfather, Constance and Ed, moved out to Los Angeles later in 1970 and, a few months later, Bobby followed.

On the West Coast he formed a new group, called Odyssey. They were a racially mixed bunch of hippies making a very Californian mix of folk and jazz-inflected funk. Bobby wrote most of the songs, including an infectious mellow groove called 'Our Lives are Shaped by What

We Love' – this was a very different vision of the post-civil rights era from the one CLR's disciples were caught up in: sunnily optimistic, not militantly revolutionary.

It looked for a moment as if Odyssey would be big. They were signed to Motown's MoWest label, who paid for a house for them to live and work in. They recorded an album together, but once again Bobby pulled back. While most of the songs on the album are written by him, his only physical contribution is to play the flute on a couple of tracks. However Peter McGovern, a young cousin of Ed Pearlstien's, came to visit Bobby and remembers it as a happy time:

> I took a trip to California and stayed with Bob and his girlfriend while they were recording the Odyssey album. We were at the recording sessions. We also took a break and the three of us drove to the Grand Canyon, walked down the Bright Angel Trail, camped out overnight at the bottom, and walked back out.[19]

Royce Jones was the young singer brought in to front the band. Later on he would work with Steely Dan and Ambrosia among many others. He remembers how the Odyssey album came to be:

> All the tunes were already rehearsed by Bobby and Kathleen Warren and they needed a singer so they called me. Bobby didn't talk very much, he was just into the music. He loved to play his guitar on the street. We all lived together in a house in Reseda, but Bobby was never there. He would come and rehearse and then go off. Bobby was a total hippie, he lived on the street, he and his girlfriend always hung together.
>
> We rehearsed for a year or two. Our manager was trying to get us a record deal and he went to Motown. We met Berry Gordy and he said, 'We'll give it a shot.' Motown moved us into a house in Pasadena and told us to rehearse. But Bobby didn't move in, once we signed with Motown he just disappeared, he didn't want to be a part of signing contracts and all that. When we went to the studio he did his little part and after that he just disappeared.[20]

In the event the album didn't make much headway and the band split up (though its key song, 'Our Lives Are Shaped', has become something of an underground classic over the years). The band's guitarist Donnie Dacus went on to play in the enormously successful Chicago for a while. Bobby James just drifted on.

That was until August 1972, when the US draft board caught up with him, living in some sort of commune in far northern California amid the redwood trees. Just like his father twenty years earlier, Bobby was arrested by the federal government. He was charged with draft dodging and threatened with prison. The case came to court in New York in March 1973. It transpired that Bobby had been served with draft papers just before he left for England to join the Scientologist navy. He had written a screed explaining why, as a Scientologist, he was opposed to the war and left it at that, assuming that the draft board would just accept his reasoning.

This was a disastrous mistake. And one that would have devastating consequences for an already fragile young man. Ed Pearlstien wrote to the judge, pleading for sensitivity:

> When he was arrested in August 1972 his mother and I went to Eureka to arrange his release, and found him in a state of hysteria after three days in jail. He spoke gibberish, making no sense at all. The experience of the last five or six months has wreaked havoc on him psychologically. Robert is clearly in need of psychological help. A jail sentence would, I am certain, destroy him, and institutionalisation might very well also, since confinement of any sort has always had extremely untoward effects on him. (Even as a child, he could not bear to have the bedclothes tucked in.) One alternative would be for the court to order him to have outpatient psychiatric care, perhaps as a condition of probation. Robert's offence is not one of commission but a failure to comply with the law. To punish him for this will have consequences far beyond the penalty imposed. I therefore ask your indulgence and help in preventing his destruction.[21]

The plea fell on deaf ears. The trial went ahead, with CLR attending at least some of the time, but there was no mercy. Bobby James was sentenced to prison and ended up serving nine months, at least some of it in Petersburg, Virginia. He was meant to be attending a federal mental hospital, but whether he actually did so is unclear.

What is clear is that, as Ed Pearlstien had predicted, he was now damaged beyond repair. According to his cousin Heno, 'That was the beginning of his decline. And he had the gene for schizophrenia – Constance's father had schizophrenia.'[22]

CLR made one determined effort to help. He had given a lecture as part of a series of events promoted by the radical jazz musicians Archie Shepp and Max Roach. He discovered that they were running a music school in Amherst, Massachusetts. CLR thought they might be able to straighten Bobby out. He got Bobby a place at the school and sent him an air ticket, but it didn't work out and before long Bobby was living on the streets, a casualty of the Vietnam war without ever having set foot in Asia.

Meanwhile the young radicals centred around the Drum and Spear bookstore – who were inspired by CLR's talks on the history of the Pan-Africanist movement, and the five Pan-African Congresses that had been significant markers along the way – decided that it was time for a sixth Congress. This would be one that would pull together all the new radical voices of the African diaspora. CLR was happy to give his blessing to the project.

The first task was to write a manifesto, a call to arms, that could be sent out to all the major African and Caribbean leaders. CLR's name would be crucial in getting those leaders to pay attention, but in terms of the actual organisation he was happy to let his young comrades take the lead. In particular, he persuaded a twenty-year-old student called Geri Stark (later Geri Augusto) to write the manifesto. 'CLR and I were friends,' she recalled, 'as much friends as a mentor, as an older person and a younger person, and I would spend almost every Sunday at his apartment in the Chastleton, and he would give me things to read.'[23]

Entitled 'The Call', the manifesto started with an uncompromising declaration, 'The 20th century is the century of Black Power,' and ends with the targets for the proposed Congress to tackle: self-reliance, freedom for South Africa and 'the third point, may be the most important and the most immediate: complete control over economic and financial life'. Geri Stark recalled CLR's reaction when she showed him the first draft:

> The one quarrel he had when I finished the draft and had to show it to him, he said there was, to put not too fine a tune on it, a lot of Black, not enough attention on class consciousness.[24]

To the delighted surprise of the Washington group, the proposals was greeted with open arms and plans went ahead for the conference, to be held in Tanzania – still CLR's model of African socialism in action. Three of the Washington activists, Kathy Flewellen, Geri Stark and Courtland Cox, actually went out to Dar es Salaam to set things up.

The Congress took place in June 1974 and was broadly successful, but CLR left before the start of proceedings, in protest against the refusal to allow representatives of Caribbean opposition groups, people like Walter Rodney, to attend. It was, in many ways, his farewell to frontline politics. At seventy-three years old he would, from now on, reserve his remaining energy for the lecture theatre. Much of the rest of the time would be spent in his room, as one of the young Black students who flocked to his lectures, the poet E. Ethelbert Miller, remembers: 'I never saw CLR in a classroom, I either saw him in bed or speaking.'[25] But on stage he was transformed, a glamorous, charismatic figure: 'When we looked at CLR, we were all struck by his presence, his height and always a woman on his arm. It was the same as if you'd see Miles Davis in person, CLR had that.'

Chapter Twenty-Five

By the autumn of 1975 CLR was firmly entrenched at Federal City College and his status as a doyen of the US Black study circuit was well established. However, the revolutionary fervour of the late sixties was starting to fade and the wider world had defaulted to its long-established assumption that Black lives could be safely ignored. If CLR wasn't entirely forgotten, it must have seemed very much like it.

So a call from a BBC producer called Mike Dibb, late in the year, was especially welcome. CLR had first heard from Dibb a year or two earlier. He had directed the enormously influential TV series *Ways of Seeing*, in which the Marxist art critic John Berger carefully unravelled the way we understand artworks. Dibb had the idea of following up with a series that explored the links between sport and art. When he mentioned it to Berger, he immediately thought of an old friend who he should contact:

> John said, 'Well, if you haven't met CLR James, you must contact him because he's written an extraordinary book about cricket.' Not that John was the slightest bit interested in cricket! He had an address and a contact number for CLR and then I realised that CLR was married to Selma James, who was already a regular figure in my life, because she was a brilliant transcriber. A lot of the interviews we did at the BBC we gave to Selma. She could be quite critical about the opinions expressed! So I went and met CLR at Staverton Road. It was wonderful because he was unlike anybody I've ever met before or since.[1]

The powers that be, however, weren't too keen on the sport and art idea so there was no further contact for a year or two till, late in 1975, the *Omnibus* producer Barrie Gavin, a fellow cricket fan, suggested that Dibb simplify his idea down to a documentary based on CLR James and *Beyond a Boundary*.

CLR was unsurprisingly enthusiastic about the idea. So, in January 1976, just around the time of CLR's seventy-fifth birthday, Dibb went to Trinidad for a recce. This immediately went badly wrong. Trinidad, at least, still believed CLR was a political force to be reckoned with:

> I was met by somebody at the airport when I went to do some research, saying CLR was *persona non grata*. So I had to sit by the swimming pool waiting to negotiate and in the end I had to come back to London and there were all sorts of exchanges with the BBC.[2]

This was followed by high-level communications between the BBC and the Trinidad government. CLR even agreed to write a letter promising not to have anything to do with politics while in Trinidad. Finally Eric Williams himself got involved and expressed his upset and outrage at the whole situation. He couldn't imagine who would have asked CLR to write such a letter. The director of Trinidad and Tobago TV was blamed for an inexplicable overreaction. The Doctor claimed to be entirely enthusiastic about the projected programme:

> Whatever assistance can be provided by us to the BBC will be provided. I wish you to know that the Government of Trinidad and Tobago is very happy indeed to know that a film on West Indian cricket is being made in connection with Mr James' *Beyond a Boundary* . . . I merely wish you to know that I have always considered Mr James' book his masterpiece; and many of my cabinet colleagues share this opinion.[3]

Filming finally took place in April. Mike Dibb and the crew arrived first and established a base at the art deco Queen's Park Hotel. Then CLR flew in from Washington:

> The first thing he said when he got there was 'Why have you booked me into the Queen's Park Hotel?' I said that it seemed to

belong to the world that you grew up in and it's overlooking the Savannah. He said, 'But I'd so much prefer to be at the Hilton!' He thought he was slumming it, while I thought I was entering into a historical space![4]

The trip went well. The film crew took CLR back to Tunapuna and the cricket pitch he had watched as a child – the house he watched from sadly no longer there. He talked to his old opening partner from Maple, Clifford Roach, and allowed himself to be gently teased. In between times he held court at the hotel, gave a speech to the pupils of QRC and, as promised, stayed well away from politics. 'It was wonderful really,' remembers Mike Dibb, 'because people did admire CLR: Stollmeyer, Clifford Roach and the other cricketers.' Among the visitors was CLR's brother Eric. Mike Dibb was struck by the contrast in the two men:

> I met his brother, so different from him but also very charming, very warm. It did make you think how different brothers can be – one so intellectual and the other, not ordinary exactly, but straightforward and decent without any of CLR's intellectual curiosity.

The film was completed in England in mid-May, just as the country was entering into a famously long hot summer. CLR was filmed at Lord's and Old Trafford, and also, most intriguingly, back in Nelson, where he sat in the stand with a couple of fellow old-timers, watching the cricket and reminiscing. One of them, Johnny Greenwood, asks CLR if his politics have mellowed over the years. CLR denies it: 'I have developed,' he tells them; as for his politics, they have 'matured'.[5]

All the Nelson chaps were very much struck by CLR's signature Stetson, which he wore throughout the filming. 'He looked terrific in it,' Mike recalled, 'he was aware of that. He liked clothes. He wasn't quite a dandy but he was aware of his physical presence. He had a very striking face and that pale cowboy hat suited him fine.'[6]

The hour-long programme went out at 10.20 p.m. on 8 July, the first day of the third Test between England and the West Indies. The timing was extraordinary: on the one hand there was CLR's elegant, erudite elaboration of the links between the Caribbean and the 'mother country' and between cricket and colonialism, not to mention between ancient Greece and Rugby School. On the cricket pitch, meanwhile, a West Indian team featuring three of the fastest, most aggressive bowlers the game had ever seen were hellbent on making the English cricket team grovel.

This was a response to the England cricket captain, a charmless South African called Tony Greig, who had made the unwise boast that his team would make the West Indies grovel when they came to England. It had been a dangerous thing to say. The West Indies won the five-match series by three games to nil. England had kept them at bay for the first two matches by picking a team full of grizzled veterans like Brian Close and David Steele, who they knew wouldn't flinch in front of the fast-bowling assault from Michael Holding, Andy Roberts and Wayne Daniel. In the third Test they were almost literally broken. The forty-five-year-old Brian Close batted for over an hour against the most ferocious bouncer-laden attack from Holding on an unreliable pitch with no helmet, chest pad or arm guard, and just a thin towel tucked over his thigh for protection.

When he came off the pitch the team's doctor suggested he go to hospital. Close, true to form, said a whisky would do fine. Next morning, though, England were bowled out in a trice and from then on, the West Indies were the only winners. A swaggering team led by its bowlers and its young batting hero Viv Richards made their colonialist rivals look like Dad's Army. Heroic, but left over from a vanishing world.

A question lingers in the air, though, after the documentary. Which side was CLR on? Was he wholly a part of this new West Indian wave, or was some part of him forever loyal to the old world?

It was a question echoed in the pages of *Race Today*. This was a radical newspaper edited by Darcus Howe as part of the Race Today Collective, the group that had evolved out of the Black Panthers. The paper was consciously influenced by Jamesian ideas, an echo of the long-lost *Correspondence*. The Metropolitan Police had started to make conscious efforts to recruit Black officers. Darcus had angrily rejected the scheme in the paper – for him, the police were simply the enemy. CLR disagreed and the next edition ran a letter from him arguing the case for changing the police from within.

Beyond a Boundary was watched by around 2 per cent of the British population – a million or so people. The reviews were largely very positive and several old friends got in touch via the BBC, including Arthur Ballard from the Marxist Group of the thirties, and Marjorie Froggatt, who had helped so much with the translation of Souvarine's *Stalin*.

Back in the USA, however, there was more trouble with Nobbie. March had seen him living briefly with his stepbrother Sam, but planning to go and live in a trailer in Sonoma with some friends. Constance and CLR had together made an offer to support him for a year if he would just use the time to get his life on track. By June, however, it was clear that this wasn't happening.

CLR's last letter to Nobbie was written some months earlier, just after his seventy-fifth birthday. This particular anniversary had prompted his old comrades Lyman, Freddy, Grace and Jimmy Boggs to write to him, congratulating him and burying the hatchet at the same time. CLR was obviously moved and wrote back to them all restating his belief that their years together were the most productive of his life.

Nobbie, by contrast, represented his greatest disappointment, failure even. This is what CLR wrote to him:

> How are you Nob? Remember my dear boy I was 75 on January 4. It is obvious I'm nearing the end of my long life. What is most important to me is that the living relic of the life I have lived is you. Books are one thing and lectures another, but there is nothing to compare with a young man like you, tall, handsome and most intelligent. That I should know from my personal experience of you and from what people have told me. I am anxious to know you are settled in some way (as I go through the next few years I'm doing my autobiography). I know I will leave behind a CLR Jr who will be a credit to himself,

friends, and his father. Settle down Nob, do tell me if I can help in any way, do settle down ... Call me collect any time you wish.[7]

He would never see his son again.

There was another seventy-fifth birthday party that November. This was Lyman Paine's and he used the occasion to get the Johnson-Forest Tendency – or at least many of them – back together for one last time. CLR attended and so did Ed Pearlstien. He provided a hilariously ill-tempered account of the proceedings in a letter to a friend:

I went to LA to attend a 75th birthday party for a friend. In fact, he gave the party for himself and paid the way for friends to come in from all over the country. He figures he's dying (and may very well be), and the party therefore was in the nature of an anticipatory wake. If the man had a sense of humour, the party would have been a glorious act of defiance to death. But he has none, so the idea was maudlin and self-indulgent. Most of the people at the party, and all who came in from out of town, were old comrades going back as long as 35 years. In 1961 there was a split in the group. Ostensibly it was based on politics, but the real reason was that the people who broke away, headed by the birthday boy – Lyman – and an insane woman named Grace Lee, were jealous of and resented the leader of the group, CLR James, Constance's former husband. Although Lyman hates Constance – principally because of her relationship with CLR and because he is a sublimated homosexual who cannot stand feminine women – he and I have been friends. I am also a friend of CLR's. But I am no friend of Grace Lee, who is one of the few people I know in the world whom I despise.[8]

Ed had already had eight martinis before he arrived, proceeded to pick fights and felt that CLR was being snubbed because he had been placed at the far end of the table from the birthday boy.

It's quite possible that CLR did indeed feel snubbed, as his own letter to Lyman, thanking him for the occasion, masks an acid putdown with courtly language. He begins by acknowledging their common history:

> First of all, it was a great pleasure to be spending some time with you and Freddy and the others, those who are very close to us and those who are our good friends. It was not only good to meet but there was an atmosphere which I'm positive represented a certain attitude to the problems which the world faces.[9]

Then he notes the passing of time: 'Naturally, it was quite painful to see that you're not your old, powerful self, the Lyman who single-handedly built our seaside resort at Long Island; at the same time it was marvellous to see Freddy does not look or move about as if she were a day older from the time she functioned at 629 Hudson'.

And finally, brutally, he tells Lyman that he has no right to consider himself as a thinker in his own right. He was a facilitator to CLR's genius and that was all:

> To be brief and to the point. You and Freddy at 629 Hudson were the solid rock and foundation on which the Johnson Forest was built and the ideas of which today remain an indestructible part of what will be tomorrow . . . You and Freddy were a foundation that one meets but rarely in a political life.. . . When I say 'rock and foundation' I mean those terms in the literal sense. On Saturday evening I got an impression that some of the younger ones might think of you as a great theoretician or advocate of the ideas which we developed and which still hold us together. That would be a mistake and a very serious mistake.

What seems to be in the forefront of CLR's mind here is the question of his legacy. Lyman, his contemporary, was preparing for death and claiming an implausible importance as a theoretician. So what did CLR himself have?

The answer was not a great deal, right then, but there were some promising shoots. In particular, there were plans in motion for a small

London publisher, Allison & Busby, to republish some of his work. They wanted to put out the first proper edition of *Notes on Dialectics* – aka the Nevada document – and were planning to compile some of his shorter essays into two or more volumes. First, however, they would publish his long-mooted book on the Ghanaian independence movement. *Nkrumah and the Ghana Revolution* appeared in 1977, and was essentially a repackaging of the work he'd done on Ghana back in 1958, plus some subsequent letters and articles indicating his frustrations with how Nkrumah's project had worked out in practice. The book was then bulked out by more recently written pieces on the future of Africa, restating his faith in Tanzania's Nyerere and the Arusha Declaration.

The publishing company was headed by Margaret Busby. Then, as now, she was unusual in being a Black woman in publishing, let alone one with her own company, that she had founded with Clive Allison in 1967, while she was still a student. Margaret's father George had been a friend of CLR's at QRC – they had been members of the Maverick Club together – so CLR was of course delighted to be published by her.*

Young women, in general, were continuing to change CLR's worldview. Feminism, as freely expressed in the lives of the students who came to his lectures, was making him reconsider his own life to date. One part of the autobiography he was working on dealt with his relations with women. It's a complex history. On one level he had always supported women and seen them as intellectual equals – take Grace, Raya and, perhaps most of all, Selma. But what he was now coming to realise was, that while respecting their intellects, he still treated them as servants, expecting them to cook his meals and clean his apartment.

Ironically, much of his thinking over this territory was conducted in the company of a series of bright young women who nevertheless often acted as his secretaries. Through the late sixties and seventies

* Chris Goodey was also significantly involved in working with CLR at Allison & Busby.

there had been several, Terisa Turner and Cynthia Hamilton among them. In 1978 the role was taken on by a graduate student called Sally Schwartz. Forty-odd years later she is the director of educational charity Globalize DC. She remembers how she met CLR and was promptly swept up into his world:

> So I was a graduate student at Howard University, I was doing a masters in Caribbean/Latin American history. I knew about CLR as I did a political science paper on his political thought, which led me to read everything I could lay my hands on, pamphlets and so forth. His works weren't as available as they are today. Maybe a week before I had to turn it in, somebody said to me, 'You know CLR is in Washington DC?' I had no idea! Of course, at that point I thought CLR was like a god. They said, 'Oh no, he is very accessible. You should call him.'
>
> So I did call and two days later I met him in the Political Science Department, the lobby area, we talked for an hour or so. At that point I'd read a lot of his work and he loved that. When I was leaving he said if I had any other questions 'feel free to call me', and he gave me his number. So I did, of course, calling back with additional questions. And he said, why don't we meet again at this hotel, the Statler Hilton at 16th and K? He said, 'They have a champagne brunch there, I go there regularly.'
>
> So I met him over there and we had a long talk, probably a couple of hours, over champagne. Because of his hand tremor, instead of a champagne glass he had a big glass with champagne at the bottom. It was at that meeting he talked about his interest in women, that this was a new thing he was really grappling with. He always talked about 'twenty-first-century women.' He felt we were on the cusp of reaching the new century. So we had a great talk and at the end, I was talking about my research, which was to investigate this community in Port of Spain, Belmont. I wanted to do a social history of Belmont.
>
> He said to me, 'Well have you ever been to Trinidad?' And I said no. He said, 'Why not, why haven't you been?' I said, 'I'm just a poor

graduate student, I can't afford it.' He said, 'How much will it cost, to go to Trinidad?' I said, '$500 maybe.' He pulled out his wallet and he just pulled out five $100 bills, laid them down and just pushed them forward to my side of the table. And he said, 'Now you can go.' Of course my reaction was 'No, take your money back!'

And then he said, 'You know, you really surprise me. We've been talking for two hours and you really struck me as a twenty-first-century woman and now you have these bourgeois conventions and attitudes towards money. I'm a person at the end of my life that has money at his disposal for a young person beginning their work. You need the money; there's nothing inappropriate about this exchange of money.' I said, 'Well, okay to that. All right!' I would never have accepted it, but he knew just the thing to say.

So I did go to Trinidad that summer, but it ended up that I would be his secretary at the same time. So that summer I went to where he was staying in Trinidad and worked with him. Every weekday while I was there I would go down to where he was staying in a place called Hobson House in San Fernando, owned by the Oil Workers' Union. He was staying there; an Indian family took care of the place. I would sit at the foot of his bed and record or take notes.[10]

Back in Washington, Sally continued to work with CLR, coming to his apartment at the Chastleton and taking dictation as he composed articles, book reviews and regular letters to the editor. Somewhat to her consternation, much of what he wrote was on Marxist theory rather than the Caribbean politics in which she was personally interested. Worse yet, though, were the pieces on cricket:

I wasn't really interested in a lot of what he was writing about. I remember writing a lot about cricket. When he was at the Chastleton he would be in bed and he would have his books and materials all over and under the covers and the TV on right next to him, but when he wrote about cricket he would talk like 'and then so-and-so came into bat and scored such and such' then he would not get the right number, so he would say 'can you get this book?' and I would root around for the book and he would tell me what page to verify whatever information. Then he would just dictate these fully formed sentences, he was quite amazing in that way. Physically he was very frail but not his mental faculties.

They also worked on his autobiography. Sally was soon aware that she wasn't the first to attempt to help him with this seemingly endless task:

> I always felt there was a string of us young women who were like his, what he called his 'amanuensis' or secretary or whatever. I know there were a string of them and all working on his autobiography. I did some work on the autobiography too, I guess the women's chapter. I never understood why that didn't come to fruition. He was so prolific, but there was something that was preventing him from finishing it.

The women issue continued to be at the front of his mind:

> He was always investigating you. He wanted to know everything about you and your family – what your father did, what your mother did, how many brothers and sisters you had, what are they doing, who did they marry – all trying to figure out how you fitted into the scheme. He did keep coming back to this issue of his own past relationship with women. And his wives – he was not particularly progressive on the male-female front, but was beginning to understand that with everything he did on the political front his attitude towards women was way back in an earlier century, so he was really trying to figure that out.
>
> He was informed by literature, these black women writers. He was in process of figuring it out, but he did recognise that he had not treated his prior wives very well. He felt he was always a dutiful husband, but he realised he didn't really treat them like partners.

As for her own relationship with this eminent man fifty years her senior, Sally offers a measured, obviously fond appraisal:

> We had definitely a mentor-mentee relationship. He was very – not flirtatious, sort of devilish: he had a great sense of humour. He still saw himself, despite his age and weakness, as a handsome young man. I just thought, wow, this guy! Nothing was explicit but there were little notes he would send, things that a lover might send, but there was nothing overt about it. It was just part of his personality. It didn't come out as sexual in any way in our relationship.
>
> He was very old school. He definitely would not be considered politically correct I suppose today, but it wasn't today. And in his political work in Washington and with me I didn't feel there was anything in the way he behaved that was offensive. And there was a lot of offensive behaviour going on in the 1970s! When I think back on what was going on at that time with men in positions of power or authority. I was at graduate school and the behaviour of professors at that time was outrageous. That was not what he was.

What CLR was, was someone completely different to anyone else she'd met. As a white radical student Sally was full of anti-Western attitudes, and yet here was this veteran of Third World liberation struggles who wanted to educate her on the good things of European civilisation:

> We didn't go out that much, most of my time with him was spent in his apartment, but he took me to a very fancy, very expensive very chi-chi French restaurant in Washington, called Sans Souci. Probably he was trying to show me something. He talked about the wine, a Medoc. He'd obviously been there before, people already seem to know him and showed respect to him. And he wanted me to taste this wine – I was not the right target audience for that! He was trying to teach me.
>
> Sometimes I would go to see him, and I think, this time I'm really going to get him to talk about the Haitian Revolution. And I

would come into his apartment and he would pull down this book on Picasso. But I was anti-Western, I was just not that interested. And he was who he was. He was so comfortable with the fact that he'd grown up in colonial Trinidad, that he learned Greek and Latin, all these languages. He had that colonial education, and he knew so much and that was part of him. It was not a contradiction at all.

Sally saw very clearly how these twin inheritances – the European and the Caribbean – came together when she was in Trinidad with CLR:

There was this interesting moment when we were in Trinidad. I was staying with this prominent middle-class black family of attorneys. CLR came over. He always talked about loving cow-heel soup and they fixed him cow-heel soup. Then we went to see the Desperados, probably the most famous steel band at the time. They came from Lavantille, a really poor neighbourhood, so we went to go visit their pan yard to hear them practising. We went up this really dark road up the steep hills and as we approached, we could hear them playing 'Flight of the Bumblebee' on the steel pans. For CLR that was just like, he could have written a *Beyond a Boundary* about that moment, because here they were, these working-class black Trinidadians who were able to create instruments out of these discarded oil drums and learn the Western canon in order to remake this classic work into this beautiful thing that resonated through Trinidad, and it was like all of colonial history and revolution was all there in that moment. That was a Jamesian moment to me.

Her abiding sense of CLR is of his optimism. He refused to get angry about the politics of the moment:

He didn't waste energy ... Someone like Trump wouldn't have bothered him. He was so optimistic. I would come in and say, 'Oh my God, things are so terrible.' And he would always say, 'Times need to ripen, things have to happen in their time, the road is long.

> Eventually things will happen.' His view of life was so broad. He could have been a very religious person because he was able to navigate all this with a very cool and always optimistic way of looking at the world. He had so much faith. Nobody else I knew was like that.

While this is the great truth of CLR's life, it doesn't mean he didn't have his moments of self-doubt. When Robert Hill spoke to him in the summer of 1979, and talked about bringing more and more of his work into print, about the certainty of his legacy, CLR just seemed dispirited and unconvinced:

> I was with him and I was then keen to publish an edition of his papers and to reprint his books, because in that period, they still weren't widely available. And that's when he told me, he said, 'Who's going to be interested in my work?' And at the time I was showing him the Penguin edition of Sigmund Freud's work, and I said, 'CLR – I can do that for you.' And he said, 'Look, who's going to be interested?' That's the only time I felt like he wasn't aware that his day was just about to break ... I mean, James would be amazed to discover where his fame and reputation and status has moved to.[11]

Even when the spirit *was* willing, the flesh was tiring. In November 1978, after a trip to the United Nations in New York to hear Michael Manley speak, he collapsed with suspected pneumonia and was hospitalised in Washington for a week. It was becoming very clear that he was simply too old and infirm to carry on his teaching job plus speaking engagements around the US.

Living in the Chastleton, he was ever more dependent on a network of acolytes. Ethelbert Miller noted that this was becoming an increasingly racialised situation: 'He had a body of people around him, and I would say there were like a cult ... they prevented access to CLR. I remember coming to see him with a young graduate student called Kent Worcester* and because he was white, they were like "what's he doing here?"'[12]

* Later the author of a valuable book on CLR's life and work.

Friends in DC started a fundraising drive* to enable him to take a year off, to go to Trinidad and work on his autobiography. At the same time, he attempted to negotiate a sabbatical from Federal City College. Come May, he accepted that he wasn't coming back to teach. He submitted his resignation, citing exhaustion, though hoping he might still do some guest lecturing.

Money remained a significant problem. While he had earned well in the past decade he had, as ever, spent freely and with lavish if erratic generosity, as per his largesse to Sally Schwartz. One person who had seen little of this largesse, however, was his wife. In 1977 he and Selma had finally agreed that he would pay her £100 a month towards her expenses, though CLR had then unilaterally reduced that to £80. In May 1979 Selma wrote him a long letter, part angry, part anguished, demanding four times that amount, clearly unaware of how fragile he was becoming. The letter ended with a note of heartfelt sadness, lamenting the fact that, as she saw it, CLR had given his family lip service, not genuine care.

She evidently had a point, but what was CLR to do, seventy-eight years old and exhausted? That summer he did indeed return to Trinidad and whether he knew it or not, his second extended sojourn in the US was now at an end.

* There was a fundraising event featuring the great Black feminist a capella group Sweet Honey in the Rock, but little else.

PART SEVEN

Old Age

Chapter Twenty-Six

CLR's decision to go home to Trinidad to rest and recuperate was one largely born of necessity. He could not afford to live in Washington without a job. He could no longer assume he would be welcome at Staverton Road, at least not for an extended period, relations with Selma having sunk so low. He was, essentially, dependent on the kindness of friends and supporters. Among them was George Weekes, the leader of the Oilfields Workers' Trade Union (OWTU).

One of his fellow union leaders, the recently retired David Abdulah, remembers what happened:

> CLR needed somewhere to settle. He had this romantic notion of Trinidad, so he contacted George Weekes, who had great solidarity. And George said the Union would house and take care of him. We had this building that we used for training sessions and so on, and we said he could stay there. The Union arranged for a woman to cook for him and two young women to type.[1]

The building in question, Hobson House, was and is just up the hill from the headquarters of the OWTU, just outside the centre of San Fernando. San Fernando is a gritty, hilly, working town, more Indian in feel than Port of Spain. It is not, however, anyone's idea of a cultural metropolis. Sam Selvon grew up there, but that's about it for literary heritage.

Before arriving in Trinidad, CLR took a side trip to Toronto, where he stayed with another young woman, a feminist activist called Judy Ramirez, who was associated with Selma's Wages for Housework campaign. Robert Hill's recollection is that CLR had shown him her photograph some years earlier, implying if not actually stating that this was a romantic relationship.

By the time he finally arrived in San Fernando, CLR was once again completely exhausted and his worried hosts checked him into hospital. Yet again the doctors could find nothing actually wrong with him, and just advised him to rest.

Judy Ramirez wrote as soon as she heard he was in hospital, offering to come see him if he needed her. How seriously the offer was meant is hard to say, but CLR certainly took it that way. He wrote back immediately in the hyperbolic style of his old age:

> Once you are here I can take care of you as long as you stay in Trinidad. Naturally you will help me at my work and I will help you at yours. By now, you will have read my chapter on women and you will understand that at last I'm a fully civilised person and will not exploit you. In fact I am hoping you will exploit me ... I feel your readiness to come is the biggest thing that has happened to me for many years.[2]

CLR received another letter while recuperating, this time from Constance. She had seen their son for the first time in years and even persuaded him to stay with her for a weekend:

> We found Nobbie, quite by accident. He was leaning against the wall in the vicinity of Edward's old office ... We took him home, bought a whole set of clothes (he smelled so bad we almost retched), he bathed, we burned the old clothes, and we fed him a good meal. Afterwards we asked him to go with us to the crisis clinic at Mt. Zion hospital and he agreed. He talked to the psychiatrists and their opinion was that he has managed to control his terrors by wandering, that he may always be a nomad and that if we tried to put him in a hospital, the little control he had achieved might crumble ... If you ask him anything, or even when he volunteered to talk (rare) it is with excessive courtesy, all overblown and courtly. I just don't know what to say.
>
> The day he left, looking so tall, elegant, and handsome in his new clothes and clean-shaven, carrying a duffel bag, I watched him walk out of sight and spent the rest of the day crying.[3]

CLR had hopes that while he was in Trinidad Olive's house could finally be sold and some money got to Nobbie, but Constance told him this was the remotest of hopes: even if Nobbie did receive some money he would just give it away.

Judy did indeed come to Trinidad. CLR sent her money for her fare and she arrived in late November for three weeks, an evidently happy time. She wrote to thank him as well as the cook Sarritt, and the two young assistants, Vashti and Anette, but worried that he still wasn't eating.

In CLR's letters that follow it's easy to sense his loneliness and isolation, stuck out in San Fernando. David Abdulah concurs:

> It was a bit stifling for him. People came, but it wasn't as stimulating as perhaps he would have wanted. While he had staff, we were all busy activists.[4]

Likewise, when Darcus Howe visited from London with his wife Leila, they found a man adrift. Leila Hassan Howe:

> I remember the bedroom in Hobson House, just him and I think someone was looking after him. He just seemed quite a lonely, isolated figure. He told Darcus he was bored, I remember that. Darcus said, 'What's wrong Nello? And he said, 'I can't get a proper newspaper and there's no decent salami!'[5]

He made do with correspondence. He sent long letters to Judy in January 1980. In one he returns yet again to the writer who he seems to have most identified with in his private life, Arnold Bennett.

> I very much wanted this letter from you Judy, as much as I have wanted anything of the kind for many a long day. It is good to want something because there is the pleasure of getting it. And by the way, as I write to you, I shall just gossip along as if you were here. Waiting has a place in my mind because it is one of the choicest

> parts of a book that I have read about 20 times and which I carry about with me always. Its name is Lord Raingo by Arnold Bennett. I shall get a copy of it to you one day. For the time being, Bennett describes a politician who had many qualities and gifts. But, says Bennett, his chief quality was his capacity to wait. After he had waited and got something, he immediately started to want to wait for something else. I feel as I do, my dear Judy, because you are you and I who have seen much of the world can appreciate you.[6]

There were plans for Judy to come to Trinidad for carnival, or for CLR to accompany her to an oil workers' conference in Libya, sponsored by the Gaddafi regime, but none of them came to pass. He wrote to other women too – long correspondences, with CLR in his characteristic role of mentor. He wrote to Renee Haussman, a fellow academic at Federal City College; to Consuelo Lopez, a Midwestern academic who was writing about his work; to a confused young Midwesterner called Donna Chambley, in the unlikely role of agony uncle. And so on. The files of correspondence that he left behind in Hobson House* are stuffed with these passionately dictated pen-pal letters, while the senior academics and suchlike who wrote to him tended to get a cursory few lines.

The autobiography, meanwhile, failed to make much progress. He rewrote his chapter on women after discussing it with Judy, but even she was less than convinced. She wrote to him to say that something had got lost between their discussions and the actual writing.

As ever, CLR was more inclined to explore new ideas than to go back over his life. His discussions with assorted young women had given him a new interest in and awareness of feminism. This was now reflected in his reading habits. He wrote to Judy about Adrienne Rich and Marilyn French. He wrote to Renee about a young Black American novelist called Alice Walker, whose new book *Meridian* had

* His papers and books from this period are accessible at a little archive in the OWTU headquarters. They offer a vivid snapshot of his nomadic life of the mind, always assembling a new library wherever he went.

made a big impression. He felt that the new generation of Black women writers were remaking the world for the better.

Rather more obscurely, he became briefly obsessed with the work of Jackson Pollock. He decided that he had divined a connection between Pollock and Picasso that no one else had seen. It's plain that here was a man starved of intellectual companionship. By March he was sufficiently lacking in an actual social world as to take refuge in someone else's. He started reading Proust and as he wrote to Renee Hausmann, 'I am constantly entangled in what people say and do and what Proust says they are really thinking, unbeknownst to I. That is the strength of Proust and that is why I am very cautious about him.'[7]

Finally, thankfully, an invitation arrived from the outside world. Margaret Busby was making a big move forward with the programme of bringing CLR's work back into print. That summer Allison & Busby would be publishing three more of his books: a second volume of CLR's selected writings; the first commercial edition of *Notes on Dialectics*; and, in its first UK publication since 1938, his revolutionary masterpiece *The Black Jacobins*. While this was obviously something to look forward to, hopes must have been qualified. When Allison & Busby published the first volume of his selected writings, plus *Nkrumah and the Ghana Revolution*, there had been next to no interest.

However, for once events conspired to place CLR in tune with his times, rather than ahead or behind. On 2 April 1980, the anger of Black British youth boiled over. The police raided the Black and White Café in St Paul's, Bristol, one of the country's best-established Black neighbourhoods. Local young people, full of anger towards the police thanks to the deployment of 'sus'* laws to harass them on the streets, decided to fight back. First one missile was thrown and then another; soon a full-scale riot broke out and the police were driven out of the area for a while, before steaming back in and arresting a selection of so-called ringleaders.

* The sus laws allowed the police to stop and search whoever they wanted simply on the grounds of suspicion.

There had been nothing like this in years and, given the heightened tension of the early Thatcher period, with its massive increase in unemployment, it looked like just what it was – the harbinger of urban unrest to come.

An immediate result was that the liberal media had one of its periodic bouts of realising it needed new Black voices. This was a time before there were any Black MPs in Parliament, barely any regular Black faces on TV at all, give or take the children's TV presenter Floella Benjamin and the avuncular newsreader Trevor McDonald. Generally, famous Black people were either musicians or sports stars. There was a glaring lack of well-known Black intellectuals for the media to call on. There were firebrands like Darcus Howe, whose Race Today Collective was an increasingly visible presence on the radical fringes, but the mainstream media was still wary of them.

Step forward CLR James. He came over to London in June 1980 and this time, rather than just talking to a group of old comrades in a church hall, he was interviewed at length by the *Guardian* – the first time he had ever been profiled in a British newspaper – and he was invited to appear on the first episode of BBC1's new flagship books programme *All About Books*.

This was presented by one of the great TV stars of the time, Russell Harty, and the first episode saw CLR appear alongside one of his contemporaries, the literary legend Christopher Isherwood, and the brilliant new comedian Victoria Wood.

The *Guardian* interview was conducted by Alex Hamilton. He found CLR in his preferred position, holding court from his bed in the Mayfair Hotel, wearing blue pyjamas. One hand on a copy of *Wisden*, the other on the telephone. He was awaiting further news on the death of Walter Rodney, assassinated in Guyana a week earlier, while also looking forward to the Lord's Test between England and the West Indies (he believed they should sack Boycott and reinstate Gower – 'a natural born player').

The piece gives a decent, if occasionally garbled, overview of CLR's remarkable life, making it seem quite extraordinary that no one – other than hard-core cricket fans and the more cerebral Black Power advocates – had ever heard of him. What comes over very clearly is his optimism and the broadness of his outlook. If the *Guardian* wanted comments on St Paul's or the racism of the British police, they were out of luck. CLR had his sights set on the global picture. Coming up to eighty, he was still possessed by fiery optimism. Where once he would have settled for four score years, he now wanted more:

> I am fanatically trying to live to the year 2000. Between now and then immense things are going to happen. Today the leaders cannot settle anything. Great upheavals are on the way ... In 1953 there was an upheaval in East Germany, 1956 in Poland, then Hungary, 1968 Czechoslovakia ... I say the next one is Moscow. That's where we have to look. I haven't seen anywhere that Brezhnev dominates the situation in Moscow. As for America with Carter and Reagan, they are a comedy, they have their feminine counterpart in Mrs Thatcher.[8]

The double whammy of TV and newspaper coverage did wonders for bringing CLR's name to public notice. The BBC decided to repeat the *Beyond a Boundary* documentary, which now appealed beyond the cricketing audience: 'CLR James may seem to have been just discovered,' said the *Guardian*, 'but the veteran West Indian writer made this film with Michael Dibb back in 1976.'

CLR finally arrived back in Trinidad in mid-July, some weeks later than originally planned, his British trip having been so unexpectedly rewarding. He was more restless than ever. There was an invitation to a W. E. B. Du Bois commemoration in Amherst, Massachusetts. He wanted to go but lacked the funds. Federal City College showed no signs of wanting him back as a guest lecturer, so he sent out a circular letter to his American comrades, telling them about his recent British successes and asking for $2000 to fund an American trip.

There was no response. From now on it was clear that the place CLR was going to find supporters was in the UK, not the USA. He made it back to London in January 1981, just in time for his eightieth birthday.

A few days later Darcus Howe and the Race Today Collective promoted a series of lectures at Kingsway College. CLR gave three talks in six days, dealing with the interlinked themes 'Socialism or Barbarism', 'Britain and America' and 'Formerly Colonial Peoples'. Taken as a whole they dealt with the question of the way forward for Britain. Was it the Labour Party, the trade union movement or the grassroots organisation of women, Black people, gay people and other marginalised groups? CLR had little hope for the Labour Party, but believed in the power of the trade union movement and was positively enthused by the idea that self-organised workers could, in combination with women's groups and Black groups, come together to create a new politics, working from the bottom up. He was particularly enthusiastic about the writing of Hilary Wainwright, one of the authors of a new book called *Beyond the Fragments*, which was having a major influence on Britain's intellectual left that year.

Each lecture was followed by a question and answer session, much of which was devoted to debating the question of how much Black Britons needed to work with British society as they found it. At one point CLR was challenged with the accusation that his hope of an alliance 'beyond the fragments' was naive, as he failed to recognise the racism of the white working class. His response was unequivocal:

> But while you can accuse me, I dare say, of having a blind spot in regard to the racism of the white working class, I would say you have a much blinder spot in regard to the progressive, revolutionary element of the British working class.[9]

The lectures were a great success. More and more opportunities were opening up for CLR in Britain. What he lacked was a base there, so in February 1981, he returned reluctantly to San Fernando* and spent the rest of the year restlessly travelling between Trinidad, London and the US.

* Eric Williams, still prime minister, died suddenly a month later, on 29 March. Oddly I could find no record of CLR's reaction.

He spent much of the summer in London. Darcus Howe was now a pivotal figure in his life, so when CLR found he could no longer abide staying at Staverton Road, effectively on sufferance and surrounded by the Wages for Housework cadres, it was Darcus he called for help. And Darcus, in turn, called on a friend of his, a comrade since Black Power days, a schoolteacher and writer called Farrukh Dhondy. Dhondy, now an eminent and elegant veteran of the literary and media worlds, remembers what happened next:

> He asked Darcus to take him out of Staverton Road where Selma was in some tension with him. CLR didn't want to stay. Darcus called me: Darcus couldn't drive. He said, 'Can you come in your car and take him away?' Then on the way Darcus said, 'Listen, Farrukh, I don't have a place for him. Can you take Nello up to your house? You have a room.' I said OK. So Darcus said, 'Fine, couple of days, then I'll fix something.' He stayed three months![10]

In his biography-cum-memoir of CLR, Dhondy offers an entertaining picture of those months living with a very demanding CLR:

> James was polite and took me entirely for granted. I was a man of political convictions; I had read his books; I said I had met him before, though I doubt if he remembered. I was a friend of his grandnephew's [Darcus]. And that was that. He would accept my hospitality.
>
> I knew that this would entail receiving his visitors and taking his phone calls, making his meals and doing his laundry . . . We got on well. We talked about books and art and writers and plays and poets, Marx and Lenin, Beethoven and Mozart, claret and Confucius, cabbages and kings.[11]

Now and again they would go out to eat, either an Italian restaurant in Soho, or in Chinatown. One time they were turned away from a Soho trattoria, even though the restaurant was empty. The young waiter looked this old Black man up and down and denied him entry:

'I don't want to go there,' James said, with extreme insistence. 'Let's just go.'

'I think we should insist. Bastards!' I said. I didn't want to turn my back on it. I knew I'd feel awful later. I was staring at the young Italian.

'I said no,' said the old man.

Dhondy also offers a gently, sadly funny account of CLR's fruitless courtship of one of his young female intellectual admirers, a woman he refers to as Marushka. There is an undeniable poignancy in Dhondy's description of CLR having his shirt ironed and his suit dry-cleaned, the bottle of Medoc bought, all ready for what he mistakenly imagines is a date.

While staying with Farrukh, CLR gave two talks at Riverside Studios in West London on the topic 'Black women in America in Fact and in Fiction'. The talk actually focused on the work of the three Black American writers he had come to admire in recent times: Alice Walker, Toni Morrison and Ntozake Shange. His speech offered a clear account of why these women's work was important, even revolutionary. It also showed very clearly how prominent feminist arguments were in CLR's understanding of the world at the beginning of the eighties:

> Women all over the world seem to have realised that they have been exploited by men. Marx pointed out many years ago that women were more exploited than the proletariat. (This is a remarkable thing for him to have said.) Now women are beginning to say: 'Who and what are we? We don't know. Hitherto we have always tried to fit ourselves into what men and what masculine society required. Now we are going to break through that.' These three women have begun to write about Black women's daily lives. Black women in America for hundreds of years have been scrubbing, sweeping, cleaning, picking up behind people; they have been held in the background; kept for sex. And now Toni Morrison, Alice Walker and Ntozake Shange have taken these Black women and put

> them right in the front of American literature. They can't be ignored any more.[12]

Dhondy goes on to tell the story of how the question-and-answer session at the end of the lecture was gatecrashed by a colourful and very elderly veteran of the American civil rights struggle, Queen Mother Moore, who had been a pioneer in the campaign to demand that the American state pay reparations for slavery to Black Americans. She wanted CLR to support her demand that America finally recognise Abraham Lincoln's offer of land and a mule for every former slave. According to Dhondy, CLR was irritated by this distraction from the subject he had come to talk about and his reply was 'impatient and contemptuous':

> 'I came here to speak about literature and some important writers. I know nothing about donkeys but if you want them, I hope you get them,' he says.[13]

When Queen Mother Moore attempted to contact CLR on the phone the following day, he instructed Farrukh to tell her he was dead. This would become something of a catchphrase of his whenever he had an unwanted caller. 'Tell them CLR James is dead.'

After London, CLR travelled to the States again. He stayed in Washington with Black Power comrades Zama and Ron Cook for a few weeks, then went to Los Angeles to give a lecture on Walter Rodney at UCLA. He was still divided as to where his future lay. Part of him was keen to return to living in the US. The problem was that he couldn't get a resident visa. He thought that if he could find Nobbie and ask him to sign a paper confirming he was his father, that might be sufficient to get him the visa. He charged Zama with going to the west coast to look for Nobbie, but this got nowhere.

From there it was back to London again. Despite all the practical difficulties of his life, CLR's intellectual powers were still strong, and he was in demand as never before. That November he filmed a series of six lectures for Britain's new and relatively radical TV station,

Channel 4. The subjects were Shakespeare, cricket, American society, the Caribbean, Africa, and Solidarity in Poland. It was perhaps the last of these that CLR was most excited about. The Polish Solidarity movement was a perfect exemplar of CLR's revolutionary ideal – a spontaneous rebellion of workers, with no vanguard party in sight.

The original plan had been for the lectures to be filmed by fellow Trinidadian Horace Ové, the best-known Black director working in the UK at the time. Ové had wanted to film in front of an invited audience, including leading Black American intellectuals like Amiri Baraka. However, this didn't work out. The producer, H. O. Nazareth, a long-term comrade of Farrukh and Darcus, but a TV novice, recalls that Sue Woodford, Channel 4's first commissioning editor for multicultural programmes, was also new to the world of television and simply didn't know how much to pay. The budget she offered wasn't enough for Horace, so he quit the project and Nazareth hired yet another rookie, a Canadian sound recordist called Christian Wangler, to step in as a director.

CLR had asked if Vanessa Redgrave could be part of the audience for the Shakespeare lecture, and the England cricket captain Mike Brearley for the cricket talk. Redgrave, a partisan Trotskyist, declined the offer, but Brearley did come to meet CLR at Lord's on the day of the filming. It was, Nazareth remembers, the one time in the whole course of the shoot that CLR made an effort to stand up rather than sit in a wheelchair:

> Yes, he stood up to meet Mike Brearley, it was tremendous to see them together. He said, 'Mr Brearley I have an ideal first eleven in my head and you are the captain!' And Brearley blushed with the compliment. But because the director knew nothing about cricket, and didn't know who Brearley was, he didn't realise it was a meeting we should have filmed![14]

He wrote to Constance soon after filming finished, with this pithy summary: 'Can't walk, but they lead me to a seat and I hold forth just as before.'[15]

* * *

From London, as he still lacked a place to live, he headed back to San Fernando once again. There was still no progress on his American visa, so when Darcus Howe offered a place to live in London, he was quick to accept. In March 1982 he booked a flight back to the UK. David Abdulah remembers his final departure from San Fernando, on a Friday afternoon:

> He was going to London. I went to make sure he was picked up on time. He was already waiting outside with his hat on. He'd arranged for a taxi. We chatted, time was slipping by and no taxi. I said, 'You want to postpone?' He said no. I said, 'I can take you, but I'll have to drive fast!' I had a Mazda, I used to drive a hundred miles an hour. I knew he was very frightened of car accidents, but he said OK. We strapped him in, I drove very fast and CLR sat there terrified, and we managed to get there – and find a wheelchair. He said, 'Well, you said you'd get me here on time. And you did!'[16]

And so he flew to London, leaving behind the support of the Oil Workers and giving himself over to the kindness of the Race Today Collective, Odysseus coming to the end of his wanderings.

Chapter Twenty-Seven

CLR arrived back in London in March 1982. He spent a few days in a hotel and then Darcus Howe came to take him to his new lodgings in the Race Today squat in Brixton, the south London neighbourhood that was then seen as the heart of London's Black community. A year earlier the junction of Railton Road and Shakespeare Road, where Race Today were squatting, was the epicentre of the Brixton riots, the 'insurrection' in which the Black community had turned with a vengeance on the police. Railton Road itself was known as the front line, a site of resistance and extra-legal commerce.

Leila Hassan Howe remembers CLR moving in:

> We brought CLR in from a hotel. Darcus had told us that we were going to be looking after him. We had squatted first of all on Shakespeare Road, then we squatted again in the building next door on Railton Road. Race Today was based on the first two floors and on the top floor there was a flat with a kitchen and bathroom and a large room and we decided CLR could come to live there. We worked out how we were going to look after him. Our concern always was about CLR being alone at night. But CLR didn't have any of those concerns at all. The big room was really light, it had windows on two walls, the sun would come streaming through.[1]

Leila enjoyed having CLR upstairs, a kind of surrogate grandfather to her and the other young activists, and in his early days there, while he was still reasonably active, enjoying the odd excursion:

> We went on a couple of dates! I said, 'Darcus, CLR is taking me to the cinema!' He took me to see *Dog Day Afternoon* with Al Pacino. Afterwards he talked to me about Pacino and American society.

> Anything you did with Nello was like that. We went out to eat sometimes, he liked to go to Chinatown, that was in the early stages.

Once firmly installed, CLR set about putting his affairs in order. He wrote to his bank, giving then Railton Road as his new permanent address. He wrote to Robert Hill, asking him to take on the considerable task of collecting all his papers and belongings from Washington, where they were stored at Ron Cook's house, and he decided that it was time he got divorced.

This turned out to be rather easier said than done. Selma was happy to accept that the marriage was over, but she was not prepared to grant CLR a divorce until he came to what she believed to be a fair financial settlement. This was a considerable stumbling block. Selma was obviously justified in saying that she had provided CLR with countless hours of unpaid assistance (it's little wonder she started Wages for Housework). However, the fact was that CLR had no savings. He had mostly been well paid while in Washington, but that money was gone. All he had was a pension from Federal City College, enough to live on modestly but no more than that. To make matters worse, when it came to his personal finances CLR was both disorganised and secretive. Preparing papers that would satisfy Selma's lawyers was not going to be easy.

The case dragged on. CLR had the well-known radical lawyer Benedict Birnberg's firm working for him, but it was an unedifying affair. CLR took Selma's demands very personally and resented her claim to have been at least part author of much of his work. And there was the possibility that he might be about to come into some money. Robert Hill was conducting protracted negotiations with Northwestern University over the potential sale of CLR's archive and papers.

While the university were deliberating, they provided funds for Hill to at least determine just how much archive material there was. The problem here was that most of CLR's papers were in Staverton Road and Selma was refusing to let go of them until a settlement was reached.

As this depressing drama carried on, Robert Hill became increasingly concerned about CLR's welfare, sensing that he was spending much of his time in London alone. There was no one to be with him during the days. Constance had been in touch with both Hill and CLR, and expressed a willingness to go over to London to see how her ex-husband was coping. Hill was able to pay for her airfare with Northwestern's money, in return for her looking into the matter of retrieving the papers from Selma:

> Your visiting him would be for him not only a great delight; he would also be reassured that yourself and Edward still care for him, and right now that is extremely important. I myself don't know how he has managed to bear the loneliness of these last years, but whatever we can do to lessen the pain of it ought to be done.[2]

Constance made it to London in early July, stayed in a hotel and visited Nello regularly. She did her best to make sense of the situation with Selma and the divorce, and reassured CLR that Robert Hill would collect his Washington papers.

> He is very weak. Farrukh feels he should go out each day to walk, with someone helping him, to strengthen his legs. But he told me once that for cricketers, when their legs go they're finished. Somehow, I feel that to him it's a sign too. When he gets up to go to the bathroom, either I give him a hand to help pull him up or he sits up, slides along the bed, transfers to a chair and then manages the walk to the next room.[3]

CLR still had ambitions to travel. There were possible academic posts in the US, invitations to speak in Trinidad or Nigeria or Hull, etc., etc. However, the flesh was getting weaker and weaker. The problem in many ways was CLR himself. His lifetime love of conducting his affairs from his bed was, ironically, more of a problem in old age than in youth. Without exercise, his legs were in danger of atrophying. He may not have been exactly lazy, as Selma accused him of being in her divorce deposition, but he was certainly stubborn.

* * *

CLR's next TV appearance was in fact conducted from his bed. This was his memorable cameo in the BBC *Arena* documentary on the Jamaican dub poet Michael 'Mikey' Smith. Smith was a protégé of Race Today's best-known member, Linton Kwesi Johnson. He was a magnetic performer and a TV natural. For the documentary the director, Anthony Wall, brought Smith and Johnson upstairs to CLR's bedroom, where they debated the merits of dub poetry versus the English Romantic tradition.

It's a fascinating conversation. CLR explains how in Trinidad he had loved Wordsworth, then in England had come to admire the revolutionaries, Keats and Shelley, more. Smith tells him he can't stand any of them, and winds him up by pretending to be unable to pronounce their names. When he goes on to call Shakespeare 'Shaka Spear', CLR looks ready to erupt. But CLR also sees that what they are doing with poetry is decolonising it, doing what the West Indian cricketers of his youth had done. They are not merely writing in dialect, like the popular Jamaican Louise Bennett, they are altering the rhythms and the structure to fit their own backgrounds and experience. They are performing the dialectic. And, in further evidence of the power of the dialectic, the film ends with Michael Smith, much less the primitive than he liked to act, reading Wordsworth's 'Composed upon Westminster Bridge', giving each syllable due weight.

CLR's next big challenge was a trip to Trinidad in October 1982, to speak to the Oil Workers Trade Union, a commitment he could not easily cancel after all the help they had given him. He wrote to Robert Hill to tell him of his plans to prepare for the trip:

> I'm doing my best with the program for health. I'm now negotiating for a trip outside every day. I'm also doing my best in regard to eating. I'm glad to be able to say that I'm working out my speech for the OWTU conference with satisfaction to myself. It is a very important meeting and I intend to say as much as I can about the need for social revolution in the Caribbean.[4]

Most of his time, however, was still spent in bed, reading discriminately and watching TV with something that looked like a complete lack of discrimination. Leila Hassan Howe remembers his fondness for *Dallas*, which stretched his argument that such shows taught you about American society to its limits. However, now and again his TV viewing would take him into surprising territory, as illustrated by this extract from a letter. The name of the recipient is missing, but the tone suggests it must have been Martina Thomson – their friendship had rekindled now CLR was back in the UK, and she was a regular visitor to Railton Road. CLR writes not as a teacher but as a friend. He treats her as an equal:

> Yesterday I was lying in bed, as usual, reading a man whose poetry I am very fond of, TS Eliot, a political scoundrel if ever there was one, but I have been reading and rereading him for over 40 years. I happened to turn my eye on the television and there was a band playing, a coloured band, the band leader dancing to correspond to the music. Believe me I have never seen or heard anything like it. He was taking short steps forwards, backwards and sideways and moving his body from hips down in time to the music with the grace and delicacy that forbade any hint of vulgarity or un-placed sexuality. His name is Kid Creole. From what I hear a popular entertainer but in my view a great artist, not so much in the music but in his motion and his leadership of the band.[5]

There begins and ends CLR James's commentary on eighties popular music.* Interesting that he should pick on Kid Creole, whose styling harked back to the Harlem of the wartime years, the Harlem CLR remembered.

The trip to Trinidad went well enough. He delivered his speech to the Oil Workers, exhorting them towards leading a Caribbean-wide

* E. Ethelbert Miller remembers that CLR was also very taken by Michael Jackson, but sadly he never wrote anything about him. Clearly CLR had a keen admiration for great dancers.

revolution, following the example of Grenada where another admirer of his, Maurice Bishop, had led a successful coup in 1979 and was attempting to establish a socialist society under the aegis of his New Jewel Movement.

Trinidad briefly invigorated him. He was joined by Judy Ramirez, which doubtless helped with the reinvigoration. He decided to fly back with her to Toronto, before returning to London.

This, unfortunately, was a step too far. In Toronto, as he told Robert Hill, he 'went to pieces'. He flew home on 2 January and had to be taken to Dulwich General Hospital the following day. He spent a week there before the doctors decided, yet again, that there was nothing wrong with him apart from exhaustion.

It was a salutary experience, however, this collapse. There would be no more transatlantic travelling. Neither did he want to see the inside of a hospital again, as Leila Hassan Howe remembers: 'When he came back, he said, "Whatever happens, Darcus, I never want to go back in the hospital. I get ill again you must never put me back in the hospital."'[6]

From now on, CLR would rarely leave his room at 165 Railton Road. Fortunately it was no longer a squat; the newly socialist-dominated Greater London Council (GLC) had allowed Race Today to stay there, and even given them grants to refurbish the building and publish their magazine.

Word got round that CLR was in residence and Black radicals would make the pilgrimage to see him. Farrukh Dhondy remembers the arrival of Maurice Bishop:

> The Grenadan revolutionaries turned up, Maurice Bishop and all, I was there and CLR said, 'Farrukh! Where's that red wine?' I said, 'We finished it.' He said, 'Go get some more, can't you see there are guests!' I went off and got some decent wine – you can't get decent wine on the front line in Brixton, you got to go to at least Sainsbury's – came back, and they were talking.
>
> CLR said, 'I keep telling you, don't write all this rubbish about Leninism, give the people good government.' So they said, 'What do

> you mean, good government?' He said, 'Look, you got a fishing industry. I know what happens there, half the fish rot on the beach. You want to send it to Miami, so you need to give them a refrigeration plant.' They all started looking at each other. He said, 'Get the fishermen together, ask them what they want. They'll say a refrigeration plant, you give it to them!' His one phrase was 'You can't have nutmeg socialism,' because Grenada used to export nutmeg and nothing else. I remember something that sticks in my mind for ever – as they left and said their goodbyes, he shouted after them 'And don't kill any nuns!'[7]

Staying close to home no longer bothered CLR; he was a past master at staying in bed. However, what he was starting to feel the absence of, was a secretary. He badly missed having an amanuensis sitting at the end of his bed, taking dictation, finding the right book, or simply talking to him about Shakespeare or Picasso or Lenin. As it was, he was dependent on either paid-by-the-hour secretarial services or Farrukh or Leila or Darcus finding time to help out.

His isolation was also leading to a reckless degree of self-medication. He would send notes to Farrukh asking him to bring half-bottles of good Bordeaux. That was not a problem in itself, but his long-term dependence on sleeping pills was in danger of getting out of hand. In April he wrote to his old friend David Pitt, by now Lord Pitt, asking for a prescription for Halcion – 'plenty of them'. Pitt responded promptly, if completely irresponsibly, by sending him a prescription for two hundred pills.* Writing a prescription for so many seems extraordinary, but CLR was doubtless grateful.

Visitors were increasingly worried by CLR's living conditions. When Alice Walker – who much appreciated CLR's championing of her work – came to see him on a visit from the US, she was so concerned that she gave him £200 to help out with his living expenses.

* This despite the fact that he hadn't actually seen CLR in person and Halcion is an extremely potent benzodiazepine. People get addicted in as little as two weeks and there is a real danger of overdose. They would be banned completely in Britain in less than a decade.

It was Paul Buhle who came up with the solution to CLR's problem. Buhle, though he only rarely met CLR in person, was perhaps his greatest champion on the American left. His *Radical America* special of 1971 had now been followed by an edition of a new magazine called *Urgent Tasks*, which had celebrated CLR's eightieth birthday by commissioning memoirs and critical pieces by a whole range of notables. Everyone from old comrades like Grace Lee and Marty Glaberman to Black radicals like Manning Marable and Bobby Hill to British leftists like E. P. Thompson and David Widgery were included in the special issue.

Buhle kept up a regular correspondence with CLR and sensed his need for a secretary-cum-companion. At the time he was co-editing yet another new journal, *Cultural Correspondence*, with a New Yorker called Jim Murray. Murray was in his early thirties, had some personal wealth and no commitments. He was also a great devotee of CLR's work. Buhle describes him as 'a New Left wastrel who was independently wealthy' and smoked dope every day.[8] He was the perfect candidate for the job.

Jim Murray arrived in London on 2 April, found a flat around the corner from CLR, and started his new job. He wrote to Robert Hill in June, describing the routine they had built up:

> First two months I gave Nello breakfast every day, still do five days a week. I stay most of the day, in his room where I have my desk next to his bed. We occasionally have dates to watch certain movies at night; at least once a week I fill in for Leila giving him dinner. (I guess you know her ... She is very warm and helpful to Nello, responsible for dinner and certain domestic stuff like new clothes, prescription refills, et cetera.)
>
> I do his mail with him, paying bills and answering letters when he puts his mind to it. Several letters to press and a few articles and book reviews. Lots of household and errands and about one red alert every day when he has to sit up while I take his bed apart looking for his pen or his pills. Once a week or so we have a concentrated afternoon talk about US politics or something.[9]

Murray's major achievement in these first few months was to assist with CLR's divorce proceedings. Selma was still refusing to hand over CLR's papers until a settlement was agreed. Jim Murray appeared in court to argue that CLR needed his papers in order to work on his autobiography. He was well prepared for the task: 'I had watched with Nello, his favourite show, *Crown Court*, every day for two months, so the atmosphere was familiar to me.'[10] The dedicated TV viewing paid off. The judge agreed to let CLR have his papers.* Jim collected seven black bags full of documents from Selma's lawyer's office and two carloads of books from Staverton Road.

The only part of this haul that CLR himself was excited about was the library of cricket books, but Jim busied himself sorting through the papers and organising them (he notes in passing what a superb secretary Selma was: 'there's barely a typo'). In order to house the books, he built some makeshift bookcases – basically planks of wood on bricks.

CLR's series of TV lectures was broadcast across the month of July. Perhaps unsurprisingly it was the talk on cricket that garnered the most attention. The *Guardian* reviewer complained about the production values, but much enjoyed the audacity of CLR's thesis.

> When this grizzle-haired West Indian described [a 1938 Test Match] as 'one of the great aesthetic experiences of my lifetime' in a game fit to rank with Michelangelo in the mind's eye, there seems no incongruity in the comparison. Yet how many could have got away with it?[11]

That same month, as the programmes were going out on Channel 4, Farrukh Dhondy brought round a new contact. This was a young woman called Anna Grimshaw. She was working as a researcher for

* The divorce itself, however, stalled. CLR had recently received $10,000 from the sale of Olive's house in Tunapuna. He unwisely attempted to hide this windfall from Selma's lawyers, was found out, and pulled back from the proceedings rather than hand over any of the money.

Granada television, after a degree in anthropology at Cambridge. She interviewed Farrukh for a documentary on migration to Britain. They got on well and Farrukh suggested CLR would be an ideal person for her to talk to:

> So I took her up to the flat and CLR was immediately taken with her. He said, 'Why is such a beautiful lady in the company of this rogue?' That's how he talked whenever I took anybody up, he'd say, 'What are you doing with this scallywag?'[12]

Almost immediately, CLR tried to persuade her to come and work for him as his secretary, calling her and sending her flowers. Jim Murray reported on this development to Robert Hill:

> Farrukh introduced her to Nello. She's 26, the anthropologist daughter of two Manchester doctors and Nello seems to be quite smitten with her: calls her every day, et cetera. Darcus and Leila are not pleased at all, expect her to crack first time Nello gets the way he gets, unreasonable let's say. (Today he balked quite harshly at the idea of spending 25 quid to put feet onto his wheelchair so he can use the damn thing. Whereas a few weeks ago he bought the *Encyclopaedia Britannica* for 700+ on an hour's notice . . . That kind of thing). She sure does perk him up though, talks about actually going for little outings with her . . . The point about Anna is that she completes the package he wants: me concentrating on the papers and autobiography, her doing all the other stuff I now do.[13]

Murray decided that he could offer Anna a small wage to look after CLR. She agreed to the deal, handed in her notice and came to work at Railton Road. She would be a constant presence there for the rest of CLR's life.

Now a professor of anthropology and a filmmaker, dividing her time between Atlanta, Georgia, and Maine, she remembers how her association with CLR began:

> Jim very much persuaded me to leave my job at Granada, which actually wasn't hard to persuade me to do, and to take over from him managing James' affairs. I thought, why not? I mean, it seemed an interesting opportunity. I had no idea what it would entail. Jim was willing to fund me to take on the job of sorting the papers and stabilising his situation in London. Race Today were downstairs. They would make his evening meal, but my job was to get there first thing, get him up, make his breakfast, make his lunch. I essentially worked from eight to five, and then my responsibilities would be over at five and they would make a meal for him and make sure that he was secure there at night.[14]

Part of the initial attraction of this new role was the prospect of working with CLR on his autobiography. She didn't know that she was only the latest in a long line of people to be engaged in this fruitless task:

> He did dictate some sections, but I very quickly realised that they were sections he'd already dictated. They were just stories fixed in his head and he duplicated them. He had no interest in writing his autobiography. It kept, I think, being suggested that he should do it. His heart was never in it.

Jim Murray may well have got to the heart of the matter when he observed that 'the autobiography was a good way to get people to come help him'.[15] There had been Terisa Turner and Sally Schwartz in the US, others too, and there was Jim and now Anna in London. So it seems that the autobiography was less a work in progress than a strategy to provide him with interesting company, to ward off the loneliness, as Anna told Jim:

> I think he was very vulnerable in his last years, and lonely. One of my greatest pluses was that I was completely reliable. If I said I would be there at such a time I would be, and, having been there stranded so often or feeling dependent on people who didn't turn

up to make his breakfast or get him out of bed, that was something that he very much valued.[16]

CLR and Anna soon settled into a domestic pattern:

I would make breakfast. We'd sit, we'd talk, we'd review the papers, and then I would get on with whatever work had to be done – going through the papers or my own writing. There were also appointments. Particularly once he stopped going out, which really happened probably a year after I started working there, people would come to see him instead. So there were always appointments to set up and to manage that kind of thing. But really he wanted companionship. He wanted someone there. He wanted to listen to music with somebody, to listen to opera, watch television, all of those things. That was really my role.[17]

At first they would still go on outings, mostly to the opera. CLR loved these, apart from a trip to see David Blake's modernist opera *Toussaint*, which he hated so much he insisted on leaving after the first act. However, what soon became clear to Anna, the doctors' daughter, was that was CLR was badly neglecting his health. For starters, his dependence on Halcion was an obvious problem:

He was frail. As I say, he didn't get out of bed, and he was addicted to sleeping pills. I've forgotten what they were but they've basically been taken off the market now. He had problems of insomnia and he was being prescribed them.

Fortunately Anna was well placed to source informal help:

When I first met James, he was still going out giving talks, and so one of the first things I did was go to Hull with him when he got an honorary doctorate. And it was on his way back from there he stayed with my mother, and she got involved in advising about his health. Subsequently she came to London quite a few times. I mean,

> she wasn't formally his doctor, but there were things that she could advise me to do, and that is essentially what I did.
>
> Which was make sure he got up every day, make sure he got dressed every day, make sure he was out of bed, not just lying there, and bit by bit getting him off the sleeping pills, which was a huge task. But we succeeded in the end. I do credit my mother for extending his life significantly, and making those last years more satisfying.

As 1983 moved into 1984 there was no let-up in CLR's improbable rise to fame. There were more TV appearances, speaking engagements and three more books. Race Today put out an edition of CLR's *80th Birthday Lectures* and Allison & Busby came up with a reissue of *Mariners, Renegades and Castaways*, plus the third volume of his selected works, *At the Rendezvous of Victory*. And while the first two volumes had austere academic covers and production values to match, this third volume came with a full-colour portrait of CLR on the cover, taken by Lord Snowdon, no less.

This was a moment at which Britain, or at least young Britain, was starting to see itself as a multicultural society. Black and white people were mixing more in schools and colleges and clubs and gyms and shops and love. Where, in the early phases, immigrant communities tended to stick to themselves, for comfort and safety, now they were coming together. Music always led the way, but TV was responding to the challenge of representing this new Britain too. Farrukh Dhondy replaced Sue Woodford as head of multicultural programmes for Channel 4. New shows like the magazine *Black on Black* and the anarchic sitcom *No Problem* started to bring Black British talent into the living room.

And with increased exposure, there came an interest in the attendant history. Step forward once again CLR James. A generation who had come to political writing through the poetry of Linton Kwesi Johnson or the songs of the Clash now had a white-haired sage to introduce them to a history of which they knew nothing: the great Haitian slave rebellion, the struggle for West Indian independence, Pan-Africanism, et al.

Through CLR and Race Today they could learn, too, about the new Caribbean martyrs, Walter Rodney and now Maurice Bishop, who had been killed following an internal coup, just before the Americans invaded and snuffed out the Grenadian dream once and for all.

As a result of all this there were book signings and media interviews and endless demands on his time. After a while, as Leila Hassan Howe remembers, it all got too much:

> I remember after he gave a lecture at the Africa Centre, Darcus literally carried him up the stairs to bed. And he said, 'That's the end of that, Darcus. I'm not doing it any more.' We put him to bed and gave him a brandy and he said, 'No more.'[18]

Chapter Twenty-Eight

There was more, though. In fact, there were five more years. Five years of sitting in bed, reading and watching TV, Anna Grimshaw beside him in the days, Leila and other collective members, such as Jean Ambrose and Lorine Stapleton, in the evenings.

There was not much more writing now – the occasional book review, short pieces on cricket for *Race Today*, all dictated to Anna – but when the mood took him he could still talk. As V. S. Naipaul had observed, it was perhaps the greatest of his talents, the natural flow of unscripted oratory. And it was in hope of hearing him talk that the visitors continued to come.

There were the political visitors, of course. These included the Labour leader Michael Foot, the Jamaican sociologist Stuart Hall, and the Trotskyist historian Peter Fryer, who was about to publish a truly ground-breaking history of the Black presence in Britain, *Staying Power*. Anna Grimshaw remembers CLR being particularly keen to talk to Fryer, and when he received a copy of the book he wrote to say that:

> The more I read it, the more I am astonished at the great mass of material that you have not only gathered but disciplined . . . Let me end by saying: a lot of people talk, others express themselves, but on this question of black people very, very few sit down and do this sort of solid work that you have done.[1]

Some of those who preferred to talk than work made their way to CLR's door as well. Leila remembers his expertise at dealing with them:

> A wonderful thing about CLR was his ability to dismiss people. People would come and a lot of people would kind of talk at CLR

> and then want his advice. And by then he really didn't want to know. And he used to just put out his hand in mid-sentence and say, 'Thank you, very nice of you to have come!' I remember one young guy coming to see CLR and he was berating the fact that the black community wasn't more radical, wasn't doing more, on and on, and CLR looked at him and said, 'OK, I tell you what. You bring six people who think the way you do and we will have another meeting. Bye-bye!' It was a brilliant way of dismissing people, because of course the guy would never get one person to come with him![2]

The visitors that excited him the most were probably the cricketers. Viv Richards, David Gower and Ian Botham all came to see him. 'He was in his element that day,' says Leila.

Perhaps surprisingly it was not the West Indies captain, the colossus that was Viv Richards, but David Gower, the England batsman often seen as being a bit too flashy for his own good, who was CLR's particular favourite. Really, though, it was predictable: Gower was the most elegant of left-handers with one of the game's great cover drives, and a natural favourite for anyone as interested in the aesthetics of the game as CLR. Such was his devotion that Anna Grimshaw recalls being regularly dispatched to send telegrams to Gower with words of encouragement or advice.

The most consistent and welcome visitor at Railton Road was Martina Thomson. She was still married to the writer and broadcaster David Thomson and they lived together in Camden Town.*

Martina would send CLR postcards from her travels, always with carefully chosen images, a Picasso or a Greek statue or a Benin bronze or a bust of Beethoven. She would read the books he recommended, *Vanity Fair* or Michelet, and suggest he listen to some Schubert. The closeness is obvious: on the back of one postcard she calls him 'the still centre of this world'.[3]

* David Thomson wrote a lovely, impressionistic account of life there at the beginning of the eighties, *In Camden Town*.

The irony in their relationship is that she had made her way in a career she had helped to invent – as an art therapist. CLR, of course, was an implacable opponent of psychoanalysis – don't psychologise me! On some level, though, he surely knew its utility and its power and was simply scared of it. In one letter Martina sent him a quote from Richard Wollheim's book on Freud, clearly meant to have resonance for CLR:

> 'I have not,' Freud wrote . . . 'The courage to rise up before my fellow men as a prophet, and I bow to the reproach that I can offer them no consolation; for at bottom that is what they are all demanding – the wildest revolutionaries no less passionately than the most virtuous believers.'
>
> No greater disservice can be done to Freud than by those, who in the interest of this or that piety, recruit him to the kind of bland or mindless optimism that he so utterly and so heroically despised.[4]

In CLR's first, more active years in Railton Road, he and Martina would go out together. They would meet sometimes to eat at CLR's favourite Soho Italian restaurant, La Tavernetta on Dean Street. Later she would come and visit and sit with him and watch films or listen to music. 'They were very, very close,' Anna Grimshaw remembers. 'The nature of their relationship, well, people say that in the fifties they had a long relationship.'[5]

It was with Anna herself, though, that CLR was developing the closest bond in these last years. They spent a very happy Christmas Day together, drinking sparkling burgundy and eating wood pigeon, then watching *Citizen Kane*.

There was a sudden influx of people from CLR's past at the beginning of 1986. To celebrate CLR's eighty-fifth birthday Race Today organised a programme of events at Riverside Studios. There was an exhibition devoted to his life and work, plus a series of talks, while the centrepiece was a revival of his play *Toussaint Louverture* – now in the version rewritten for the Nigerian production in the sixties and retitled *The Black Jacobins*. It would be the first performance in London since the initial run nearly fifty years earlier.

This production had come about in a hurry. Following the 1985 re-election of Margaret Thatcher, she had promised to abolish the left-wing Greater London Council. Confronted with their imminent demise, the GLC decided to go out with a bang, blowing all their available budget on dream projects. Yvonne Brewster, a Jamaican British theatre director, was one of the beneficiaries of this sudden largesse:

> I received a phone call suggesting I submit, virtually immediately, a fully costed proposal for a theatrical production. I was told that there might be funding available for the staging of something 'impressive' from the black community. Having been convinced that this proposal was not a hoax, there was no difficulty identifying *The Black Jacobins* ... as the ultimate choice. My preliminary blue-sky budget for this production – which would require a minimum of 23 actors, a first-rate set design, lighting, sound and costume designers, excellent stage managers, innumerable 18th-century military costumes, a full six weeks rehearsal in decent rehearsal rooms and the rental of a splendid venue – topped the £80,000 mark. Even today, this is an enormous sum for an independent black production in England: an impossible dream. The money was, surprisingly, granted in full with no quibbles.[6]

Brewster rapidly set up her own theatre company to put on the play. She called it Talawa and ran it in collaboration with the actors and theatre-makers Mona Hammond, Inigo Espegel and Carmen Munroe. At this stage she hadn't even secured the rights to the play. A series of conversations with CLR at Railton Road eventually saw her receive his blessing and so *The Black Jacobins* would be launched with Britain's best-known Black actor of the time, Norman Beaton, in the role of Toussaint.

The GLC also funded the programme of talks that preceded the play's opening. Tim Hector came over from Antigua to give the keynote speech. An old friend of CLR's, the *sui generis* Guyanese novelist Wilson Harris, gave a talk on CLR as a writer and literary critic. More unexpectedly, the GLC paid for Grace Lee Boggs and Marty Glaberman to travel from Detroit to give a talk on the Johnson-Forest Tendency, a period of CLR's life little known to a British audience at the time.

CLR was pleased to see the ever-loyal Marty. The reunion with Grace, after decades of distance, was unsurprisingly more awkward, as she recalled in her memoirs:

> His surroundings were much the same as I had known them in the past when he had been married to Constance or Selma. He was lying on his bed. There were books all over the place. A female assistant (in this case, Anna Grimshaw) was typing away in a corner, and in the tiny kitchen next door there were dirty dishes and leftovers. Each time we spent about half an hour chatting, but there were periods when the conversation noticeably lapsed.[7]

When she came to give her speech, however, on 20 February, she paid warm tribute to the years they had worked together and the inspiration he had provided:

> In those days people used to say that in any gathering you could tell a Johnsonite by the enthusiasm and energy we exuded. Our very eyes were stars because CLR had helped us rediscover America and the world, and because in the Johnson-Forest Tendency we had created a unique political community, a fellowship of revolutionary intellectuals and grassroots people united by a common goal, the unleashing of the creative energies of those at the bottom of our society.[8]

The play ran for nearly a month, with a fine cast that saw Norman Beaton supported by Mona Hammond, Trevor Laird (as Dessalines) and a young Brian Bovell. The programme featured a single paragraph introduction from CLR, showing a mix of hope and trepidation for the project:

Two reflections. Mozart once said: 'I have a lot of tunes in my head. I want a story.' With the great musician the music came first. The same is true of the drama. I'm not a dramatist by nature or inclination. But a play was required and when I sat down to write it I was very conscious of what Mozart had said. The play had been successful with audiences in Europe, Africa, America and in the Caribbean. But nowhere has it swept the audience off its feet. However it was written fifty years ago. Fifty years is a long time and what did not happen then can happen now. Lift the curtain gentlemen.[9]

In the event, the revived *The Black Jacobins* followed in its predecessors' footsteps. It intrigued and intermittently triumphed, but was still not sweeping the audience off its feet. The *Financial Times* reviewer, Michael Coveney, was guardedly enthusiastic. He praised the performances – 'Beaton growls to magnificent effect as he blasts out his intention of bringing Africans to San Domingo to be both French and free' – and admired greatly the ambition on display – 'How marvellous to see a large-scale project – presented by the newly formed Talawa . . . that lends dignity and credibility to the British black theatre movement.'

There was another big profile in the *Guardian* to accompany all this activity. Clive Davis looked back over CLR's long career and ended by discussing the inspiring hopefulness of his vision:

He remains almost perversely optimistic about the state of the world, discussing the 20th century as if it were a young brother who may occasionally have gone off the rails and broken a few windows, but who is still lovable at heart. 'I'm optimistic because I simply cannot believe that those who proposed the development of democracy will be defeated. With the spread of information and ideas, movies, gramophone records, I cannot see the movement being beaten. I can say this because I have seen the past 85 years, when we started with nothing. I dare say others think differently.'[10]

Sadly, this optimism about the world was not always reflected in his personal life, and after the excitement of the exhibition and play CLR went into a depressive dip. As so often before, he was convinced the problem was physical and the doctors were called but could find nothing wrong with him. Anna Grimshaw wrote to Constance to tell her what was going on:

> I think he is finding it difficult to come to terms with the fact that he is no longer at the centre of things and that people get on with their lives without him. I think he feels that with respect to Darcus who is running a film company and hardly ever comes to see him. But as you say Nello keeps most things to himself and when he's depressed he becomes very introverted. I have tried to get books for him, play music, have a conversation with him when he's in such a mood but he really doesn't want to respond. He is still interested in cricket and the beginning of the season and prospect of the cricket book have cheered him a little. But he is very up and down.[11]

The cricket book was the first fruit of CLR having his papers returned to him and Anna organising them. Given the enduring popularity of *Beyond a Boundary*, which had remained in print in Britain and was finally receiving a US publication, she decided to collect together the best of his cricket journalism over the past half-century. It was a project that CLR thoroughly approved of, and Margaret Busby was happy to bring the book out, simply titled *Cricket*. Following publication, *Arena* decided to make a film in which CLR selected his all-time finest cricket eleven. CLR was filmed in his room and, as Anna once more reported to Constance, he looked bright and alert. The team he came up with was a curious mix.

The batsmen were led out, inevitably, by the sport's very own Old Man, W. G. Grace, opening with Jack Hobbs. Next came Don Bradman and then a trio of West Indians – George Headley, Learie Constantine and Gary Sobers (the latter two of whom would also have added greatly to the bowling attack). So far so predictable.

The wicketkeeper, however, was the surprise choice of the Edwardian great Herbert Strudwick, while the bowlers came in two matched pairs. There were two Australian fast bowlers from the 1920s, Jack Gregory and Ted McDonald, whose ferocity is hardly conveyed by modest Test records, and then the two West Indian spinners from the 1950s, Sonny Ramadhin and Alf Valentine, whose heyday was as brilliant as it was brief.

Meanwhile Anna and Constance were developing a close relationship via correspondence, one that became closer still when Constance started sending over copies of the letters CLR had written to her in the forties. She hoped they might be published. Anna recognised their extraordinary quality and agreed that they might indeed make a book, one that would both illustrate the development of CLR's thinking and also widen the understanding of him as a man in his time:

> I became very interested in how that whole dimension of James' life didn't figure in the kind of official stories, and that increased my interest in what it would be to construct a different life than just the political, left stuff, and actually work with more personal documents like the letters to Constance. They're so vivid, those letters – to see James in his old age compared to the voice of the letters and to imagine the kind of person Constance was.[12]

In time, Constance did come over and the two women became friends. Anna remembers the Constance she met:

> Just a very vibrant, attractive woman. Very unlike all the other women in that world ... She was glamorous, independent, smart, political without being predictable. She was just a very, very attractive woman. I liked her enormously. And she had no kind of resentment, nothing. I mean, her relationship with James at the end of their lives was very warm, positive ...[13]

Now that it was clear that there would be no autobiography, it was up to others to tell the story of his life. Constance started work on turning the letters into a book. Anna herself started tentatively working on a biography, using CLR's papers and contacting old friends for interviews.

Others too were starting to write about CLR. Paul Buhle was the first of these to really step forward. In 1986 Allison & Busby published an extended version of the *Urgent Tasks* collection of tributes to and essays on CLR, under the title *C. L. R. James: His Life and Work.* At the same time Buhle started working on his own biography, albeit one that would focus more on the work than the life itself.

As CLR became ever weaker and more dependent, tensions started to break out between those responsible for looking after him. On the one hand there was Darcus, Leila and the Race Today Collective, on the other there was Anna Grimshaw.

She wrote to Constance to tell her the situation as she saw it:

> I have just been going through a very bad patch with Race Today and very seriously considered resigning as Nello's assistant. They suddenly started insisting on 'screening' Nello's visitors, implied I had neglected him and his affairs and that from now on Race Today were in charge. I was quite hurt not to say indignant, but in the end had a very long talk with Nello about it. He brought the topic up – his understanding is that Race Today has lost its direction . . . And that there are all kinds of problems which Darcus won't confront.[14]

Leila Hassan Howe sees what happened very differently:

> After a while CLR didn't want regular visitors and he told us that quite frankly if anyone wanted to see him we should tell them he's dead! This is where people have had the impression that Race Today were kind of gatekeepers and guardians and wouldn't let people upstairs. That was on CLR's request. He'd had enough.[15]

Ethelbert Miller, who visited from Washington DC around this time, feels there was definitely an air of possessiveness:

> I was over in London for the radical book fair and there was a party at Race Today and I was downstairs and someone said, 'You will need to be quiet because CLR is upstairs.' And I was like 'CLR is upstairs!' And they said, 'You can't see him.' What happened then was CLR must've asked who was downstairs. So when somebody mentioned my name, that I was downstairs, they all caught hell. All of a sudden there was the red-carpet treatment given to me. I got the rum punch. Before I was just this guy from the States, but now CLR wanted to see me it was all different![16]

The situation seems to have been exacerbated by the fact that Race Today was starting to lose momentum. The prospect of losing GLC funding was a major worry and the group's undisputed leader, Darcus Howe, no longer had time to properly attend to the magazine. He had resigned as editor in 1985, replaced by Leila, and started what would become a very successful TV career.

Farrukh Dhondy decided to scrap Channel 4's existing Black and Asian magazine shows, *Black On Black* and *Eastern Eye*, and replaced them with a strand of serious documentaries to be called *The Bandung Files* and fronted by a leading Black radical in Darcus Howe, and a leading Asian radical in Tariq Ali.

Howe and Ali formed a company, Bandung Productions, and soon they were off shooting documentaries both in Britain and abroad. Inevitably Darcus was spending much less time with CLR, though as Leila points out, 'Soon as Darcus walked into the room, he would just light up. Darcus was doing a lot of travelling, with the TV, and he'd always come back and report on what he'd done.'[17]

Leila was struggling to keep Race Today going while also coping with CLR's often tyrannical demands for particular West Indian foods just the moment he felt like them. She also did not appreciate what she saw as interference from CLR's visitors.

> CLR had an eye for the ladies, a lot of the people who visited him were young women who loved him and then they'd come downstairs and say, 'How is CLR being looked after? Is he OK? Is he

getting this? Is he getting that?' Marika was one, there were a whole load of them.

Marika Sherwood was a young academic who visited CLR regularly in his last years. She remembers putting up more bookshelves and curtains for him, buying him a cardigan, but she most certainly didn't get on with Darcus, who tried to ban her from coming to see CLR.

Gradually, though, life settled down. Jim Murray arrived from the US for Christmas and Anna bought more wood pigeons – 'Nello didn't want anything "commonplace" like turkey,' she told Constance.[18]

CLR started to sleep more and more. When he was awake, with no need to write he focused more and more on music and art. Anna remembers listening to music with him:

> He took a lot of pleasure in listening to his favourite composers – Bach, Beethoven, Mozart – and we often did that. And also one of the things he really enjoyed was opera on video. Only Mozart, he wouldn't watch any other. So he would happily spend an afternoon watching *The Marriage of Figaro* or *The Magic Flute*. He would follow along with the score. That was something that he really enjoyed doing and he enjoyed doing it with me and sharing it with me.[19]

As ever, even as he took pleasure in the art itself, he liked to educate his companion as to the significance:

> He would be interested in the music and what he thought were the developments Mozart was after in that opera, as a late opera compared to the other ones. His knowledge of music was very, very detailed. He could follow a score. And like everything else, he understood the changes in sound as coming out of changes in historical periods. So it was never a kind of crude relationship – he would say, 'Well, in The Magic Flute you hear Wagner – this is where this music is going over the course of the next century,' so he was engaged with music as he would be with Shakespeare, not just as a kind of background but as a way of understanding something of the world.

His love of looking at books of paintings remained and, again, he would focus on the absolute best, the highlights of Western civilisation: 'Picasso, obviously. But Michelangelo and Leonardo would be the main ones. It was as if at the end of his life he'd narrowed down to the really key. The best.'

And then there was always his beloved television:

> As he got older and less interested in reading, sustained reading, we would figure out what we could watch on television. Because, for him, once he stopped going out, the days were just long, continuous days and I realised it was important to have things to do and things to look forward to, While I was there the BBC dramatised *Vanity Fair*. Well, that was a huge treat ... Whoever it was who played Becky Sharp, he thought was really rather terrific.* She was sharp! I remember one Christmas we spent the whole Christmas on an Orson Welles season. Welles was somebody who interested James just because his work was extraordinary, the period in which it was being made.

He still read a lot, the daily papers and re-reading old favourites. He would return over and over to Shakespeare, *King Lear* in particular: 'That remained a kind of foundation for him, again in terms of understanding power and transitions between one form of government and another and Shakespeare was absolutely the framework for those ideas.'

Anna also believed that, whatever he said, CLR actually benefited from having visitors. Some of them were friends of hers – CLR still liked nothing better than quizzing young people about their backgrounds and their lives. Politically minded visitors often got shorter shrift. Pete Ayrton, the radical publisher,† remembers visiting CLR to conduct an interview. CLR had specified one hour maximum, but as that hour coincided almost entirely with the Test match being on the

* Eve Matheson.

† Then at Pluto Press, soon to found Serpent's Tail.

TV, he got barely a word out of the sage. Edward Said, whose book *Orientalism* was having a major impact, got rather more attention, not because of his politics but because CLR quickly discovered he was a former concert pianist. 'The only thing he really wanted to talk to Edward Said about was music,' remembers Anna, 'he wasn't interested in any of the political stuff – absolutely not.'

Afterwards Said sent CLR a recording of Glenn Gould playing the *Goldberg Variations* and he was thrilled. Around the same time Maya Angelou addressed a packed audience downstairs at Race Today, then came up to talk to CLR. However, Anna reported to Constance that 'he is rather cool about her'.[20]

In late 1987 another regular visitor appeared on the scene. This was Keith Hart, an anthropologist by training who had broadened the field into economics. He had worked extensively in Africa and had identified the now familiar, then innovative, concept of the informal economy that tended to be ignored by conventional economists, making it almost impossible to understand how a modern African city functioned at all. At this time in his mid-forties, Hart had been teaching in Jamaica when he became obsessed with the work of CLR James, and was determined to talk to him when he returned to England in the summer.

He first came to Railton Road that August. Not only did he find CLR just as fascinating as he expected, but he soon began a relationship with Anna Grimshaw. This was not a development CLR welcomed, as Hart remembers: 'He saw me instantly and correctly as a rival for her attention. So he put me down, called me "Professor", which in his lexicon was not all that favourable!'[21]

Smitten, Hart decided to give up the offer of a new post in St Louis to stay close to Anna. Gradually he got closer to her crotchety charge as well:

> I spent a great deal of time with them. We got on pretty well. He would say to me 'Go to Selfridge's and buy me the best claret, wood pigeon and some Schubert!' We would have these tremendous

> discussions about the French Revolution, he was still reading biographies of Danton. And we watched a lot of television.

It wasn't just old films and cricket, though. Together they watched a wave of protest sweep China in the spring of 1989 and Keith saw CLR analyse it with remarkable acuity:

> He had this theory that there were only two world revolutions left, the second Russian Revolution and the second American Revolution. He was very keen on Solidarity in Poland, he had that at the back of his mind all the time. And James said to me, 'The Chinese CP will put down this uprising with great ease, but the Russians won't hold on to Eastern Europe after this.' And six months later the Berlin Wall was down.

And while CLR was clearly old and ever-weakening, Keith did see flashes of his old self, and what had consistently drawn people to him over so many decades:

> Twenty American schoolkids came to see him. They sat on the floor and he starts giving them Western political history since the French Revolution and after twenty minutes he's got up to the fall of Hitler. These kids, I tell you, they were gobsmacked. I suspect it wasn't what he was saying, it was the pure intensity. The sense that he had this history in his hands and could give it to you. He could give people the sense that they were part of a history that they never even knew existed.

One thing that struck Keith forcibly was how strong CLR's visual sense remained:

> He relied very strongly on the visual sense. I remember him telling when he was nine in Port of Spain he ran off and got to the rails of the racetrack and he got very close to the race and, he then described this horse in great detail, like it was yesterday: its strain and effort, its drooling, its face.

Jim Murray, on one of his visits from New York, was also struck by CLR's focus on the visual:

> I was watching the news with James . . . A mass meeting of five thousand British Leyland workers in the North of England voted to continue their walkout over management abolition of the three-minute wash up time between shifts . . . During the report, James pointed to the telly: 'Look! Look! Look at that!' I looked, there were the workers massed in the courtyard of the plant, there was the female reporter in the foreground.
>
> I thought: Ah ah! A perfect Jamesian story, industrial workers self-organising, the issue being not money but quality of life . . . ordinary people taking everyday history into their own hands. But James continued: 'Jim, look! Look at that!' He impatiently leaned forward, touched the upper left corner of the screen. 'Look: the steeple, the hills in the distance, the sky.' He was referring to the depth of the camera's view, the undivided totality of the picture coming to us on such a small box. He said nothing about the story.[22]

It was a welcome event then, when, in late 1988, an artist and peace activist called Maggie Glover came to do a portrait of CLR. She had previously painted CLR's comrade from the ILP days of the 1930s, Fenner Brockway, so that may have been the introduction. Either way, CLR relished the experience, as Anna told Constance:

> A rather batty woman comes several afternoons a week. I like her style. She invited me for tea the other week and we looked through her work. Some of it is very fine, particularly a great oil painting of Dora Russell. She also does some part-time teaching and talks to Nello about art and painting which he enjoys.[23]

Once the portrait was done, CLR would look at it for hours. Keith Hart remembers him studying it minutely, 'identifying his mother's Roman nose, his brother Eric's weak chin'.[24]

In the last year of his life CLR slept more and more, but there was still some work being done. Anna worked with him, selecting pieces to put together for a *C. L. R. James Reader*, covering his whole writing career. Meanwhile Keith and Anna had unearthed the *American Civilization* document from the early fifties and were thoroughly struck by it. Now, with CLR's blessing, they were trying to get it ready for publication.

The problem was who would be the publisher. Allison & Busby had gone into receivership the year before, which was a huge blow both to Margaret Busby personally and to the wider cause of radical publishing. Nevertheless, Anna found CLR an agent in Andrew Best at Curtis Brown, and in turn a new home for his work at Blackwell's,* where the editor Simon Prosser was a great admirer.

In the autumn of 1988 Channel 4 screened a film of CLR in conversation with Britain's other leading Black intellectual of the time, Stuart Hall – a thoroughly engaging talk ranging across CLR's long life. Recorded in 1984, it now had an inevitably valedictory feel. And, in the spring of 1989, Paul Buhle's intellectual biography, *C. L. R. James: The Artist as Revolutionary*, was published by Verso, and he came over to see CLR. Anna remembers that the visit was both encouraging and tiring:

> He exhausted Nello with a string of interviews which meant that when the party began downstairs in the Race Today offices, Nello refused to go and got into bed. Anyway he enjoyed all the fuss and we're waiting with interest for the reviews.[25]

Buhle's biography itself is thoroughly focussed on the work and thinking of CLR, so his domestic life plays virtually no part and there is little time given to his family. Nor was there a great deal of family in CLR's actual life in these last years. There were visits from Constance, which he enjoyed. He was happy to see Sam too. Sam was married now,

* An appropriate choice as for decades CLR had been buying books from Blackwell's bookshop in Oxford.

to a fellow activist, Barbadian American Margaret Prescod, and would bring their young daughter Chanda to visit her step-grandfather. Now a noted cosmologist and, unsurprisingly, an activist, Chanda Prescod-Weinstein remembers CLR as 'the grandfather who talked art with me (we shared a love of Picasso)'.[26] There was even a partial reconciliation with Selma. She came with Sam to see CLR for the first time in years. There was still one person missing, of course, his lost boy, Nobbie.

The end was drawing close now. CLR was plainly starting to withdraw from the world. It would not have escaped his notice that things were changing around him. Race Today was in deep trouble; they had stopped publishing the paper, laid off workers and would not survive much longer, throwing the future of the building into question. Anna and Keith were spending more time together, with Anna joining Keith in Jamaica for some weeks. And she was busy, too, with her own project, writing a book on her experiences in a Tibetan nunnery before she started working in TV.

When the end came, in the last days of May, it came suddenly. As ever CLR had appeared to be in remarkably good health for all his frailty. Anna wrote to Constance a day or two later to explain what had happened:

> Nello was very well on the afternoon of Thursday when I left for a day in Cambridge. When I returned to work on the Sunday morning he seemed tired and slightly breathless. He spent the day resting in bed and occasionally getting up to watch TV. He said he had no pains, he was just tired. I spent most the day and evening with him. The next day he was better and sat up all day and I began to feel it was just a low period (he had many of them), but on Tuesday he was no better and I called the doctor. She wanted to admit him to hospital but he refused. At this point Darcus appeared ... but he could not persuade Nello to change his mind.
>
> I spent the night with him, a difficult time as I began to think then he could be dying. On Wednesday morning the doctor returned. Nello seemed a little better, his chest had eased and he sat out of bed to watch some cricket. Andrew Salkey had called earlier,

but Nello was in bed and not really interested . . . Later, after lunch, the nurse called by to help to bathe and change him. He spoke very warmly and affectionately to her and said how much more comfortable he felt. I sat on his bed reading when suddenly his breathing changed. I immediately telephoned the doctor but by the time I put the phone down he had stopped breathing. His death was sudden but peaceful.[27]

It's perhaps not surprising, given the antipathy that had grown up in the extended household, that Leila Hassan Howe remembers things a little differently. In her account she sees CLR at the last as a man of the Caribbean:

So when CLR died, it was Anna, myself and Stafford, Darcus's younger brother. He was going down, he was conscious, he said he wanted milk and brandy. Anna, who was very – what can I say – middle-class and whatever, said, 'I don't think it's a good idea for him to have any alcohol.' So Darcus called me from his office and I said, 'CLR wants milk and brandy but Anna says he can't have it,' and Darcus said, 'If CLR wants brandy give it to him.' So I gave him milk and brandy and he held my hand and he thanked me. He had milk and brandy, and Stafford and I were going up and down the stairs and then Anna called down and said, 'I think he's gone.' Stafford got a mirror, the West Indian way, got the mirror and put it to his mouth to see if there was any breath and then he said, 'No, he's gone.'[28]

It was 31 May 1989. This life that had begun in the Victorian era had ended in the time of Thatcher and Reagan. In less than six months the world would change profoundly again. The Berlin Wall would come down and with it the whole edifice of Russian communism, all as CLR had foreseen. And thirty years later, much of what he imagined and hoped and fought for is thankfully taken for granted. Other parts are still the territory on which we fight.

But leave the legacy for a moment and regard Anna Grimshaw's snapshot of CLR as he was in his last months – a man, as he had been for so much of his life, both profoundly alone and profoundly loved:

> During the last few months CLR, an insomniac for most of his life, began to sleep. His books lay unopened as he slept deeply, sometimes throughout the day, in his armchair. I slept too. On many afternoons I crept across the room to nap on his bed, feeling the slow fading of his life almost as a sapping of my own strength. But there were moments of happiness, such as a whole day devoted to Beethoven or to a Mozart opera – the room filled with music, the scores laid out across his lap and those bright eyes, alert and curious, as CLR found a companion for his journey into the world of the creative imagination.[29]

Epilogue

The funeral of CLR James took place in Trinidad in early June. His will stipulated that he should be buried in Tunapuna, that the Oil Workers should take charge of arrangements, and that there should be absolutely no religion. There was some wrangling about all this – the Trinidad government, now led by A. N. R. Robinson, a one-time comrade of CLR's, wanted to give him a state funeral, but the Oil Workers won out.

The funeral events unfolded in three stages over several days. First, on 8 June, there was a brief ceremony at the airport after the plane carrying CLR's body landed. John La Rose had selected a series of extracts from Aimé Césaire's *Return to a Native Land* and the actor Errol Jones read them aloud. Then the most popular calypsonian of the moment, David Rudder, sang a tribute.*

From the airport, the funeral cortège headed south to San Fernando and the Oil Workers headquarters, just down the hill from Hobson House, where CLR had lived for a time. Here, his body lay in state for three days, while hundreds of people came to pay their respects.

On 12 June a formal celebration of CLR's life was held in the union's Palms Club. Around a thousand people attended. There were politicians and activists from all over the Caribbean, but close friends and family too. Martina Thomson came to say goodbye; Selma came to pay her own farewell to the man to whom she had been married for so long. His nephews Heno and Nello were there as well.

Darcus Howe spoke, and presided over proceedings. There were speeches from old friends like George Lamming and Marty Glaberman. There was music too: David Rudder performed again – as did CLR's

* Rudder had recently recorded a song called 'Haiti', based on his reading of *The Black Jacobins*. He sent a copy to CLR shortly before he died.

favourite calypsonian, the Mighty Sparrow, who sang the now poignant 'Federation'. There was steel band music from the Pamberi Steel Orchestra, who played Stravinsky's *Rite of Spring*. There was even a choir singing a Russian folk song.

Later that day, in pouring rain, CLR was buried in Tunapuna, in the same graveyard as his beloved mother Bessie. This was an occasion for close comrades only – Lennox Pierre, Richard Small, Robert Hill, John La Rose, Darcus Howe, Martin Glaberman and Selwyn Cudjoe among them. Finally, the poet and activist Eintou Pearl Springer read her fellow poet Martin Carter's 'Death of a Comrade', leaving these last lines in the air as CLR's body was laid in the ground:

Now from the mourning vanguard moving on
dear Comrade I salute you and I say
Death will not find us thinking that we die.

When most political thinkers die, their work quickly becomes obsolete, of interest only to historians. Not so with CLR James. In his case the world has slowly caught up with him in the thirty years since. Predictions he made came true: the Soviet Union collapsed almost immediately after his death, for instance. And the ideas he put forward in his own time – of the importance of identity alongside class, of rebellion coming from below, of the leading roles of Black people, women and youth in political struggle – have gradually made their way to the forefront of our political thinking.

Remarkably enough, this process has come to a head during the writing of this book, with a great uprising of Black protest. The killing of George Floyd, caught on camera, has sparked a furious reappraisal of the failures of Western societies to deal fairly with their Black citizens, or to acknowledge responsibility for the depredations of slavery and colonialism.

Can one guess what CLR would have made of Black Lives Matter? There's no question that he would have wholeheartedly supported it. He was always most excited by movements like this that came from below, without obvious leaders, that represented the spontaneous anger of the oppressed. He was also always appreciative of movements led by the young, that lacked the cynicism and caution of age. He would have appreciated too the leading role of women in the struggle. His vision of a better world was one that foregrounded women and young people, as well as one that was founded on principles of racial justice.

He would, I think, have cautioned against seeing all Black struggles as the same. He was absolutely in favour of solidarity between all those engaged in struggle, but was very well aware of the differences between the specific histories and situations of, say, Black Americans and Black British.

What I am sure of is that, given the chance, he would have done what he always did: talked to the people and shared his knowledge. He would have made it very clear that, to use a favourite phrase of his, 'you don't play with revolution'. Revolutionary struggle requires dedication and learning. Yes, you need to know Black history, but you also need to know Marx and Trotsky, you need to read Toni Morrison *and* Shakespeare.

Whether his moral and intellectual seriousness would have been suited to the world of social media is doubtful to say the least, but he would not, for one moment, have been surprised by the emergence of Boris Johnson or Donald Trump. Such men, he would have pointed out, were well known to Shakespeare.

At which point it's worth stating loud and clear that CLR was not just a major thinker, he was also a remarkable prose stylist. It's not simply the message that gives writing its power to change lives; it is so much more effective when it pays attention to beauty. And CLR always did that. The reason his works endure, like *Beyond a Boundary*, like *Every Cook Can Govern*, like *Minty Alley*, is in no small part because of the elegance and rhythm of his prose. Just as Gary Sobers or Rohan Kanhai took the English precepts of batsmanship and transformed them into something new, gave them an elegance that was specifically Caribbean, so does CLR's writing work the same magic on the prose of Arnold or Hazlitt.

Another easily neglected part of CLR's legacy is that he remains the most persuasive of teachers. Taking on CLR's perspective allows us to go back to the classics of the Western canon, Aeschylus and Shakespeare,

Mozart and Beethoven, and see and hear them afresh. It was CLR, for instance, who made me go back to Thackeray's *Vanity Fair* and to discover Hazlitt for the first time and see just how thrilling both writers are. After finishing the first draft of this book I went to Athens, and visited the Archaeological Museum, a place I'd been to before but, I realised now, never properly taken in. I'd just seen it as a huge collection of more or less beautiful objects. This time I did my best to look at the works there in a Jamesian way, to note the historical contexts, to trace the artistic developments and see them set against the parallel developments in philosophy and political thought. The experience was revelatory – I was fully engaged by the work, not simply admiring.

CLR returns us to who we are and challenges us as to who we could be. He exhorts us to learn from history and from culture – yes, very much including Western culture – but to make sense of it in the context of what we have learnt from the particular circumstances of our own lives. Of course his work has particular resonances for people with a colonial history, but really he challenges us all to think harder, to bring everything we know to everything we study.

And alongside CLR's work there is much to learn from his life itself. It's the life of man continually striving to see a way forward even in the darkest of times ('a way out of no way', as the African-American axiom has it). CLR continually insisted on making his own way in the world, regardless of his family's wishes, or the strictures of racism, or economic self-interest. What mattered to CLR was that he lived his life according to his own lights. It would have been an easier life if he had remained a teacher in Trinidad, or perhaps even a novelist in London. It would have been easier for a while if he'd been a Stalinist not a Trotskyist and so on. But those were the choices he made, because he could be true only to himself and his belief, honed on the cricket pitches of Port of Spain, in truth and fairness above all. He did not always live up to his own standards in his personal life, but when it came to his political principles he was incapable of cheating. He stuck fast to a vision of a world transformed by its great working masses, realising and celebrating their common humanity. Forward ever, backward never.

Acknowledgements

My first acknowledgement is to Cyril Lionel Robert James himself, the writer whose work did so much to shape how I see the world.

I first encountered Jamesian politics in 1980, when I was nineteen. I was working in an anarchist print shop in Cardiff and my co-worker Jon introduced me to the new politics of groups like Big Flame and Solidarity, whose mix of Marxist and anarchistic thinking was profoundly influenced by CLR James.

But while I'd heard his name, I didn't go so far as to seek out his books until I saw him on TV a year or two later, in the *Arena* documentary on the dub poet Michael Smith. Being a typical product of the punk-rock upheaval, I was devoted to reggae and had attended many a Rock against Racism show, so I knew something about dub poetry. I had even interviewed Linton Kwesi Johnson for our community paper in Cardiff.

CLR, as shown in the documentary, startled me: here was this old man with his red polo-neck and his shock of white hair, taking Mikey Smith and LKJ to task for disrespecting the English poetic tradition while affirming the ways they'd changed it to new and radical ends. The closing sequence – the one in which Mikey Smith, taking CLR's direction, read Wordsworth's 'Composed upon Westminster Bridge'– was revelatory. It showed me how the British radical tradition could live alongside the new worlds of reggae and punk. And if that seems obvious now, it didn't then.

I was living in London by the time I saw the documentary, working in a radical bookshop called Compendium, where I sold books by CLR James as well as new work by the Jamesian likes of Paul Gilroy and A. Sivanandan; Stuart Hall was a regular and much-loved customer.

At the same time, I started going to college and ended up writing my dissertation on John Arlott and the particular construction of liberal Englishness that *Test Match Special* had promoted, both in Britain and across the Commonwealth. It drew heavily on the work of CLR, and I had wanted to send it to him, just in case he was interested. I knew his address, at least, as we sold copies of *Race Today* in the bookshop – but I was too shy to do it, and then too busy, and then it was too late. I was first sad and then annoyed with myself when I heard the news of his death. I would love to have met him. I felt that I should at least have written to him to thank him for his work.

So, three decades later, this biography is by way of making up for that shortcoming – a way of saying thank you to the man whose influence has carried on through my own subsequent thirty years of writing. So here it is: thank you, CLR James.

There are any number of people I've talked to about CLR James over the past thirty-odd years, and thanks to all of them, but I'd particularly like to credit Pete Ayrton, most Jamesian of publishers: a friend for all that time, colleague for much of it.

In researching and writing this book I am enormously indebted to the help and example of today's foremost CLR James scholar, Christian Høgsbjerg, whose own book, *C. L. R. James in Imperial Britain*, is an absolute model of accessible scholarly writing.

Val Wilmer, photographer and writer extraordinaire, whose knowledge of twentieth-century Black British culture is unrivalled, was once again enormously helpful, not least in pointing me in the direction of Ernest Borneman. It's an honour to include one of her unpublished photos of CLR.

I am hugely indebted to all those who made the time to talk to me about CLR James. Thanks, then, to Erica James, Heno James, Robert Hill, Margaret Busby, Isa-Kae Meksin, Anna Grimshaw, Leila Hassan Howe, Farrukh Dhondy, John Cowley, Jean Besson, Kenneth Ramchand, David Abdulah, Sally Schwartz, E. Ethelbert Miller, Mike Dibb, H. O. Nazareth, Mike Brearley, Tariq Ali, Keith Hart, David Goodway, Paul Buhle, Kent Worcester, Marika Sherwood, Charles Barr, Mark Ainley et al.

For practical support I'm indebted to Alasdair Roberts for

transcriptions, and to Des Barry for his critical input. For friendship and support on my research trips to the US and Trinidad I'm indebted to Lloyd Robson, Sarah Weinman, Jon Langford, Marcia Pilliciotti, Mark Olson, Victoria Williams, Nicholas Laughlin, Georgia Popplewell and Chris Cozier.

Many thanks to the staff of the various libraries I've used – particularly the Rare Book & Manuscript Library at Columbia University; the Walter P. Reuther Research Library at Wayne State University; the Alma Jordan Library at the University of the West Indies, St. Augustine; the CLR James collection at the Oil Workers Trade Union in San Fernando, Trinidad. Also Senate House Library, University of London; the Schomburg Center for Research in Black Culture; NYU Special Collections; Lawrence B. De Graaf Center for Oral and Public History at California State University, Fullerton; LSE Library; the British Library.

Thanks to my agent Matthew Hamilton, to my editors Andreas Campomar and Claire Chesser, and to everyone at Constable. Many thanks to Zoe Gullen for a fantastically thorough and sensitive copy edit.

The actual writing of this book took place across the lockdown year of 2020. I am enormously indebted to my pub-quiz team for offering a Wednesday-night online escape portal throughout the year. Cheers Paul, Patrick, Julie, Katell, Euros, Andrew, Gruff and the occasional Rob.

Most of all thanks to Anna Davis for living with me and CLR all this time and offering such insightful editorial support to boot. I know how lucky I am.

Finally, I would like to acknowledge the receipt of a John C. Laurence Award from the Society of Authors, an organisation I wholeheartedly recommend to all writers. This award covered my travel expenses and is enormously appreciated.

Notes

Introduction

1 Walcott, 'A Tribute to C. L. R. James', in Cudjoe and Cain (eds), *C. L. R. James: His Intellectual Legacies*.
2 James, *The Black Jacobins*.

Chapter 1

1 Unpublished autobiography, C. L. R. James Collection, Alma Jordan Library, UWI St Augustine (UWI).
2 Ibid.
3 James, *Special Delivery*.
4 Unpublished autobiography.
5 James, *Beyond a Boundary*.
6 James, *Special Delivery*.
7 Unpublished autobiography.
8 Conversation with Stuart Hall. Recorded for television but never broadcast, 1976. UWI.
9 James, *Beyond a Boundary*.
10 Unpublished autobiography.

Chapter 2

1 Hamilton-Gordon, speech to Trinidad Legislative Council, 1870.
2 Unpublished autobiography, UWI.
3 Ibid.
4 Cripps, *C. L. R. James: Memories and Commentaries*.
5 Unpublished autobiography.
6 James, *Special Delivery*.
7 Unpublished autobiography.
8 James, *Beyond a Boundary*.
9 Besson, *Caribbean Reflections*.
10 Unpublished autobiography.
11 Ibid.
12 E. James, interview, 2019.
13 Unpublished autobiography.
14 James, *Beyond a Boundary*.
15 Besson, *Caribbean Reflections*.
16 Unpublished autobiography.

Chapter 3

1 Besson, *Caribbean Reflections.*
2 James, *Beyond a Boundary.*
3 Besson, *Caribbean Reflections.*
4 Unpublished autobiography, UWI.
5 Ibid.
6 James, 'The Maverick Club', *The Nation*, 28 February 1959.
7 James, *Beyond a Boundary.*

Chapter 4

1 James, *Beyond a Boundary.*
2 Unpublished autobiography, UWI.
3 Mendes, *The Autobiography of Alfred H. Mendes.*
4 Unpublished autobiography.
5 James, *Beyond a Boundary.*
6 In Mendes, *Selected Writings of Alfred H. Mendes.*
7 Unpublished autobiography.
8 Mendes, *The Autobiography of Alfred H. Mendes.*
9 Ibid.
10 R. W. Sander, 'The Turbulent Thirties in Trinidad: An Interview with Alfred H. Mendes', *World Literature Written in English*, 12:1 (April 1973).
11 Unpublished autobiography.
12 James, 'Triumph', *Trinidad*, 1:1 (Christmas 1929).
13 Sander, 'The Turbulent Thirties in Trinidad'.
14 Unpublished autobiography.
15 Ibid.
16 Letter to James, 30 June 1928. Quoted in M. Levy, 'C. L. R. James, Alfred H. Mendes and "La Diablesse"', *Journal of West Indian Literature*, 9:2 (April 2001).
17 Unpublished autobiography.
18 I. Munro and R. Sander (eds), *Kas-Kas: Interviews with Three Caribbean Writers in Texas. George Lamming, C. L. R. James, Wilson Harris* (Austin: African and Afro-American Research Institute, University of Texas at Austin, 1972).
19 In Mendes, *Selected Writings of Alfred H. Mendes.*
20 Webb, *Not Without Love.*

Chapter 5

1 de Boissière, *Life on the Edge.*
2 Mendes, *Selected Writings of Alfred H. Mendes.*
3 de Boissière, *Life on the Edge.*
4 Mendes, *Selected Writings of Alfred H. Mendes.*
5 James, *Beyond a Boundary.*
6 James, *The Life of Captain Cipriani.*

7 Unpublished autobiography, UWI.
8 James, *The Life of Captain Cipriani.*
9 de Boissière, *Life on the Edge.*
10 Gomes, *Through a Maze of Colour.*
11 'Books and Writers' column (on Arnold Bennett), *The Beacon*, 1:4 (1931).
12 James, *Beyond a Boundary.*
13 James, 'The Intelligence of the Negro: A Few Words with Dr Harland', *The Beacon*, 1:5 (1931).
14 James, *Beyond a Boundary.*
15 Ibid.

Chapter 6

1 James, *Letters from London.*
2 These pieces were later collected in *Letters from London.*
3 Unpublished autobiography, UWI.
4 James, *Letters from London.*
5 G. Valere, BBC Radio 4 interview, 19 February 2006.
6 James, *Beyond a Boundary.*
7 C. James, letter to William Gillies, 10 August 1932, Labour History Archive (LHA) Manchester.
8 James, 'The greatest of all bowlers: an impressionist sketch of S. F. Barnes', *Manchester Guardian*, 1 September 1932.
9 'Beyond a Boundary', *Omnibus*, BBC, 8 July 1976. Directed by Mike Dibb.
10 A. Lamb, interviewed by Anna Grimshaw, c. 1985.
11 James, *80th Birthday Lectures.*
12 James, *Beyond a Boundary.*

Chapter 7

1 Constantine, *Cricket and I.*
2 Unpublished autobiography, UWI.
3 'The Old World and the New', in James, *At the Rendezvous of Victory.*
4 Letter to *The Listener*, May 1933
5 James, 'A century of freedom?', *The Listener*, May 1933.
6 'The Old World and the New'.
7 Unpublished autobiography.
8 'A revolutionary youth – Harold Edwards'. Available at: https://libcom.org/history/revolutionary-youth
9 Unpublished autobiography.
10 Borneman's recollections are in *Die Ur-Szene.* Translations by John L. Williams.

Chapter 8

1 James, 'Foreword to the 1980 Edition', *The Black Jacobins.*
2 C. James, letter to Leonard Woolf, 3 December 1933, Columbia University (CU).

3 'Foreword to the 1980 Edition'.
4 James, 'My Knowledge of Damas is Unique', in D. L. Racine (ed.), *Léon-Gontran Damas, 1912–1978: Father of Negritude: A Memorial Casebook* (Washington DC: University Press of America, 1979).
5 Unpublished autobiography, UWI.
6 Ibid.
7 *Sunday Guardian (Trinidad)*, 17 June 1934.
8 *Nelson Leader*, 16 March 1934.
9 G. O'Connor, *The Secret Woman: A Life of Peggy Ashcroft* (London: Weidenfeld & Nicolson, 1997).
10 James, 'Paul Robeson: Black Star', *Black World* (November 1970).
11 Cripps, *C. L. R. James: Memories and Commentaries.*
12 Borneman, *Die Ur-Szene.* Translation by John L. Williams.

Chapter 9

1 Cripps, *C. L. R. James: Memories and Commentaries.*
2 Unpublished autobiography, UWI.
3 Cripps, *C. L. R. James: Memories and Commentaries.*
4 F. Brockway, *Towards Tomorrow: The Autobiography of Fenner Brockway* (London: Hart-Davis, MacGibbon, 1977).
5 Warburg, *An Occupation for Gentlemen.*
6 Unpublished autobiography.
7 James, 'Paul Robeson: Black Star', *Black World* (November 1970).
8 Warburg, *An Occupation for Gentlemen.*
9 D. James, 'Marxist Group Internal Report', 20 February 1936.
10 Unpublished autobiography.
11 H. Wicks, *Keeping My Head: The Memoirs of a British Bolshevik* (London: Socialist Platform, 1992).
12 A. Richardson, 'C. L. R. James and British Trotskyism' (London: Socialist Platform, 1987).
13 Warburg, *An Occupation for Gentlemen.*
14 James, *Special Delivery.*
15 James, *World Revolution.*
16 Unpublished autobiography.
17 P. Davison (ed.), *The Complete Works of George Orwell: Volume XI: A Kind of Compulsion, 1903–1936* (London: Secker & Warburg, 1986).

Chapter 10

1 Unpublished autobiography, UWI.
2 Cripps, *C. L. R. James: Memories and Commentaries.*
3 Ibid.
4 Unpublished autobiography.
5 Cripps, *C. L. R. James: Memories and Commentaries.*

6 Unpublished autobiography.
7 Adi, *Pan-Africanism*.
8 'Towards the Seventh: The Pan-African Congress', in James, *At the Rendezvous of Victory*.
9 Makonnen and King, *Pan-Africanism from Within*.
10 Ibid.
11 Unpublished autobiography.
12 James, 'Black Intellectuals in Britain', in Parekh (ed.), *Colour, Culture and Consciousness*.
13 Høgsbjerg, *C. L. R. James in Imperial Britain*.
14 Unpublished autobiography.
15 Ibid.
16 James P. Cannon letter to Charles Curtiss, 6 March 1940. Available at: https://www.marxists.org/archive/cannon/index.htm.

Chapter 11

1 In Mendes, *Selected Writings of Alfred H. Mendes*.
2 Bernard (ed.), *Remember Me to Harlem*.
3 Unpublished autobiography, UWI.
4 James, 'Black Intellectuals in Britain', in Parekh (ed.), *Colour, Culture and Consciousness*.
5 In Mendes, *Selected Writings of Alfred H. Mendes*.
6 Worcester, *C. L. R. James: A Political Biography*.
7 Unpublished autobiography.
8 G. M. Slezak and D. W. Jackanicz, '"The Town is Beastly and the Weather was Vile": Bertrand Russell in Chicago, 1938–9', *Russell*, 25–28 (1977).
9 Webb, *Not Without Love*.
10 Trotsky, *Leon Trotsky – Collected Writings (1929–1940)*.
11 Unpublished reminiscence, Raya Dunayevskaya Papers, Walter P. Reuther Library, Wayne State University (WSU).
12 Unpublished autobiography.
13 Ibid.
14 Trotsky, *Collected Writings*.
15 James, *Special Delivery*.
16 Ibid.
17 Unpublished autobiography.
18 Letter to Trotsky, 1930, Raya Dunayevskaya Papers.

Chapter 12

1 Trotsky, *Leon Trotsky – Collected Writings (1929–1940)*.
2 Unpublished autobiography, UWI.
3 'The Man Trotsky', 1938 article, Raya Dunayevskaya Papers, WSU.
4 Letter to Trotsky, 1939, Raya Dunayevskaya Papers.

5 A. Richardson, 'C. L. R. James and British Trotskyism' (London: Socialist Platform, 1987).
6 James, *Special Delivery*.
7 Unpublished reminiscence, Raya Dunayevskaya Papers, Walter P. Reuther Library, WSU.
8 James P. Cannon letter to Charles Curtiss, 6 March 1940. Available at: https://www.marxists.org/archive/cannon/index.htm.
9 James, *Special Delivery*.
10 Cripps, *C. L. R. James: Memories and Commentaries*.
11 James, *Special Delivery*.
12 Macdonald, *Memoirs of a Revolutionist*.
13 Perspectives and Proposals', in James, *Marxism for Our Times*.

Chapter 13

1 James, *Special Delivery*.
2 Boggs, *Living for Change*.
3 James, *Special Delivery*.
4 Boggs, *Living for Change*.
5 Weir, *Singlejack Solidarity*. James, *Special Delivery*.
6 Ibid.
7 Boggs, *Living for Change*.
8 James, 'Socialism and the National Question', *The New International*, October 1943.
9 Boggs, *Living for Change*.
10 James, *Special Delivery*.
11 Webb, *Not Without Love*.

Chapter 14

1 James, *Special Delivery*.
2 Webb, *Not Without Love*.
3 C. Webb letter to Anna Grimshaw, 18 March 1986, CU.
4 Webb, *Not Without Love*.
5 Ibid.
6 James, *Special Delivery*.
7 Ibid.
8 Webb, *Not Without Love*.
9 C. Webb, letter to Robert Hill, 1986, CU.
10 Webb, *Not Without Love*.
11 Ibid.
12 James, *Special Delivery*.
13 This document is included in ibid.
14 Boggs, *Living for Change*.
15 James, *Special Delivery*.
16 Ibid.

17 Ibid.
18 Ibid.
19 Ibid.
20 Ibid.

Chapter 15

1 James, *Special Delivery*.
2 James, 'The Revolutionary Answer to the Negro Problem in the United States', *Fourth International*, December 1948.
3 James, *Notes on Dialectics*.
4 Interviewed by Paul Buhle. Tape held in Tamiment Library, NYU.
5 Webb, *Not Without Love*.
6 C. James, letter to Daniel Guérin, 17 January 1950, UWI.
7 E. Raskin, letter to CLR James, 17 December 1949, UWI.
8 C. James, letter to Constance Webb, undated (1950), CU.
9 C. Webb, annotation – probably 1980s – on a letter from CLR James originally written on 16 April 1951, Schomburg Center for Research in Black Culture, New York.
10 I. K. Meskin, interview, 2019.
11 S. James, interview, 2020.
12 S. James, *Sex, Race and Class*.
13 James, *Special Delivery*.
14 C. James, letter to Constance Webb, 16 April 1951, Schomburg Center for Research in Black Culture.
15 Webb, *Not Without Love*.
16 C. James, letter to Lyman Paine, undated, WSU.
17 Webb, *Not Without Love*.
18 J. Dwyer, 'Johnsonism: A Political Appraisal', pamphlet, April 1956.
19 C. and D. R. James, 'The Balance Sheet Completed: Ten Years of American Trotskyism', August 1951.
20 Cannon, 'Factional Struggle and Party Leadership, *Fourth International*, November 1953.
21 Boggs, *Living for Change*.
22 R. Potter, letter to CLR James, 15 February 1952, CU.
23 C. James, letter to Lyman Paine, 2 June 1952, WSU.
24 James, *Mariners, Renegades and Castaways*.
25 Ibid.
26 C. James, letter to Raya Dunayevskaya, undated, WSU.
27 S. James, interview, 2020.
28 Webb, *Not Without Love*.
29 Ibid.
30 James, *Mariners, Renegades and Castaways*.
31 Webb, *Not Without Love*.

Chapter 16

1 From Security Service records, held at the National Archives: KV 2/1825.
2 C. James, letter to Grace Lee, undated, WSU.
3 C. James, letter to Grace Lee, 3 August 1953, WSU.
4 C. James, letter to Lyman Paine, 23 November 1953, WSU.
5 C. James, letter to US comrades, 14 Oct 1953, WSU.
6 C. James, letter to Lyman Paine, 4 November 1953, WSU.
7 Of *Mariners, Renegades, and Castaways*, the chapter that describes CLR's experiences on Ellis Island.
8 C. James, letter to US comrades, 20 December 1953, WSU.
9 Ibid.
10 Ibid.
11 C. James, letter to US comrades, 1 January 1954, WSU.
12 James, 'The New Monthlies', *Saturday Review*, 22 May 1954.
13 C. James, letter to Grace Lee, 1 January 1954, WSU.
14 C. James, letter to Lyman Payne, 6 February 1954, WSU.
15 G. Lee, letter to Raya Dunayevskaya, 25 February 1954, WSU.
16 Ibid.
17 G. Lee, letter to Raya Dunayevskaya, 6 April 1954, WSU.
18 G. Lee, letter to CLR James, 26 August 1954, WSU.
19 G. Lee, letter to Raya Dunayevskaya, 15 June 1954, WSU.
20 James, *Special Delivery*.
21 C. James, letter to Grace Lee, 6 October 1954 (rec), WSU.
22 C. James, letter to Lyman Paine, October 1954, WSU.

Chapter 17

1 James, *Every Cook Can Govern*.
2 C. James, letter to Lyman Paine, 4 August 1955, WSU.
3 C. James, letter to US comrades, 15 July 1955, WSU.
4 D. Scott, 'The Sovereignty of the Imagination: An Interview with George Lamming', *Small Axe*, 6:2 (September 2002).
5 Boggs, *Living for Change*.
6 C. James, letter to CLR James Jr, undated but probably around November 1955, UWI.
7 C. James Jr, letter to Constance Webb, 24 July 1956, CU.
8 Dorothy Padmore's recollections are in L. James, *George Padmore and Decolonization from Below: Pan-Africanism, the Cold War, and the End of Empire* (London: Palgrave Macmillan, 2015).

Chapter 18

1 From the speech 'Reflections on Pan-Africanism', 20 November 1973. Transcript available at: https://www.marxists.org/archive/james-clr/works/1973/panafricanism.htm

2 C. James, letter to US comrades, 3 March 1957, WSU.
3 Ibid.
4 G. Padmore, letter to Richard Wright, 9 February 1955, Richard Wright Papers, Beinecke Rare Book and Manuscript Library, Yale University.
5 D. Padmore, letter to Ellen Wright, 9 April 1957, Richard Wright Papers.
6 C. James, letter to Grace Lee, March 1957, WSU.
7 C. James, letter to US comrades, 3 March 1957.
8 H. Muir, 'Martin Luther King in London', *Guardian*, 2 December 2014.
9 C. James, letter to US comrades, 25 March 1957, WSU.
10 C. James, letter to US comrades, March 1957, WSU.
11 C. James, letter to Marty Glaberman, 12 April 1957, WSU.
12 C. James, letter to Lyman Paine, 26 May 1957, WSU.
13 G. Lee, letter to US comrades, 2 May 1957, WSU.
14 C. James, letter to Lyman Paine, 29 November 1957, WSU.
15 C. James, letter to Freddy Paine, 13 December 1957, WSU.
16 C. James, letter to David Thomson, 24 February 1958.
17 C. James, letter to Lyman Paine, 26 March (?) 1958, WSU.
18 C. James, letter to US comrades, 20 March 1958.
19 C. James, letter to Lyman Paine, 26 March (?) 1958.
20 Ibid.
21 L. Paine, letter to CLR James, April 1958, WSU.

Chapter 19

1 C. James, letter to Lyman Paine, Constance Webb and Grace Lee, 18 July 1958, WSU.
2 H. Toledano, *In and Around the Caribbean: Stories, People and Places* (IUniverse 2012)
3 C. James, letter to Lyman Paine, Constance Webb and Grace Lee, 18 July 1958.
4 Ibid.
5 E. James, interview, 2019.
6 C. James, letter to Lyman Paine, Constance Webb and Grace Lee, 18 July 1958.
7 Ibid.
8 H. James, interview, 2019.
9 Brown, *Angry Men – Laughing Men.*
10 Manley, *Drumblair.*
11 C. Webb, letter to Marty Glaberman, 2001, CU.

Chapter 20

1 C. James, letter to 'B', September 1959, UWI.
2 James, *Beyond a Boundary.*
3 *The Nation (Trinidad)*, 5 February 1960.
4 *The Nation (Trinidad)*, 4 March 1960.
5 James, *Party Politics in the West Indies.*
6 Ibid.

7 C. Webb, letter to CLR James, July 1960, CU.
8 Boggs, *Living for Change*.
9 N. Manley, letter to CLR James, 24 May 1960, Senate House Library.
10 N. Manley, letter to CLR James, 10 June 1960, Senate House Library.
11 Boggs, *Living for Change*.
12 C. James, *Modern Politics*.
13 I. K. Meskin, interview, 2019.
14 Ibid.
15 From E. E. Williams (ed. P. K. Sutton), *Forged from the Love of Liberty: Selected Speeches of Dr Eric Williams* (Port of Spain: Longman Caribbean, 1981)
16 R. Lusty, letter to CLR James, 29 May 1961, UWI.
17 C. James, letter to US comrades, 5 June 1961, WSU.
18 C. James, letter to Grace Lee Boggs, 22 October 1961, WSU.

Chapter 21

1 S. French, 'CLR and Selma: An Unfinished Reminiscence', *Caribbean Review*, 5 June 2011.
2 C. James, letter to Lyman Paine, 3 January 1963, WSU.
3 C. James, letter to John Arlott, 29 December 1962, CU.
4 '*Othello* and *The Merchant of Venice*', in James, *Spheres of Existence*.
5 L. Gutteridge, letter to CLR James, 26 April 1963, and John Arlott, letter to CLR James, 13 February 1964. Both UWI.
6 *Observer*, 2 June 1963.
7 C. James, letter to Alan Ross, 18 May 1963, UWI.
8 *Guardian*, 17 May 1963.
9 C. James, letter to *Guardian*, 18 May 1963, CU.
10 E. W. Swanton, 'Not Quite What I Call Cricket', *Daily Telegraph*, 1963.
11 *Trinidad Guardian*, 28 July 1963.
12 O. James, letter to CLR James, 19 September 1963, CU.
13 C. James, letter to Sheila Innes, 20 May 1963, CU.
14 James, 'The 1963 West Indians', *Journal of the Cricket Society* (spring 1963).
15 C. James, letter to Sydney King, 10 April 1963, CU.
16 C. Webb, letter to CLR James, 19 May 1963, CU.
17 C. James, letter to Constance Webb, 1 September 1963, CU.
18 G Rawick, letter to Marty Glaberman, 6 December 1963, WSU.
19 Ibid.
20 Rawick, 'Personal Notes', in Buhle (ed.), *C. L. R. James: His Life and Work*.
21 G. Rawick, letter to Marty Glaberman, 3 January 1964, WSU.
22 C. James, letter to US comrades.
23 'Black Freedom and the WPA Slave Narratives: Dave Roediger Interviews George Rawick', in Don Fitz and Dave Roediger (eds), *Within the Shell of the Old: Essays on Workers' Self-Organization: A Salute to George Rawick* (Chicago: Charles H. Kerr, 1990).

24 'Appendix: From Toussaint L'Ouverture to Fidel Castro', in James, *The Black Jacobins*.
25 'Letter to V. S. Naipaul', in James, *Cricket*.
26 Naipaul, *A Way in the World*.

Chapter 22

1 C. James, letter to John Arlott, 24 February 1965, WSU.
2 E. James, interview 2019
3 C. James, letter to Marty Glaberman, 13 October 1965, WSU.
4 S. French, 'CLR and Selma: An Unfinished Reminiscence', *Caribbean Review*, 5 June 2011.
5 N. Girvan, 'Remembering C. L. R. James', seminar paper, Department of Behavioural Sciences, UWI St Augustine, 8 May 2000.
6 G. Lamming, letter to Marty Glaberman, July 1966, WSU.
7 C. James, letter to Selma James, 11 November 1966, UWI.
8 M. Glaberman, letter to Selma James, October 1966, WSU.

Chapter 23

1 C. James, letter to Willie Gorman, 12 May 1967, WSU.
2 'Black Power', in James, *Spheres of Existence*.
3 James, *You Don't Play with Revolution*.
4 *The Cricketer*, May 1967.
5 C. James, letter to Marty Glaberman, 4 June 1967, WSU.
6 T. Ali, 'A Conversation with C. L. R. James', *Socialist Challenge*, 3 July 1980.
7 'Black Power'.
8 A. Salkey, *Havana Journal* (London: Penguin, 1971).
9 C. James, letter to Marty Glaberman, 24 February 1968, WSU.
10 C. James, letter to Marty Glaberman, 2 May 1968, WSU.
11 C. James, letter to US comrades, May 1968, WSU.
12 L. Ron Hubbard, letter to CLR James, 24 June 1968, CU.
13 C. James, letter to Constance Webb, 2 July 1968, CU.
14 C. James, letters to Rowland Bowen, 20 May and 25 June 1968, UWI.
15 C. James, letter to Marty Glaberman, 31 July 1968, UWI.
16 James, *Nkrumah and the Ghana Revolution*.
17 C. James, letter to George Rawick, 5 July 1968, WSU.
18 T. Turner, radio interview for Radio4all.
19 C. James, letter to George Rawick, October 1968, UWI.

Chapter 24

1 *Washington Post*, 6 March 1969.
2 J. Bracey, letter to CLR James, 16 May 1969, UWI.
3 P. Buhle, interview, 2020.
4 George Rawick interviewed by Paul Buhle, 1987. Available at: https://soundcloud.com/user-488941364/sets/george-rawick 'The Olympia Statues, Picasso's *Guernica*

and the Frescoes of Michelangelo in the Capella Paolina', in James, *The Future in the Present (Selected Writings)* (London: Allison & Busby, 1977).
5 J. Bracey, 'Nello', *Urgent Tasks*, 12 (1981).
6 V. Harding, 'Conversation', *Urgent Tasks*, 12 (1981).
7 R. Hill, interview, 2019.
8 M. Glaberman, letter to CLR James, 4 March 1970, WSU.
9 M. Glaberman, letter to Selma James, 2 March 1970, WSU.
10 M. Glaberman, letter to Facing Reality comrades, 27 April 1970, WSU.
11 M. Kadalie, interview, 2010.
12 C. James, letter to Constance Webb, 17 April 1970, CU.
13 M. Phillips and T. Phillips, *Windrush: The Irresistible Rise of Multi-Racial Britain* (London: HarperCollins, 1999).
14 Bunce and Field, *Renegade*.
15 James, 'The Old World at the New', in *At the Rendezvous of Victory*.
16 R. Hill, interview, 2019
17 T. Kosinec, interview, 2020.
18 P. McGovern, interview, 2021.
19 R. Jones, interview, 2021.
20 E. Pearlstien, letter to Judge Gagliardi, 16 February 1973, CU.
21 Heno James, interview, 2019.
22 Interview with Geri Augusto. Available at: http://www.noeasyvictories.org/interviews/int10_augusto.php
23 Geri Augusto, 'Drafting the Call', SNCC Digital Gateway: Our Voices. Available at: https://snccdigital.org/wp-content/uploads/2017/12/Internationalism_Transcript04.pdf
24 E. Miller, interview, 2020.

Chapter 25

1 M. Dibb, interview, 2020.
2 Ibid.
3 Dr Eric Williams, letter to the British High Commissioner Sir Christopher Diggines, 27 February 1976, Collection of Mike Dibb.
4 M. Dibb, interview, 2020.
5 'Beyond a Boundary', BBC *Omnibus* documentary, 1976. Directed by Mike Dibb.
6 M. Dibb, interview, 2020.
7 C. James, letter to CLR James Jr, 18 February 1976, CU.
8 E. Pearlstien, letter to 'Alfred', 3 December 1976, CU.
9 C. James, letter to Lyman Paine, 1 December 1976, WSU.
10 S. Schwartz, interview, 2020.
11 R. Hill, interview, 2019.
12 E. Miller, interview, 2020.

Chapter 26

1 D. Abdulah, interview, 2020.
2 C. James, letter to Judy Ramirez, 5 August 1979, OWTU Archive, San Fernando.
3 C. Webb, letter to CLR James, 28 August 1979, OWTU Archive.
4 D. Abdulah, interview, 2020.
5 L. H. Howe, interview, 2020.
6 C. James, letter to Judy Ramirez, 14 January 1980, OWTU Archive.
7 C. James, letter to Renee Hausmann, 25 March 1980, OWTU Archive.
8 *Guardian*, 23 June 1980.
9 James, *80th Birthday Lectures*.
10 F. Dhondy, interview, 2019.
11 Dhondy, *C. L. R. James*.
12 James, 'Three Black Women Writers', in *At the Rendezvous of Victory*.
13 Dhondy, *C. L. R. James*.
14 H. Nazareth, interview, 2020.
15 C. James, letter to Constance Webb, 9 July 1982, CU.
16 D. Abdulah, interview, 2020.

Chapter 27

1 L. H. Howe, interview, 2020.
2 R. Hill, letter to Constance Webb, 14 June 1982, CU.
3 C. Webb, letter to Robert Hill, 13 July 1982, CU.
4 C. James, letter to Robert Hill, 10 September 1982, CU.
5 C. James, letter to Martina Thomson, 28 October 1982, UWI.
6 L. H. Howe, interview, 2020.
7 F. Dhondy, interview, 2019.
8 P. Buhle, interview, 2019.
9 J. Murray, letter to Robert Hill, undated (some time in June 1983), CU.
10 J. Murray, letter to to Robert Hill, 17 July 1983, CU.
11 *Guardian*, 25 July 1983.
12 F. Dhondy, interview, 2019
13 J. Murray, letter to Robert Hill, 17 July 1983, CU.
14 A. Grimshaw, interview, 2019.
15 A. Grimshaw, K. Worcester and J. Murray, 'C.L.R. James in the 1980s: a conversation with Anna Grimshaw', pamphlet, 1991.
16 A. Grimshaw, interview, 1991.
17 A. Grimshaw, interview, 2019.
18 L. H. Howe, interview, 2020.

Chapter 28

1 C. James, letter to Peter Fryer, 13 April 1984, UWI.
2 L. H. Howe, interview, 2020.
3 M. Thomson, postcard to CLR James, 2 September 1988, UWI.

4 Wollheim, *Sigmund Freud*.

5 A. Grimshaw, interview, 2019.

6 Y. Brewster, 'Directing the Black Jacobins'. Available at: https://www.bl.uk/20th-century-literature/articles/directing-the-black-jacobins

7 Boggs, *Living for Change*.

8 G. L. Boggs, talk at Riverside Studios, 20 February 1986. Transcript at WSU.

9 James, preface to the programme for *The Black Jacobins*, Riverside Studios, 21 February–15 March 1986

10 *Guardian*, 17 February 1986.

11 A. Grimshaw, letter to Constance Webb, 21 May 1986, Columbia University (CU).

12 A. Grimshaw, interview 2019

13 Ibid.

14 A. Grimshaw, letter to Constance Webb, 27 June 1986, CU.

15 L. H. Howe, interview, 2020.

16 E. Miller, interview, 2020.

17 L. H. Howe, interview, 2020.

18 A. Grimshaw, letter to Constance Webb, 15 December 1986, CU.

19 A. Grimshaw, interview, 2019.

20 A. Grimshaw, letter to Constance Webb, 8 February 1988, CU.

21 K. Hart, interview, 2019.

22 J. Murray, 'The Boy at the Window', in Farred (ed.), *Rethinking C. L. R. James*.

23 A. Grimshaw, letter to Constance Webb, undated (presumably late 1988), CU.

24 K. Hart, interview, 2019.

25 A. Grimshaw, letter to Constance Webb, 6 March 1989, CU.

26 G. Childs, 'Black Intellectual History and STEM: A Conversation with Dr Chandra Prescod-Weinstein', Black Perspectives, 29 August 2016. Available at: https://www.aaihs.org/black-intellectual-history-and-stem-a-conversation-with-chanda-prescod-weinstein/

27 A. Grimshaw, unpublished letter to Constance Webb, 2 June 1989, CU.

28 L. H. Howe, interview, 2020.

29 A. Grimshaw, 'CLR James, 1901–1989: A Personal Memoir', in Cudjoe and Cain (eds), *C. L. R. James: His Intellectual Legacies*.

Bibliography

Books by CLR James

James, CLR (1932). *The Life of Captain Cipriani: An Account of British Government in the West Indies*. Nelson: Cartmel & Co.

James, CLR (1936). *Minty Alley*. London: Secker & Warburg

James, CLR (1937). *World Revolution 1917–1936*, London: Martin Secker & Warburg

James, CLR (1938). *The Black Jacobins*. London: Secker & Warburg

James, CLR (1953). *Mariners, Renegades & Castaways: The Story of Herman Melville and the World We Live In*. New York: CLR James

James, CLR (1956). *Every Cook Can Govern*. Detroit: Correspondence Publishing Co.

James, CLR, Lee, Grace and Castoriadis, Cornelius (1958). *Facing Reality*. Detroit: Correspondence Publishing Co.

James, CLR (1960). *Modern Politics*. Port of Spain: PNM Publishing

James, CLR (1962). *Party Politics in the West Indies*. Port of Spain: CLR James

James, CLR (1963). *Beyond a Boundary*. London: Hutchinson

James, CLR (1969). *A History of Pan-African Revolt*. Washington DC: Drum and Spear Press

James, CLR (1970). *Notes on Dialectics*. Detroit: Friends of Facing Reality

James, CLR (1977) *The Future In The Present*. London: Allison & Busby

James, CLR (1977). *Nkrumah and the Ghana Revolution*. London: Allison & Busby

James, CLR (1980). *Spheres of Existence*. London: Allison & Busby

James, CLR (1984). *80th Birthday Lectures*. London: RT Publications

James, CLR (1984). *At the Rendezvous of Victory*. London, Allison & Busby

James, CLR (ed. Grimshaw, A.) (1986). *Cricket*. London: Allison & Busby

James, CLR, Dunayevskaya, Raya and Lee, Grace (1986). *State Capitalism and World Revolution*. Chicago: Charles H. Kerr

James, CLR (1993). *American Civilization*. Oxford: Blackwell

James, CLR (ed. Grimshaw, A.) (1996). *Special Delivery: The Letters of C. L. R. James to Constance Webb, 1939–1948*. Oxford: Blackwell

James, CLR (ed. McLemee, S.) (1996). *C. L. R. James on the 'Negro Question'*. Jackson: University Press of Mississippi

James, CLR (ed. Grimshaw, A.) (1997). *The C. L. R. James Reader*. Oxford: Blackwell

James, CLR (ed. Glaberman, M.) (1999). *Marxism for Our Times*. Jackson: University Press of Mississippi

James, CLR (ed. Laughlin, N.) (2003). *Letters from London*. Port of Spain: Prospect Press

James, CLR (ed. Webb, C.) (2006). *The Nobbie Stories for Children and Adults*. Lincoln: University of Nebraska Press

James, CLR (ed. Austin, D.) (2009). *You Don't Play with Revolution: The Montreal Lectures of C. L. R. James*. Oakland: AK Press

James, CLR (ed. Høgsbjerg, C.) (2013). *Toussaint L'Ouverture: A Play in Three Acts*. Durham, NC: Duke University Press

James, CLR (ed. McLemee, S. and Le Blanc, P.) (2018). *C. L. R. James and Revolutionary Marxism: Selected Writings of C. L. R. James 1939–1949*. Chicago: Haymarket

Books concerning CLR James

Buhle, Paul (ed.) (1986). *C. L. R. James: His Life and Work*. London: Allison & Busby

Buhle, Paul (1989). *C. L. R. James: The Artist as Revolutionary*. London: Verso

Cripps, Louise (1997). *C. L. R. James: Memories and Commentaries*. London: Cornwall Books

Cudjoe, Selwyn R. and Cain, William E. (eds) (1995). *C. L. R. James: His Intellectual Legacies*. Amherst: University of Massachusetts Press

Dhondy, Farrukh (2001). *C.L.R. James: A Life*. London: Weidenfeld & Nicolson.

Douglas, Rachel (2019). *Making The Black Jacobins*. Durham, NC: Duke University Press

Farred, Grant (1996). *Rethinking C. L. R. James*. Cambridge, MA: Blackwell

Featherstone, David, Gair, Christopher, Høgsbjerg, Christian and Smith, Andrew (2018). *Marxism, Colonialism, and Cricket: C. L. R. James's Beyond a Boundary*. Durham, NC: Duke University Press

Forsdick, Charles and Høgsbjerg, Christian (eds) (2017). *The Black Jacobins Reader*. Durham, NC: Duke University Press

Henry, Paget and Buhle, Paul (eds) (1992). *C. L. R. James's Caribbean*. Durham, NC: Duke University Press

Høgsbjerg, Christian (2014). *C. L. R. James in Imperial Britain*. Durham, NC: Duke University Press

Renton, Dave (2013). *C. L. R. James: Cricket's Philosopher King*. London: Haus

Rosengarten, Frank (2010). *Urbane Revolutionary: C. L. R. James and the Struggle for a New Society*. Jackson: University Press of Mississippi

Worcester, Kent (1996). *C. L. R. James: A Political Biography*. Albany: SUNY Press

Young, James D. (1999). *The World of C. L. R. James: The Unfragmented Vision*. Glasgow: Clydeside Press

Books consulted

Adi, Hakim (2018). *Pan-Africanism: A History*. London: Bloomsbury

Allen, David Rayvern (1994). Arlott: The Authorised Biography. London: HarperCollins.

Ayrton, Pete (2016). *¡No Pasarán!: Writings from the Spanish Civil War*. London: Serpent's Tail

Banton, M. (1955). *The Coloured Quarter*. London: Cape

Bennett, Arnold (1926). *Lord Raingo*. London: Cassell

Bennett, Dorothy Cheston (1935). *Arnold Bennett*. London: Cape

Bernard, Emily (ed.) (2002). *Remember Me to Harlem: The Letters of Langston Hughes and Carl Van Vechten, 1925–1964*. New York: Vintage

Besson, William. W. (1989). *Caribbean Reflections: The Life and Times of a Trinidad Scholar (1901–1986). An Oral History Narrated by William W. Besson*. Edited and Introduced by Jean Besson. Foreword by C. L. R. James. London: Karia Press

Boggs, Grace Lee (2016). *Living for Change*. Minneapolis: University of Minnesota Press

Boggs, James, Boggs, Grace Lee, Paine, Freddy and Paine, Lyman (1978). *Conversations in Maine*. Boston: South End Press

Borneman, Ernest (2015). *Die Ur-Szene*. Frankfurt: S. Fischer Verlag

Brown, Wenzell (1947). *Angry Men – Laughing Men*. New York: Greenberg

Bunce, Robin and Field, Paul (2017). *Renegade: The Life and Times of Darcus Howe*. London: Bloomsbury

Cardus, Neville (1947). *Autobiography*. London: Collins

Chisholm, Anne (1979). *Nancy Cunard*. London: Sidgwick & Jackson

Constantine, Learie (1933). *Cricket and I*. London: P. Allan

Cunninghame Graham, Jean (2004). *Gaucho Laird: The Life of R. B. Cunninghame Graham*. Glasgow, KY: Long Riders' Guild Press

de Boissière, Ralph (1990). *Crown Jewel*. London: Pan

de Boissière, Ralph (2010). *Life on the Edge*. Caroni: Lexicon
De-Light, D. and Thomas, P. (2005). *The Rough Guide to Trinidad and Tobago*. London: Rough Guides
Duberman, Martin B. (1996). *Paul Robeson*. New York: The New Press
Field, Paul, Bunce, Robin, Hassan, Leila and Peacock, Margaret (2019). *Here to Stay, Here to Fight: A Race Today Anthology*. London: Pluto Press
French, Patrick (2008). *The World is What it is: The Authorized Biography of V. S. Naipaul*. London: Picador
Fry, C. B. (1986). *Life Worth Living: Some Phrases of an Englishman*. London: Pavilion
Gomes, Albert (1974). *Through a Maze of Colour*. Port of Spain: Key Caribbean Publications
Green, Nan (2004). *A Chronicle of Small Beer: The Memoirs of Nan Green*. Nottingham: Trent Editions
Hamilton, Cynthia (2013). *Every Cook Can Govern*, Bloomington: Trafford
Hazlitt, William (1985). *Selected Writings*. London: Penguin
Himes, Chester and Fabre, Michel (1995). *Conversations with Chester Himes*. Jackson: University Press of Mississippi.
Høgsbjerg, Christian (2014). *Chris Braithwaite: Mariner, Renegade and Castaway*. London: Socialist History Society
Hurston, Zora Neale (1979). *I Love Myself When I am Laughing*. New York: The Feminist Press
James, Selma (2012). *Sex, Race and Class: The Perspective of Winning: A Selection of Writings, 1952–2011*. Oakland: PM Press
Jelly-Schapiro, Joshua (2017). *Island People: The Caribbean and the World*. Edinburgh: Canongate
Lahr, Sheila (2015). *Yealm: A Sorterbiography*. London: UNKANT Publishers
Lamartine, A. D. (1870). *Toussaint Louverture Poëme Dramatique*. Paris: Michel Lévy Frères
Lamming, George (1954). *The Emigrants*. London: Michael Joseph
Lamming, George (1960). *The Pleasures of Exile*. London: Michael Joseph
Lamming, George (1972). *Natives of My Person*. London: Longman
Leavis, F. R. (1952). *The Common Pursuit*. London: Chatto & Windus
Little, K. L. (1948). *Negroes in Britain*. London: Kegan Paul, Trench, Trubner & Co.
Macdonald, Dwight (1957). *Memoirs of a Revolutionist: Essays in Political Criticism*. New York: Farrar, Straus & Cudahy
Macinnes, Colin (1979). *Out of the Way: Later Essays*. London: Martin Brian & O'Keeffe
Makonnen, Ras & King, Kenneth (1973). *Pan-Africanism from Within*. Oxford: Oxford University Press
Manley, Rachel (2004). *Drumblair: Memories of a Jamaican Childhood*. Kingston: I. Randle
Mannin, Ethel (1945). *Comrade O Comrade*. London: Jarrolds
Martin, Tony (2007). *Amy Ashwood Garvey – Pan-Africanist, Feminist and Mrs Marcus Garvey*. Dover, MA: Majority Press
Mason, Peter (2008). *Learie Constantine*. Oxford: Macmillan Caribbean
McCabe, Cameron (1986). *The Face on the Cutting-Room Floor*. London: Penguin
Mendes, Alfred. H. (ed. Levy, M.) (2002). *The Autobiography of Alfred H. Mendes: 1897–1991*. Mona: University of the West Indies Press
Mendes, Alfred H. (ed. Levy, M.) (2013). *Selected Writings of Alfred H. Mendes*. Mona: University of the West Indies Press
Mittelhölzer, Edgar (1950). A Morning at the Office. London: Hogarth Press
Naipaul, V. S. (1962). *The Middle Passage: Impressions of Five Societies – British, French, and Dutch – in the West Indies and South America*. London: André Deutsch
Naipaul, V. S. (2007). *Ways of Looking and Feeling*. London: Picador
Naipaul, V. S. (2003). *The Writer and the World: Essays*. London: Picador
Naipaul, V. S. (2011). *A Way in the World: A Sequence*. London: Picador

Parekh, B. C. (ed.) (1974). *Colour, Culture and Consciousness: Immigrant Intellectuals in Britain*. London. Allen & Unwin

Pilkington, E. (1988). *Beyond the Mother Country: West Indians and the Notting Hill White Riots*. London: I.B. Tauris.

Rawick, George P. (1974). *From Sundown to Sunup: The Making of the Black Community*. Westport: Greenwood

Sander, Reinhard W. (1978). *From Trinidad: An Anthology of Early West Indian Writing*. London: Hodder & Stoughton

Schwarz, Bill (ed.) (2003). *West Indian Intellectuals in Britain*. Manchester: Manchester University Press

Sinclair, Neil (1993). *The Tiger Bay Story*. Cardiff: Butetown History & Arts Project

Talalay, Kathryn (1998). *Composition in Black and White: The Life of Philippa Schuyler*. Oxford: Oxford University Press

Thomson, David (1983). *In Camden Town*. London: Hutchinson

Thurman, Wallace (2013). *Infants of the Spring*. Mineola: Dover Publications

Trotsky, Leon (1979). *Leon Trotsky – Collected Writings (1929–1940)*. New York: Pathfinder Press

Vandercook, John W. (1928). *Black Majesty*. New York: Literary Guild Of America

Vandercook, John W. (1938). *Caribbee Cruise: A Book of the West Indies*. Reynal & Hitchcock: New York

Warburg, Fredric (1960). *An Occupation for Gentlemen*. Boston: Houghton Mifflin

Warner, P. F. (1900). *Cricket in Many Climes*. London: W. Heinemann

Wandor, Michelene (ed.) (1990). *Once a Feminist: Stories of a Generation*. London: Virago

Webb, Constance (2003). *Not Without Love: Memoirs*. Hanover: Dartmouth College/ University Press of New England

Weir, Stan (2004). *Singlejack Solidarity*. Minneapolis: University of Minnesota Press

White, Edward (2014). *The Tastemaker: Carl Van Vechten and the Birth of Modern America*. New York: Farrar, Straus and Giroux

Williams, Eric (1969). *Inward Hunger*. London: André Deutsch

Williams, John A. (1970). *The Most Native of Sons: A Biography of Richard Wright*. New York: Doubleday

Williams, John L. (2008). *Michael X: A Life in Black and White*. London: Century

Wollheim, Richard (1981). *Sigmund Freud*. Cambridge: Cambridge University Press

Online resources

There is a very useful website devoted to the life and work of CLR James at www.clrjames.uk

There is a decent collection of CLR James's political essays at https://www.marxists.org/archive/james-clr/index.htm

Index

Credits

Quotations from published and unpublished materials under copyright of the Estate of C. L. R. James are reproduced by the permission of Robert Hill on behalf of the James Estate.

Extracts from *Beyond a Boundary* by C. L. R. James published by Yellow Jersey. Copyright © 1963 Executor to the Estate of C. L. R. James. Reprinted by permission of The Random House Group Limited.

Extracts from *Living for Change: An Autobiography* by Grace Lee Boggs are reproduced by permission of the University of Minnesota Press. Copyright 1998, 2016 by the Regents of the University of Minnesota.

Extract from 'Not Quite What I Would Call Cricket' by E. W. Swanton, *Daily Telegraph,* 1963 © Telegraph Media Group Ltd.

Extracts from *Singlejack Solidarity* by Stan Weir are produced by permission of the University of Minnesota Press. Copyright 2004 by the Regents of the University of Minnesota.